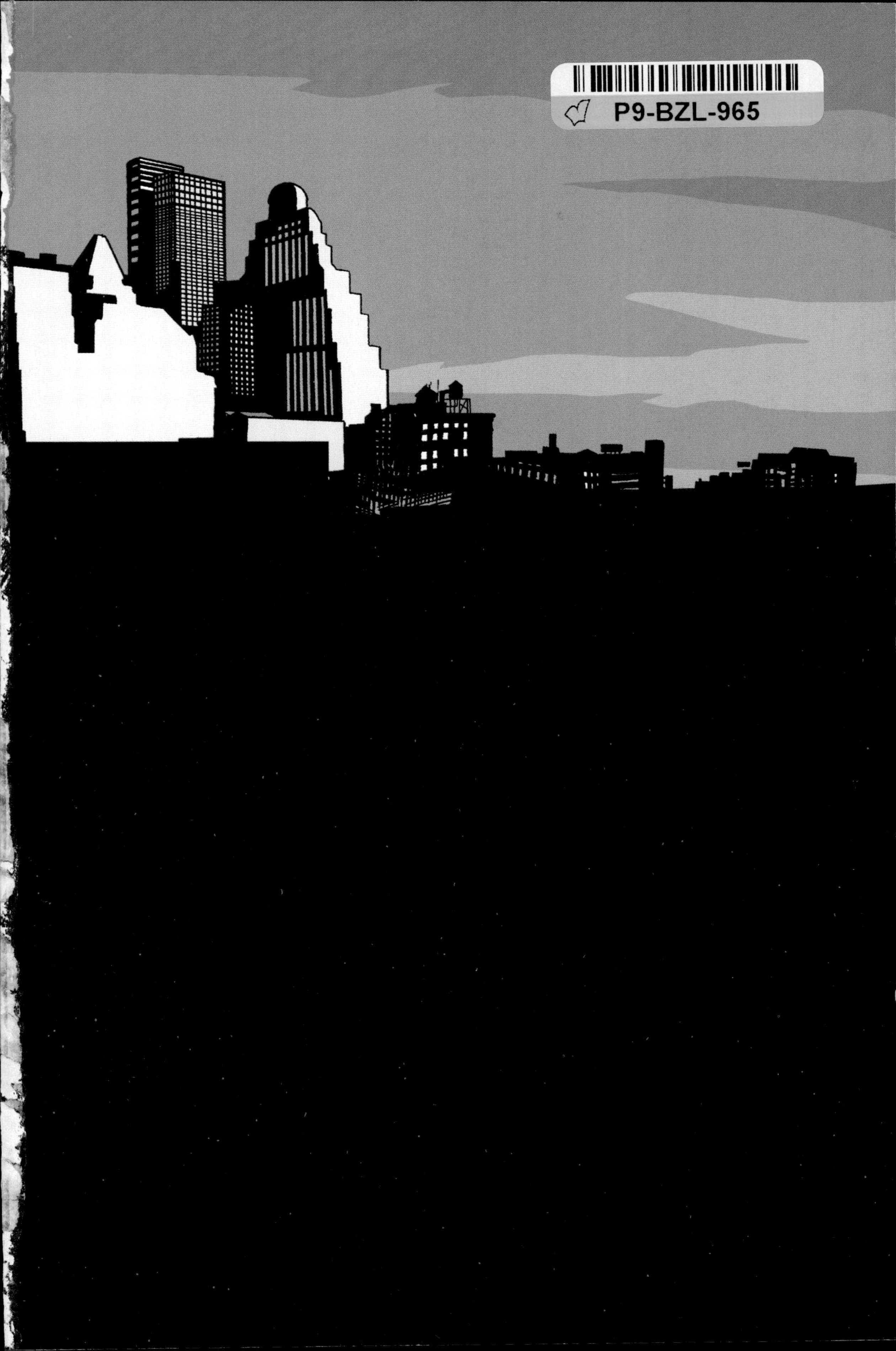

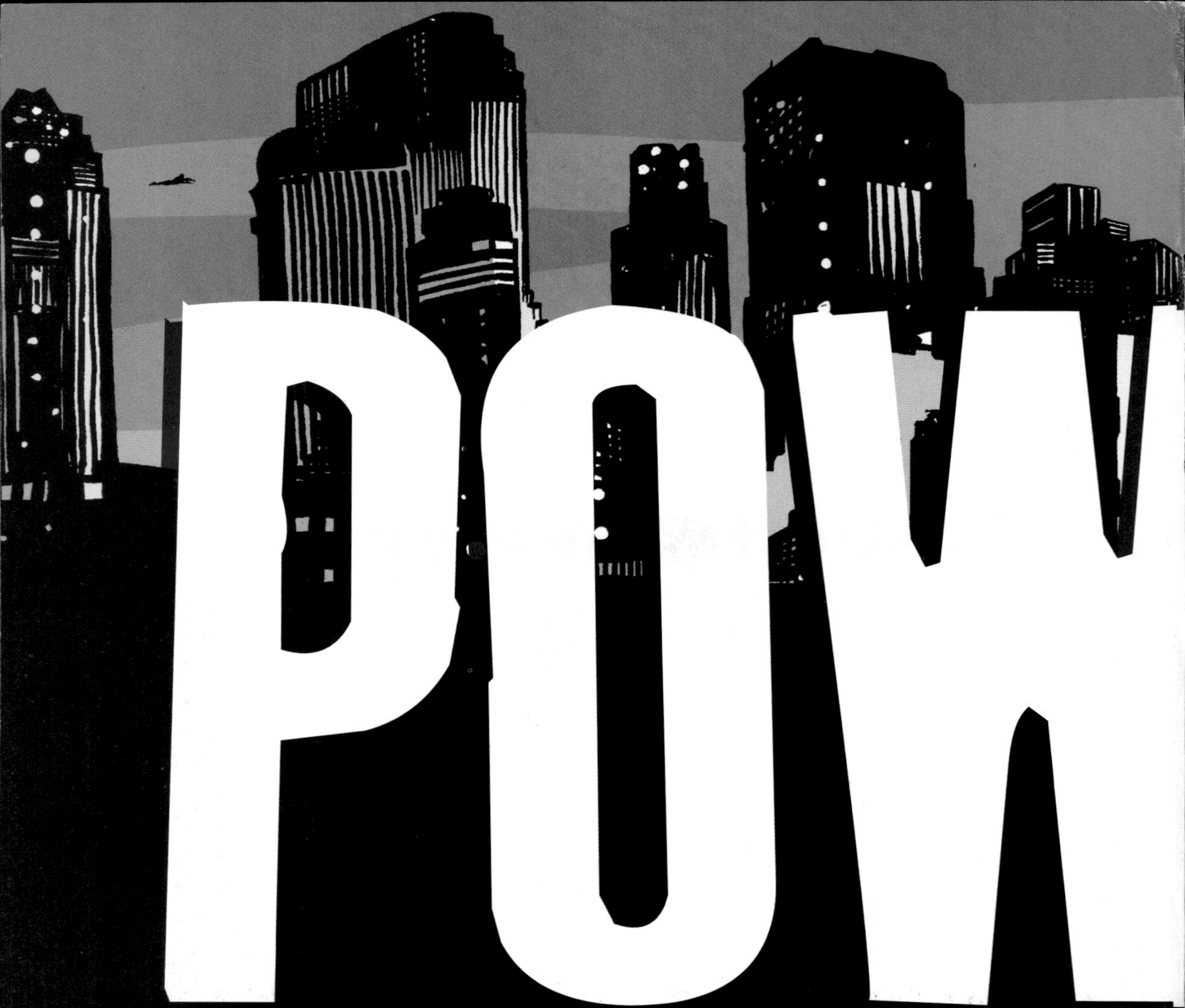
POW

CREATED AND PRODUCED
BY
BRIAN MICHAEL BENDIS
AND
MIKE AVON OEMING

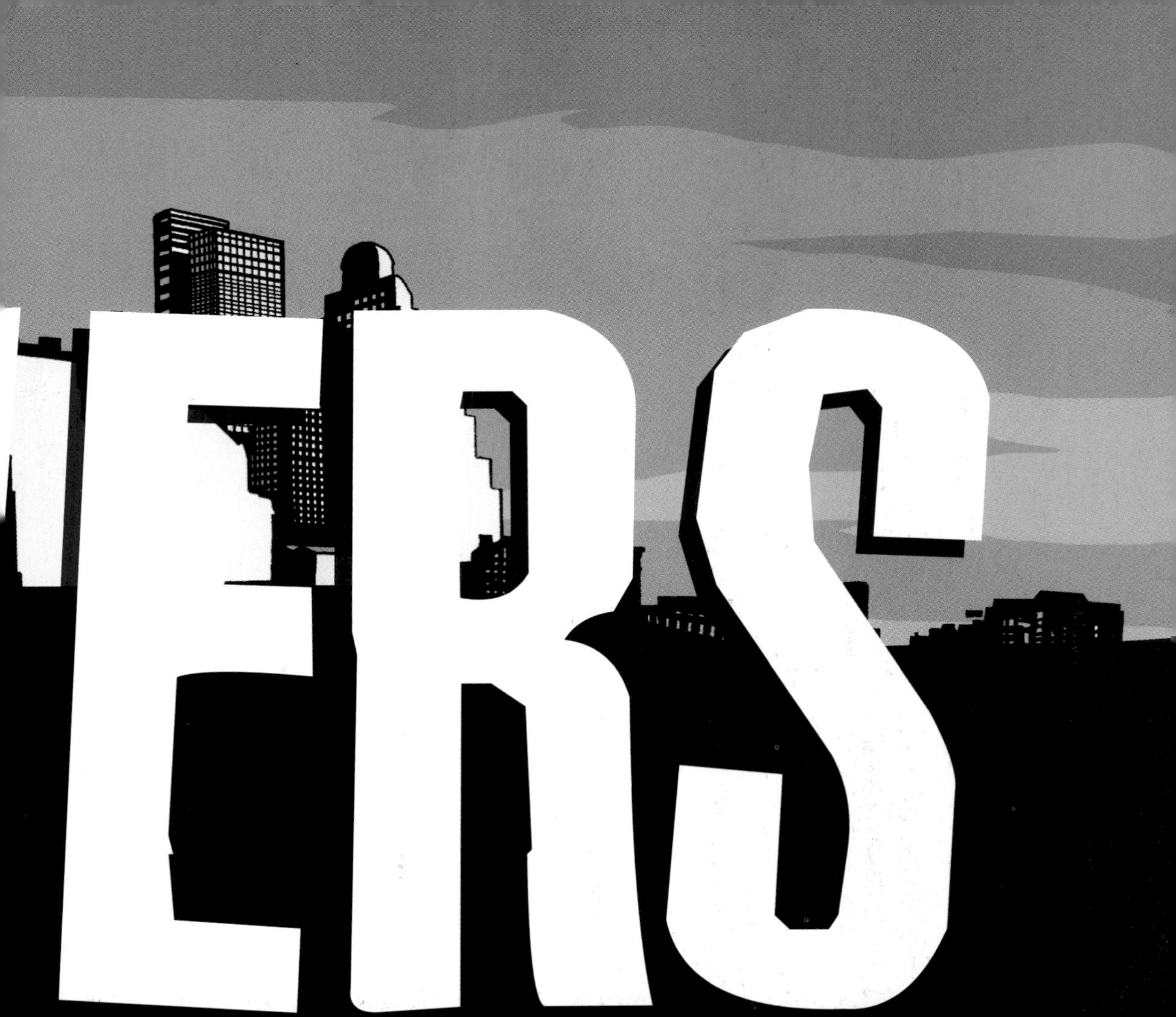
ERS

COLOR ART
PETER PANTAZIS

TYPOGRAPHY
KEN BRUZENAK

EDITED BY
JAMES LUCAS JONES AND C.B. CEBULSKI

BUSINESS AFFAIRS
ALISA BENDIS

DESIGN ASSISTANCE
PATRICK McGRATH

SPECIAL THANKS TO JEN GRÜNWALD

Previously in Powers:

Homicide Detectives Christian Walker and Deena Pilgrim investigate murders specific to superhero cases... powers.

The damage brought on by this out of control power forced the world governments to declare all powers illegal. The city, reeling from a powers turf war, is in the worst shape it has ever been.

But shockingly, Retro Girl, one of the most beloved superheroes the world has ever known, has returned from the dead. Walker discovers that Retro Girl is someone he knows—A girl he rescued years ago named Calista. She has grown up only to develop powers and an unexplainable attachment to the Retro Girl legacy. Now she wants Walker to train her to be a superhero.

And Deena now carries a dark secret. She has mysterious, dangerous powers that she contracted from a villain. She doesn't know what they are or what they ar

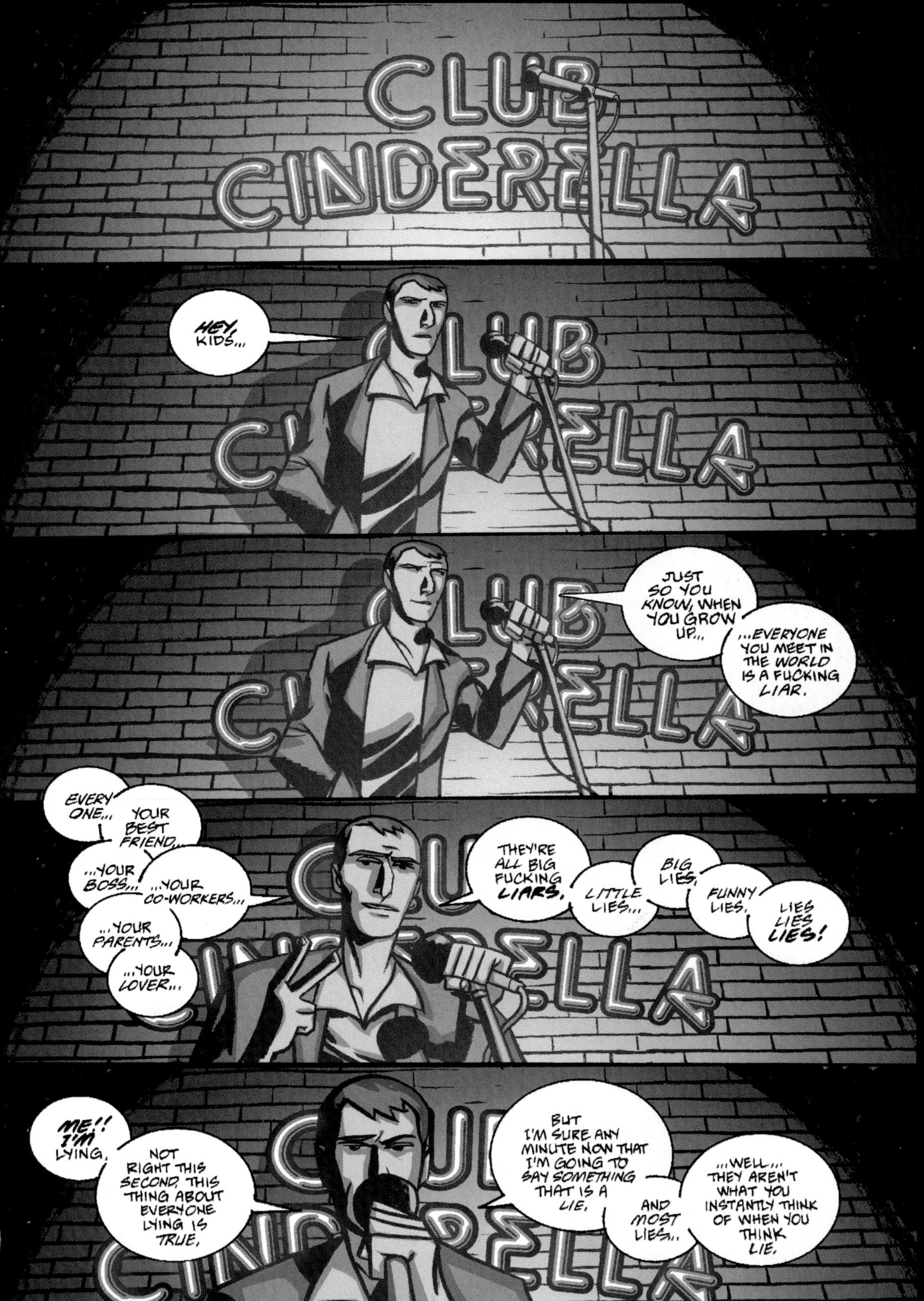
CLUB CINDERELLA
HEY, KIDS...
JUST SO YOU KNOW, WHEN YOU GROW UP...
...EVERYONE YOU MEET IN THE WORLD IS A FUCKING LIAR.
EVERY ONE...
YOUR BEST FRIEND...
...YOUR BOSS...
...YOUR CO-WORKERS...
...YOUR PARENTS...
...YOUR LOVER...
THEY'RE ALL BIG FUCKING LIARS.
LITTLE LIES...
BIG LIES.
FUNNY LIES.
LIES LIES LIES!
ME!! I'M LYING.
NOT RIGHT THIS SECOND, THIS THING ABOUT EVERYONE LYING IS TRUE.
BUT I'M SURE ANY MINUTE NOW THAT I'M GOING TO SAY SOMETHING THAT IS A LIE.
AND MOST LIES...
...WELL... THEY AREN'T WHAT YOU INSTANTLY THINK OF WHEN YOU THINK LIE.

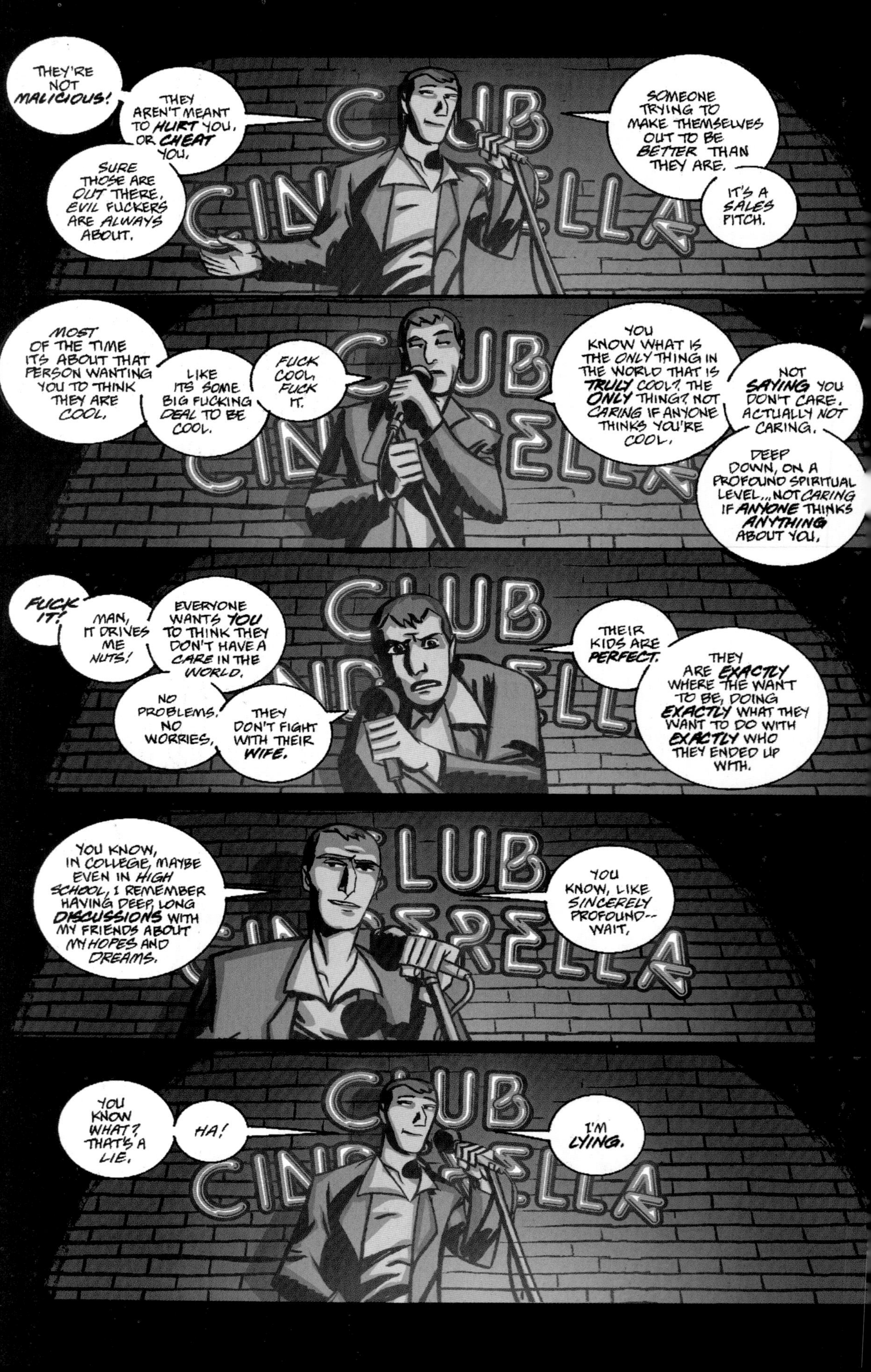
THEY'RE NOT MALICIOUS!
THEY AREN'T MEANT TO HURT YOU, OR CHEAT YOU.
SURE THOSE ARE OUT THERE. EVIL FUCKERS ARE ALWAYS ABOUT.
SOMEONE TRYING TO MAKE THEMSELVES OUT TO BE BETTER THAN THEY ARE.
IT'S A SALES PITCH.
CLUB CINDERELLA
MOST OF THE TIME ITS ABOUT THAT PERSON WANTING YOU TO THINK THEY ARE COOL.
LIKE ITS SOME BIG FUCKING DEAL TO BE COOL.
FUCK COOL. FUCK IT.
YOU KNOW WHAT IS THE ONLY THING IN THE WORLD THAT IS TRULY COOL? THE ONLY THING? NOT CARING IF ANYONE THINKS YOU'RE COOL.
NOT SAYING YOU DON'T CARE. ACTUALLY NOT CARING.
DEEP DOWN, ON A PROFOUND SPIRITUAL LEVEL... NOT CARING IF ANYONE THINKS ANYTHING ABOUT YOU.
FUCK IT!
MAN, IT DRIVES ME NUTS!
EVERYONE WANTS YOU TO THINK THEY DON'T HAVE A CARE IN THE WORLD.
NO PROBLEMS. NO WORRIES.
THEY DON'T FIGHT WITH THEIR WIFE.
THEIR KIDS ARE PERFECT.
THEY ARE EXACTLY WHERE THE WANT TO BE, DOING EXACTLY WHAT THEY WANT TO DO WITH EXACTLY WHO THEY ENDED UP WITH.
YOU KNOW, IN COLLEGE, MAYBE EVEN IN HIGH SCHOOL, I REMEMBER HAVING DEEP, LONG DISCUSSIONS WITH MY FRIENDS ABOUT MY HOPES AND DREAMS.
YOU KNOW, LIKE SINCERELY PROFOUND-- WAIT.
YOU KNOW WHAT? THAT'S A LIE.
HA!
I'M LYING.

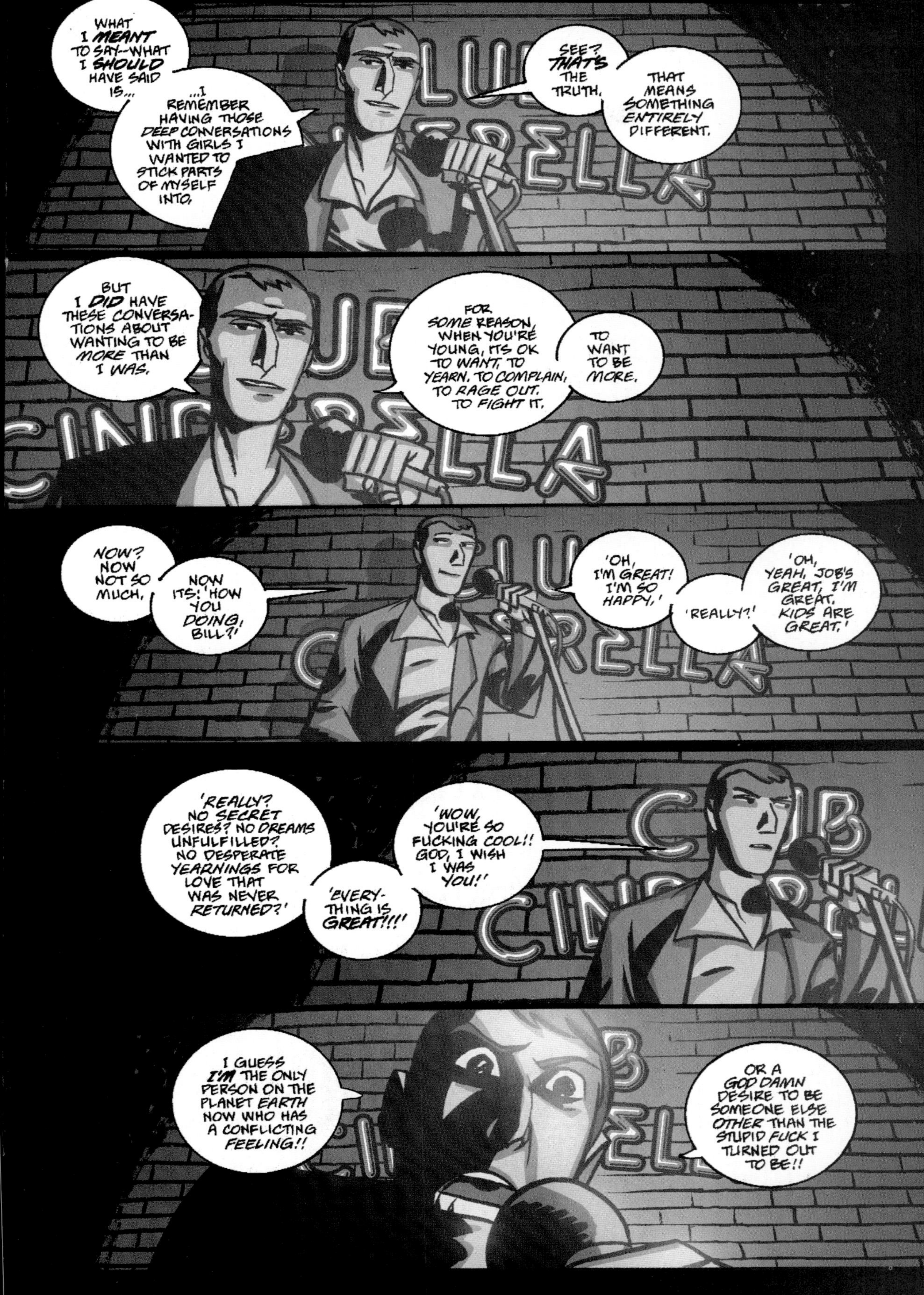
WHAT I MEANT TO SAY--WHAT I SHOULD HAVE SAID IS...
...I REMEMBER HAVING THOSE DEEP CONVERSATIONS WITH GIRLS I WANTED TO STICK PARTS OF MYSELF INTO.
SEE? THAT'S THE TRUTH.
THAT MEANS SOMETHING ENTIRELY DIFFERENT.
BUT I DID HAVE THESE CONVERSATIONS ABOUT WANTING TO BE MORE THAN I WAS.
FOR SOME REASON, WHEN YOU'RE YOUNG, ITS OK TO WANT, TO YEARN, TO COMPLAIN, TO RAGE OUT. TO FIGHT IT.
TO WANT TO BE MORE.
NOW? NOW NOT SO MUCH.
NOW ITS: 'HOW YOU DOING, BILL?'
'OH, I'M GREAT! I'M SO HAPPY.'
'REALLY?'
'OH, YEAH. JOB'S GREAT, I'M GREAT. KIDS ARE GREAT.'
'REALLY? NO SECRET DESIRES? NO DREAMS UNFULFILLED? NO DESPERATE YEARNINGS FOR LOVE THAT WAS NEVER RETURNED?'
'EVERY-THING IS GREAT!!!'
'WOW, YOU'RE SO FUCKING COOL!! GOD, I WISH I WAS YOU!'
I GUESS I'M THE ONLY PERSON ON THE PLANET EARTH NOW WHO HAS A CONFLICTING FEELING!!
OR A GOD DAMN DESIRE TO BE SOMEONE ELSE OTHER THAN THE STUPID FUCK I TURNED OUT TO BE!!

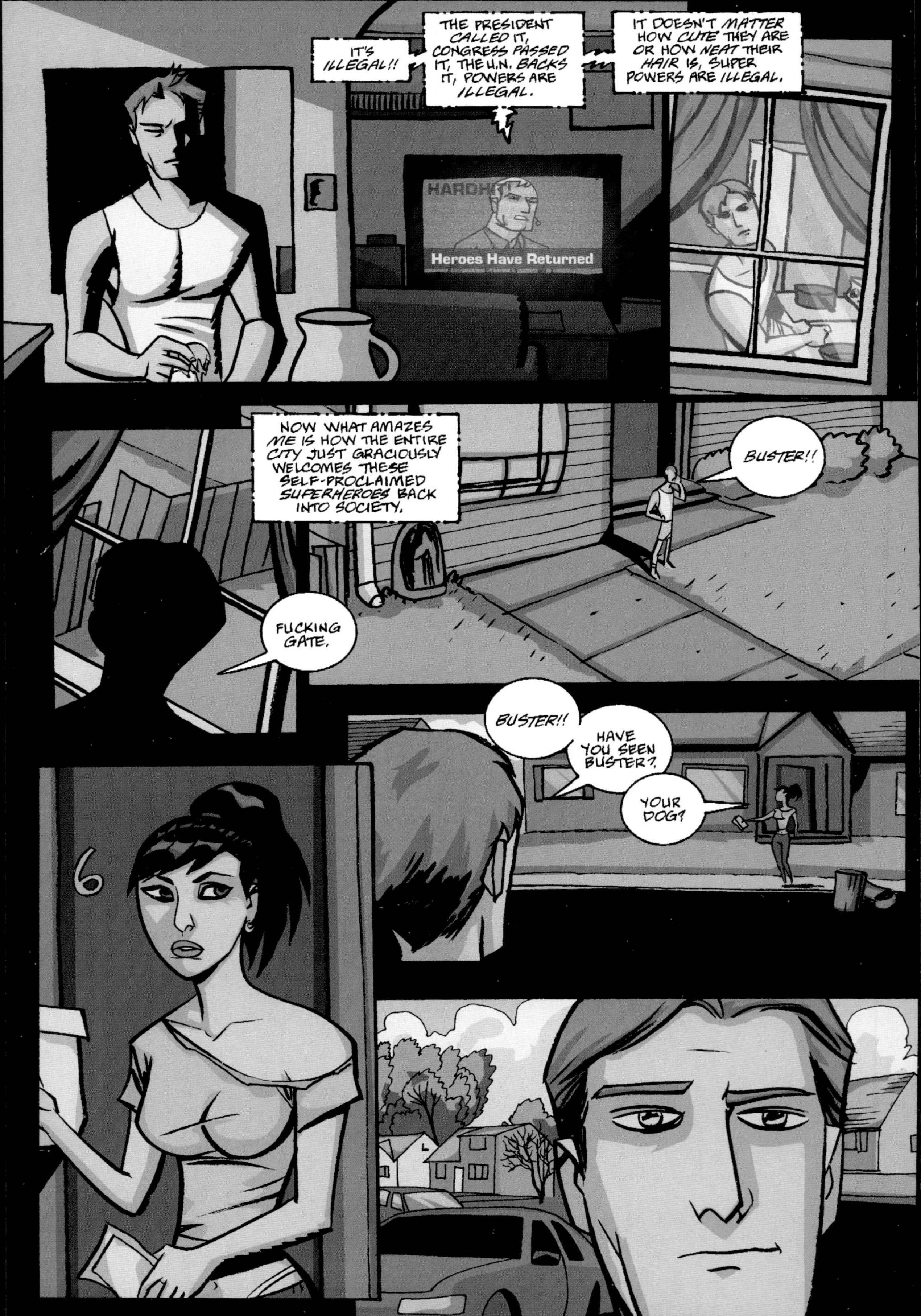
IT'S ILLEGAL!!
THE PRESIDENT CALLED IT, CONGRESS PASSED IT, THE U.N. BACKS IT, POWERS ARE ILLEGAL.
IT DOESN'T MATTER HOW CUTE THEY ARE OR HOW NEAT THEIR HAIR IS, SUPER POWERS ARE ILLEGAL.
HARDHIT
Heroes Have Returned
NOW WHAT AMAZES ME IS HOW THE ENTIRE CITY JUST GRACIOUSLY WELCOMES THESE SELF-PROCLAIMED SUPERHEROES BACK INTO SOCIETY.
BUSTER!!
FUCKING GATE.
BUSTER!!
HAVE YOU SEEN BUSTER?
YOUR DOG?
6

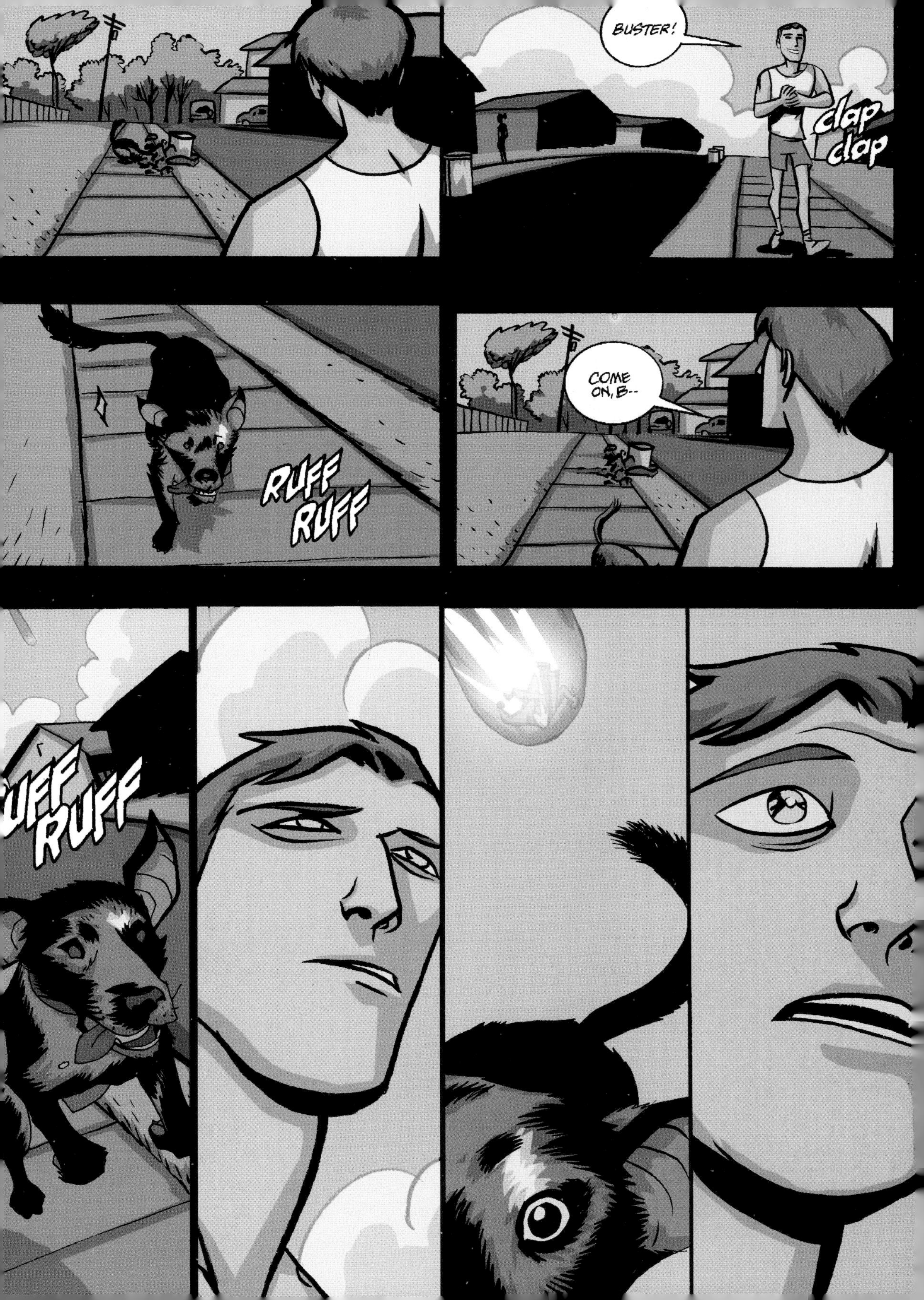
BUSTER!
clap clap
RUFF RUFF
COME ON, B--
UFF RUFF

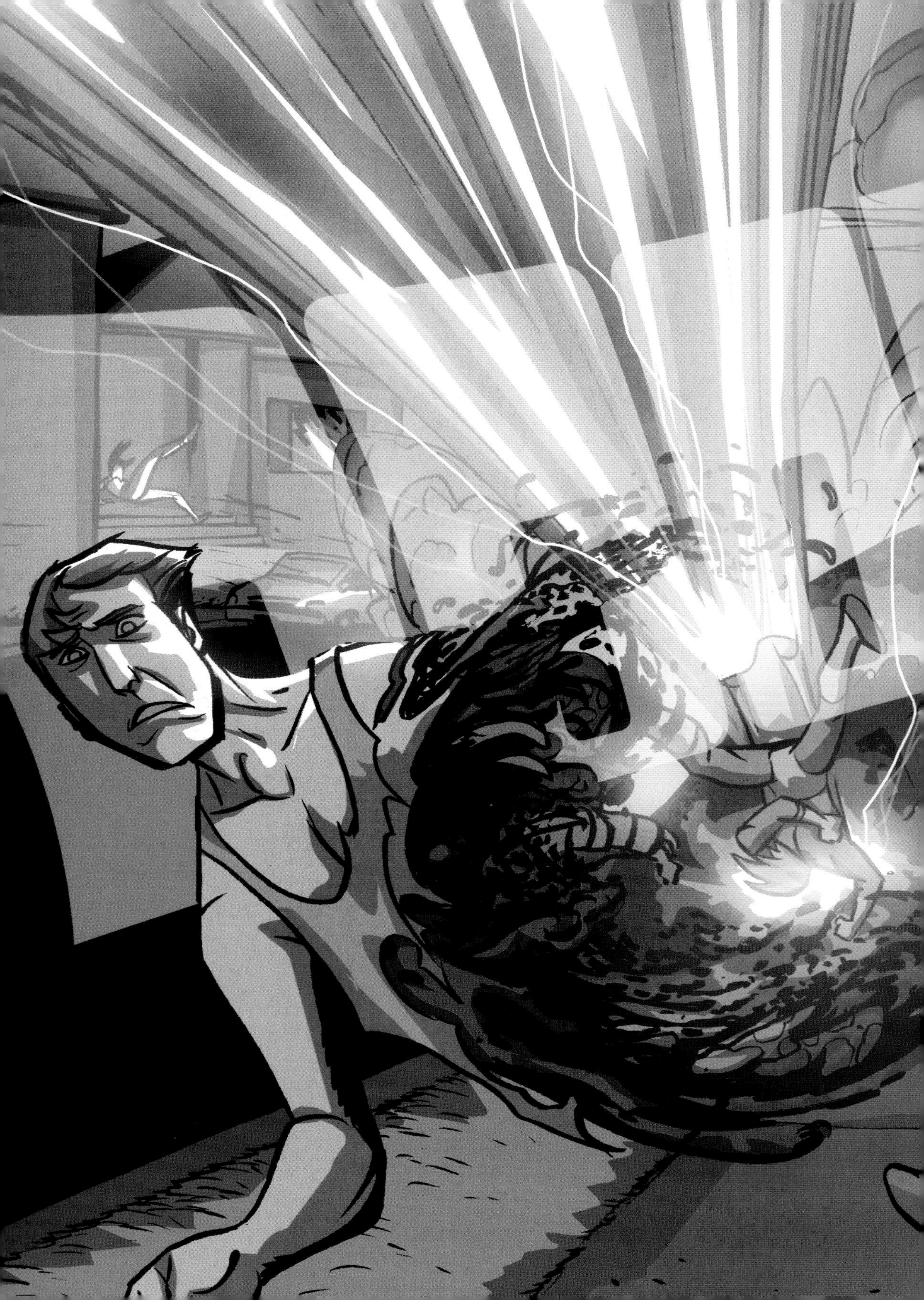

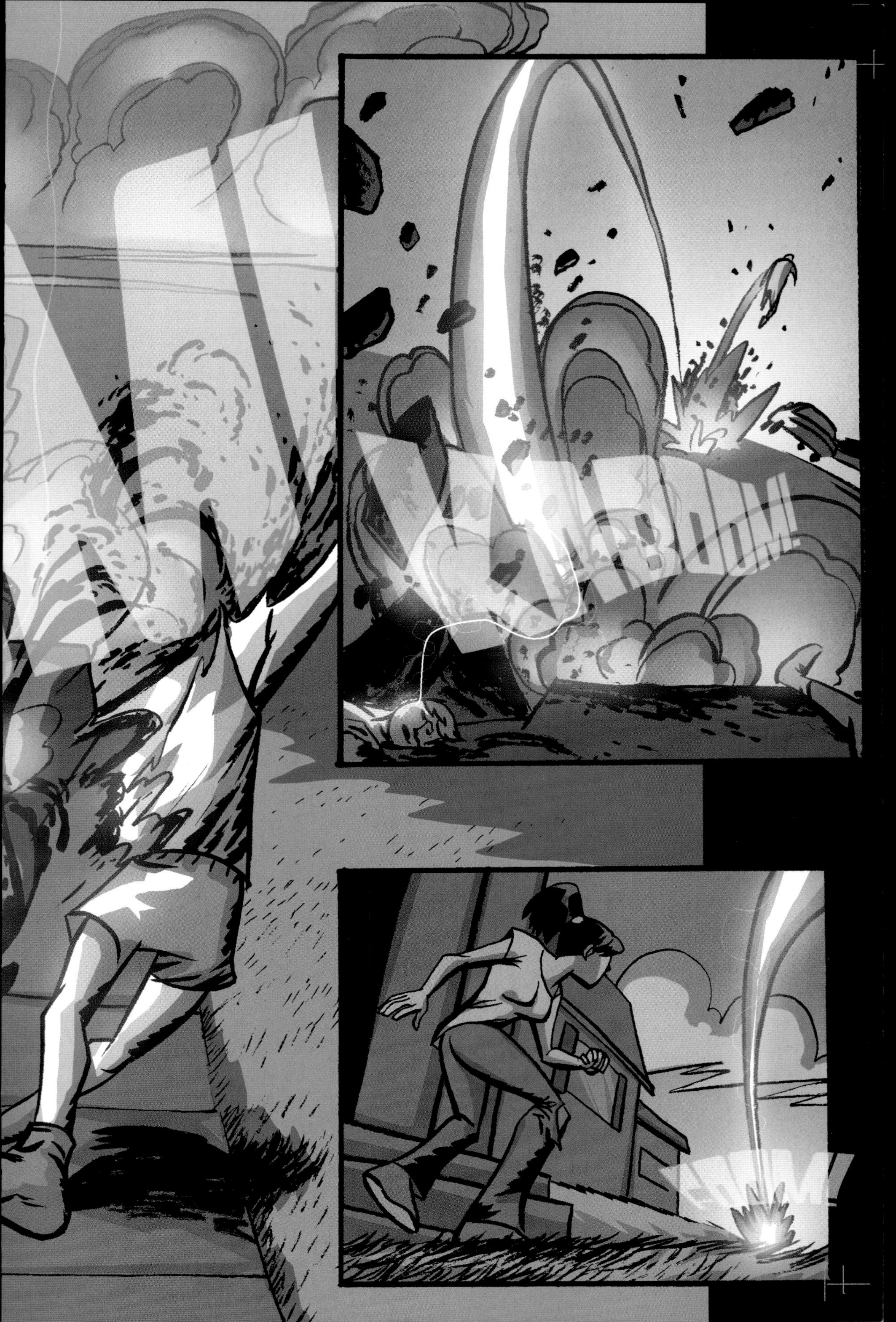
BOOM!

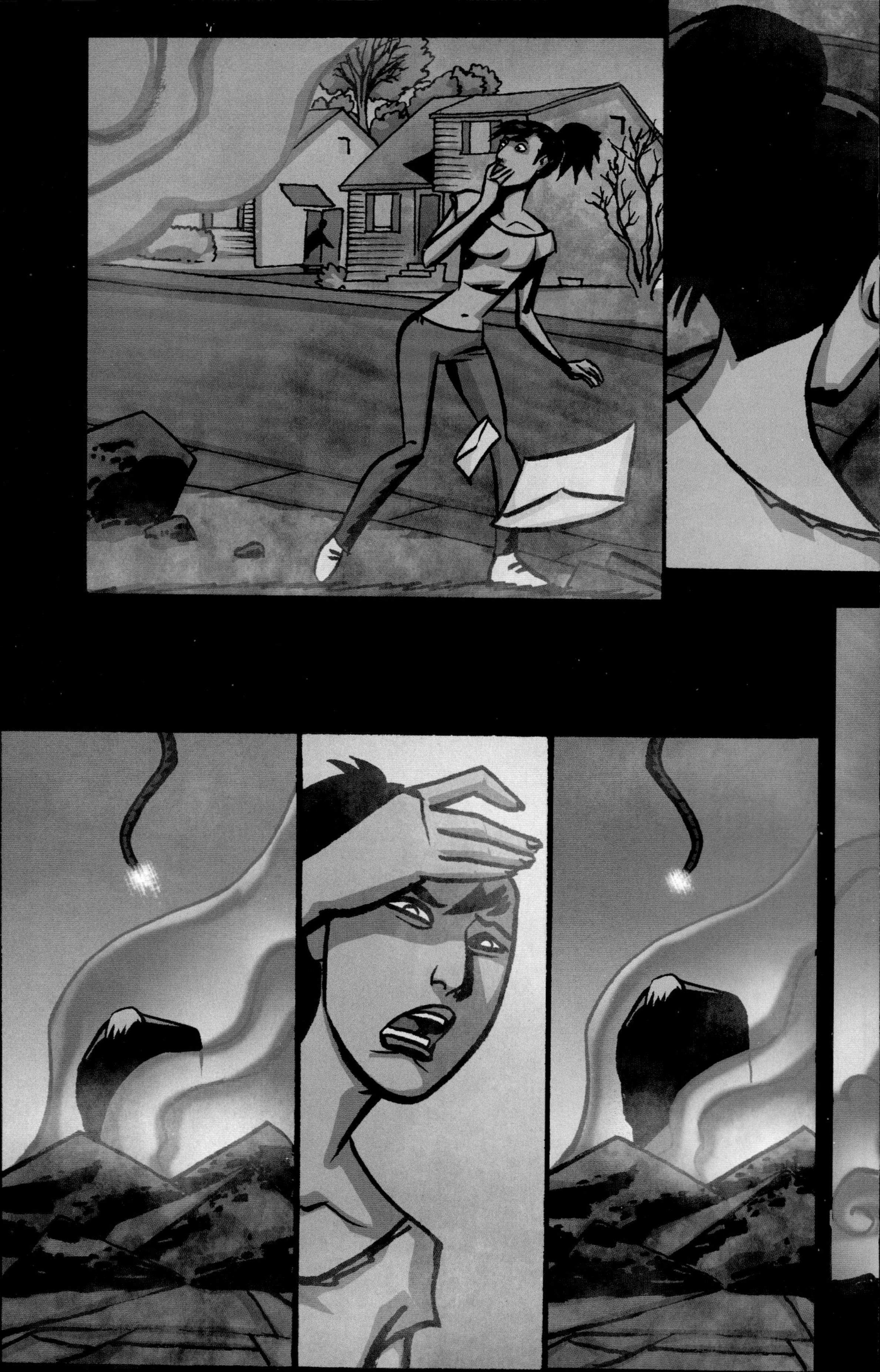

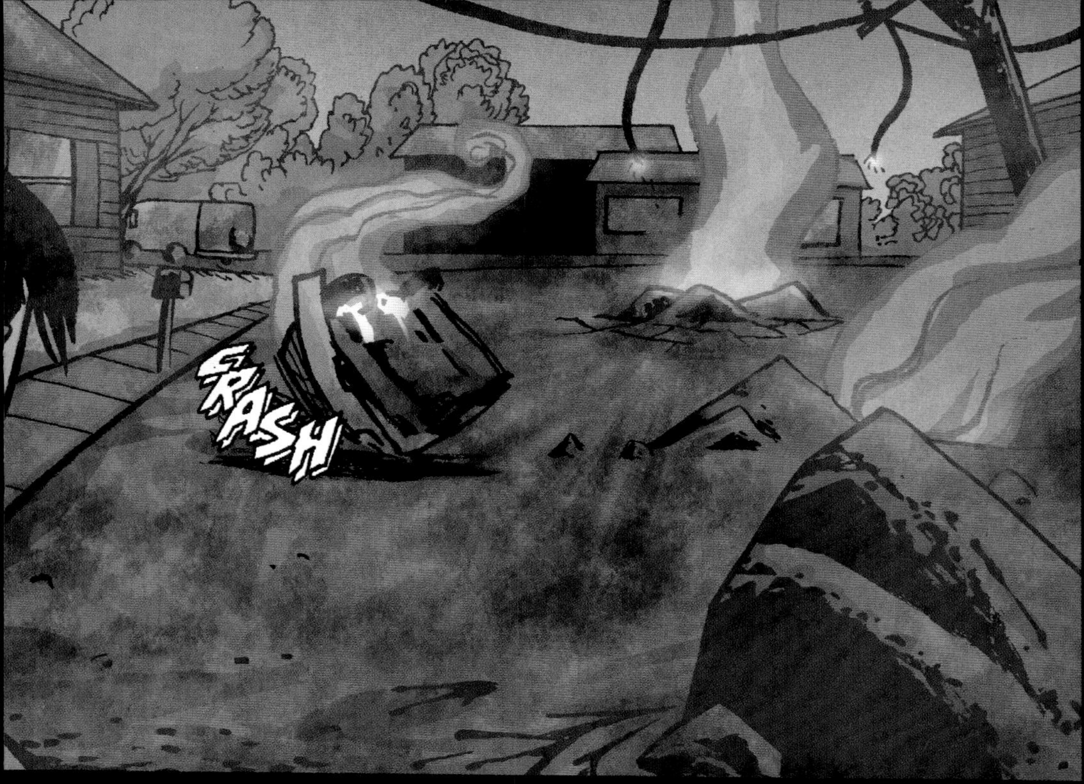
CRASH

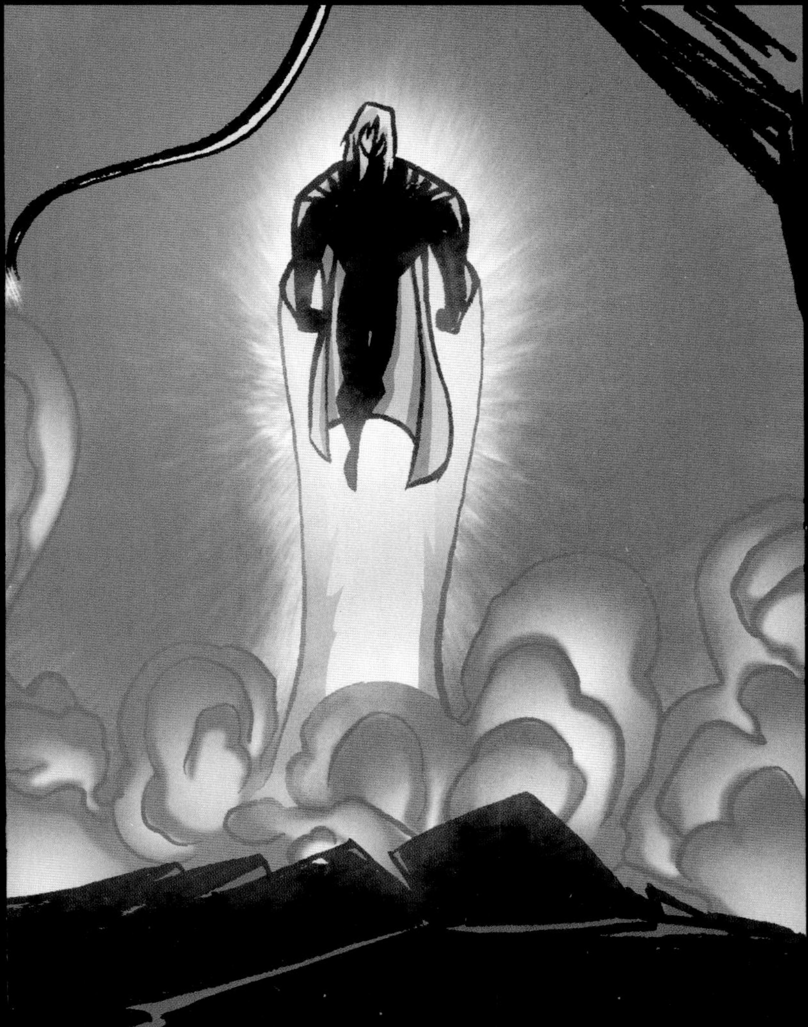

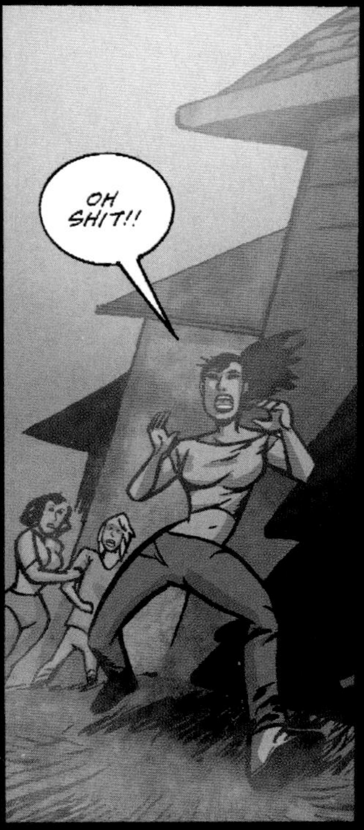
OH SHIT!!

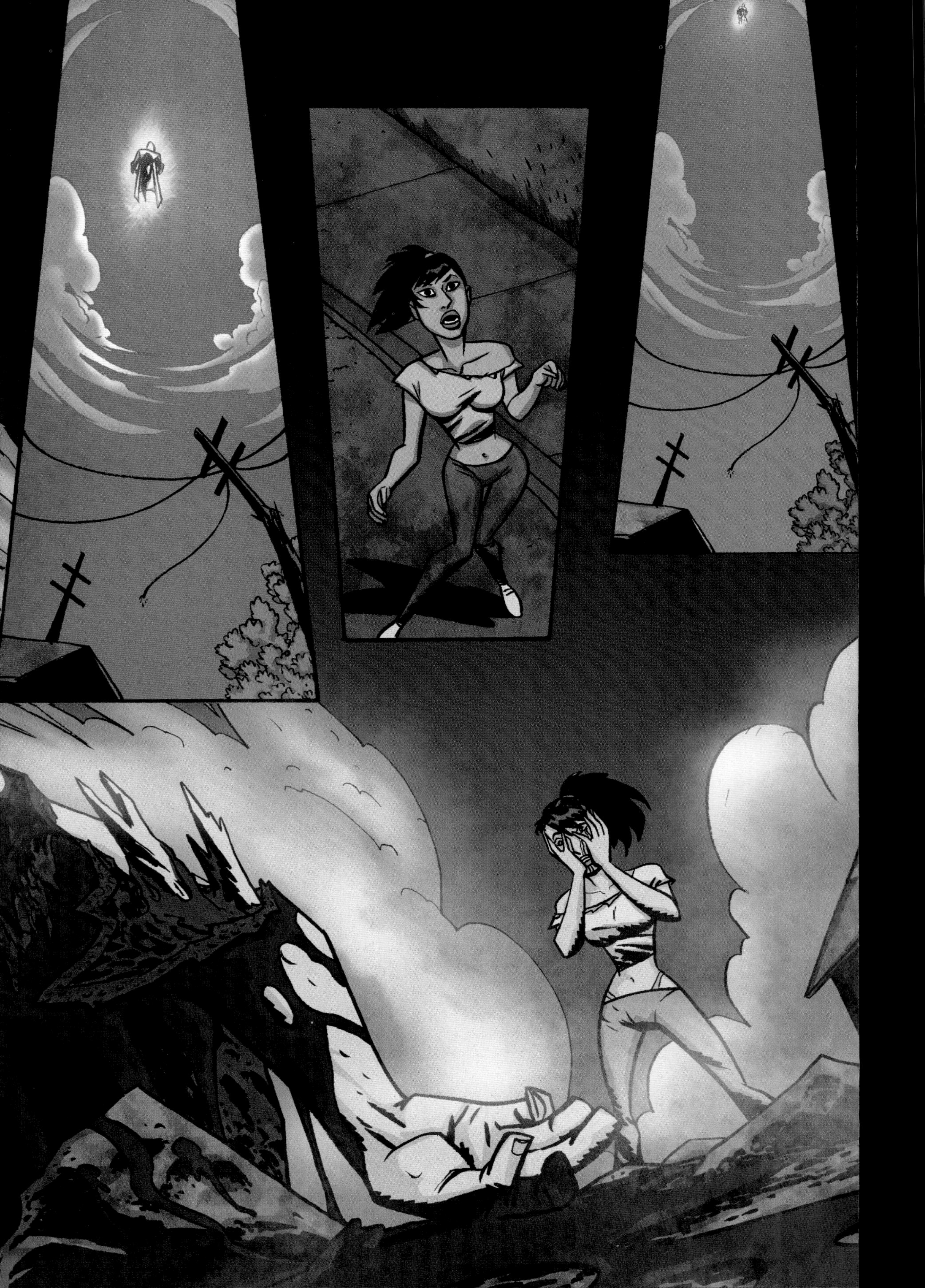

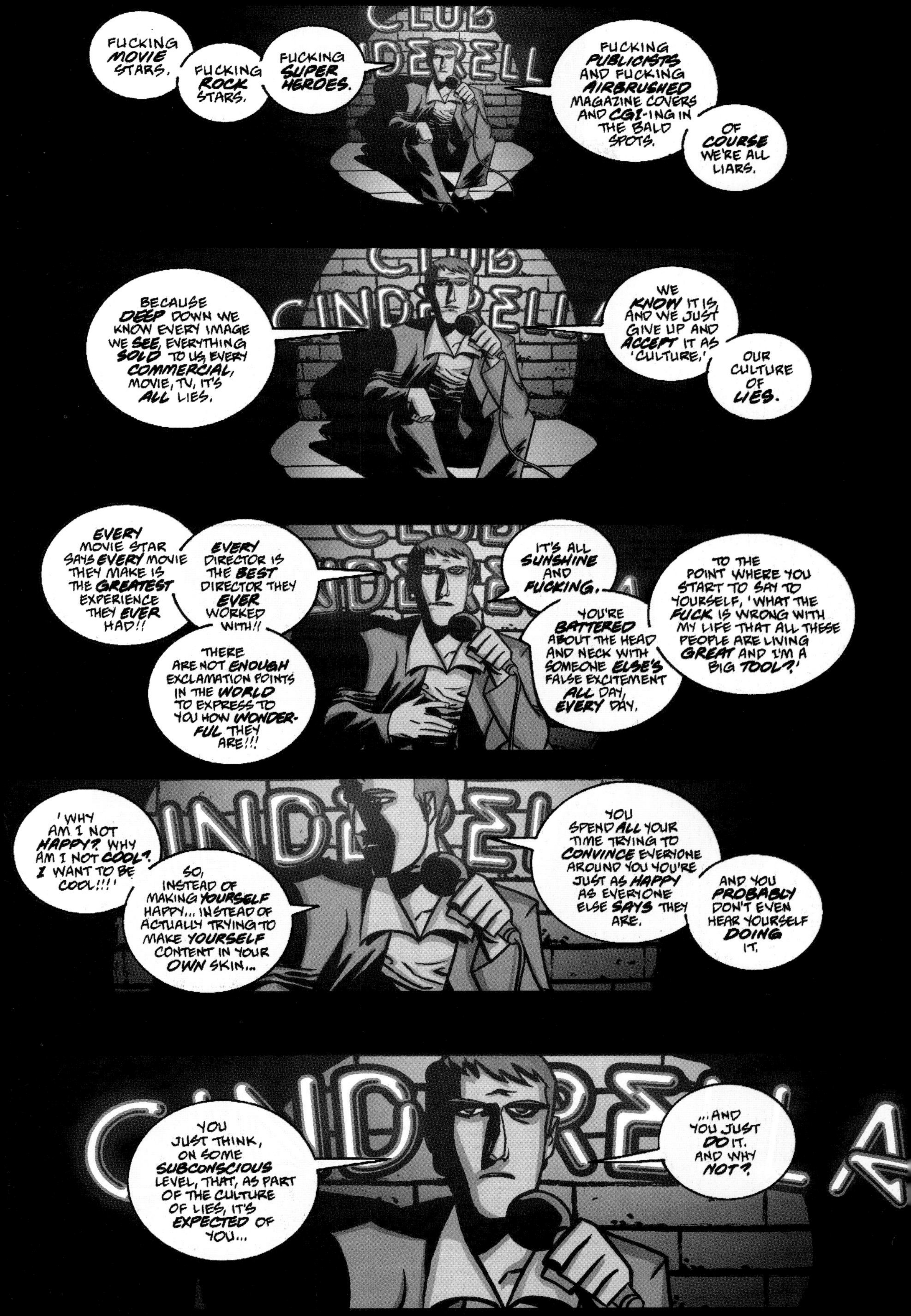
CLUB CINDERELLA
FUCKING MOVIE STARS.
FUCKING ROCK STARS.
FUCKING SUPER HEROES.
FUCKING PUBLICISTS AND FUCKING AIRBRUSHED MAGAZINE COVERS AND CGI-ING IN THE BALD SPOTS.
OF COURSE WE'RE ALL LIARS.
BECAUSE DEEP DOWN WE KNOW EVERY IMAGE WE SEE, EVERYTHING SOLD TO US, EVERY COMMERCIAL, MOVIE, TV, IT'S ALL LIES.
WE KNOW IT IS, AND WE JUST GIVE UP AND ACCEPT IT AS 'CULTURE.'
OUR CULTURE OF LIES.
EVERY MOVIE STAR SAYS EVERY MOVIE THEY MAKE IS THE GREATEST EXPERIENCE THEY EVER HAD!!
EVERY DIRECTOR IS THE BEST DIRECTOR THEY EVER WORKED WITH!!
THERE ARE NOT ENOUGH EXCLAMATION POINTS IN THE WORLD TO EXPRESS TO YOU HOW WONDERFUL THEY ARE!!!
IT'S ALL SUNSHINE AND FUCKING.
YOU'RE BATTERED ABOUT THE HEAD AND NECK WITH SOMEONE ELSE'S FALSE EXCITEMENT ALL DAY, EVERY DAY.
TO THE POINT WHERE YOU START TO SAY TO YOURSELF, 'WHAT THE FUCK IS WRONG WITH MY LIFE THAT ALL THESE PEOPLE ARE LIVING GREAT AND I'M A BIG TOOL?'
'WHY AM I NOT HAPPY? WHY AM I NOT COOL? I WANT TO BE COOL!!!'
SO, INSTEAD OF MAKING YOURSELF HAPPY... INSTEAD OF ACTUALLY TRYING TO MAKE YOURSELF CONTENT IN YOUR OWN SKIN...
YOU SPEND ALL YOUR TIME TRYING TO CONVINCE EVERYONE AROUND YOU YOU'RE JUST AS HAPPY AS EVERYONE ELSE SAYS THEY ARE.
AND YOU PROBABLY DON'T EVEN HEAR YOURSELF DOING IT.
YOU JUST THINK, ON SOME SUBCONSCIOUS LEVEL, THAT, AS PART OF THE CULTURE OF LIES, IT'S EXPECTED OF YOU...
...AND YOU JUST DO IT. AND WHY NOT?

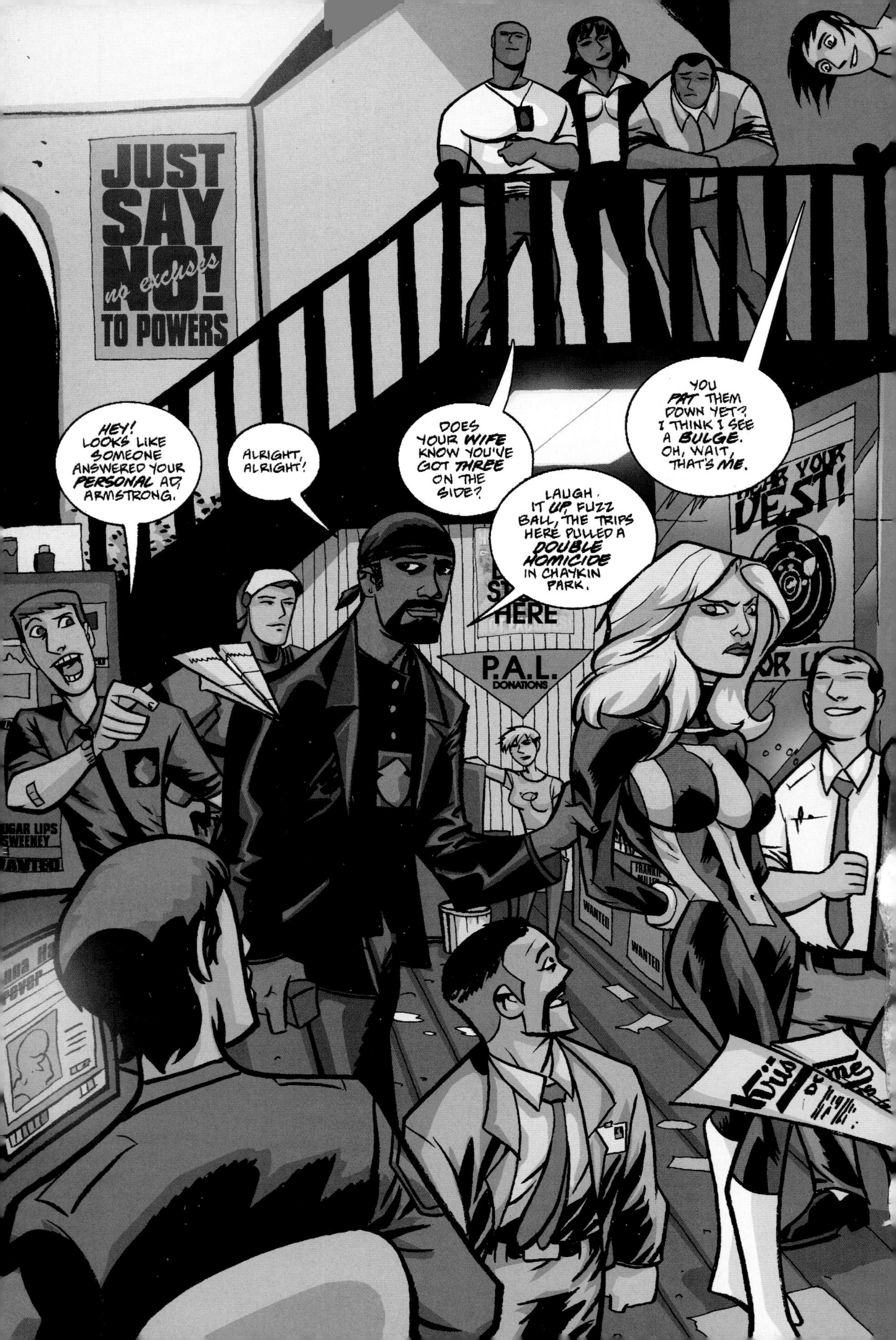
JUST SAY NO! no excuses TO POWERS
HEY! LOOKS LIKE SOMEONE ANSWERED YOUR PERSONAL AD, ARMSTRONG.
ALRIGHT, ALRIGHT!
DOES YOUR WIFE KNOW YOU'VE GOT THREE ON THE SIDE?
LAUGH IT UP, FUZZ BALL, THE TRIPS HERE PULLED A DOUBLE HOMICIDE IN CHAYKIN PARK.
YOU PAT THEM DOWN YET? I THINK I SEE A BULGE. OH, WAIT, THAT'S ME.
P.A.L. DONATIONS
HERE
SWEENEY
WANTED

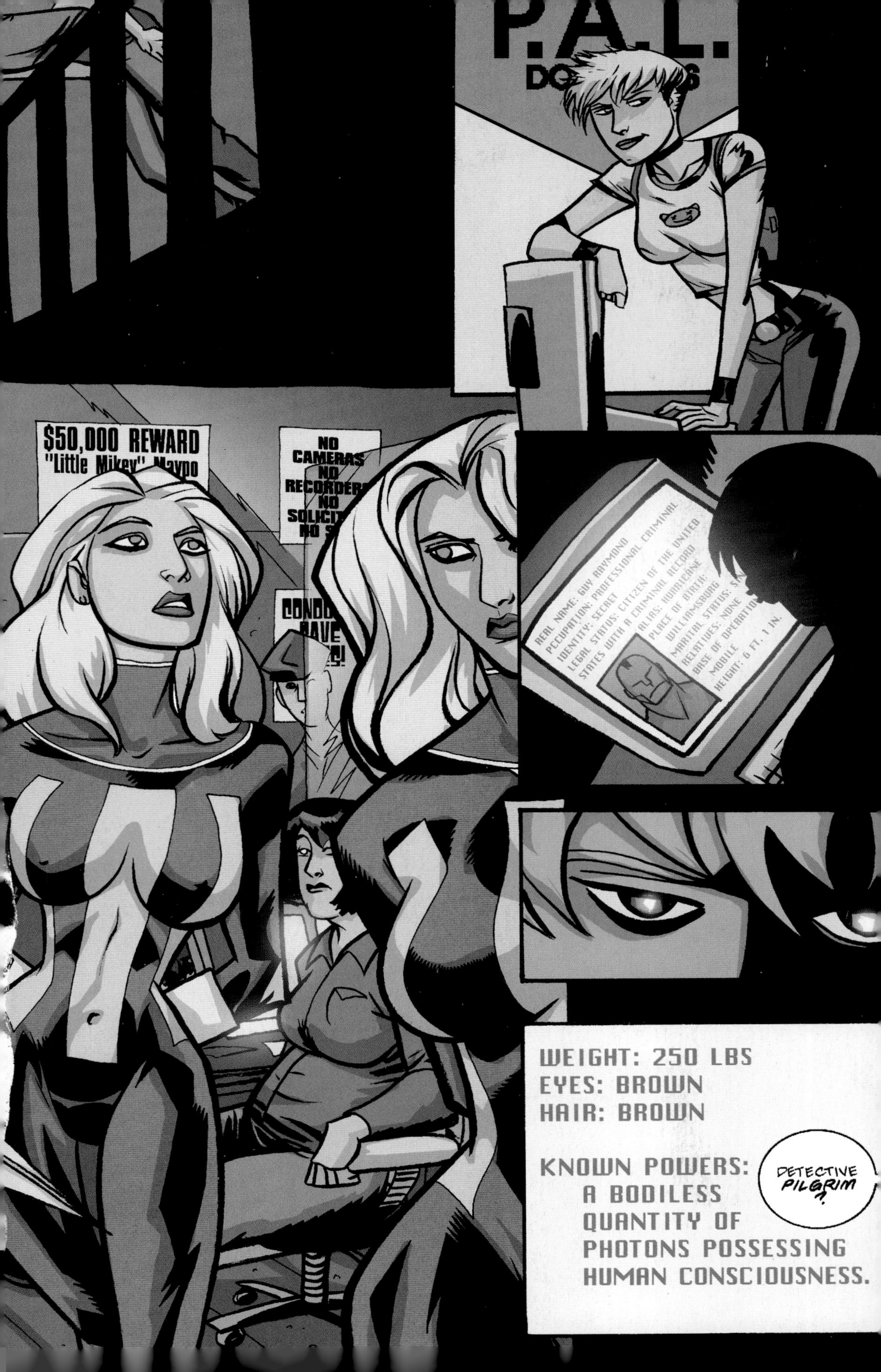
P.A.L.
$50,000 REWARD
"Little Mikey" Maypo
NO
CAMERAS
NO
RECORDERS
NO
REAL NAME: GUY RAYMOND
OCCUPATION: PROFESSIONAL CRIMINAL
IDENTITY: SECRET
LEGAL STATUS: CITIZEN OF THE UNITED STATES WITH A CRIMINAL RECORD
ALIAS: HURRICANE
PLACE OF BIRTH: WILLIAMSBURG
MARITAL STATUS:
RELATIVES: NONE
MOBILE
HEIGHT: 6 FT. 1 IN.
WEIGHT: 250 LBS
EYES: BROWN
HAIR: BROWN
KNOWN POWERS:
A BODILESS QUANTITY OF PHOTONS POSSESSING HUMAN CONSCIOUSNESS.
DETECTIVE PILGRIM?

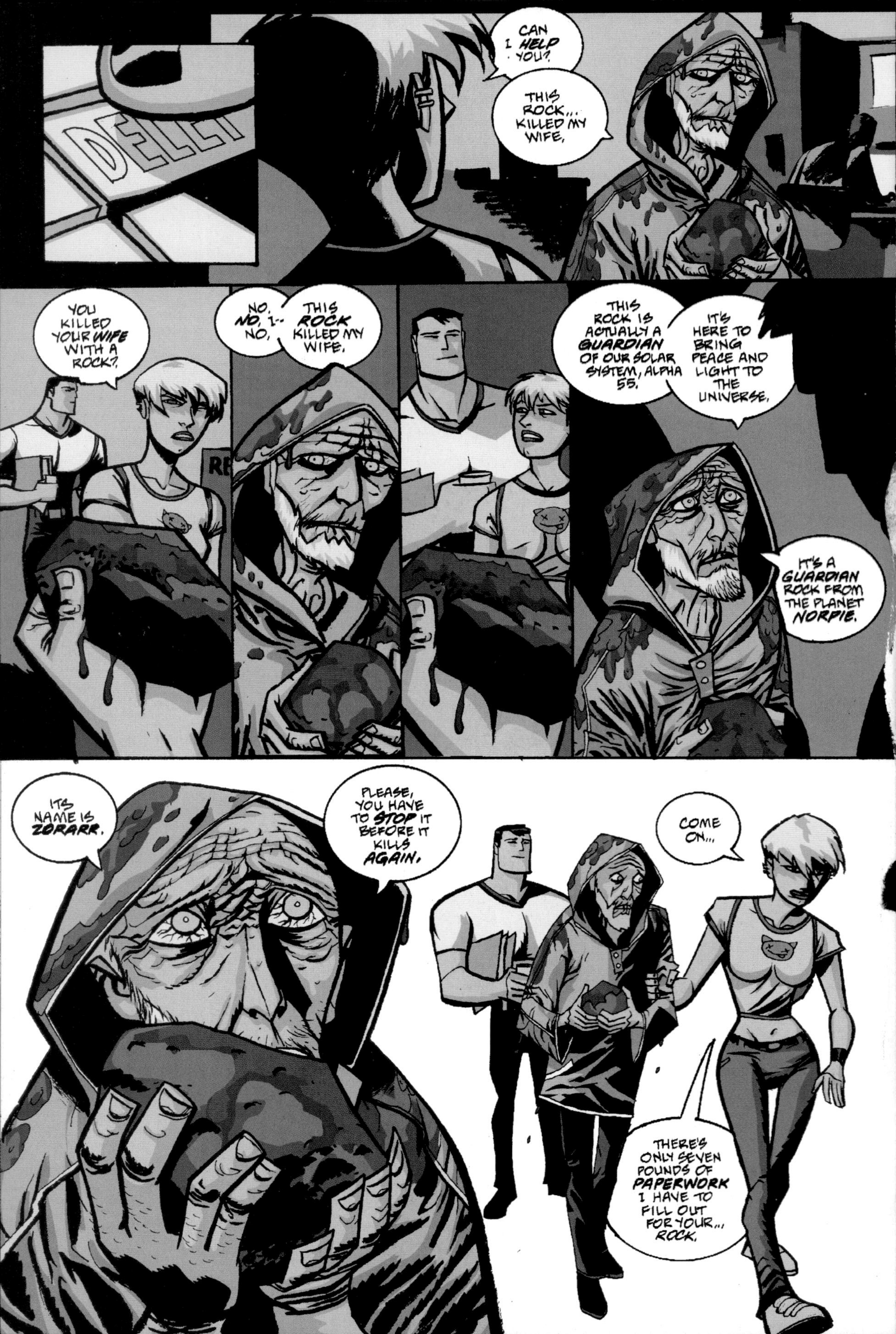
CAN I HELP YOU?
THIS ROCK... KILLED MY WIFE.
YOU KILLED YOUR WIFE WITH A ROCK?
NO, NO, I-- NO.
THIS ROCK KILLED MY WIFE.
THIS ROCK IS ACTUALLY A GUARDIAN OF OUR SOLAR SYSTEM, ALPHA 55.
IT'S HERE TO BRING PEACE AND LIGHT TO THE UNIVERSE.
IT'S A GUARDIAN ROCK FROM THE PLANET NORPIE.
ITS NAME IS ZORARR.
PLEASE, YOU HAVE TO STOP IT BEFORE IT KILLS AGAIN.
COME ON...
THERE'S ONLY SEVEN POUNDS OF PAPERWORK I HAVE TO FILL OUT FOR YOUR... ROCK.

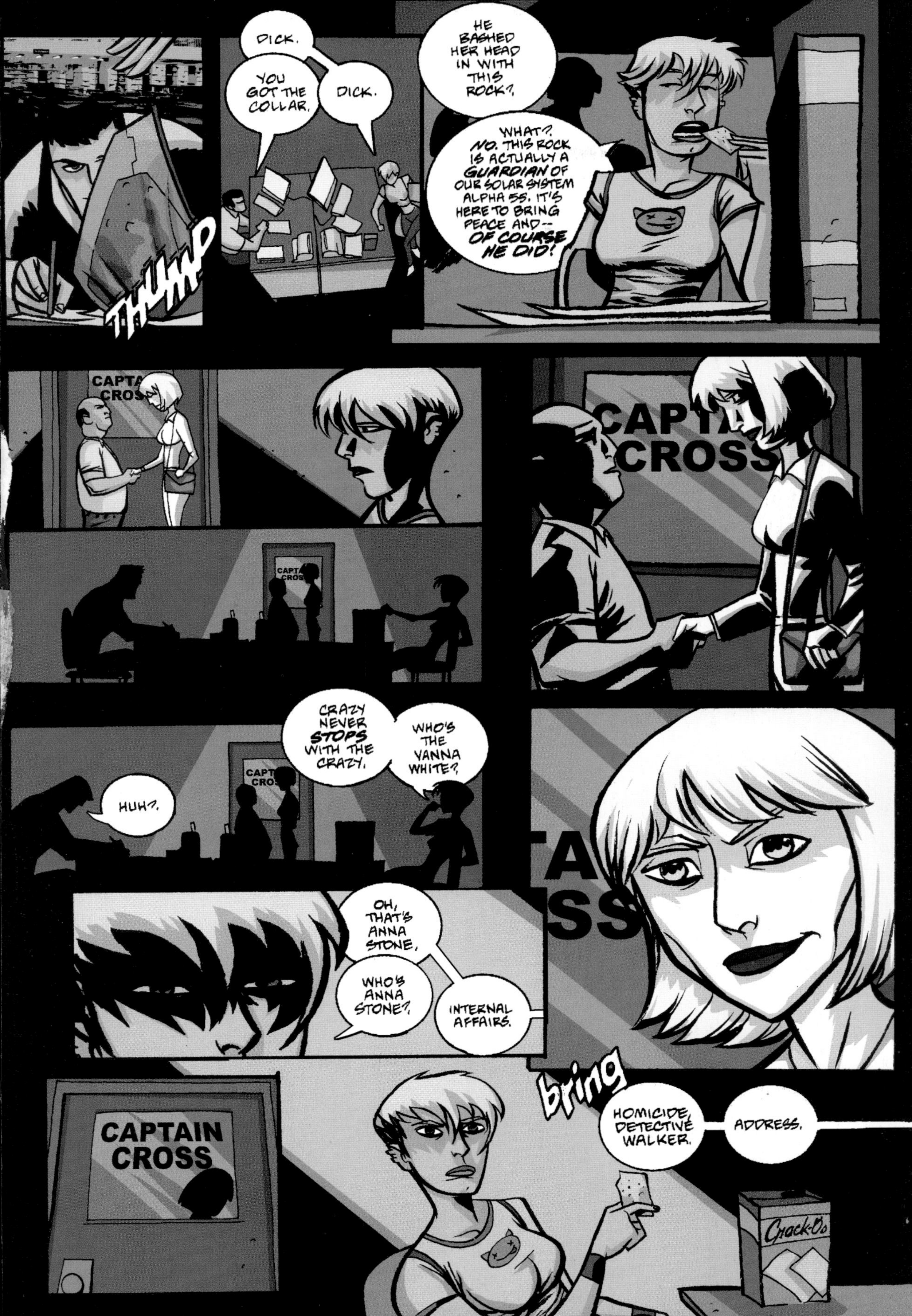
THUMP
DICK.
YOU GOT THE COLLAR.
DICK.
HE BASHED HER HEAD IN WITH THIS ROCK?
WHAT? NO. THIS ROCK IS ACTUALLY A GUARDIAN OF OUR SOLAR SYSTEM ALPHA 55. IT'S HERE TO BRING PEACE AND-- OF COURSE HE DID!
CAPTAIN CROSS
CRAZY NEVER STOPS WITH THE CRAZY.
HUH?
WHO'S THE VANNA WHITE?
OH, THAT'S ANNA STONE.
WHO'S ANNA STONE?
INTERNAL AFFAIRS.
CAPTAIN CROSS
bring
HOMICIDE, DETECTIVE WALKER.
ADDRESS.
Crack-Os

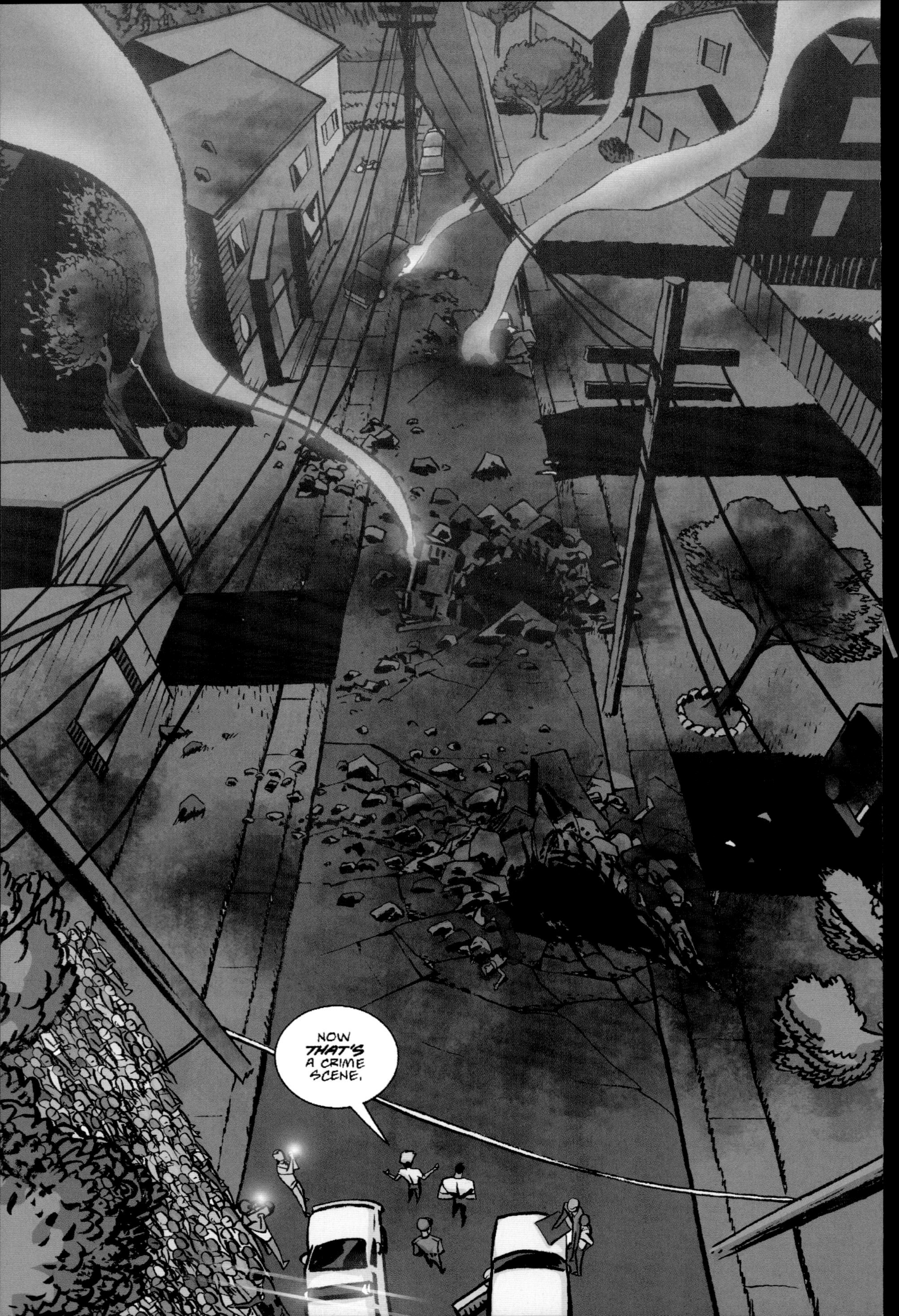
NOW THAT'S A CRIME SCENE.

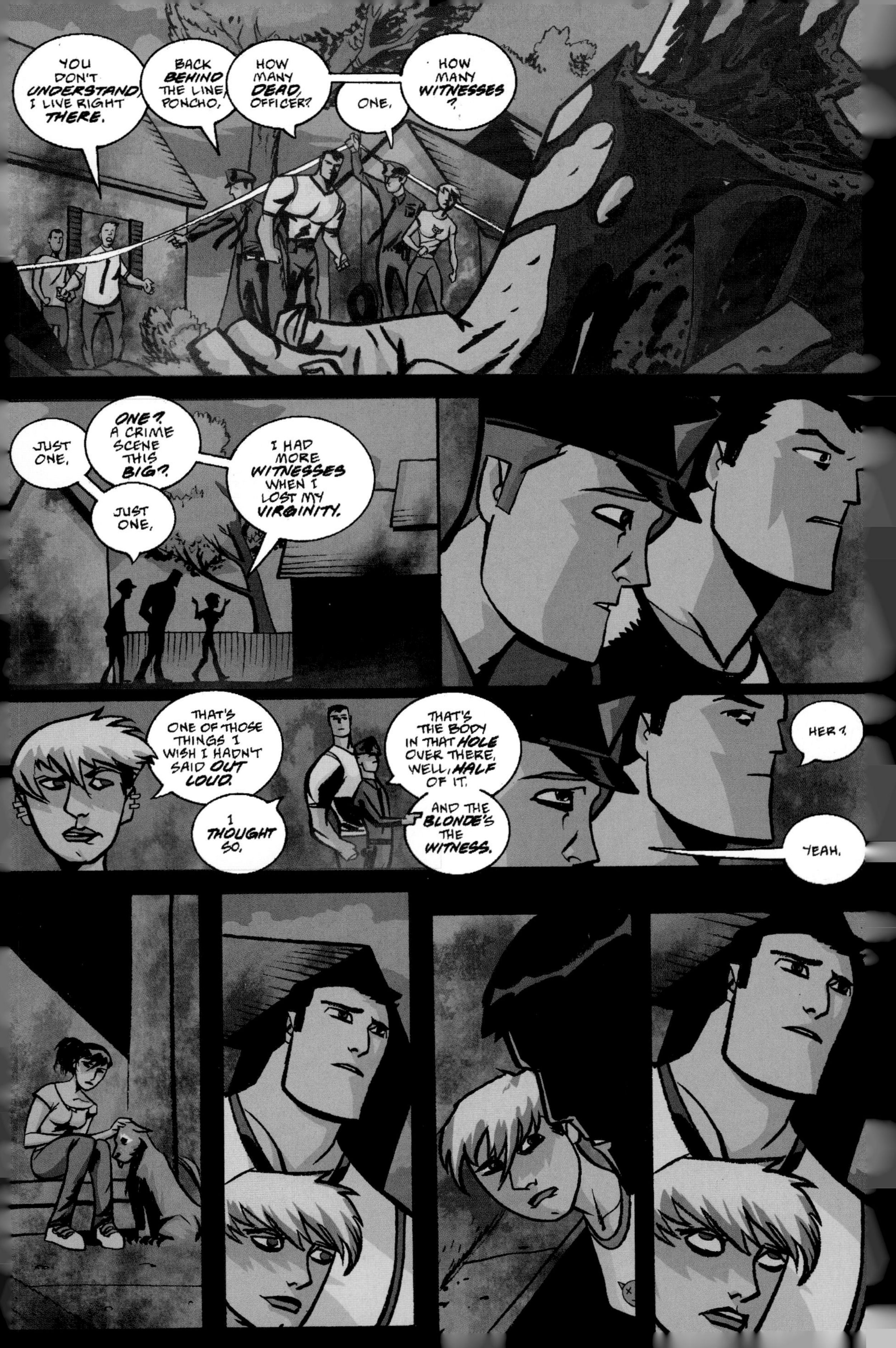
YOU DON'T UNDERSTAND, I LIVE RIGHT THERE.
BACK BEHIND THE LINE, PONCHO.
HOW MANY DEAD, OFFICER?
ONE.
HOW MANY WITNESSES?
JUST ONE.
ONE? A CRIME SCENE THIS BIG?
JUST ONE.
I HAD MORE WITNESSES WHEN I LOST MY VIRGINITY.
THAT'S ONE OF THOSE THINGS I WISH I HADN'T SAID OUT LOUD.
I THOUGHT SO.
THAT'S THE BODY IN THAT HOLE OVER THERE. WELL, HALF OF IT.
AND THE BLONDE'S THE WITNESS.
HER?
YEAH.

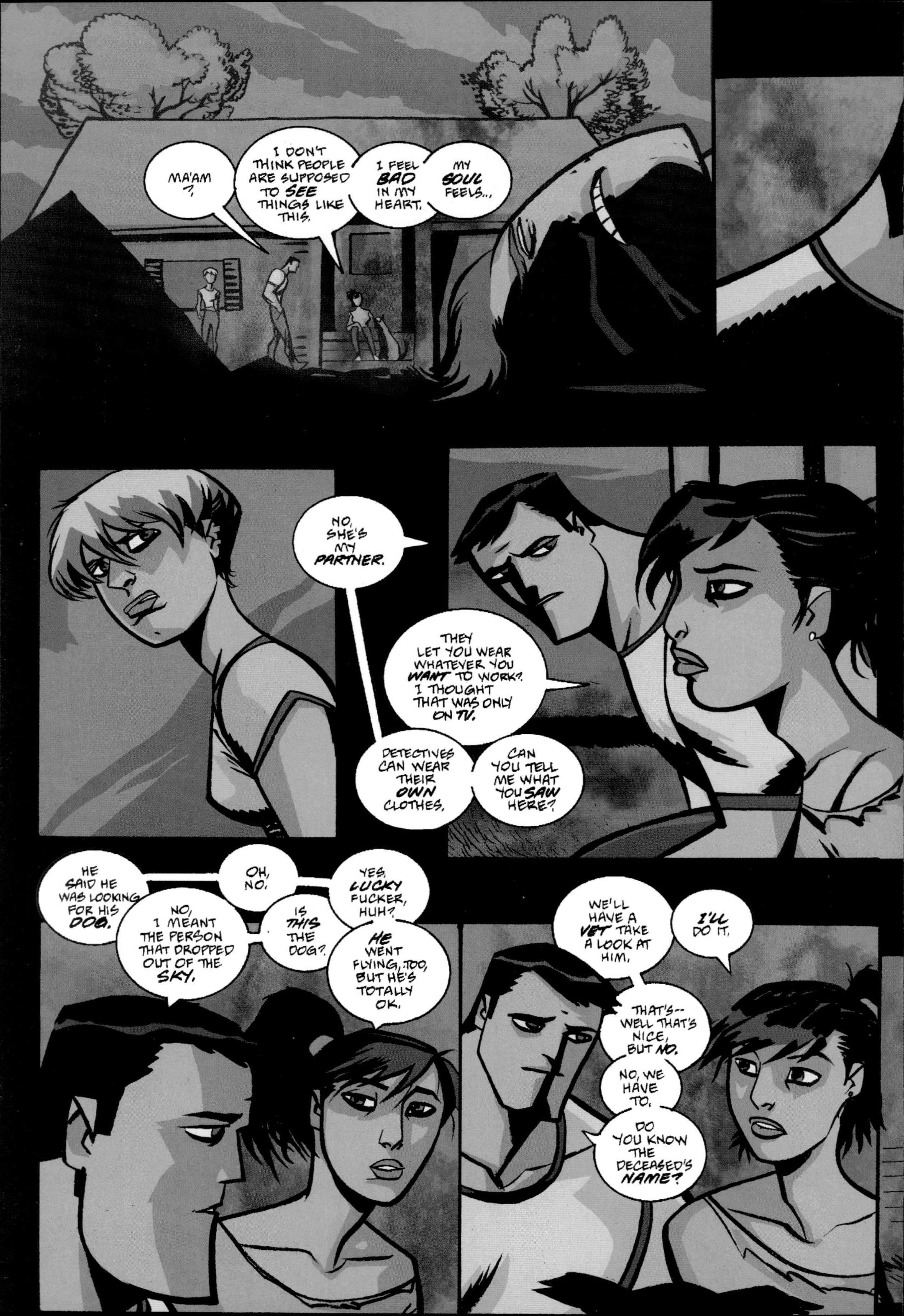

MA'AM?
I DON'T THINK PEOPLE ARE SUPPOSED TO SEE THINGS LIKE THIS.
I FEEL BAD IN MY HEART.
MY SOUL FEELS...
NO, SHE'S MY PARTNER.
THEY LET YOU WEAR WHATEVER YOU WANT TO WORK? I THOUGHT THAT WAS ONLY ON TV.
DETECTIVES CAN WEAR THEIR OWN CLOTHES.
CAN YOU TELL ME WHAT YOU SAW HERE?
HE SAID HE WAS LOOKING FOR HIS DOG.
OH, NO.
NO, I MEANT THE PERSON THAT DROPPED OUT OF THE SKY.
IS THIS THE DOG?
YES, LUCKY FUCKER, HUH?
HE WENT FLYING, TOO, BUT HE'S TOTALLY OK.
WE'LL HAVE A VET TAKE A LOOK AT HIM.
I'LL DO IT.
THAT'S-- WELL THAT'S NICE, BUT NO.
NO, WE HAVE TO.
DO YOU KNOW THE DECEASED'S NAME?

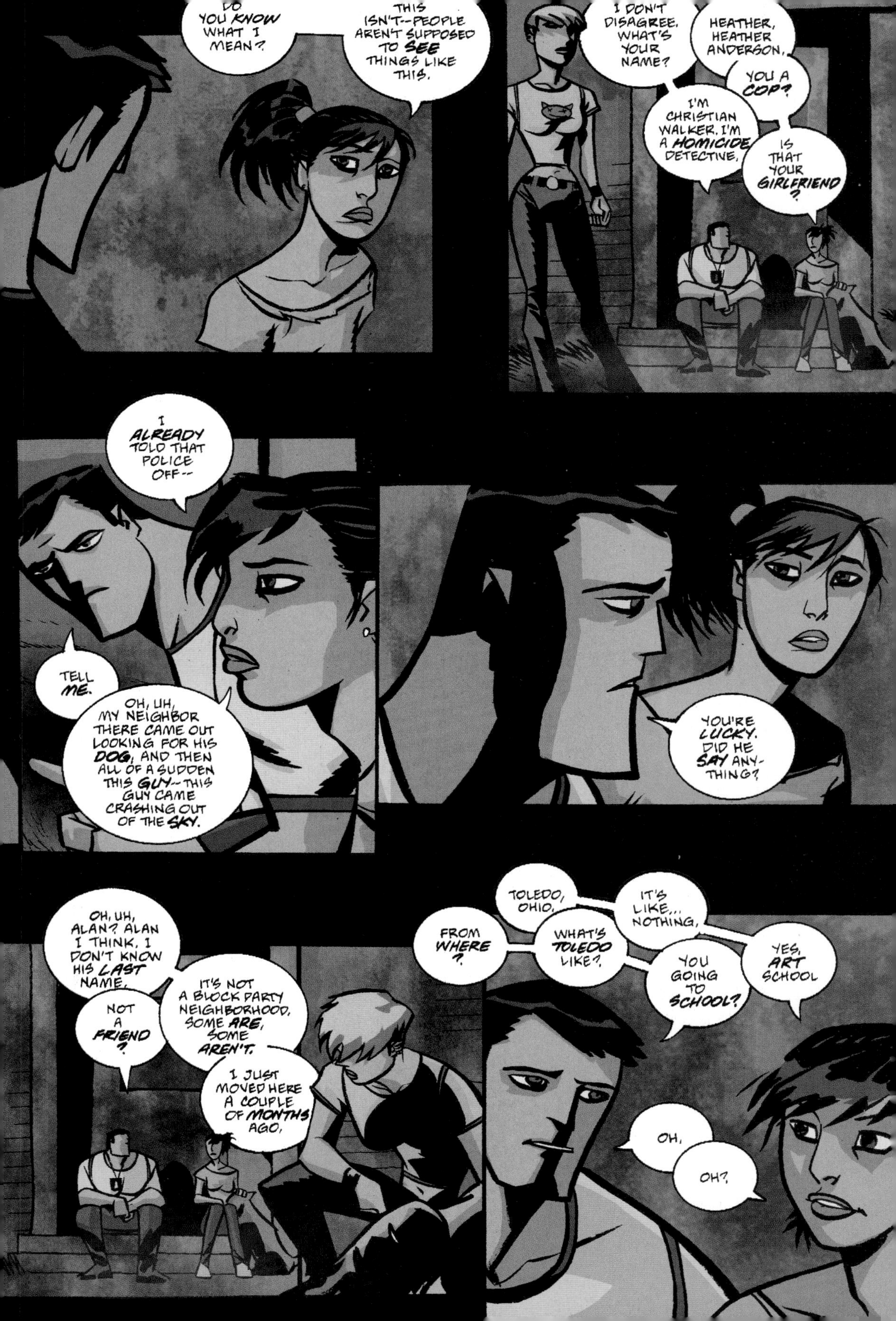
DO YOU KNOW WHAT I MEAN?
THIS ISN'T--PEOPLE AREN'T SUPPOSED TO SEE THINGS LIKE THIS.
I DON'T DISAGREE. WHAT'S YOUR NAME?
HEATHER, HEATHER ANDERSON.
I'M CHRISTIAN WALKER. I'M A HOMICIDE DETECTIVE.
YOU A COP?
IS THAT YOUR GIRLFRIEND?
I ALREADY TOLD THAT POLICE OFF--
TELL ME.
OH, UH, MY NEIGHBOR THERE CAME OUT LOOKING FOR HIS DOG, AND THEN ALL OF A SUDDEN THIS GUY-- THIS GUY CAME CRASHING OUT OF THE SKY.
YOU'RE LUCKY. DID HE SAY ANY-THING?
OH, UH, ALAN? ALAN I THINK. I DON'T KNOW HIS LAST NAME.
NOT A FRIEND?
IT'S NOT A BLOCK PARTY NEIGHBORHOOD. SOME ARE, SOME AREN'T.
I JUST MOVED HERE A COUPLE OF MONTHS AGO.
FROM WHERE?
TOLEDO, OHIO.
WHAT'S TOLEDO LIKE?
IT'S LIKE... NOTHING.
YOU GOING TO SCHOOL?
YES. ART SCHOOL
OH.
OH?

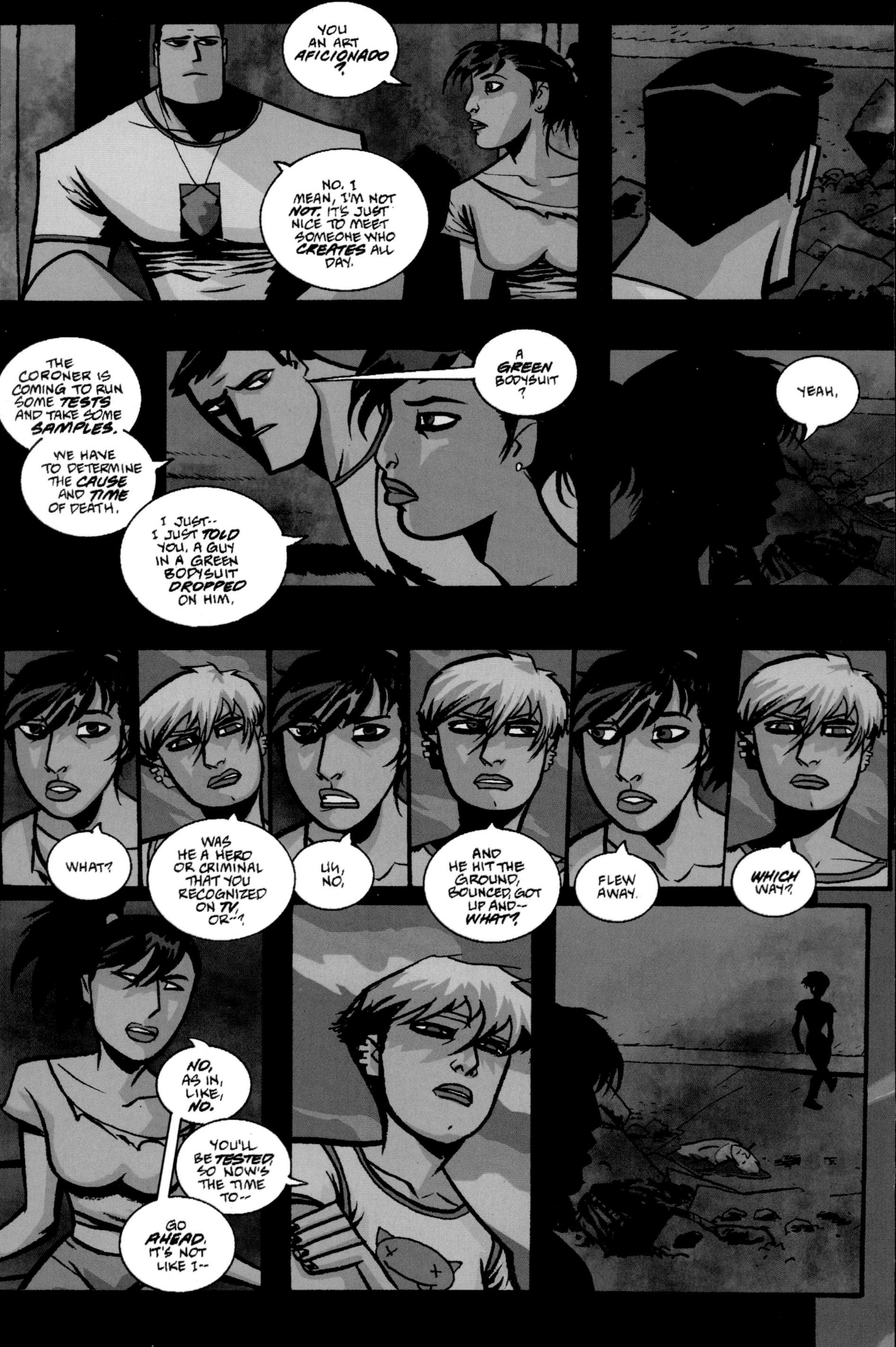

YOU AN ART AFICIONADO?
NO. I MEAN, I'M NOT NOT. IT'S JUST NICE TO MEET SOMEONE WHO CREATES ALL DAY.
THE CORONER IS COMING TO RUN SOME TESTS AND TAKE SOME SAMPLES.
WE HAVE TO DETERMINE THE CAUSE AND TIME OF DEATH.
I JUST-- I JUST TOLD YOU. A GUY IN A GREEN BODYSUIT DROPPED ON HIM.
A GREEN BODYSUIT?
YEAH.
WHAT?
WAS HE A HERO OR CRIMINAL THAT YOU RECOGNIZED ON TV, OR--?
UH, NO.
AND HE HIT THE GROUND, BOUNCED, GOT UP AND-- WHAT?
FLEW AWAY.
WHICH WAY?
NO, AS IN, LIKE, NO.
YOU'LL BE TESTED, SO NOW'S THE TIME TO--
GO AHEAD. IT'S NOT LIKE I--

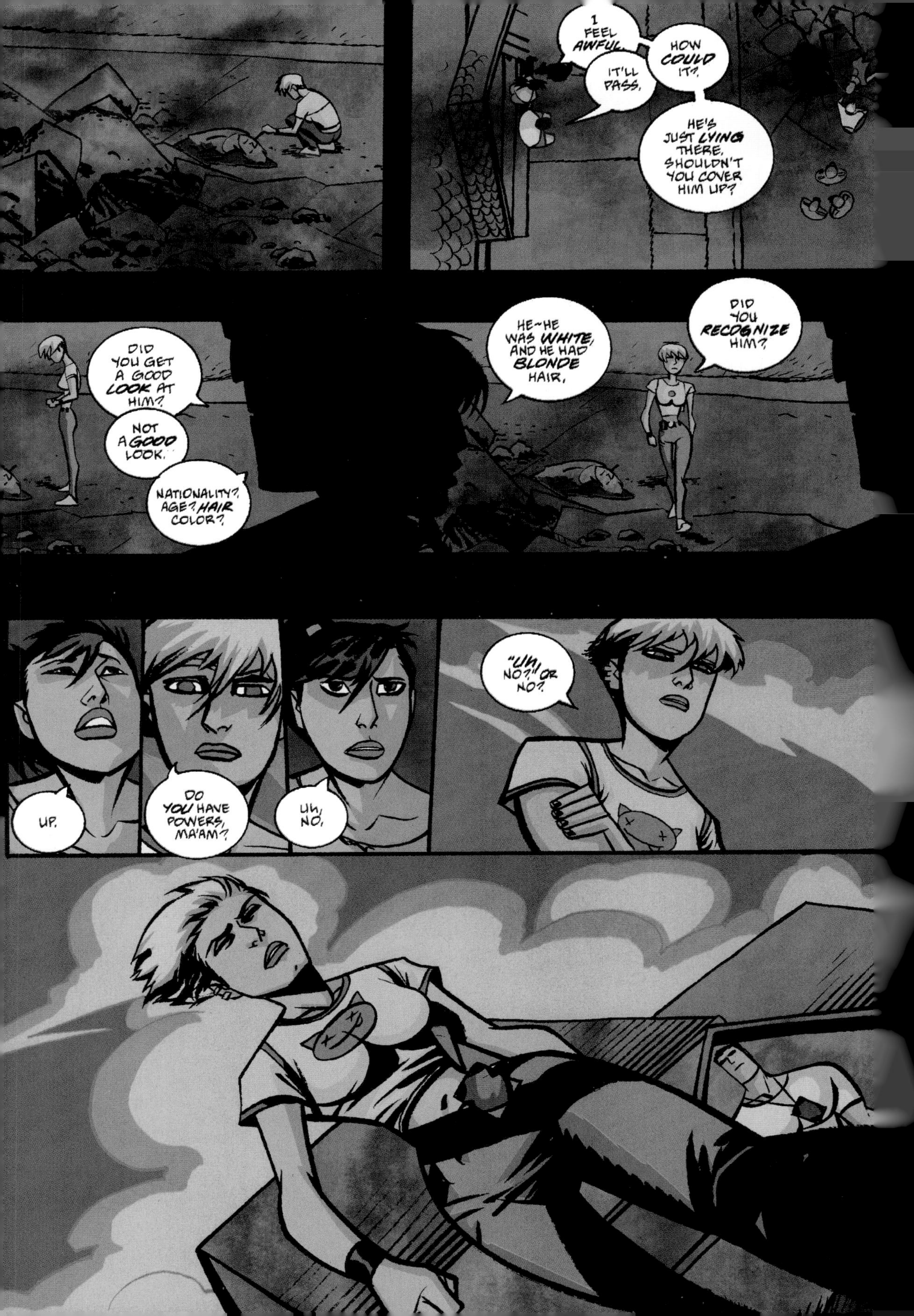
I FEEL AWFUL.
IT'LL PASS.
HOW COULD IT?
HE'S JUST LYING THERE. SHOULDN'T YOU COVER HIM UP?
DID YOU GET A GOOD LOOK AT HIM?
NOT A GOOD LOOK.
NATIONALITY? AGE? HAIR COLOR?
HE--HE WAS WHITE, AND HE HAD BLONDE HAIR.
DID YOU RECOGNIZE HIM?
UP.
DO YOU HAVE POWERS, MA'AM?
UH, NO.
"UH, NO?" OR NO?

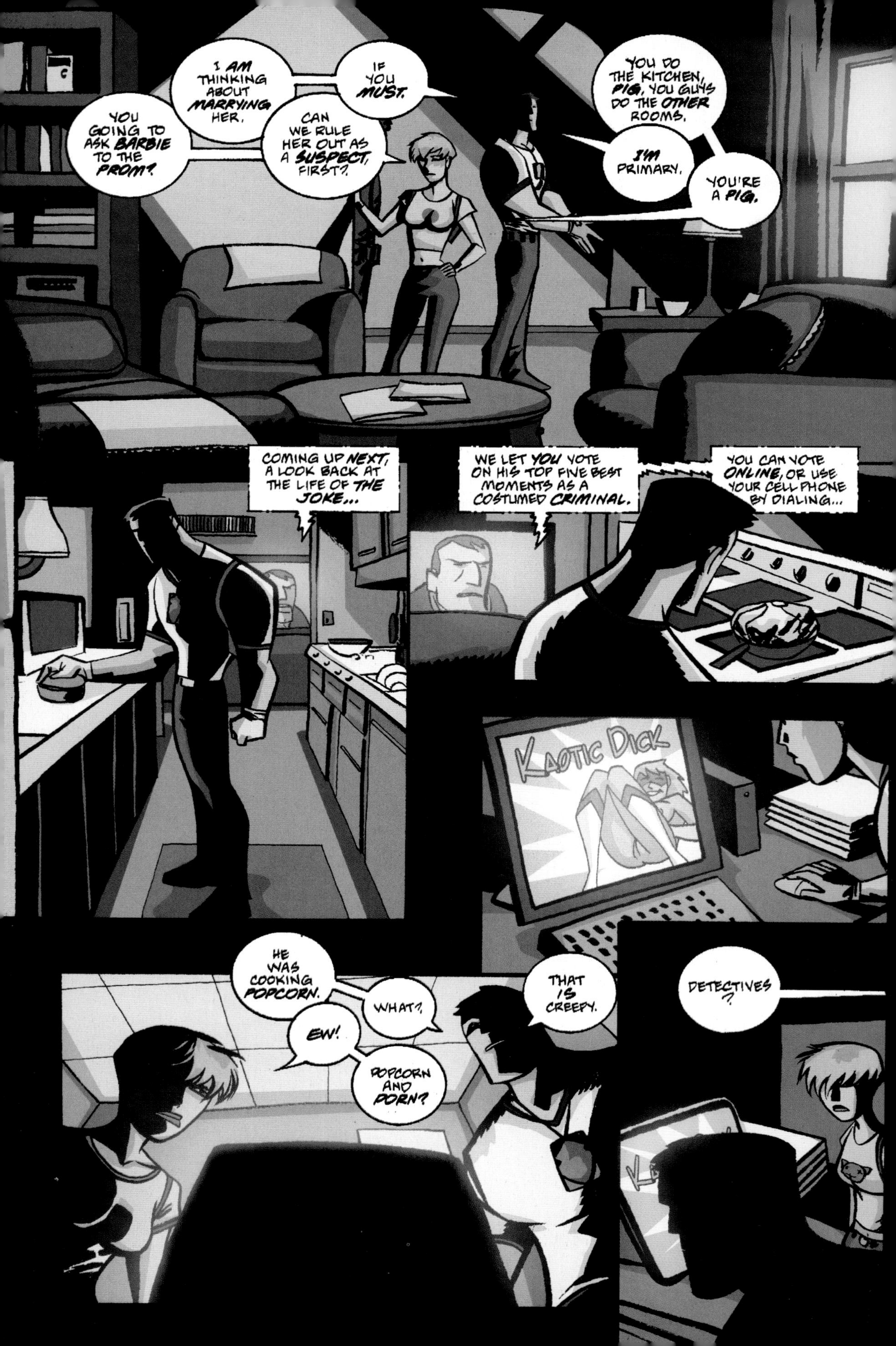
YOU GOING TO ASK BARBIE TO THE PROM?
I AM THINKING ABOUT MARRYING HER.
IF YOU MUST.
CAN WE RULE HER OUT AS A SUSPECT, FIRST?
YOU DO THE KITCHEN, PIG, YOU GUYS DO THE OTHER ROOMS.
I'M PRIMARY.
YOU'RE A PIG.
COMING UP NEXT, A LOOK BACK AT THE LIFE OF THE JOKE...
WE LET YOU VOTE ON HIS TOP FIVE BEST MOMENTS AS A COSTUMED CRIMINAL.
YOU CAN VOTE ONLINE, OR USE YOUR CELL PHONE BY DIALING...
KAOTIC DICK
HE WAS COOKING POPCORN.
WHAT?
EW!
POPCORN AND PORN?
THAT IS CREEPY.
DETECTIVES?

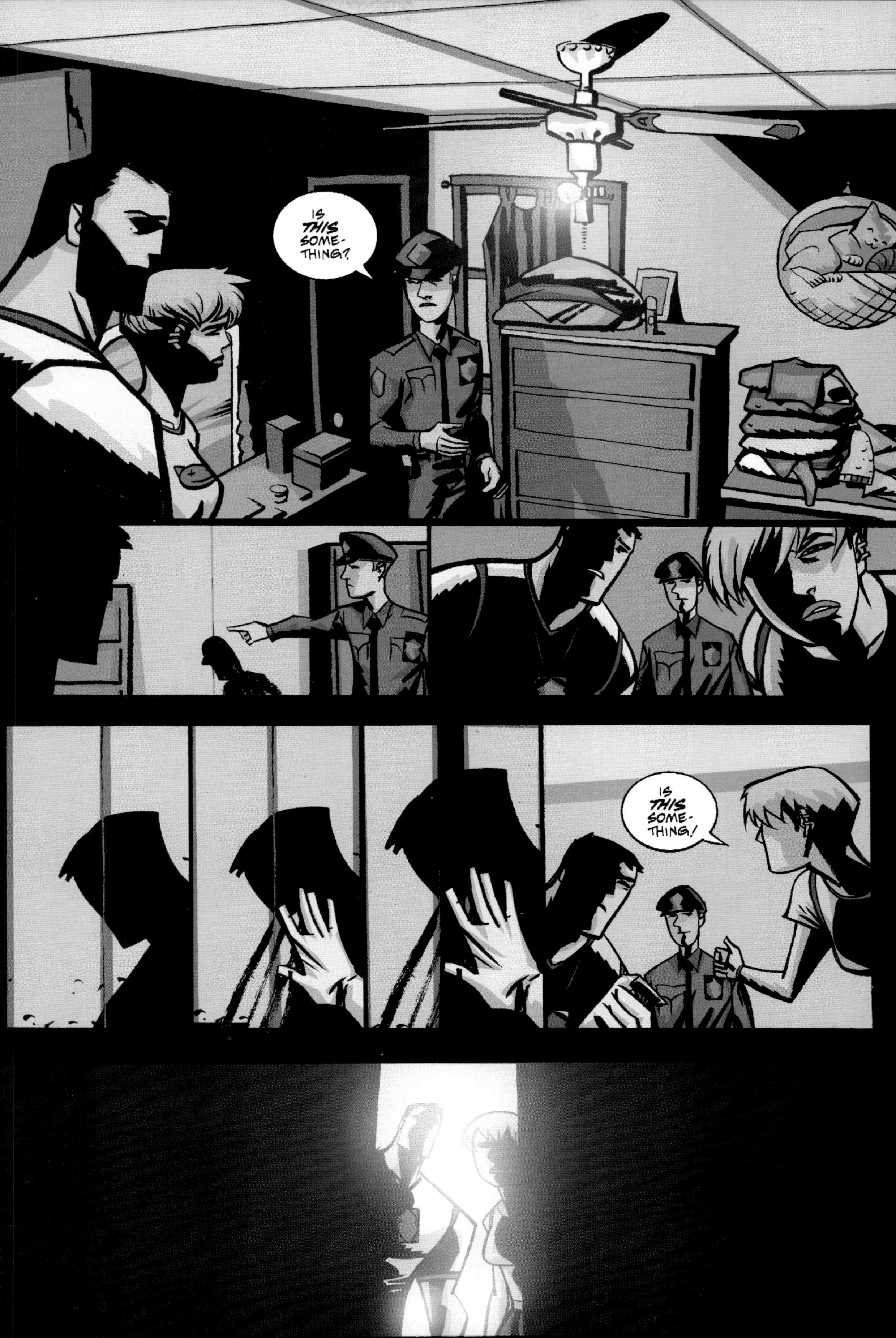
IS THIS SOME-THING?
IS THIS SOME-THING!

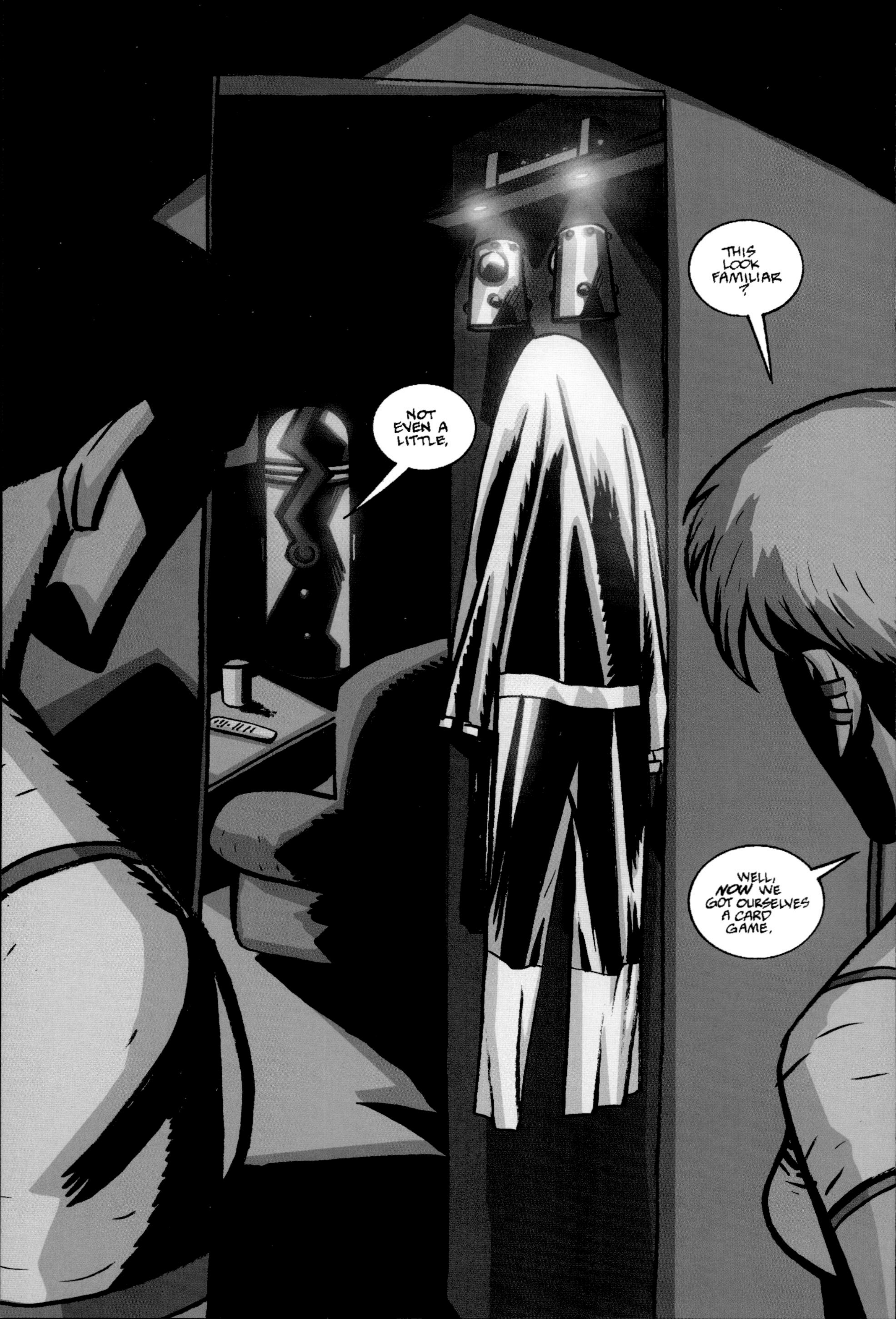
THIS LOOK FAMILIAR?
NOT EVEN A LITTLE.
WELL, NOW WE GOT OURSELVES A CARD GAME.

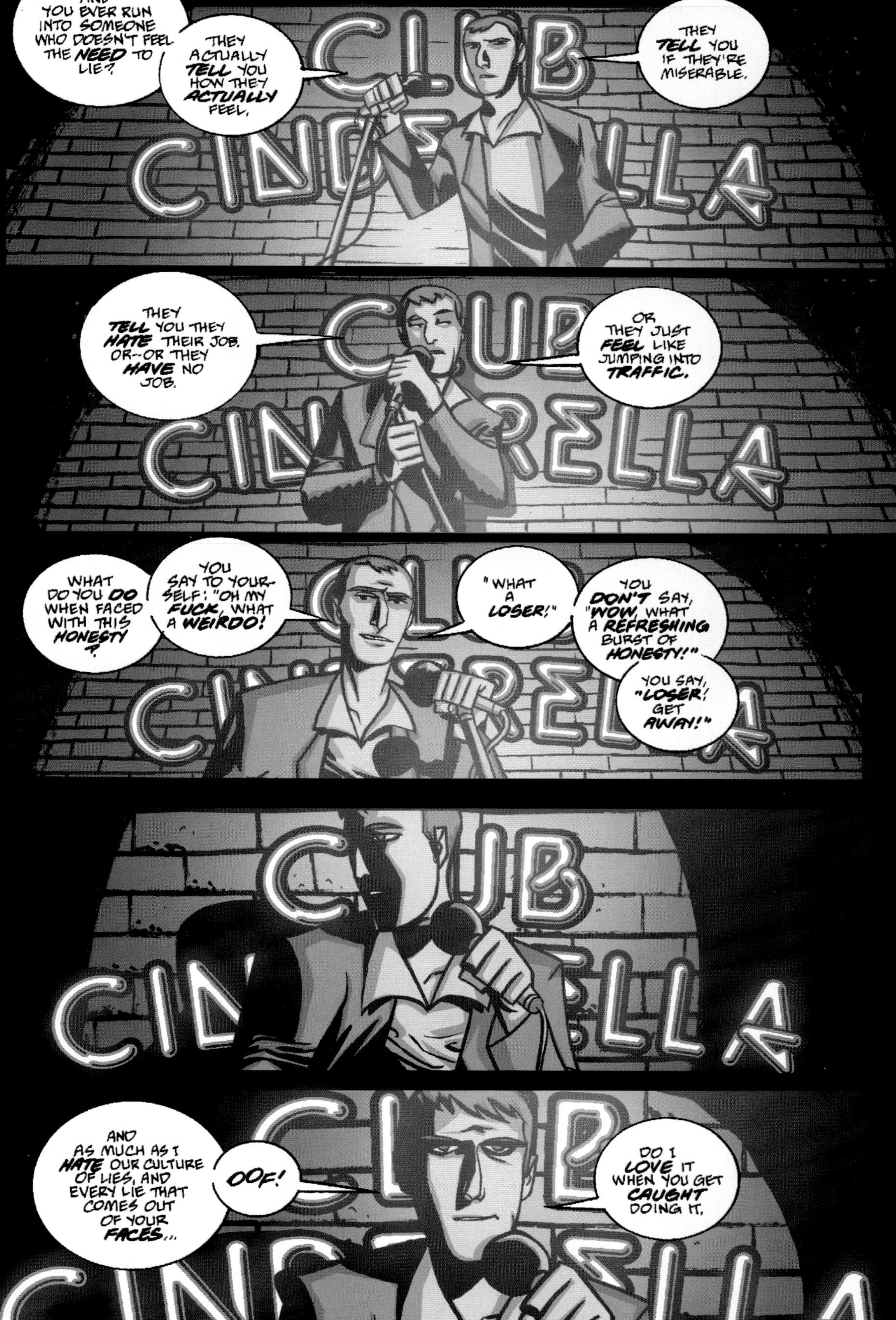

AND YOU EVER RUN INTO SOMEONE WHO DOESN'T FEEL THE NEED TO LIE?
THEY ACTUALLY TELL YOU HOW THEY ACTUALLY FEEL.
THEY TELL YOU IF THEY'RE MISERABLE.
CLUB CINDERELLA
THEY TELL YOU THEY HATE THEIR JOB. OR--OR THEY HAVE NO JOB.
OR THEY JUST FEEL LIKE JUMPING INTO TRAFFIC.
WHAT DO YOU DO WHEN FACED WITH THIS HONESTY?
YOU SAY TO YOURSELF: "OH MY FUCK, WHAT A WEIRDO!
"WHAT A LOSER!"
YOU DON'T SAY, "WOW, WHAT A REFRESHING BURST OF HONESTY!"
YOU SAY, "LOSER! GET AWAY!"
AND AS MUCH AS I HATE OUR CULTURE OF LIES, AND EVERY LIE THAT COMES OUT OF YOUR FACES...
OOF!
DO I LOVE IT WHEN YOU GET CAUGHT DOING IT.

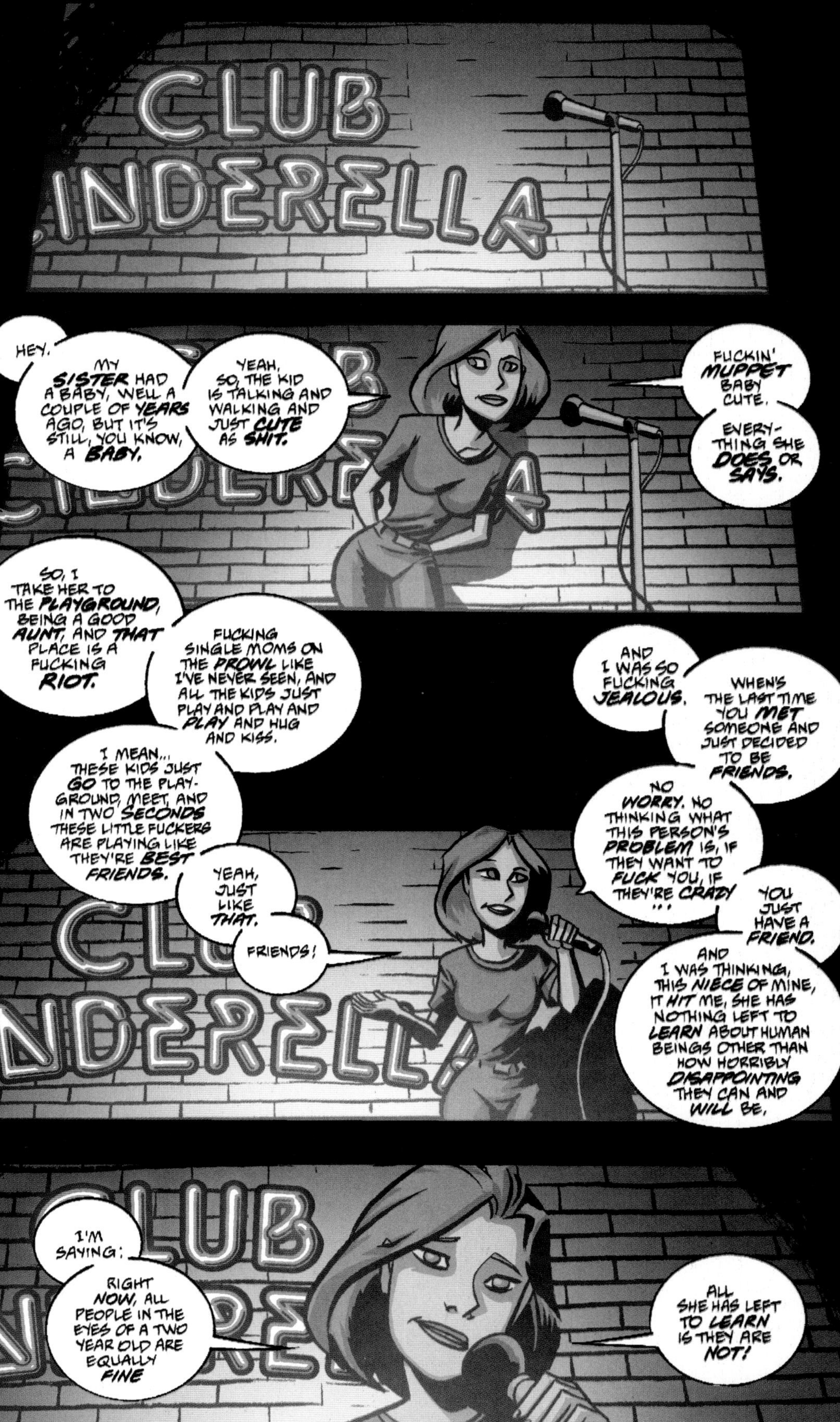

CLUB CINDERELLA
HEY.
MY SISTER HAD A BABY, WELL A COUPLE OF YEARS AGO, BUT IT'S STILL, YOU KNOW, A BABY.
YEAH, SO, THE KID IS TALKING AND WALKING AND JUST CUTE AS SHIT.
FUCKIN' MUPPET BABY CUTE.
EVERY-THING SHE DOES OR SAYS.
SO, I TAKE HER TO THE PLAYGROUND, BEING A GOOD AUNT, AND THAT PLACE IS A FUCKING RIOT.
FUCKING SINGLE MOMS ON THE PROWL LIKE I'VE NEVER SEEN, AND ALL THE KIDS JUST PLAY AND PLAY AND PLAY AND HUG AND KISS.
I MEAN... THESE KIDS JUST GO TO THE PLAY-GROUND, MEET, AND IN TWO SECONDS THESE LITTLE FUCKERS ARE PLAYING LIKE THEY'RE BEST FRIENDS.
YEAH, JUST LIKE THAT.
FRIENDS!
AND I WAS SO FUCKING JEALOUS.
WHEN'S THE LAST TIME YOU MET SOMEONE AND JUST DECIDED TO BE FRIENDS.
NO WORRY. NO THINKING WHAT THIS PERSON'S PROBLEM IS, IF THEY WANT TO FUCK YOU, IF THEY'RE CRAZY...
YOU JUST HAVE A FRIEND.
AND I WAS THINKING, THIS NIECE OF MINE, IT HIT ME, SHE HAS NOTHING LEFT TO LEARN ABOUT HUMAN BEINGS OTHER THAN HOW HORRIBLY DISAPPOINTING THEY CAN AND WILL BE.
I'M SAYING:
RIGHT NOW, ALL PEOPLE IN THE EYES OF A TWO YEAR OLD ARE EQUALLY FINE
ALL SHE HAS LEFT TO LEARN IS THEY ARE NOT!

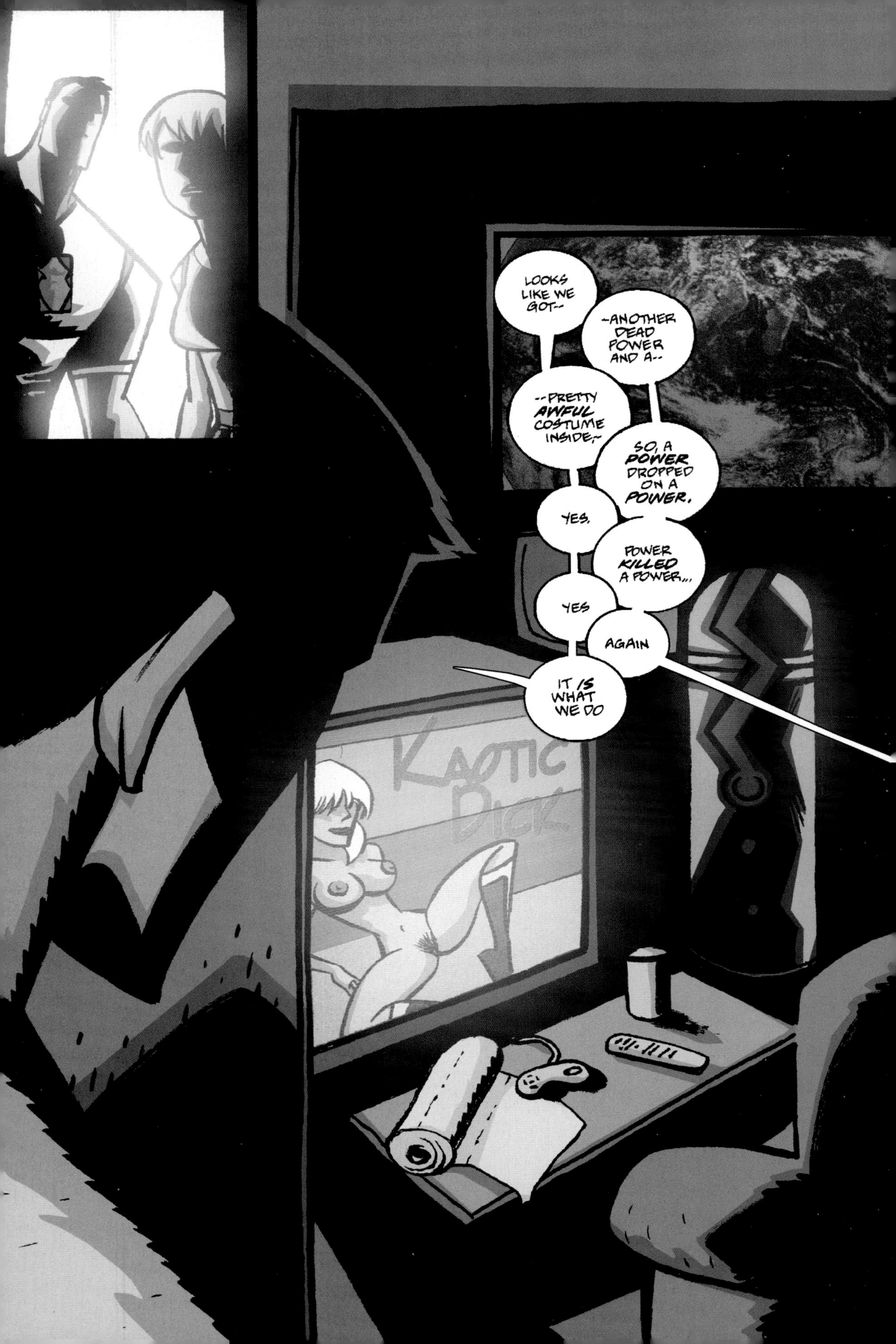
LOOKS LIKE WE GOT--
-ANOTHER DEAD POWER AND A--
--PRETTY AWFUL COSTUME INSIDE.-
SO, A POWER DROPPED ON A POWER.
YES.
POWER KILLED A POWER...
YES
AGAIN
IT IS WHAT WE DO
KAOTIC DICK

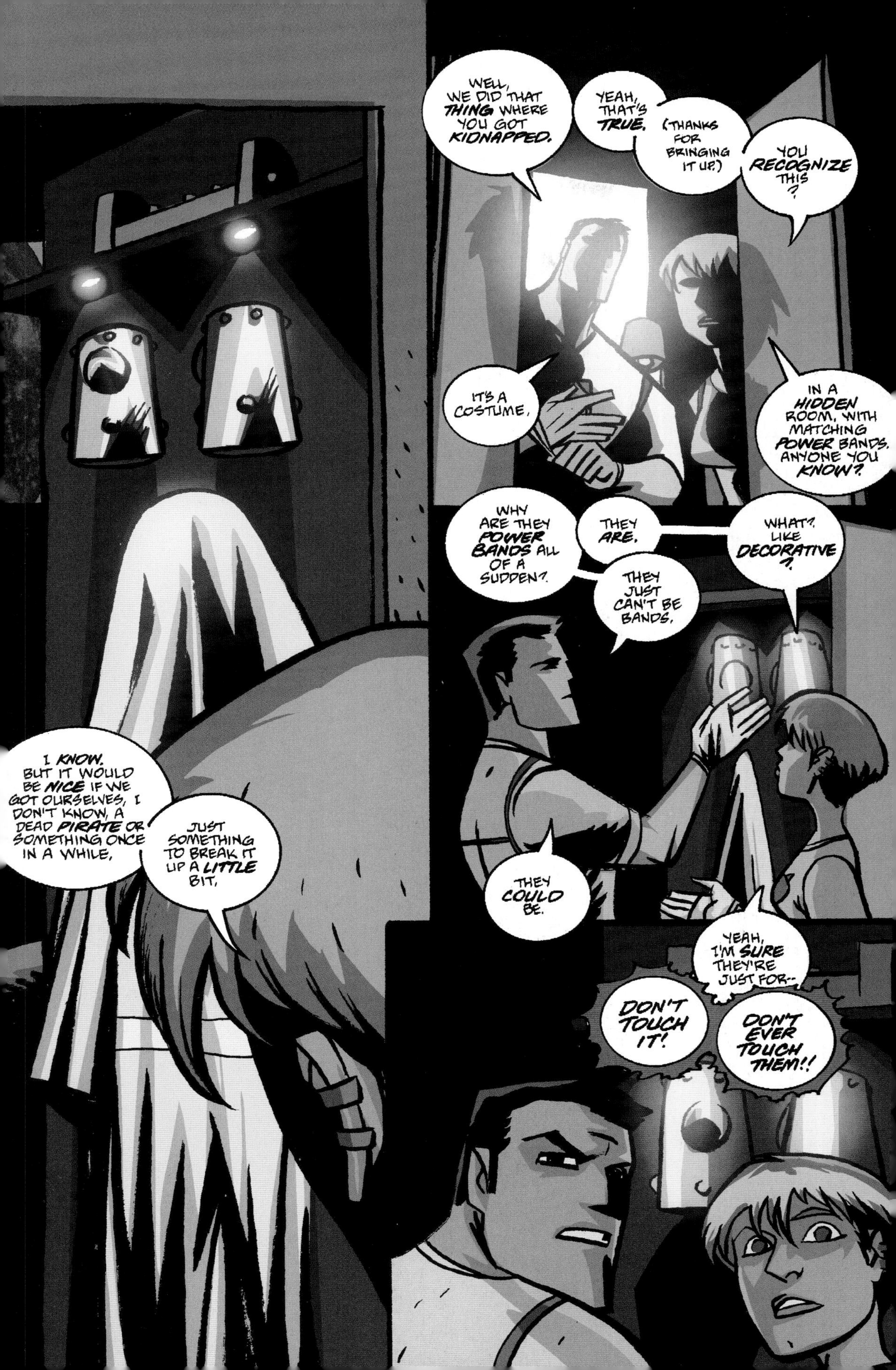
I KNOW. BUT IT WOULD BE NICE IF WE GOT OURSELVES, I DON'T KNOW, A DEAD PIRATE OR SOMETHING ONCE IN A WHILE.
JUST SOMETHING TO BREAK IT UP A LITTLE BIT.
WELL, WE DID THAT THING WHERE YOU GOT KIDNAPPED.
YEAH, THAT'S TRUE.
(THANKS FOR BRINGING IT UP.)
YOU RECOGNIZE THIS?
IT'S A COSTUME.
IN A HIDDEN ROOM, WITH MATCHING POWER BANDS. ANYONE YOU KNOW?
WHY ARE THEY POWER BANDS ALL OF A SUDDEN?
THEY ARE.
WHAT? LIKE DECORATIVE?
THEY JUST CAN'T BE BANDS.
THEY COULD BE.
YEAH, I'M SURE THEY'RE JUST FOR--
DON'T TOUCH IT!
DON'T EVER TOUCH THEM!!

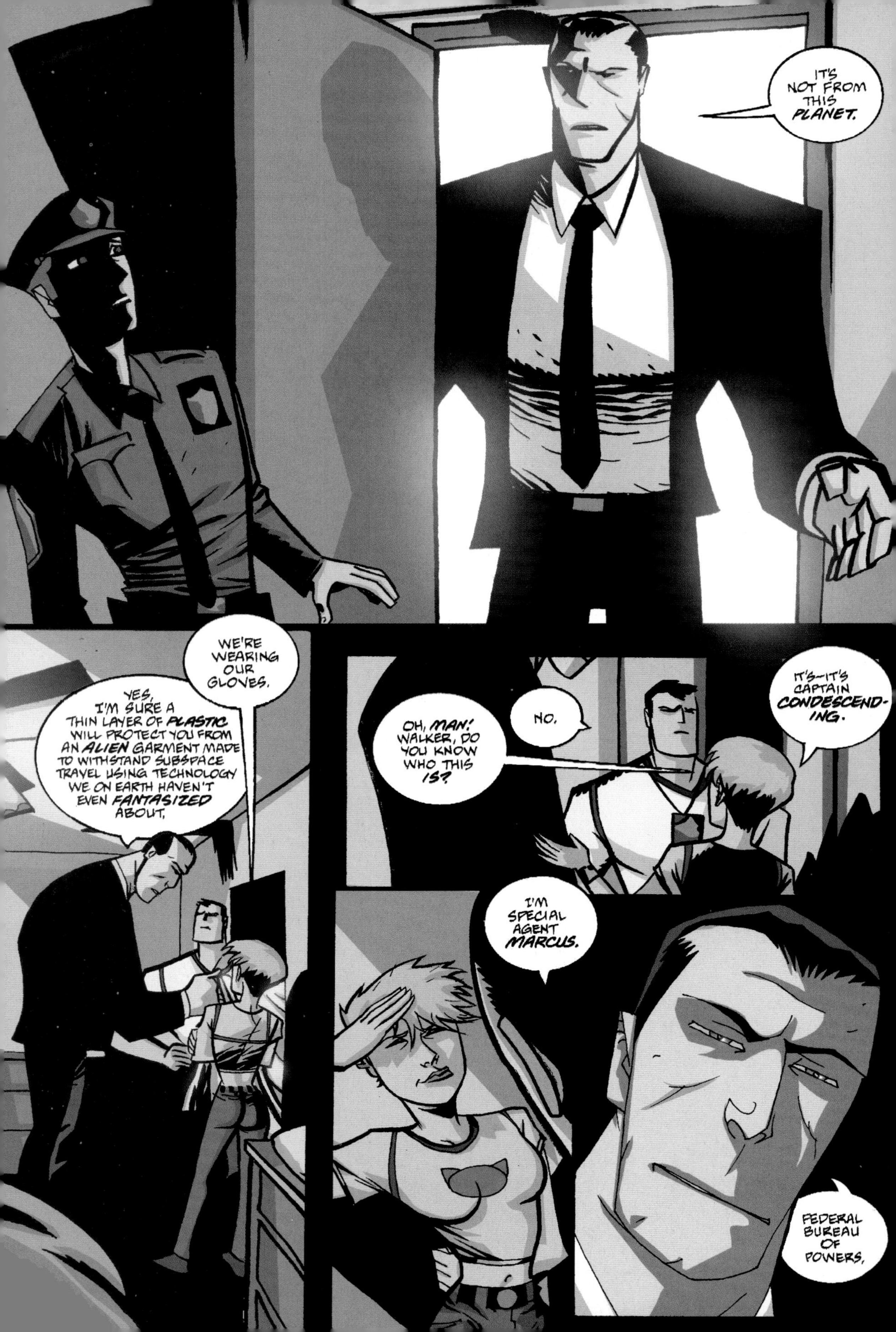
IT'S NOT FROM THIS PLANET.
WE'RE WEARING OUR GLOVES.
YES, I'M SURE A THIN LAYER OF PLASTIC WILL PROTECT YOU FROM AN ALIEN GARMENT MADE TO WITHSTAND SUBSPACE TRAVEL USING TECHNOLOGY WE ON EARTH HAVEN'T EVEN FANTASIZED ABOUT.
OH, MAN! WALKER, DO YOU KNOW WHO THIS IS?
NO.
IT'S--IT'S CAPTAIN CONDESCENDING.
I'M SPECIAL AGENT MARCUS.
FEDERAL BUREAU OF POWERS.

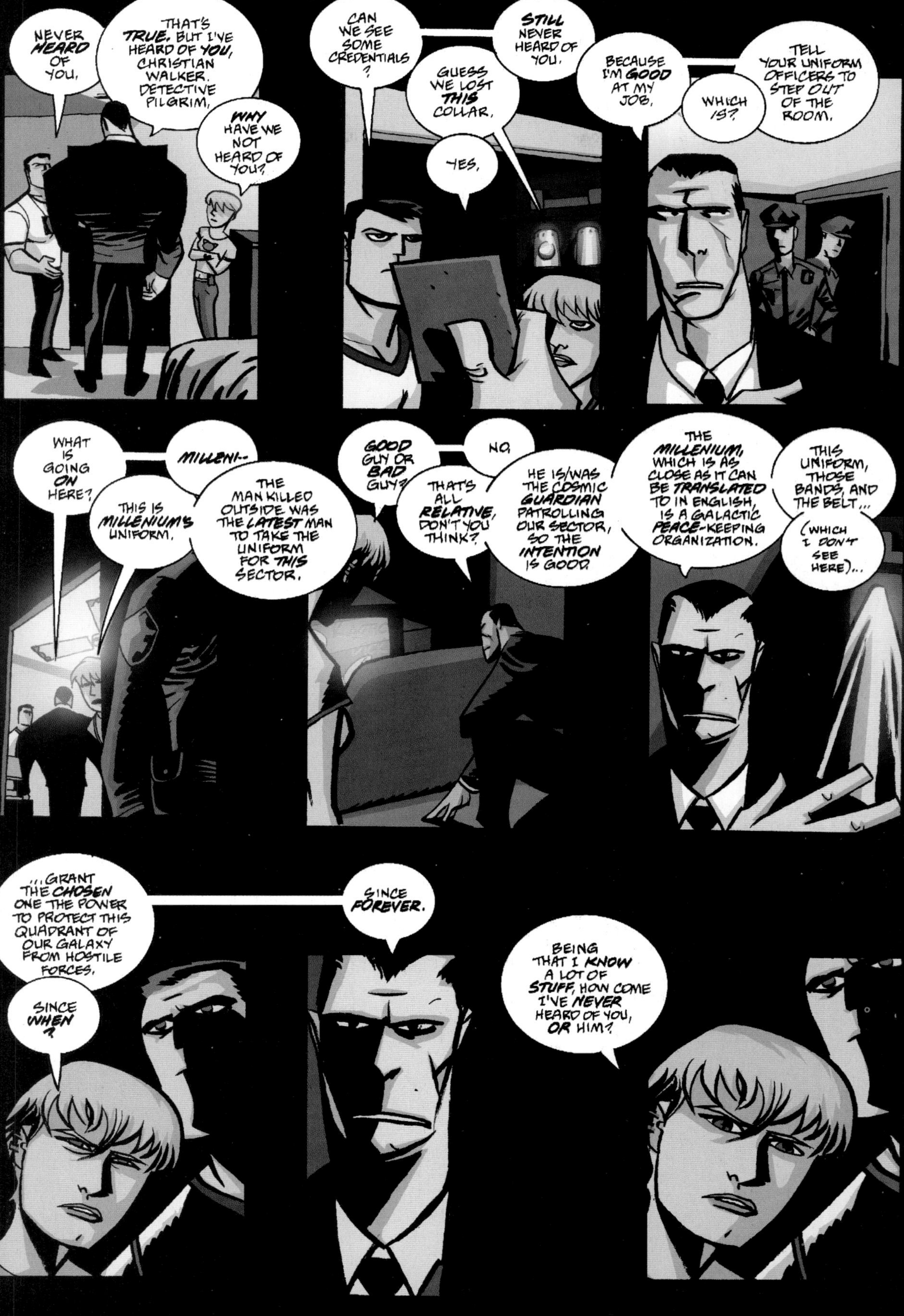
NEVER HEARD OF YOU.
THAT'S TRUE. BUT I'VE HEARD OF YOU, CHRISTIAN WALKER. DETECTIVE PILGRIM.
WHY HAVE WE NOT HEARD OF YOU?
CAN WE SEE SOME CREDENTIALS?
STILL NEVER HEARD OF YOU.
GUESS WE LOST THIS COLLAR.
YES.
BECAUSE I'M GOOD AT MY JOB.
WHICH IS?
TELL YOUR UNIFORM OFFICERS TO STEP OUT OF THE ROOM.
WHAT IS GOING ON HERE?
MILLENI--
THIS IS MILLENIUM'S UNIFORM.
THE MAN KILLED OUTSIDE WAS THE LATEST MAN TO TAKE THE UNIFORM FOR THIS SECTOR.
GOOD GUY OR BAD GUY?
NO.
THAT'S ALL RELATIVE, DON'T YOU THINK?
HE IS/WAS THE COSMIC GUARDIAN PATROLLING OUR SECTOR, SO THE INTENTION IS GOOD.
THE MILLENIUM, WHICH IS AS CLOSE AS IT CAN BE TRANSLATED TO IN ENGLISH, IS A GALACTIC PEACE-KEEPING ORGANIZATION.
THIS UNIFORM, THOSE BANDS, AND THE BELT...
(WHICH I DON'T SEE HERE)...
...GRANT THE CHOSEN ONE THE POWER TO PROTECT THIS QUADRANT OF OUR GALAXY FROM HOSTILE FORCES.
SINCE WHEN?
SINCE FOREVER.
BEING THAT I KNOW A LOT OF STUFF, HOW COME I'VE NEVER HEARD OF YOU, OR HIM?

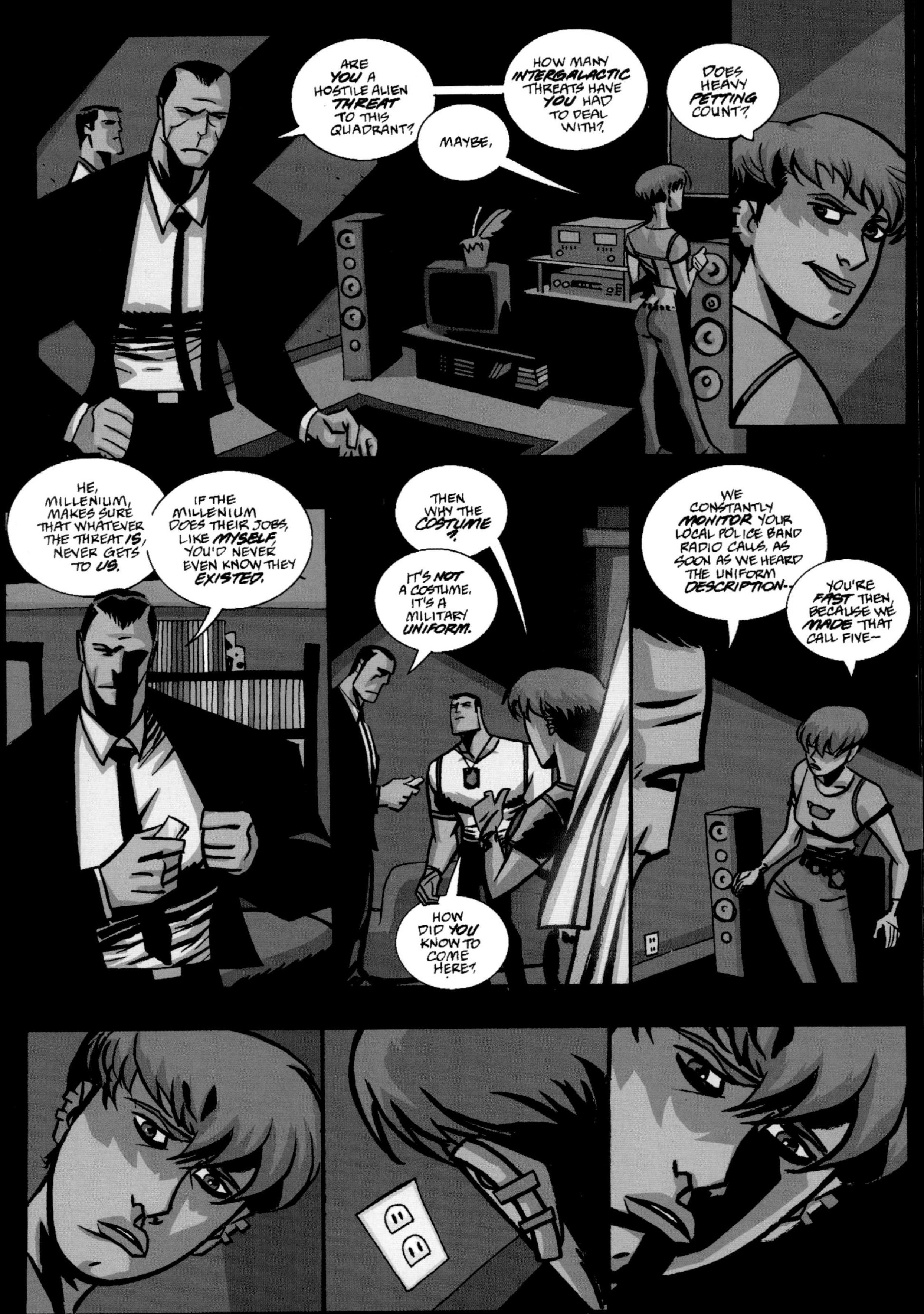
ARE YOU A HOSTILE ALIEN THREAT TO THIS QUADRANT?
MAYBE.
HOW MANY INTERGALACTIC THREATS HAVE YOU HAD TO DEAL WITH?
DOES HEAVY PETTING COUNT?
HE, MILLENIUM, MAKES SURE THAT WHATEVER THE THREAT IS, NEVER GETS TO US.
IF THE MILLENIUM DOES THEIR JOBS, LIKE MYSELF, YOU'D NEVER EVEN KNOW THEY EXISTED.
THEN WHY THE COSTUME?
IT'S NOT A COSTUME. IT'S A MILITARY UNIFORM.
HOW DID YOU KNOW TO COME HERE?
WE CONSTANTLY MONITOR YOUR LOCAL POLICE BAND RADIO CALLS. AS SOON AS WE HEARD THE UNIFORM DESCRIPTION--
YOU'RE FAST THEN, BECAUSE WE MADE THAT CALL FIVE--

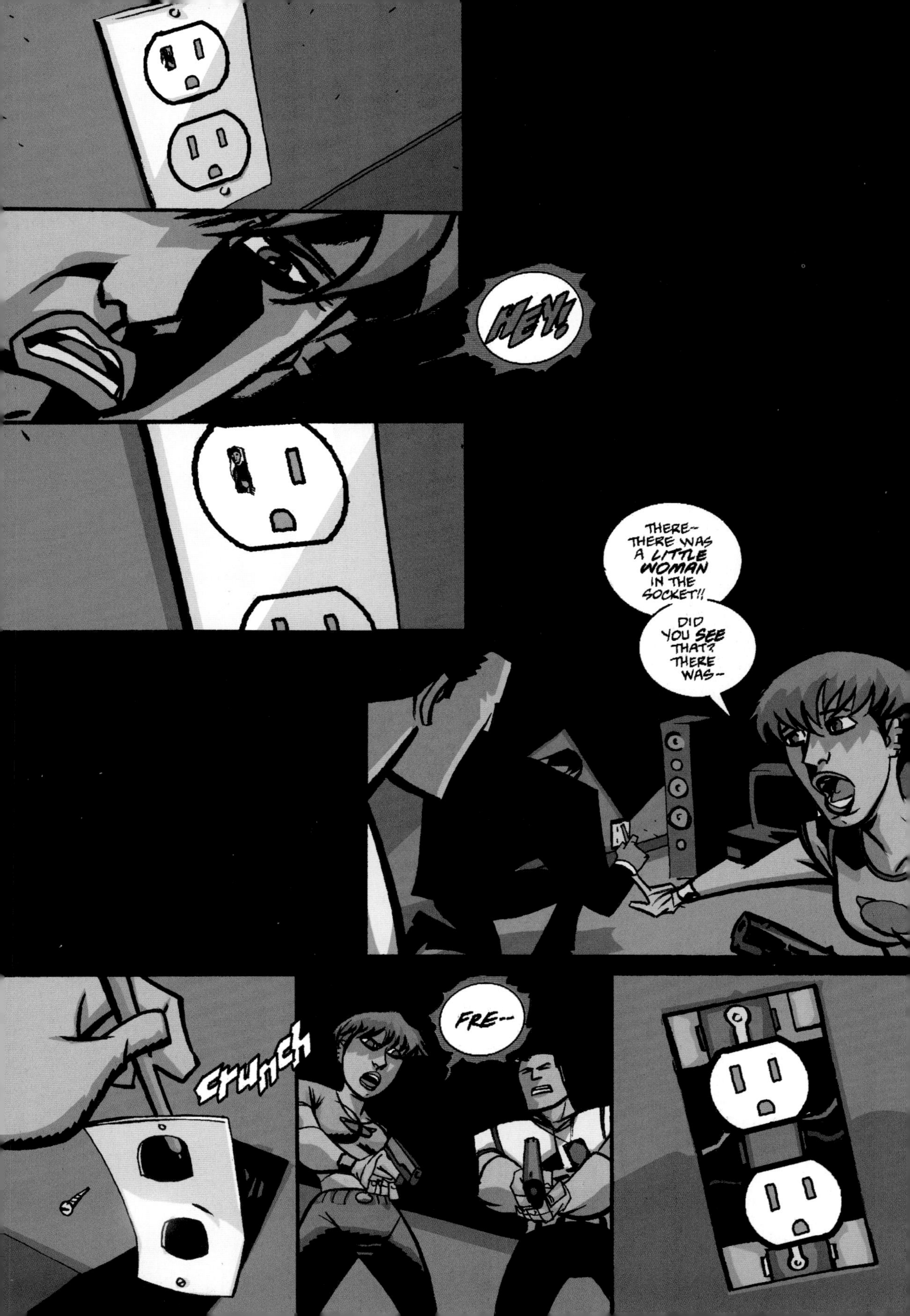
HEY!
THERE-- THERE WAS A LITTLE WOMAN IN THE SOCKET!!
DID YOU SEE THAT? THERE WAS--
CRUNCH
FRE--

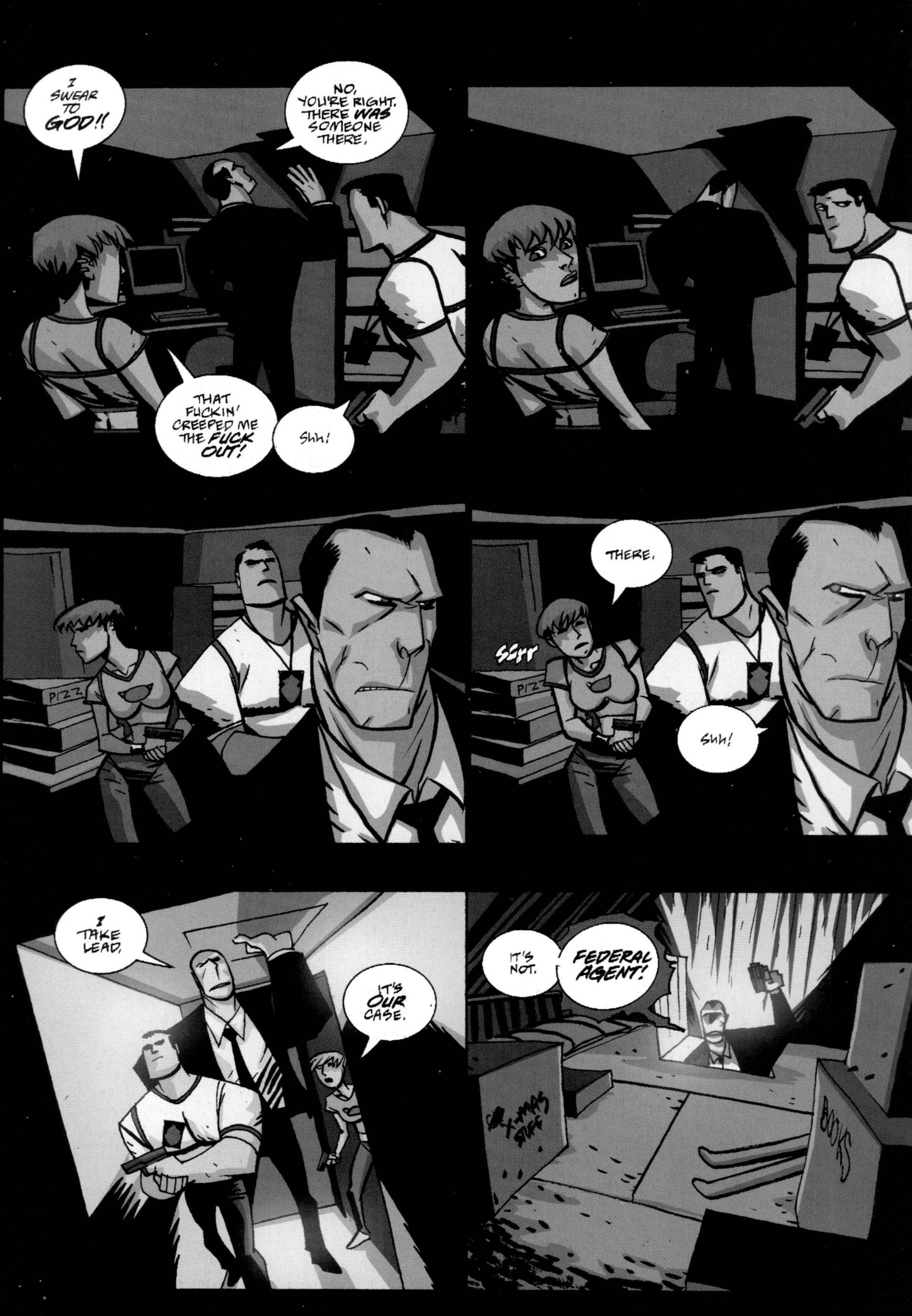
I SWEAR TO GOD!!
NO, YOU'RE RIGHT. THERE WAS SOMEONE THERE.
THAT FUCKIN' CREEPED ME THE FUCK OUT!
Shh!
THERE.
SCrr
Shh!
I TAKE LEAD.
IT'S OUR CASE.
IT'S NOT.
FEDERAL AGENT!
X-MAS STUFF
BOOKS

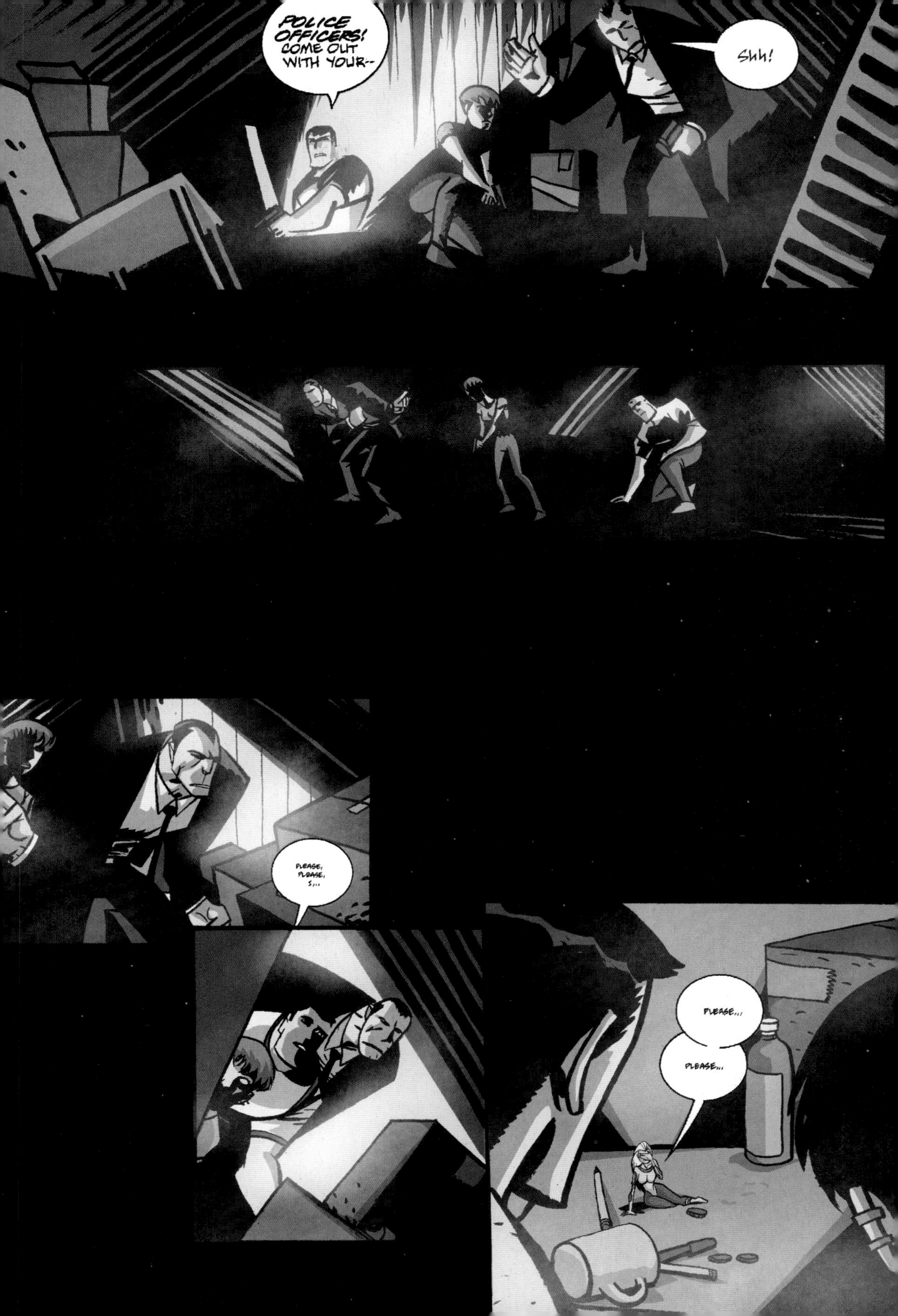
POLICE OFFICERS! COME OUT WITH YOUR--
Shh!
PLEASE, PLEASE, S...
PLEASE...
PLEASE...

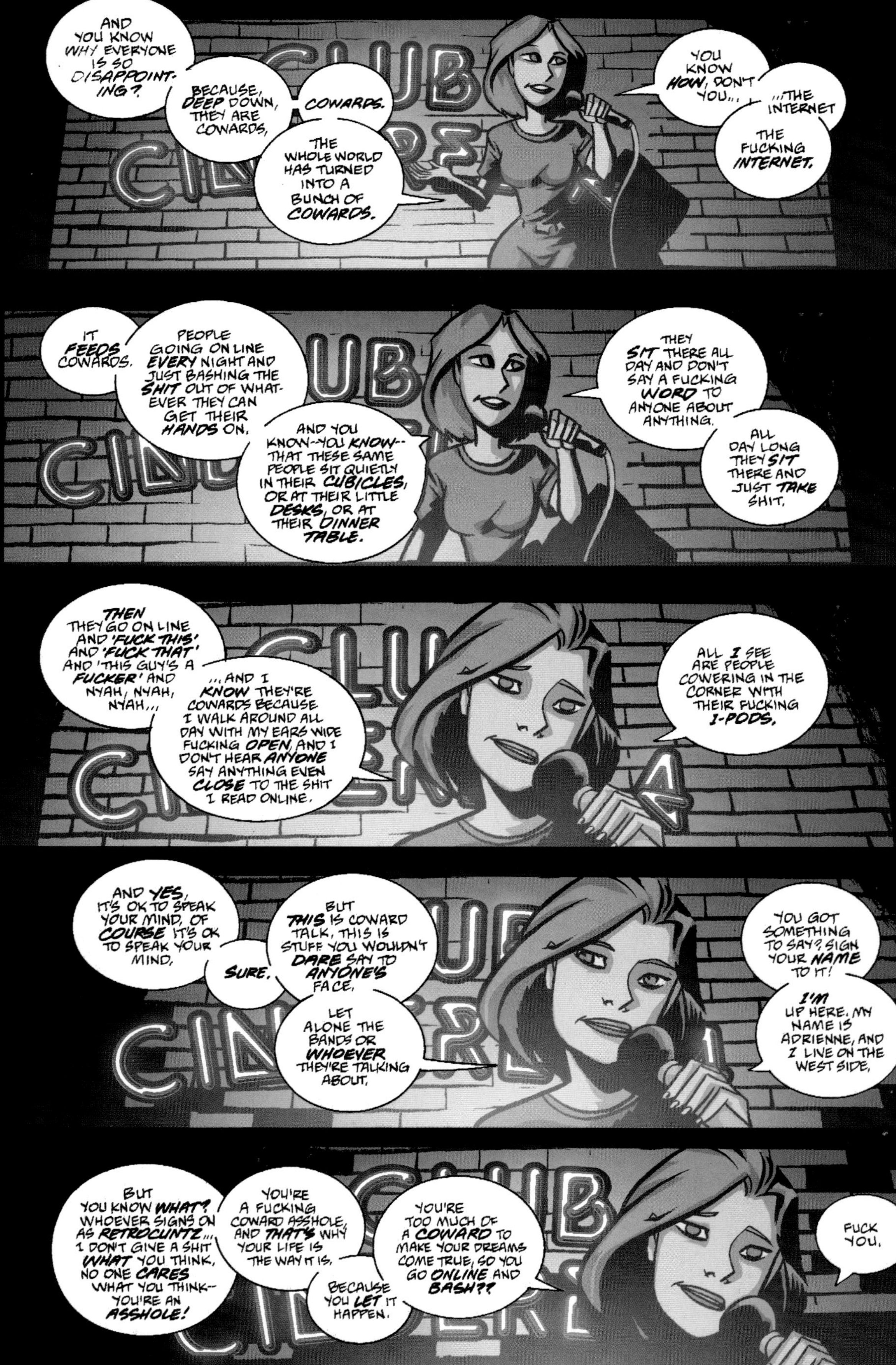
AND YOU KNOW WHY EVERYONE IS SO DISAPPOINTING?
BECAUSE, DEEP DOWN, THEY ARE COWARDS,
COWARDS.
THE WHOLE WORLD HAS TURNED INTO A BUNCH OF COWARDS.
YOU KNOW HOW, DON'T YOU...
...THE INTERNET
THE FUCKING INTERNET.
IT FEEDS COWARDS.
PEOPLE GOING ON LINE EVERY NIGHT AND JUST BASHING THE SHIT OUT OF WHATEVER THEY CAN GET THEIR HANDS ON.
AND YOU KNOW--YOU KNOW--THAT THESE SAME PEOPLE SIT QUIETLY IN THEIR CUBICLES, OR AT THEIR LITTLE DESKS, OR AT THEIR DINNER TABLE.
THEY SIT THERE ALL DAY AND DON'T SAY A FUCKING WORD TO ANYONE ABOUT ANYTHING.
ALL DAY LONG THEY SIT THERE AND JUST TAKE SHIT.
THEN THEY GO ON LINE AND 'FUCK THIS' AND 'FUCK THAT' AND 'THIS GUY'S A FUCKER' AND NYAH, NYAH, NYAH...
...AND I KNOW THEY'RE COWARDS BECAUSE I WALK AROUND ALL DAY WITH MY EARS WIDE FUCKING OPEN, AND I DON'T HEAR ANYONE SAY ANYTHING EVEN CLOSE TO THE SHIT I READ ONLINE.
ALL I SEE ARE PEOPLE COWERING IN THE CORNER WITH THEIR FUCKING I-PODS.
AND YES, IT'S OK TO SPEAK YOUR MIND, OF COURSE IT'S OK TO SPEAK YOUR MIND.
SURE.
BUT THIS IS COWARD TALK. THIS IS STUFF YOU WOULDN'T DARE SAY TO ANYONE'S FACE.
LET ALONE THE BANDS OR WHOEVER THEY'RE TALKING ABOUT.
YOU GOT SOMETHING TO SAY? SIGN YOUR NAME TO IT!
I'M UP HERE. MY NAME IS ADRIENNE, AND I LIVE ON THE WEST SIDE.
BUT YOU KNOW WHAT? WHOEVER SIGNS ON AS RETROCUNTZ... I DON'T GIVE A SHIT WHAT YOU THINK, NO ONE CARES WHAT YOU THINK--YOU'RE AN ASSHOLE!
YOU'RE A FUCKING COWARD ASSHOLE, AND THAT'S WHY YOUR LIFE IS THE WAY IT IS.
BECAUSE YOU LET IT HAPPEN.
YOU'RE TOO MUCH OF A COWARD TO MAKE YOUR DREAMS COME TRUE, SO YOU GO ONLINE AND BASH??
FUCK YOU.

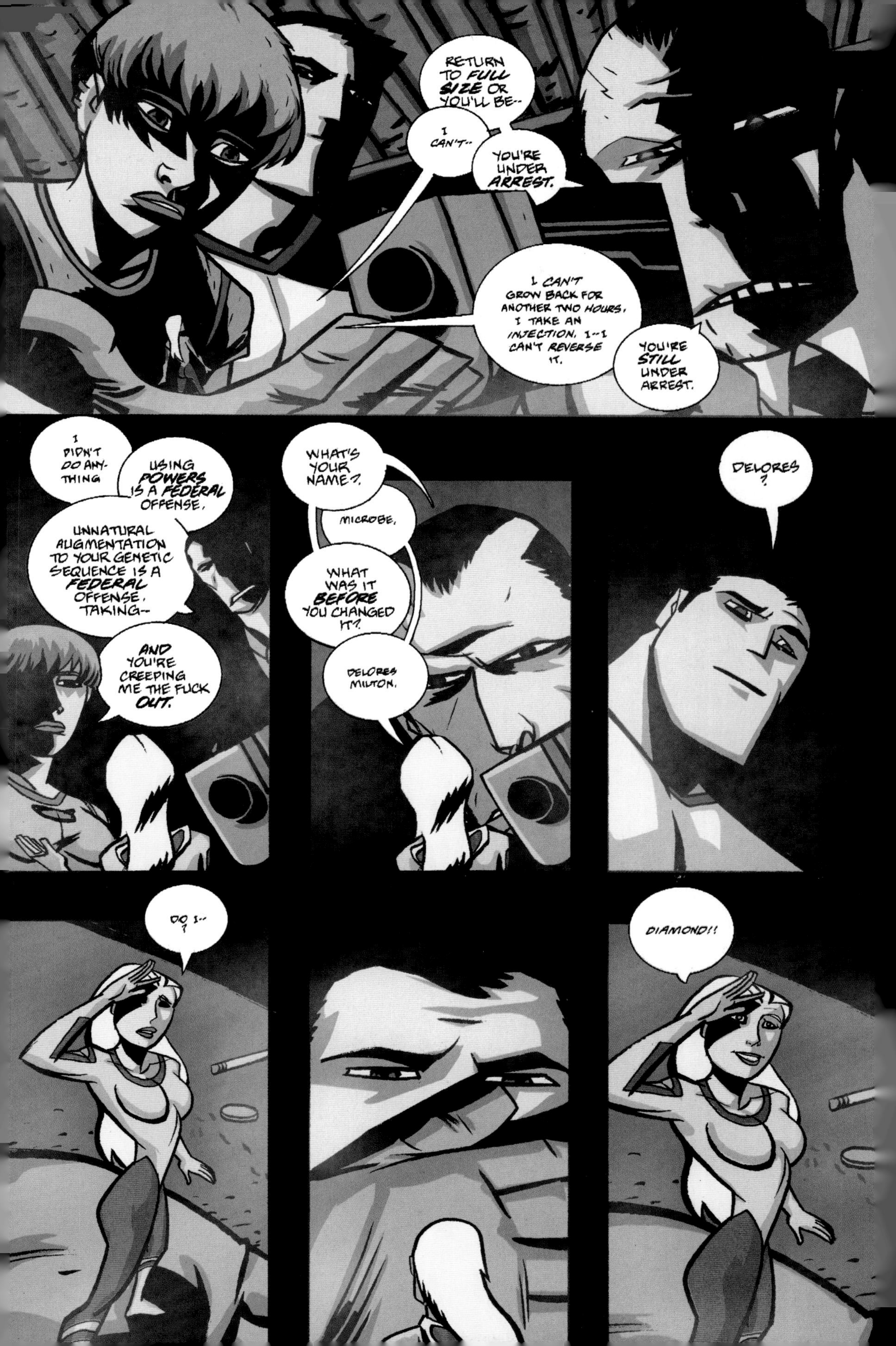

RETURN TO FULL SIZE OR YOU'LL BE--
I CAN'T--
YOU'RE UNDER ARREST.
I CAN'T GROW BACK FOR ANOTHER TWO HOURS. I TAKE AN INJECTION. I--I CAN'T REVERSE IT.
YOU'RE STILL UNDER ARREST.
I DIDN'T DO ANYTHING
USING POWERS IS A FEDERAL OFFENSE.
UNNATURAL AUGMENTATION TO YOUR GENETIC SEQUENCE IS A FEDERAL OFFENSE. TAKING--
AND YOU'RE CREEPING ME THE FUCK OUT.
WHAT'S YOUR NAME?
MICROBE.
WHAT WAS IT BEFORE YOU CHANGED IT?
DELORES MILTON.
DELORES?
DO I--?
DIAMOND!!

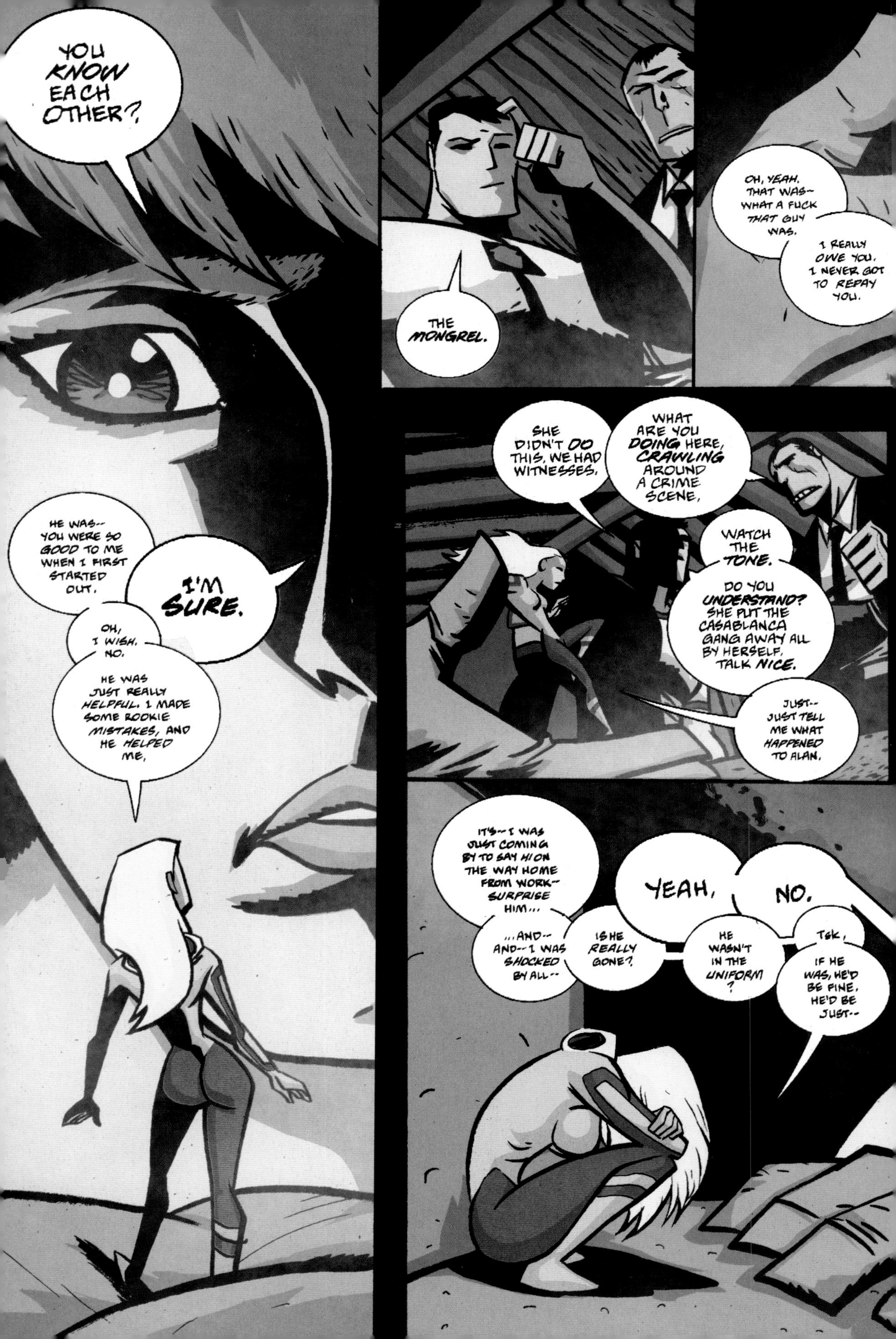
YOU KNOW EACH OTHER?
THE MONGREL.
OH, YEAH. THAT WAS-- WHAT A FUCK THAT GUY WAS.
I REALLY OWE YOU. I NEVER GOT TO REPAY YOU.
HE WAS-- YOU WERE SO GOOD TO ME WHEN I FIRST STARTED OUT.
I'M SURE.
OH, I WISH. NO.
HE WAS JUST REALLY HELPFUL. I MADE SOME ROOKIE MISTAKES, AND HE HELPED ME.
SHE DIDN'T DO THIS. WE HAD WITNESSES.
WHAT ARE YOU DOING HERE, CRAWLING AROUND A CRIME SCENE.
WATCH THE TONE.
DO YOU UNDERSTAND? SHE PUT THE CASABLANCA GANG AWAY ALL BY HERSELF. TALK NICE.
JUST-- JUST TELL ME WHAT HAPPENED TO ALAN.
IT'S-- I WAS JUST COMING BY TO SAY HI ON THE WAY HOME FROM WORK-- SURPRISE HIM...
...AND-- AND-- I WAS SHOCKED BY ALL--
IS HE REALLY GONE?
YEAH.
HE WASN'T IN THE UNIFORM?
NO.
TSK.
IF HE WAS, HE'D BE FINE. HE'D BE JUST--

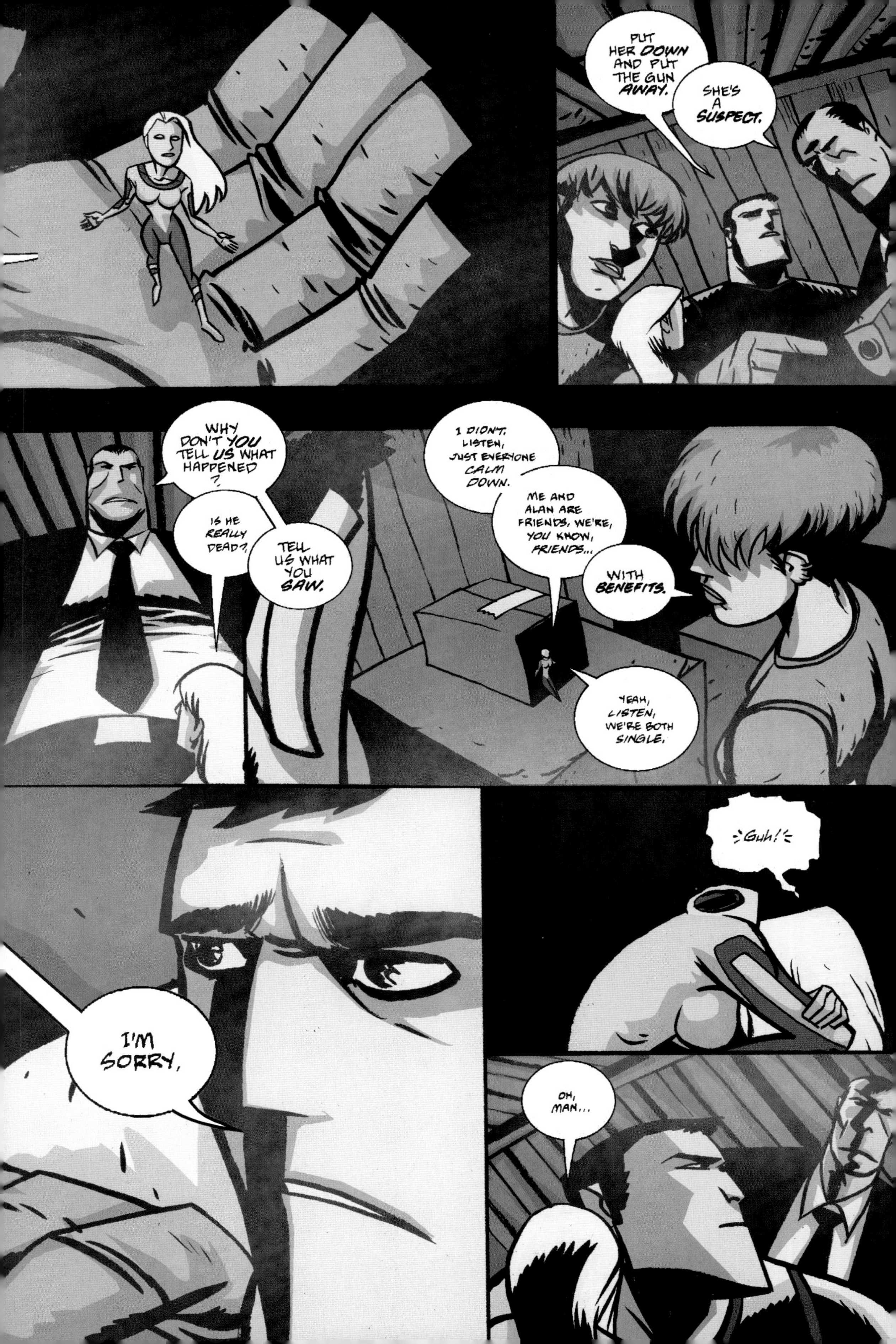
PUT HER DOWN AND PUT THE GUN AWAY.
SHE'S A SUSPECT.
WHY DON'T YOU TELL US WHAT HAPPENED?
IS HE REALLY DEAD?
TELL US WHAT YOU SAW.
I DIDN'T. LISTEN, JUST EVERYONE CALM DOWN.
ME AND ALAN ARE FRIENDS, WE'RE, YOU KNOW, FRIENDS...
WITH BENEFITS.
YEAH, LISTEN, WE'RE BOTH SINGLE.
I'M SORRY.
Guh!
OH, MAN...

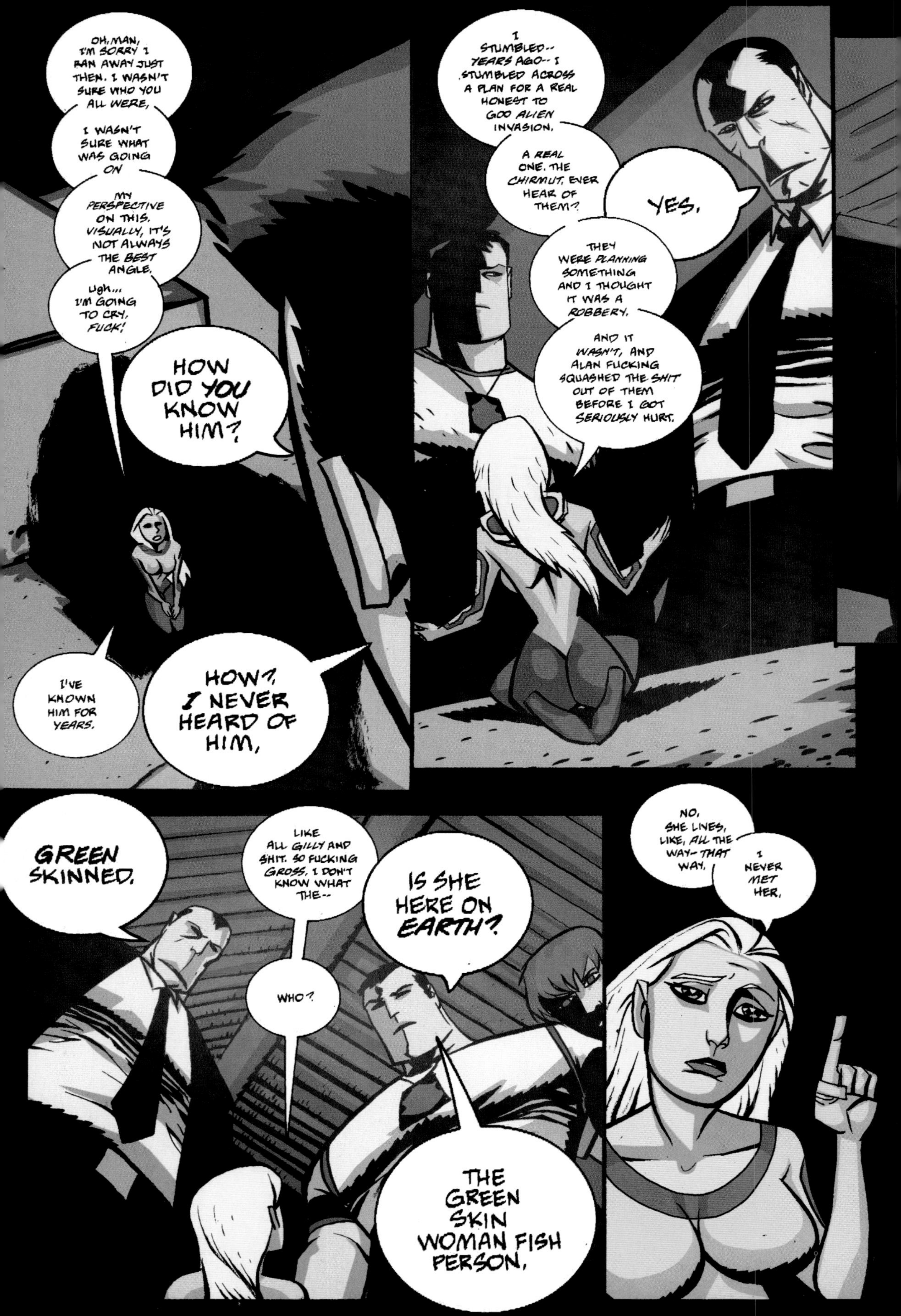
OH, MAN, I'M SORRY I RAN AWAY JUST THEN. I WASN'T SURE WHO YOU ALL WERE.
I WASN'T SURE WHAT WAS GOING ON
MY PERSPECTIVE ON THIS. VISUALLY, IT'S NOT ALWAYS THE BEST ANGLE.
Ugh... I'M GOING TO CRY. FUCK!
HOW DID YOU KNOW HIM?
I'VE KNOWN HIM FOR YEARS.
HOW? I NEVER HEARD OF HIM.
I STUMBLED-- YEARS AGO-- I STUMBLED ACROSS A PLAN FOR A REAL HONEST TO GOD ALIEN INVASION.
A REAL ONE. THE CHIRMUT. EVER HEAR OF THEM?
YES.
THEY WERE PLANNING SOMETHING AND I THOUGHT IT WAS A ROBBERY.
AND IT WASN'T, AND ALAN FUCKING SQUASHED THE SHIT OUT OF THEM BEFORE I GOT SERIOUSLY HURT.
GREEN SKINNED.
LIKE ALL GILLY AND SHIT. SO FUCKING GROSS. I DON'T KNOW WHAT THE--
WHO?
IS SHE HERE ON EARTH?
THE GREEN SKIN WOMAN FISH PERSON.
NO. SHE LIVES, LIKE, ALL THE WAY-- THAT WAY.
I NEVER MET HER.

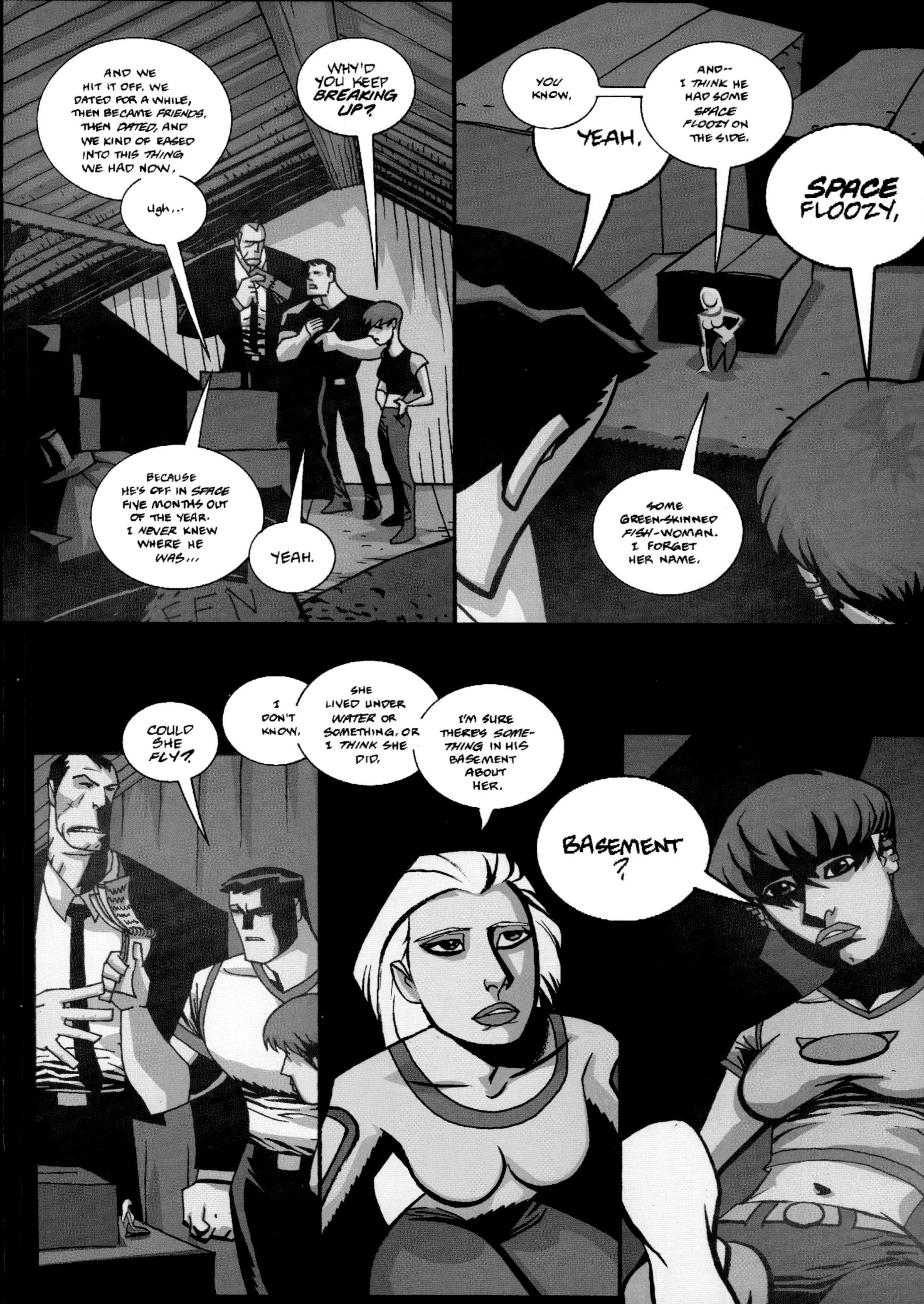
AND WE HIT IT OFF. WE DATED FOR A WHILE, THEN BECAME FRIENDS, THEN DATED, AND WE KIND OF EASED INTO THIS THING WE HAD NOW.
Ugh...
WHY'D YOU KEEP BREAKING UP?
BECAUSE HE'S OFF IN SPACE FIVE MONTHS OUT OF THE YEAR. I NEVER KNEW WHERE HE WAS...
YEAH.
YOU KNOW.
YEAH.
AND-- I THINK HE HAD SOME SPACE FLOOZY ON THE SIDE.
SPACE FLOOZY.
SOME GREEN-SKINNED FISH-WOMAN. I FORGET HER NAME.
COULD SHE FLY?
I DON'T KNOW.
SHE LIVED UNDER WATER OR SOMETHING, OR I THINK SHE DID.
I'M SURE THERE'S SOMETHING IN HIS BASEMENT ABOUT HER.
BASEMENT?

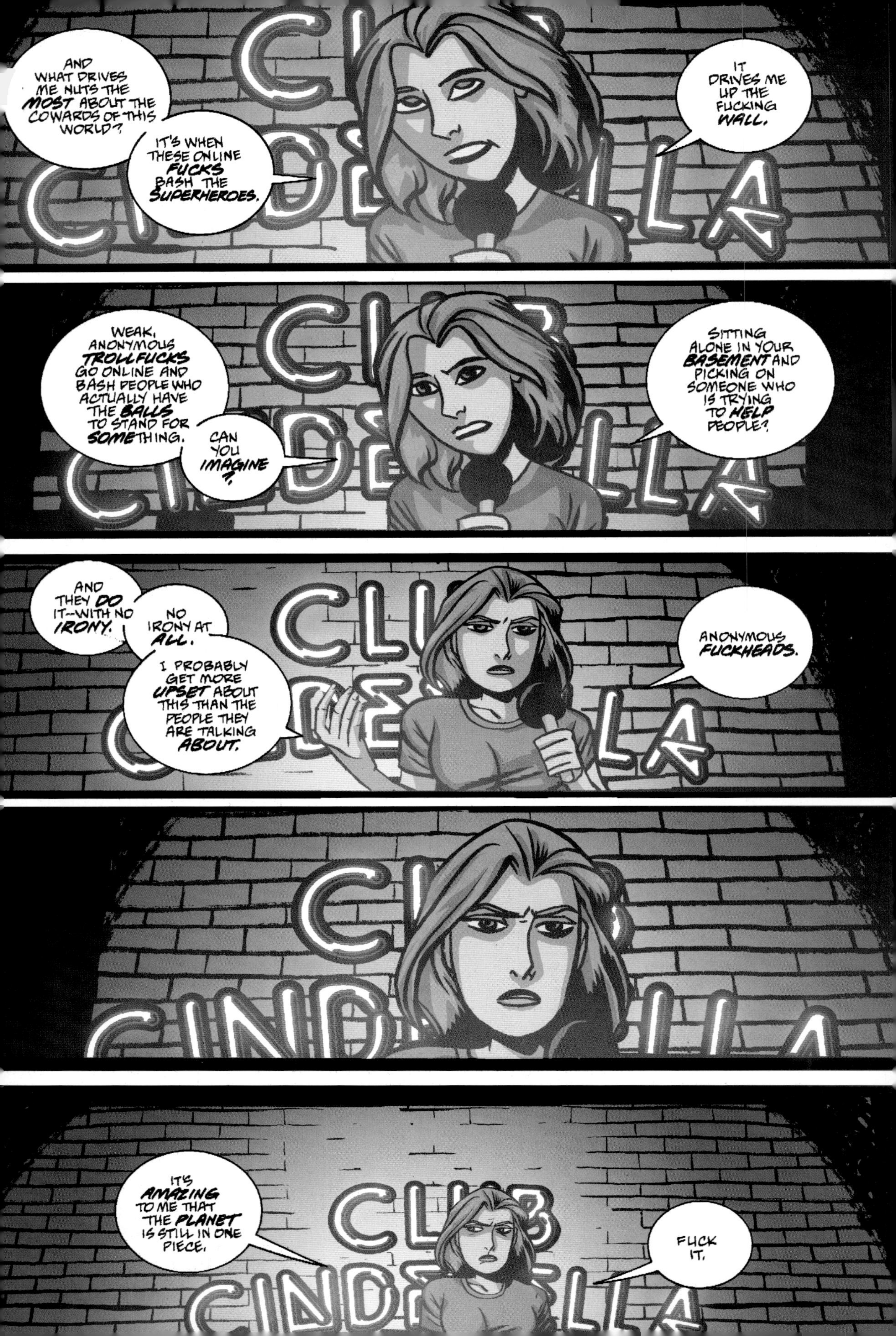
CLUB CINDERELLA
AND WHAT DRIVES ME NUTS THE MOST ABOUT THE COWARDS OF THIS WORLD?
IT'S WHEN THESE ONLINE FUCKS BASH THE SUPERHEROES.
IT DRIVES ME UP THE FUCKING WALL.
WEAK, ANONYMOUS TROLLFUCKS GO ONLINE AND BASH PEOPLE WHO ACTUALLY HAVE THE BALLS TO STAND FOR SOMETHING.
CAN YOU IMAGINE?
SITTING ALONE IN YOUR BASEMENT AND PICKING ON SOMEONE WHO IS TRYING TO HELP PEOPLE?
AND THEY DO IT--WITH NO IRONY.
NO IRONY AT ALL.
I PROBABLY GET MORE UPSET ABOUT THIS THAN THE PEOPLE THEY ARE TALKING ABOUT.
ANONYMOUS FUCKHEADS.
IT'S AMAZING TO ME THAT THE PLANET IS STILL IN ONE PIECE.
FUCK IT.

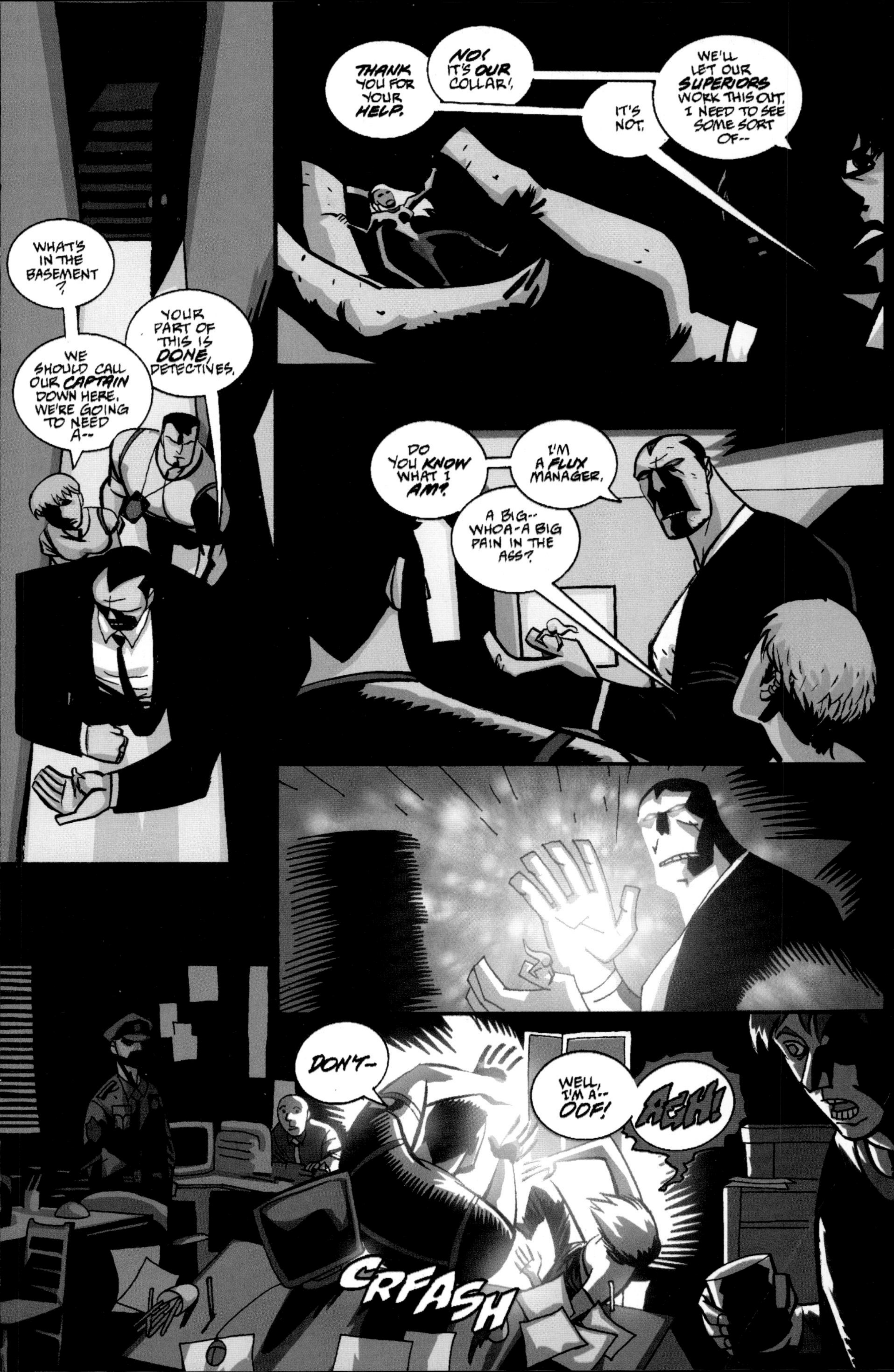
THANK YOU FOR YOUR HELP.
NO! IT'S OUR COLLAR!
IT'S NOT.
WE'LL LET OUR SUPERIORS WORK THIS OUT. I NEED TO SEE SOME SORT OF--
WHAT'S IN THE BASEMENT?
WE SHOULD CALL OUR CAPTAIN DOWN HERE. WE'RE GOING TO NEED A--
YOUR PART OF THIS IS DONE, DETECTIVES.
DO YOU KNOW WHAT I AM?
I'M A FLUX MANAGER.
A BIG-- WHOA-A BIG PAIN IN THE ASS?
DON'T-
WELL, I'M A-- OOF!
AGH!
CRFASH

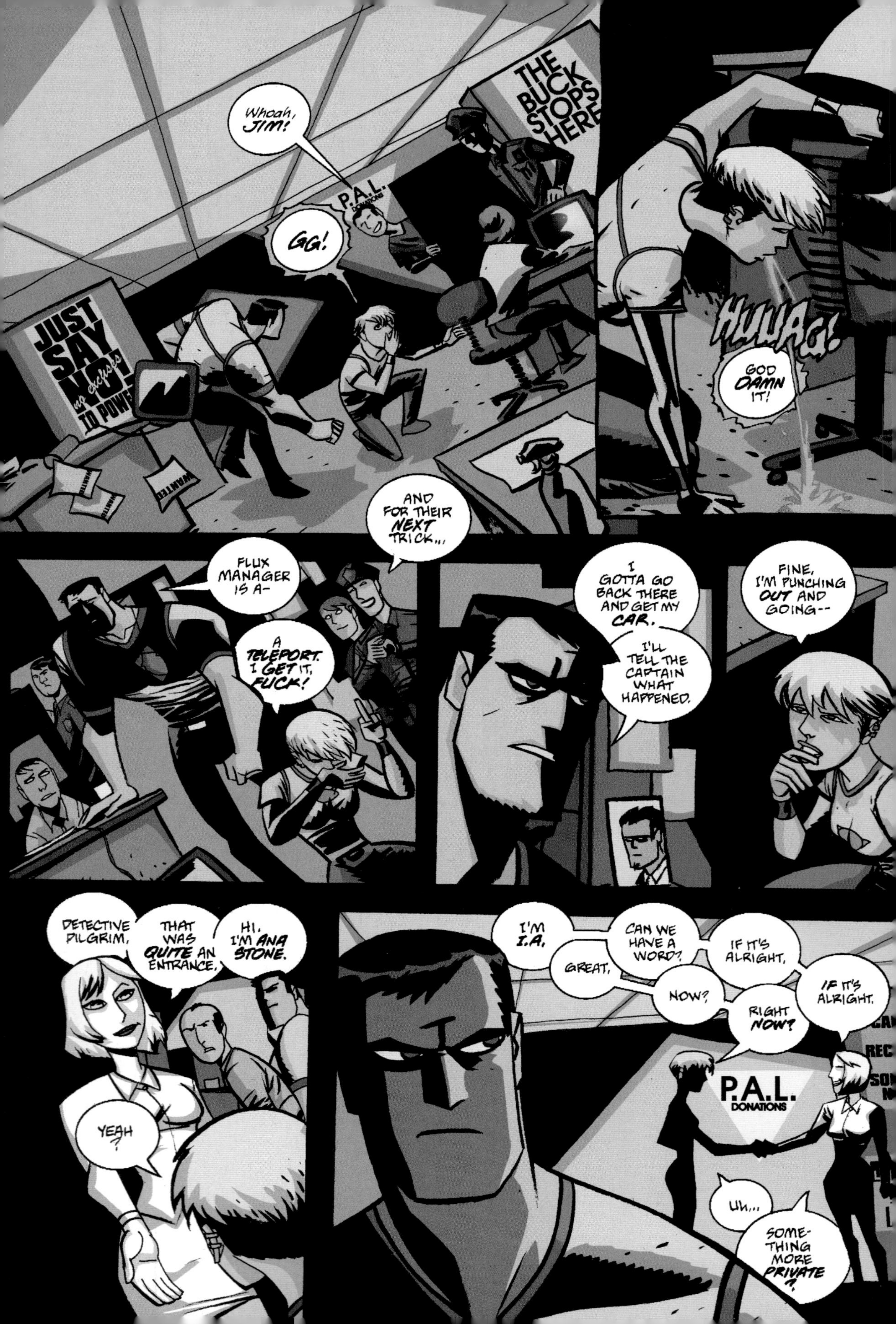

THE BUCK STOPS HERE
Whoah, JIM!
P.A.L. DONATIONS
GG!
JUST SAY NO! no excuses TO POWE
WANTED
HUUAG!
GOD DAMN IT!
AND FOR THEIR NEXT TRICK...
FLUX MANAGER IS A-
A TELEPORT. I GET IT. FUCK!
I GOTTA GO BACK THERE AND GET MY CAR.
I'LL TELL THE CAPTAIN WHAT HAPPENED.
FINE, I'M PUNCHING OUT AND GOING--
DETECTIVE PILGRIM,
THAT WAS QUITE AN ENTRANCE,
HI. I'M ANA STONE.
YEAH?
I'M I.A.
GREAT.
CAN WE HAVE A WORD?
NOW?
IF IT'S ALRIGHT,
RIGHT NOW?
IF IT'S ALRIGHT.
P.A.L. DONATIONS
UH...
SOME-THING MORE PRIVATE?

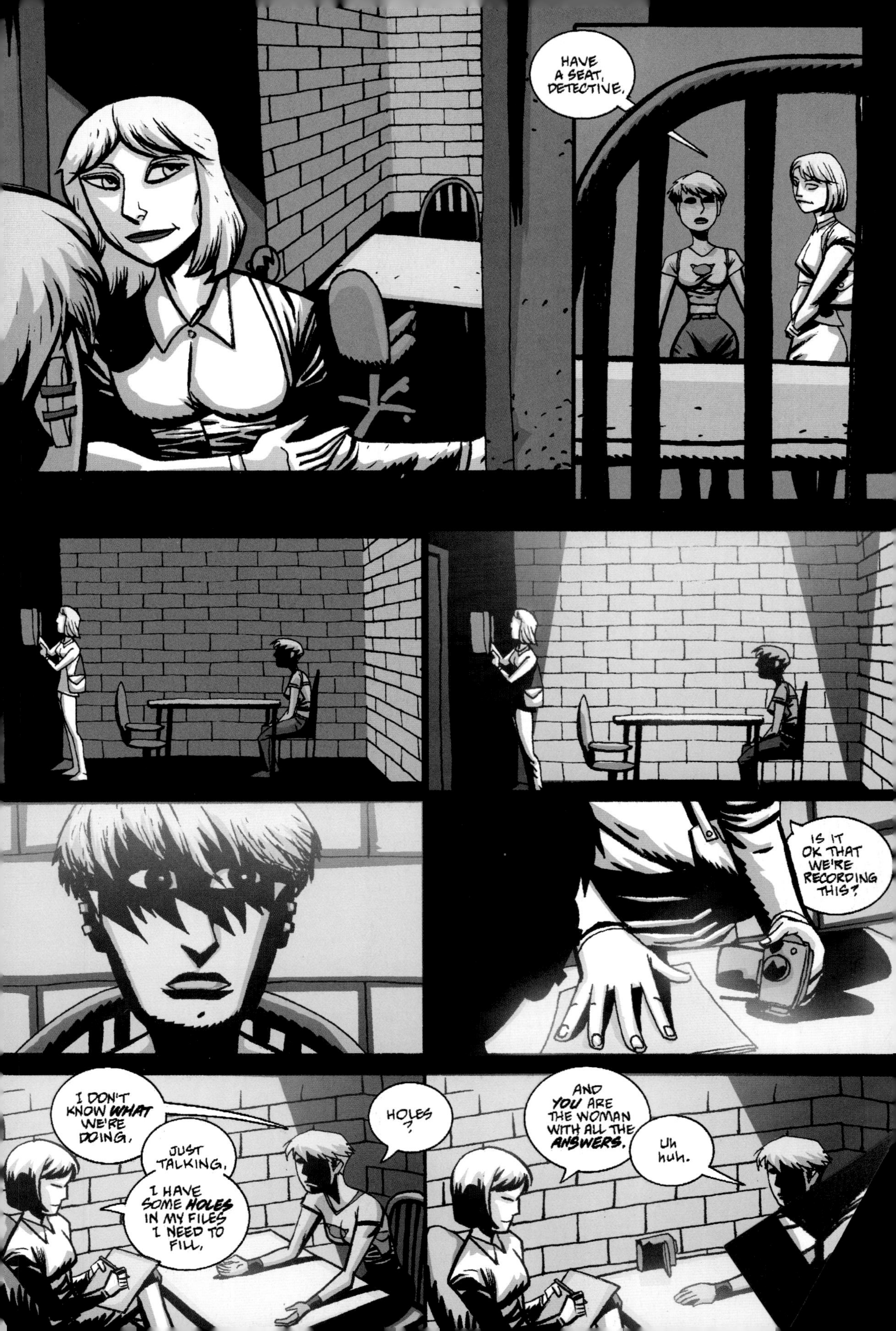
HAVE A SEAT, DETECTIVE.
IS IT OK THAT WE'RE RECORDING THIS?
I DON'T KNOW WHAT WE'RE DOING.
JUST TALKING.
I HAVE SOME HOLES IN MY FILES I NEED TO FILL.
HOLES?
AND YOU ARE THE WOMAN WITH ALL THE ANSWERS.
Uh huh.

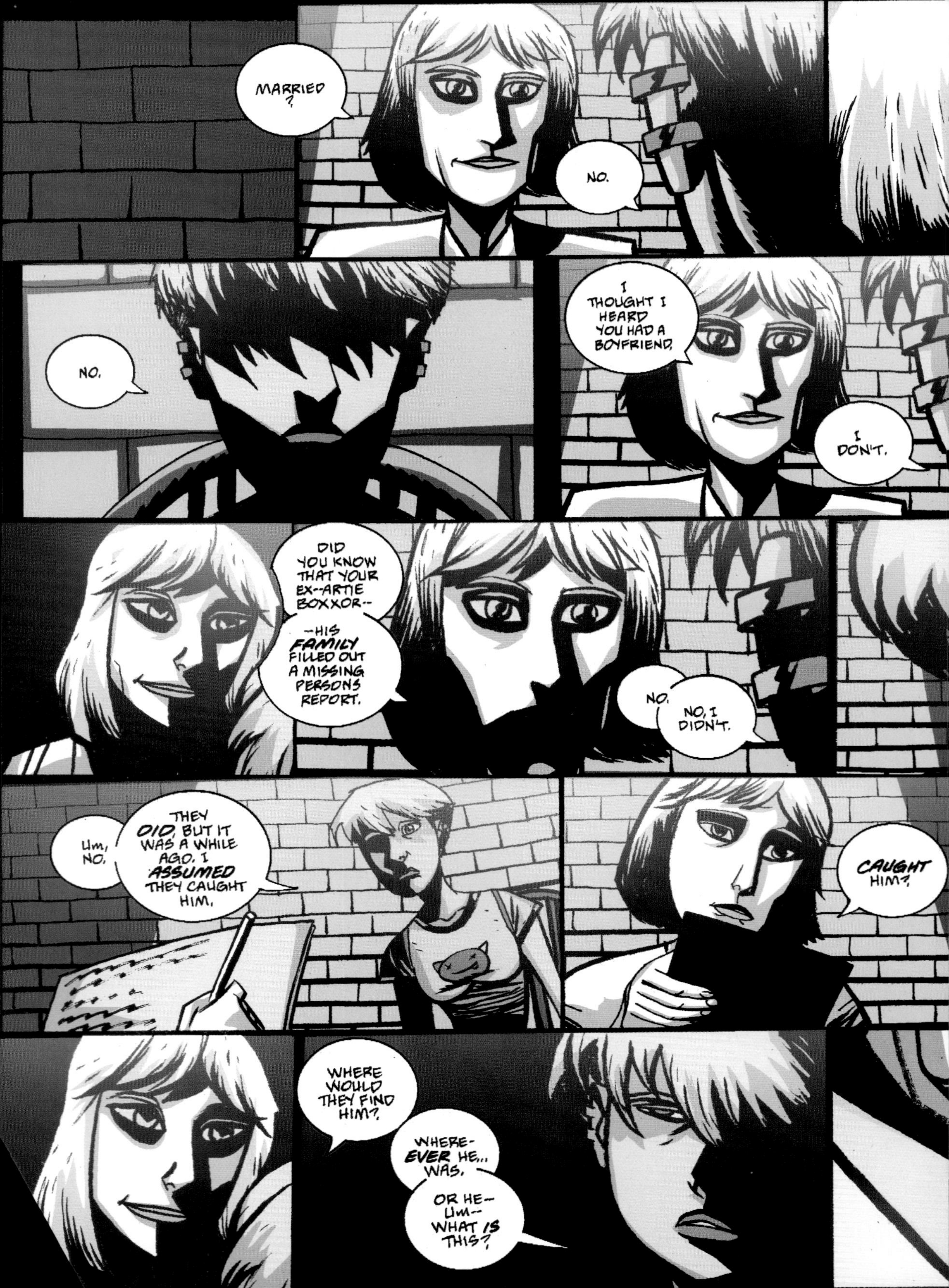
MARRIED?
NO.
NO.
I THOUGHT I HEARD YOU HAD A BOYFRIEND.
I DON'T.
DID YOU KNOW THAT YOUR EX--ARTIE BOXXOR--
--HIS FAMILY FILLED OUT A MISSING PERSONS REPORT.
NO.
NO, I DIDN'T.
UM, NO.
THEY DID, BUT IT WAS A WHILE AGO. I ASSUMED THEY CAUGHT HIM.
CAUGHT HIM?
WHERE WOULD THEY FIND HIM?
WHERE-EVER HE... WAS.
OR HE-- UM-- WHAT IS THIS?

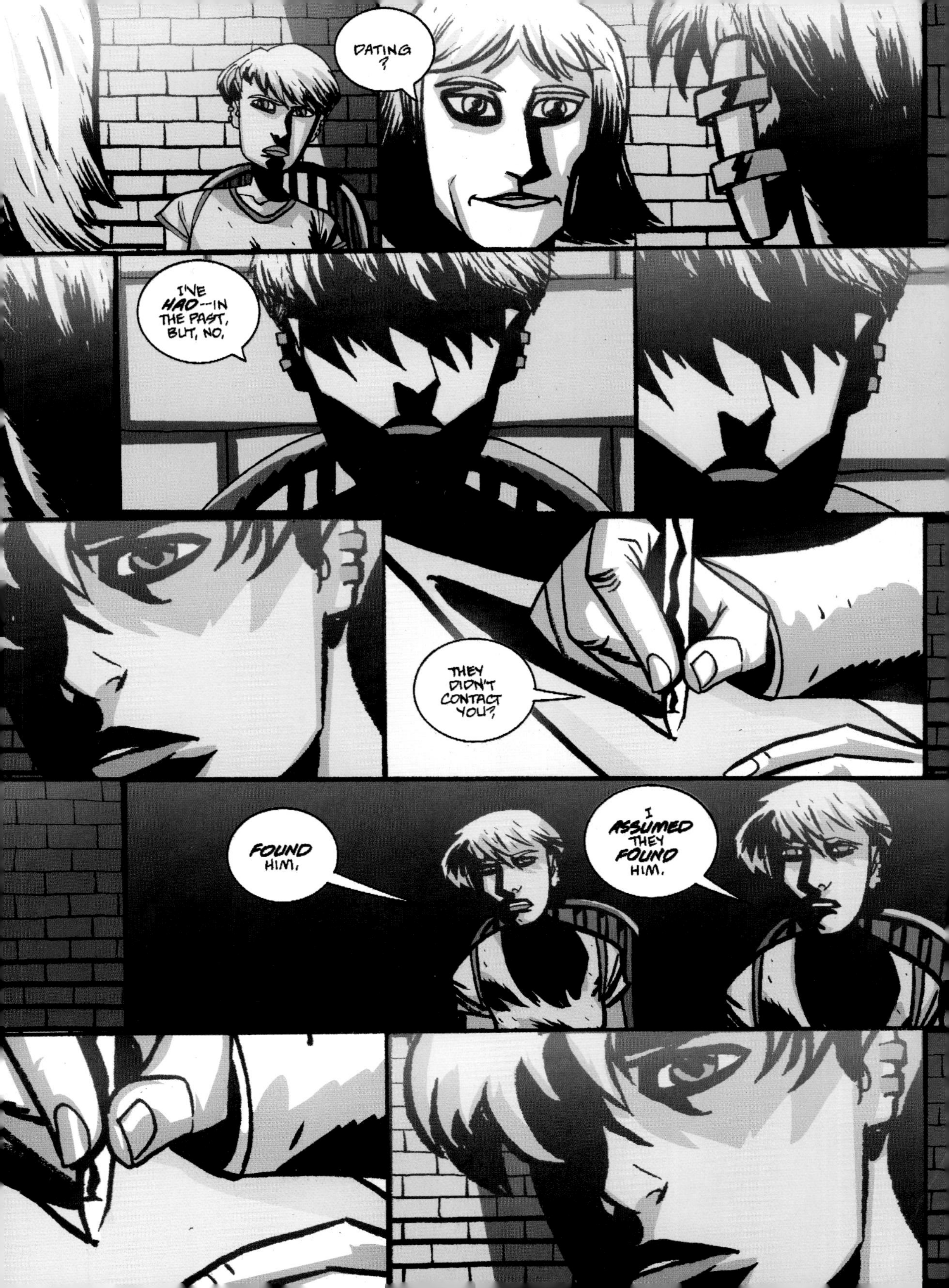
DATING?
I'VE HAD--IN THE PAST, BUT, NO.
THEY DIDN'T CONTACT YOU?
FOUND HIM.
I ASSUMED THEY FOUND HIM.

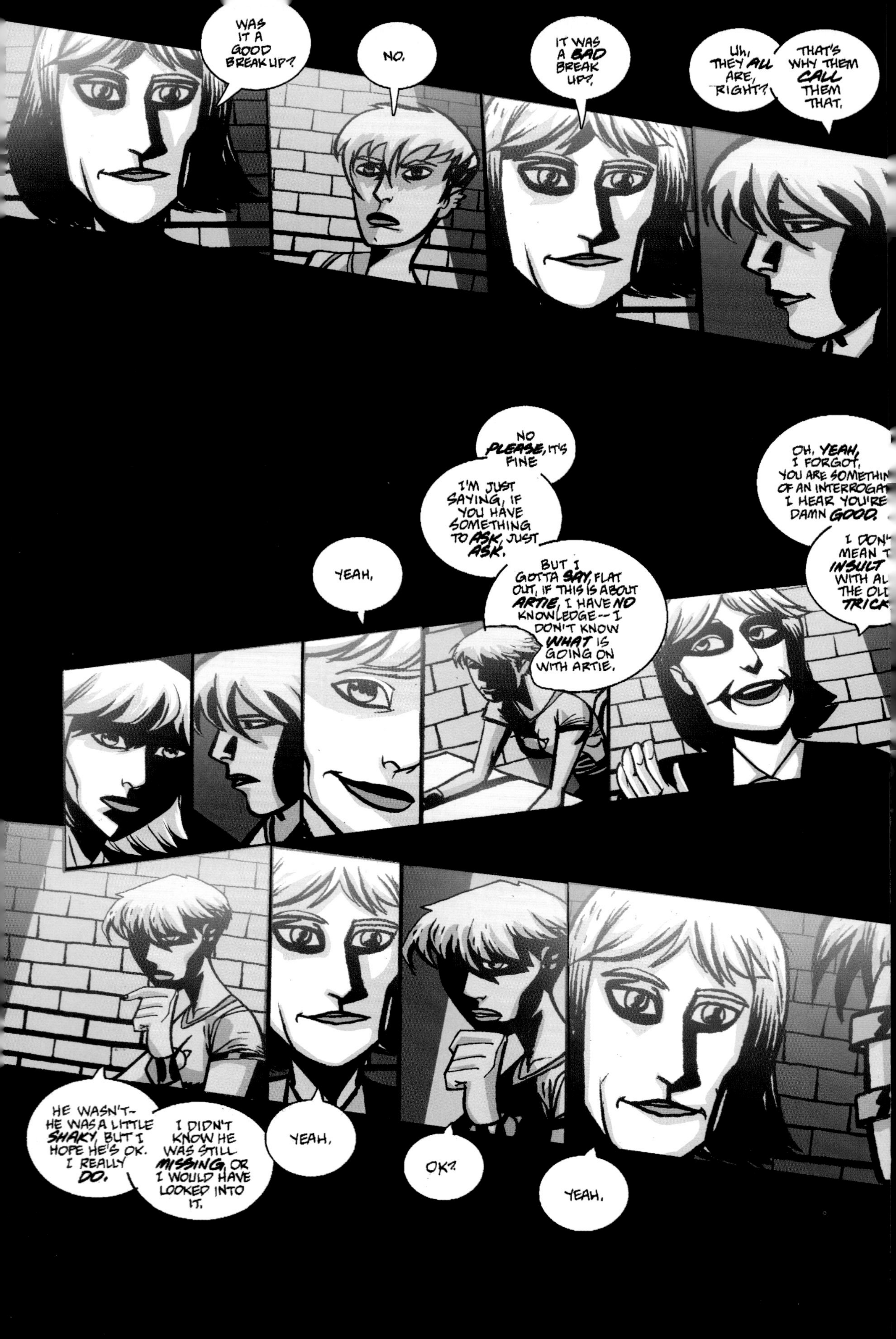
WAS IT A GOOD BREAK UP?
NO.
IT WAS A BAD BREAK UP?.
UH, THEY ALL ARE, RIGHT?
THAT'S WHY THEM CALL THEM THAT.
NO PLEASE, IT'S FINE
I'M JUST SAYING, IF YOU HAVE SOMETHING TO ASK, JUST ASK.
YEAH.
BUT I GOTTA SAY, FLAT OUT, IF THIS IS ABOUT ARTIE, I HAVE NO KNOWLEDGE-- I DON'T KNOW WHAT IS GOING ON WITH ARTIE.
OH, YEAH, I FORGOT, YOU ARE SOMETHIN OF AN INTERROGAT I HEAR YOU'RE DAMN GOOD.
I DON' MEAN T INSULT WITH AL THE OL TRICK
HE WASN'T- HE WAS A LITTLE SHAKY, BUT I HOPE HE'S OK. I REALLY DO.
I DIDN'T KNOW HE WAS STILL MISSING, OR I WOULD HAVE LOOKED INTO IT.
YEAH.
OK?
YEAH.

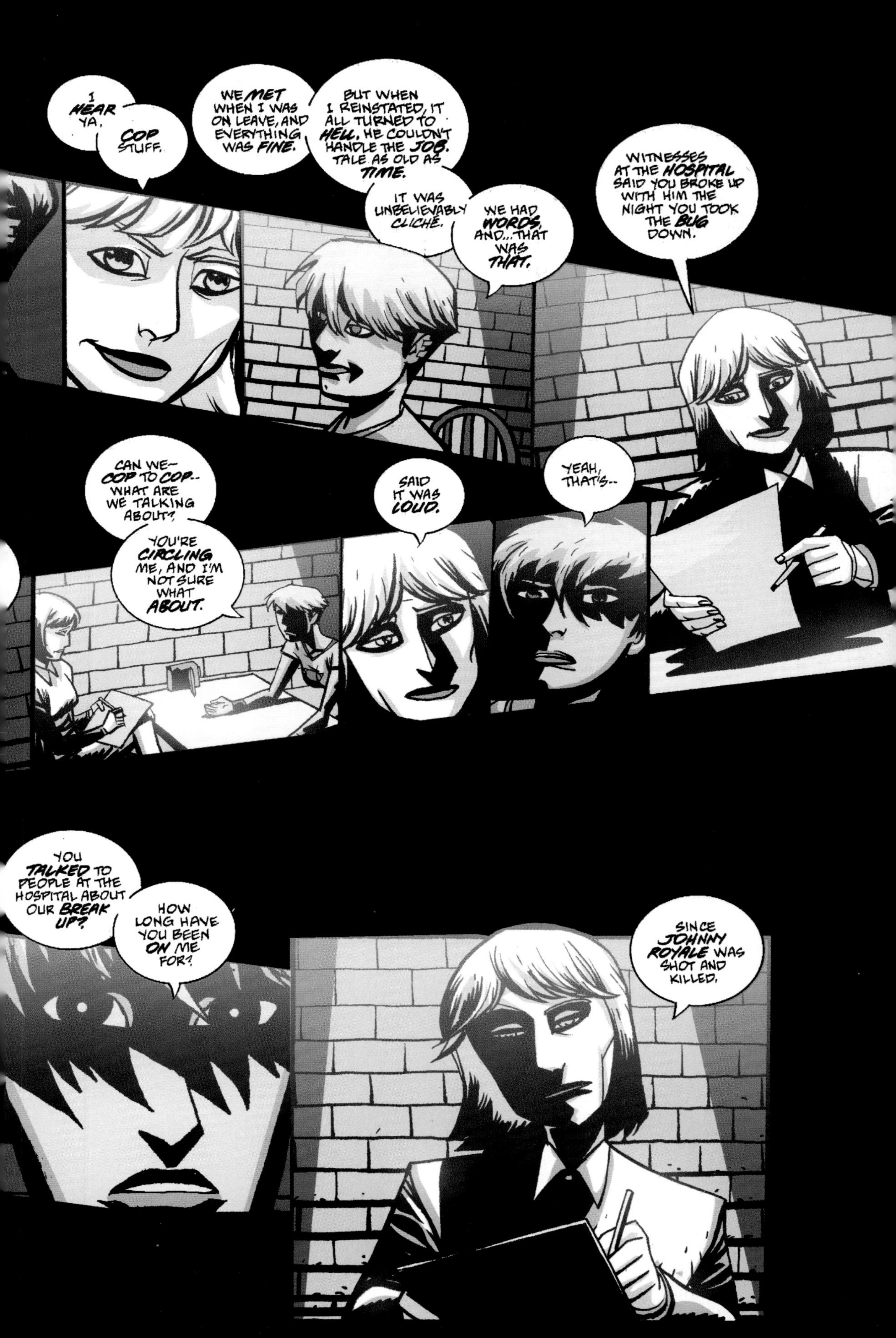
I HEAR YA.
COP STUFF.
WE MET WHEN I WAS ON LEAVE, AND EVERYTHING WAS FINE.
BUT WHEN I REINSTATED, IT ALL TURNED TO HELL. HE COULDN'T HANDLE THE JOB. TALE AS OLD AS TIME.
IT WAS UNBELIEVABLY CLICHÉ.
WE HAD WORDS, AND... THAT WAS THAT.
WITNESSES AT THE HOSPITAL SAID YOU BROKE UP WITH HIM THE NIGHT YOU TOOK THE BUG DOWN.
CAN WE-- COP TO COP-- WHAT ARE WE TALKING ABOUT?
YOU'RE CIRCLING ME, AND I'M NOT SURE WHAT ABOUT.
SAID IT WAS LOUD.
YEAH, THAT'S--
YOU TALKED TO PEOPLE AT THE HOSPITAL ABOUT OUR BREAK UP?
HOW LONG HAVE YOU BEEN ON ME FOR?
SINCE JOHNNY ROYALE WAS SHOT AND KILLED.

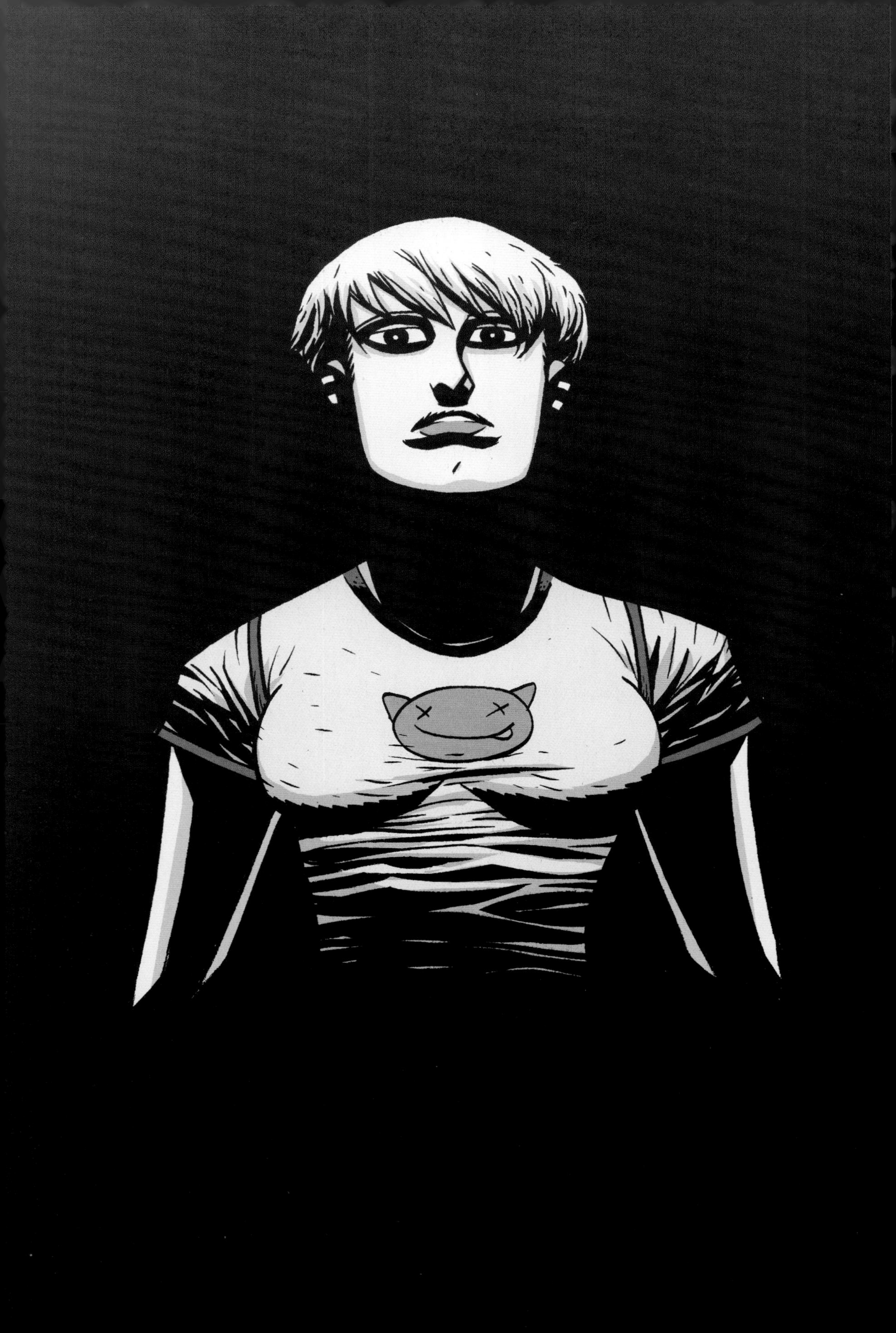

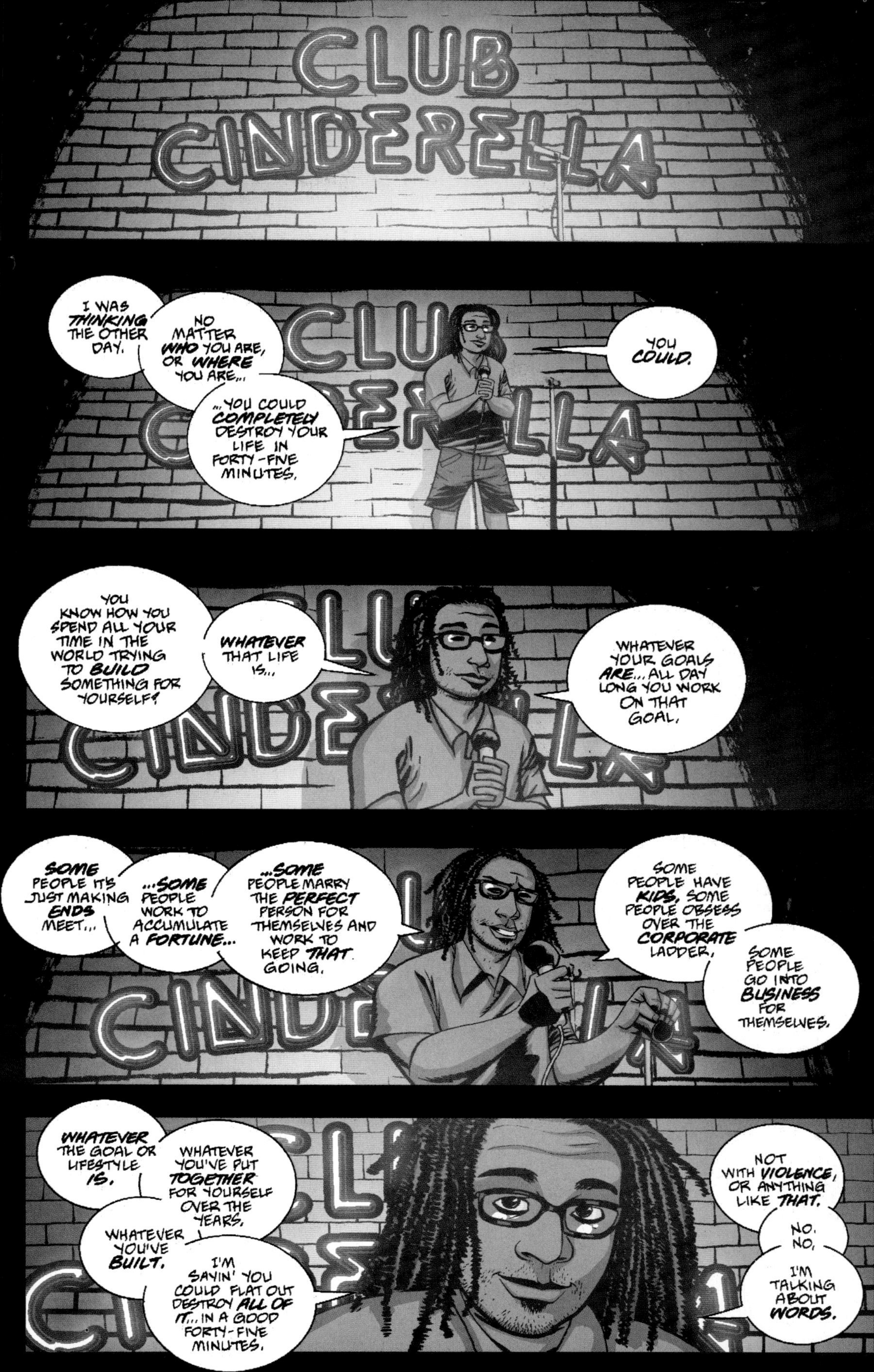
CLUB CINDERELLA
I WAS THINKING THE OTHER DAY.
NO MATTER WHO YOU ARE, OR WHERE YOU ARE...
...YOU COULD COMPLETELY DESTROY YOUR LIFE IN FORTY-FIVE MINUTES.
YOU COULD.
YOU KNOW HOW YOU SPEND ALL YOUR TIME IN THE WORLD TRYING TO BUILD SOMETHING FOR YOURSELF?
WHATEVER THAT LIFE IS...
WHATEVER YOUR GOALS ARE... ALL DAY LONG YOU WORK ON THAT GOAL.
SOME PEOPLE IT'S JUST MAKING ENDS MEET...
...SOME PEOPLE WORK TO ACCUMULATE A FORTUNE...
...SOME PEOPLE MARRY THE PERFECT PERSON FOR THEMSELVES AND WORK TO KEEP THAT GOING.
SOME PEOPLE HAVE KIDS, SOME PEOPLE OBSESS OVER THE CORPORATE LADDER.
SOME PEOPLE GO INTO BUSINESS FOR THEMSELVES.
WHATEVER THE GOAL OR LIFESTYLE IS.
WHATEVER YOU'VE PUT TOGETHER FOR YOURSELF OVER THE YEARS.
WHATEVER YOU'VE BUILT.
I'M SAYIN' YOU COULD FLAT OUT DESTROY ALL OF IT... IN A GOOD FORTY-FIVE MINUTES.
NOT WITH VIOLENCE, OR ANYTHING LIKE THAT.
NO. NO.
I'M TALKING ABOUT WORDS.

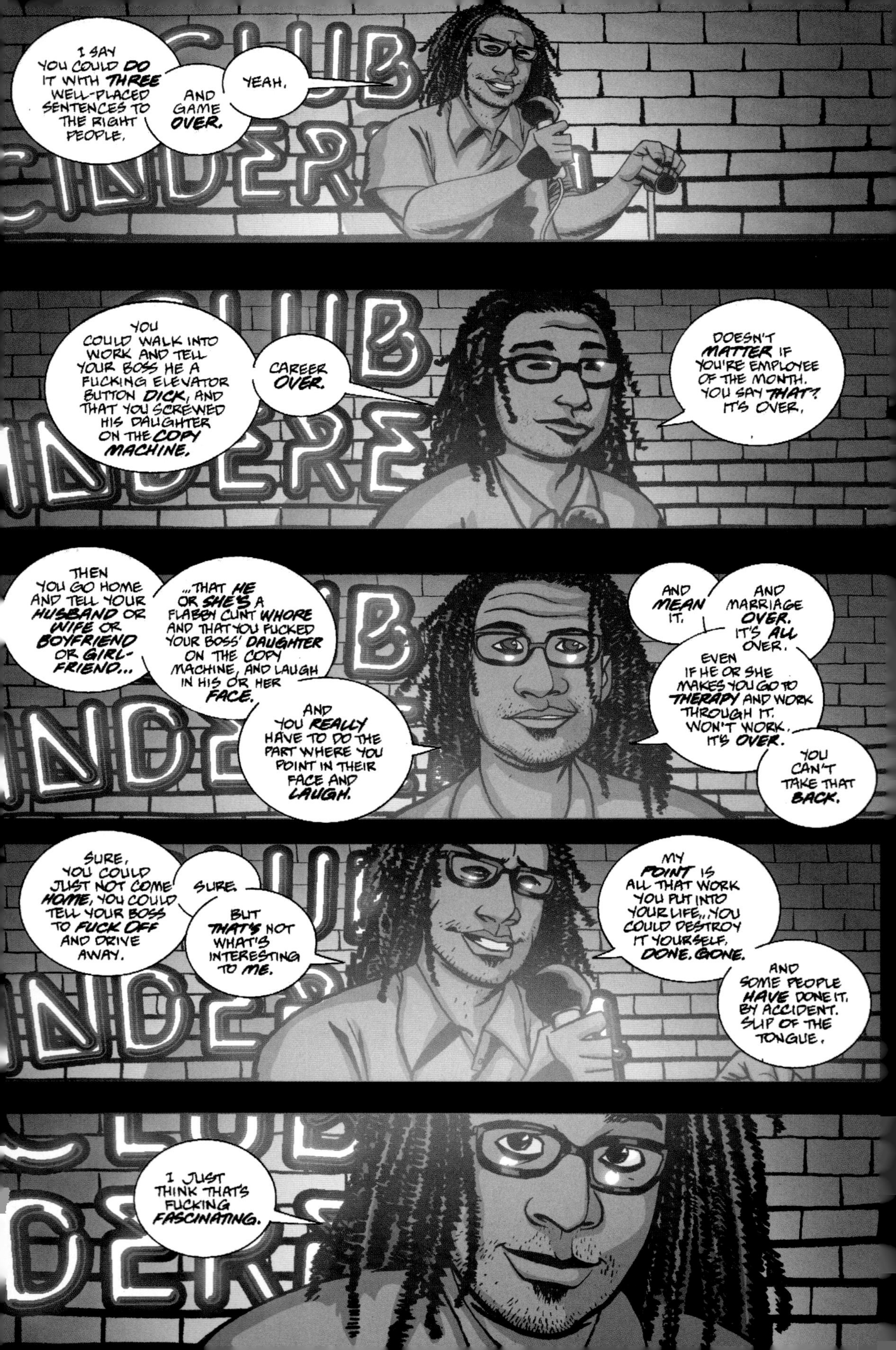
I SAY YOU COULD DO IT WITH THREE WELL-PLACED SENTENCES TO THE RIGHT PEOPLE.
AND GAME OVER.
YEAH.
YOU COULD WALK INTO WORK AND TELL YOUR BOSS HE A FUCKING ELEVATOR BUTTON DICK, AND THAT YOU SCREWED HIS DAUGHTER ON THE COPY MACHINE.
CAREER OVER.
DOESN'T MATTER IF YOU'RE EMPLOYEE OF THE MONTH. YOU SAY THAT? IT'S OVER.
THEN YOU GO HOME AND TELL YOUR HUSBAND OR WIFE OR BOYFRIEND OR GIRL-FRIEND...
...THAT HE OR SHE'S A FLABBY CUNT WHORE AND THAT YOU FUCKED YOUR BOSS' DAUGHTER ON THE COPY MACHINE, AND LAUGH IN HIS OR HER FACE.
AND YOU REALLY HAVE TO DO THE PART WHERE YOU POINT IN THEIR FACE AND LAUGH.
AND MEAN IT.
AND MARRIAGE OVER. IT'S ALL OVER.
EVEN IF HE OR SHE MAKES YOU GO TO THERAPY AND WORK THROUGH IT. WON'T WORK. IT'S OVER.
YOU CAN'T TAKE THAT BACK.
SURE, YOU COULD JUST NOT COME HOME, YOU COULD TELL YOUR BOSS TO FUCK OFF AND DRIVE AWAY.
SURE.
BUT THAT'S NOT WHAT'S INTERESTING TO ME.
MY POINT IS ALL THAT WORK YOU PUT INTO YOUR LIFE... YOU COULD DESTROY IT YOURSELF. DONE. GONE.
AND SOME PEOPLE HAVE DONE IT. BY ACCIDENT. SLIP OF THE TONGUE.
I JUST THINK THAT'S FUCKING FASCINATING.

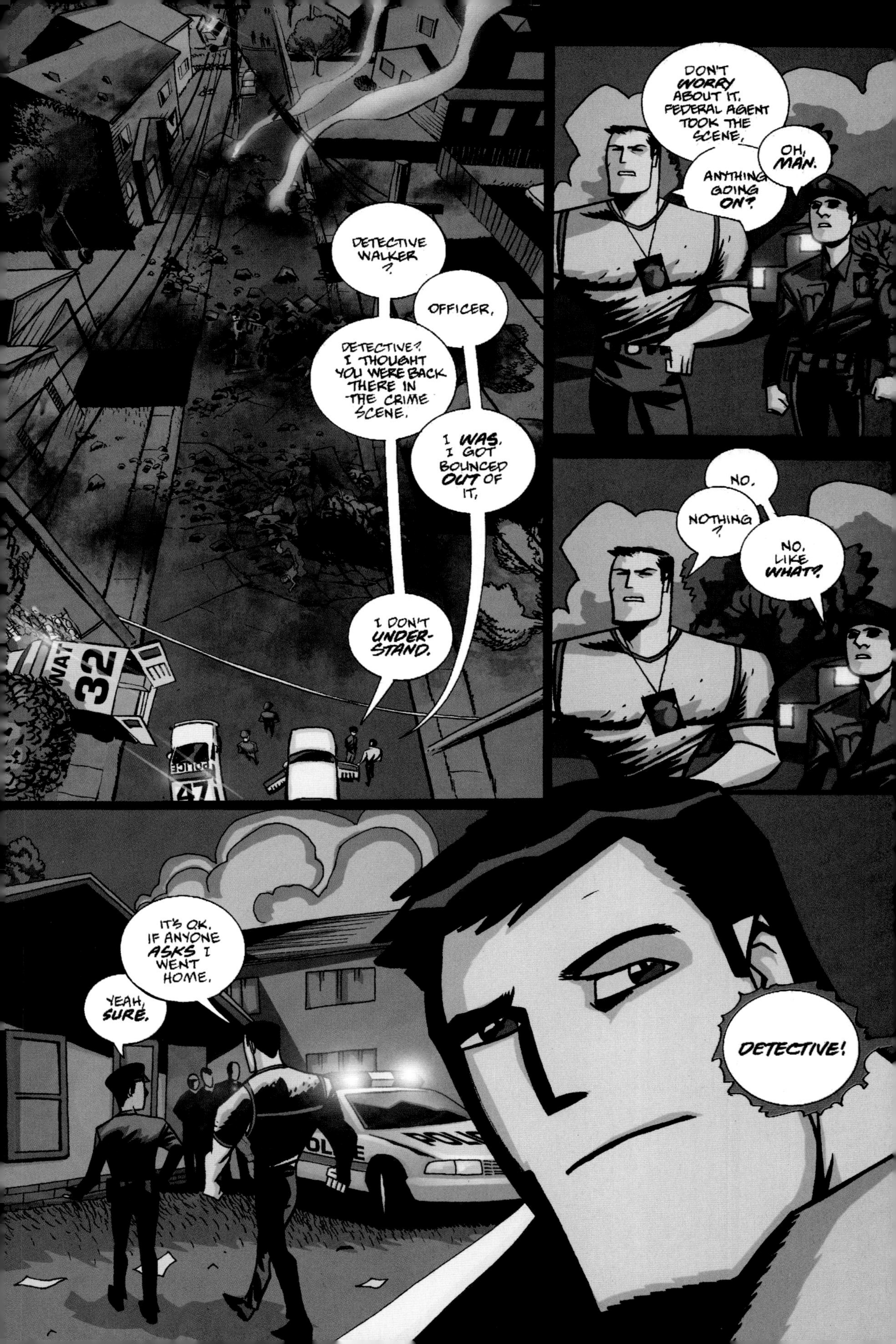
DETECTIVE WALKER?
OFFICER.
DETECTIVE? I THOUGHT YOU WERE BACK THERE IN THE CRIME SCENE.
I WAS. I GOT BOUNCED OUT OF IT.
I DON'T UNDER-STAND.
WAT
32
POLICE
47
DON'T WORRY ABOUT IT. FEDERAL AGENT TOOK THE SCENE.
OH, MAN.
ANYTHING GOING ON?
NO.
NOTHING?
NO. LIKE WHAT?
IT'S OK. IF ANYONE ASKS I WENT HOME.
YEAH, SURE.
POLICE
DETECTIVE!

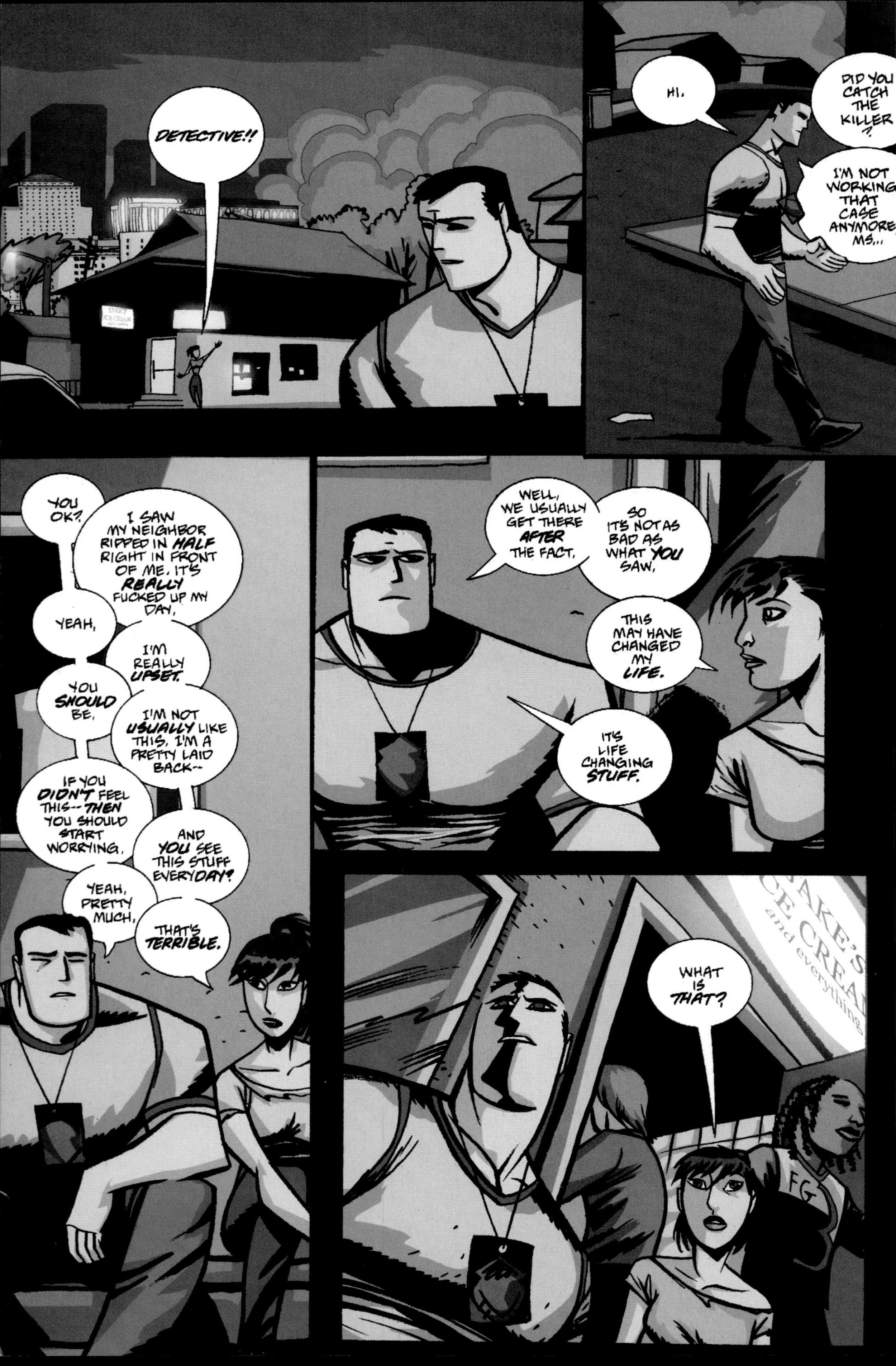
DETECTIVE!!
HI.
DID YOU CATCH THE KILLER?
I'M NOT WORKING THAT CASE ANYMORE, MS...
YOU OK?
I SAW MY NEIGHBOR RIPPED IN HALF RIGHT IN FRONT OF ME. IT'S REALLY FUCKED UP MY DAY.
YEAH.
I'M REALLY UPSET.
YOU SHOULD BE.
I'M NOT USUALLY LIKE THIS. I'M A PRETTY LAID BACK--
IF YOU DIDN'T FEEL THIS-- THEN YOU SHOULD START WORRYING.
AND YOU SEE THIS STUFF EVERYDAY?
YEAH, PRETTY MUCH.
THAT'S TERRIBLE.
WELL, WE USUALLY GET THERE AFTER THE FACT.
SO IT'S NOT AS BAD AS WHAT YOU SAW.
THIS MAY HAVE CHANGED MY LIFE.
IT'S LIFE CHANGING STUFF.
WHAT IS THAT?

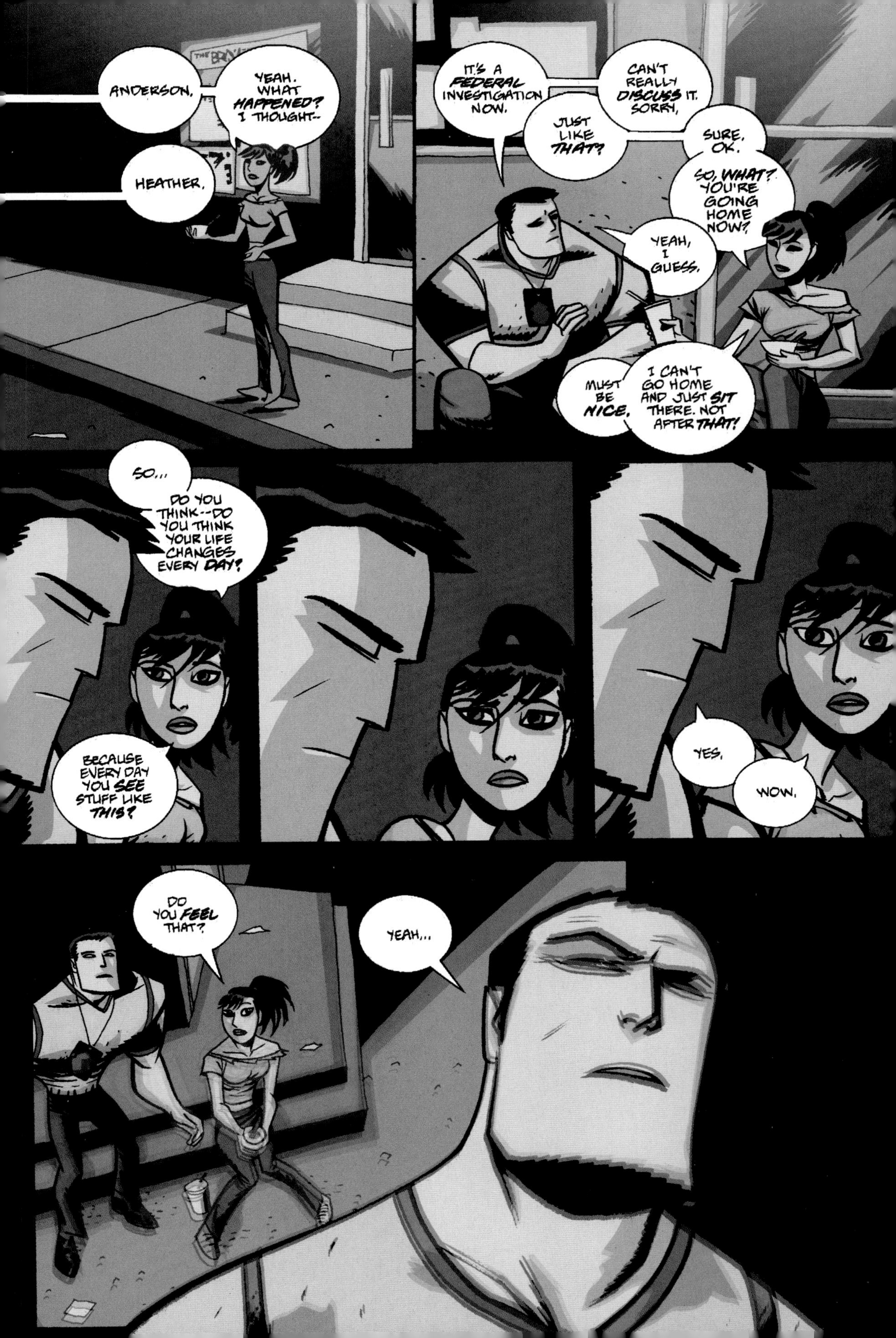

ANDERSON.
YEAH. WHAT HAPPENED? I THOUGHT--
HEATHER.
IT'S A FEDERAL INVESTIGATION NOW.
CAN'T REALLY DISCUSS IT. SORRY.
JUST LIKE THAT?
SURE. OK.
SO, WHAT? YOU'RE GOING HOME NOW?
YEAH, I GUESS.
MUST BE NICE.
I CAN'T GO HOME AND JUST SIT THERE. NOT AFTER THAT!
SO...
DO YOU THINK--DO YOU THINK YOUR LIFE CHANGES EVERY DAY?
BECAUSE EVERY DAY YOU SEE STUFF LIKE THIS?
YES.
WOW.
DO YOU FEEL THAT?
YEAH...

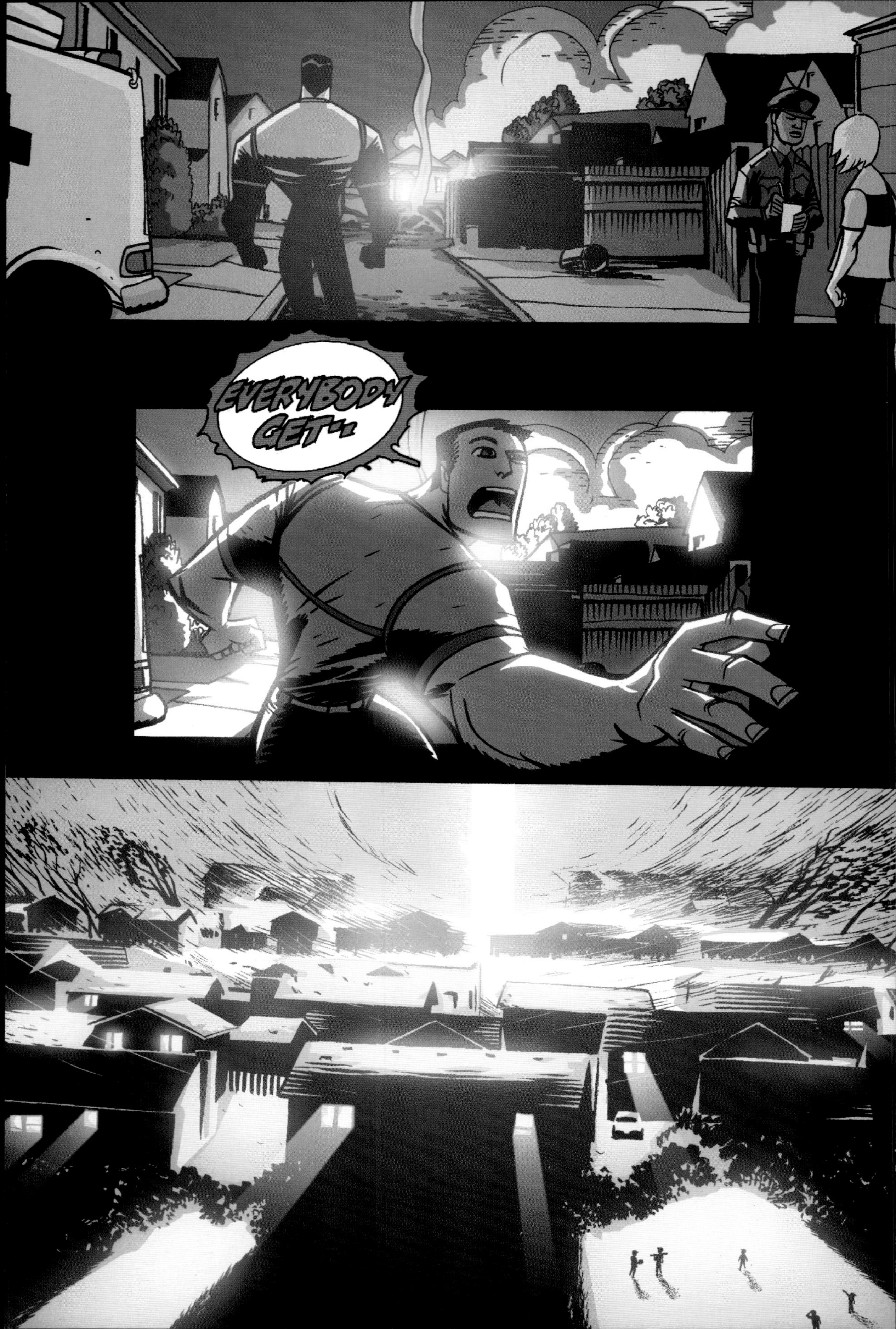
EVERYBODY GET--

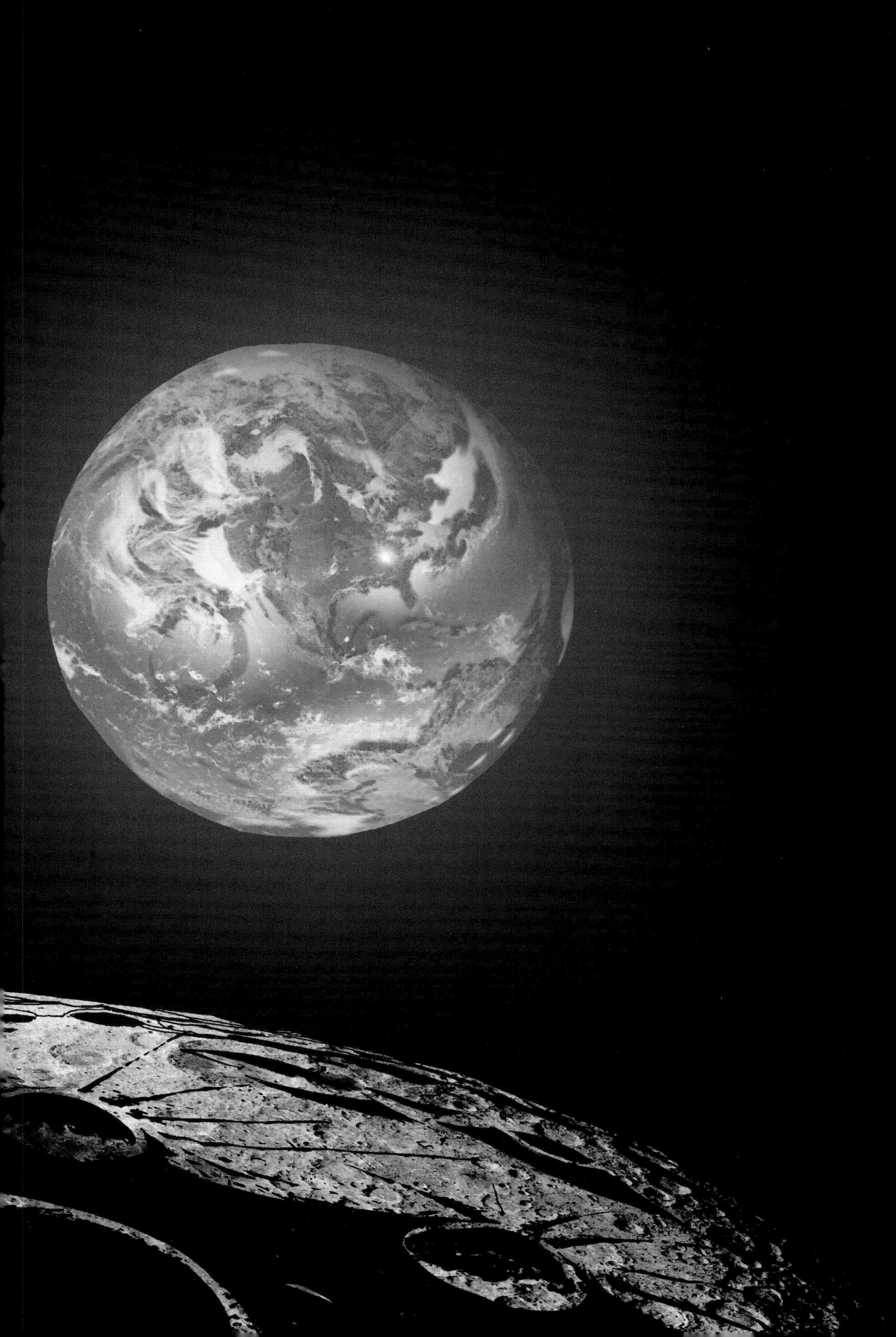

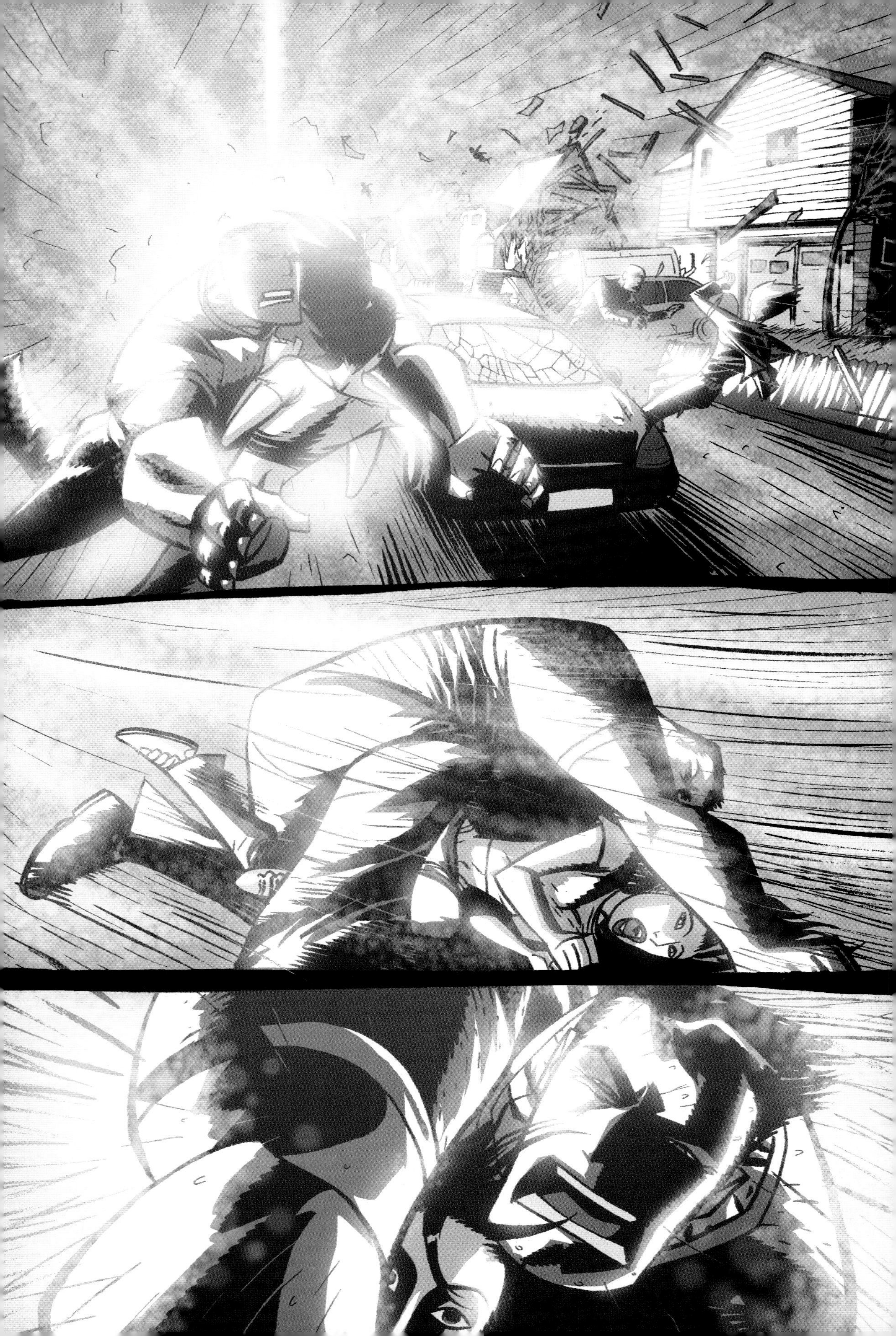

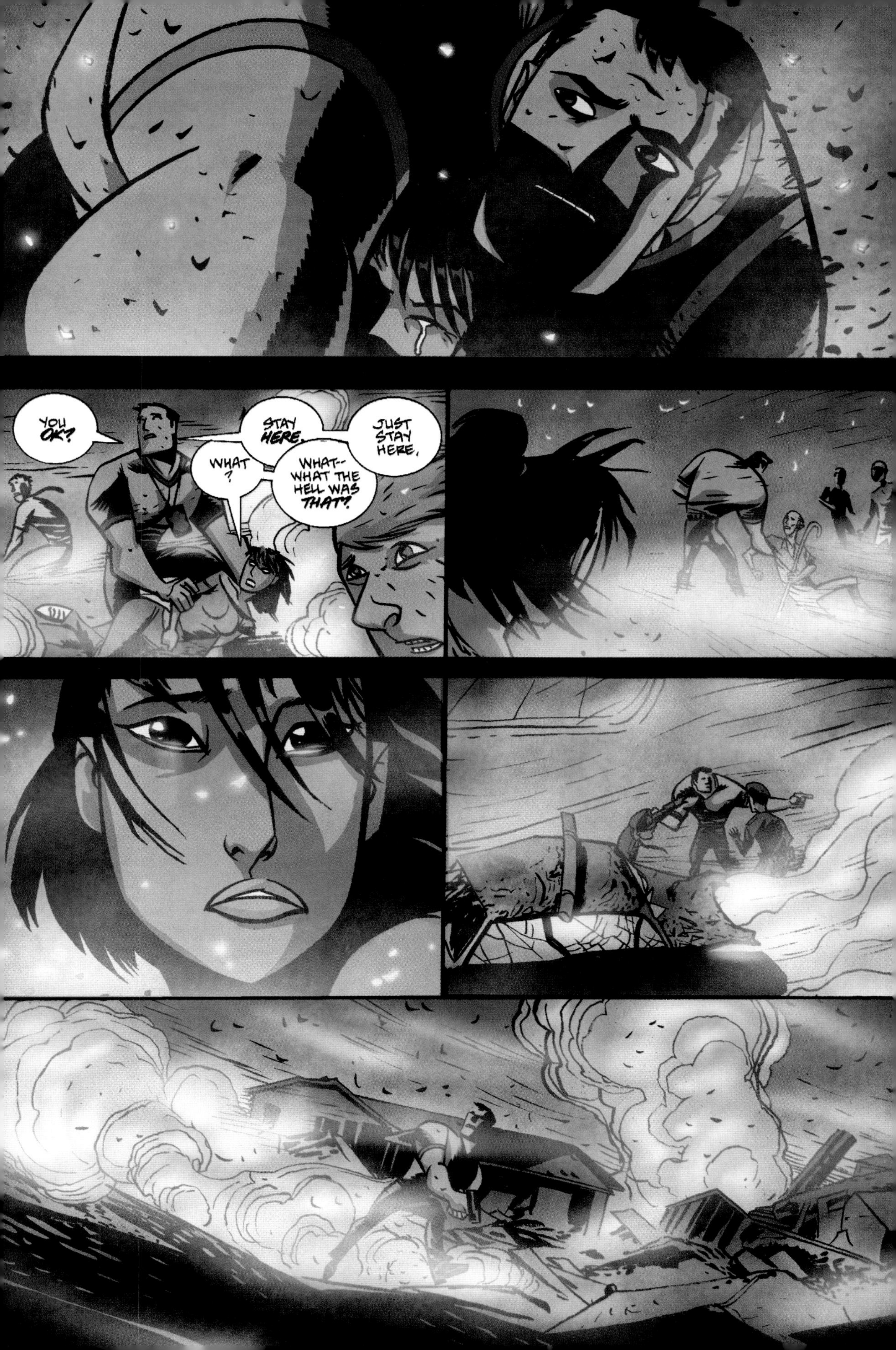
YOU OK?
STAY HERE.
WHAT?
JUST STAY HERE,
WHAT-- WHAT THE HELL WAS THAT?

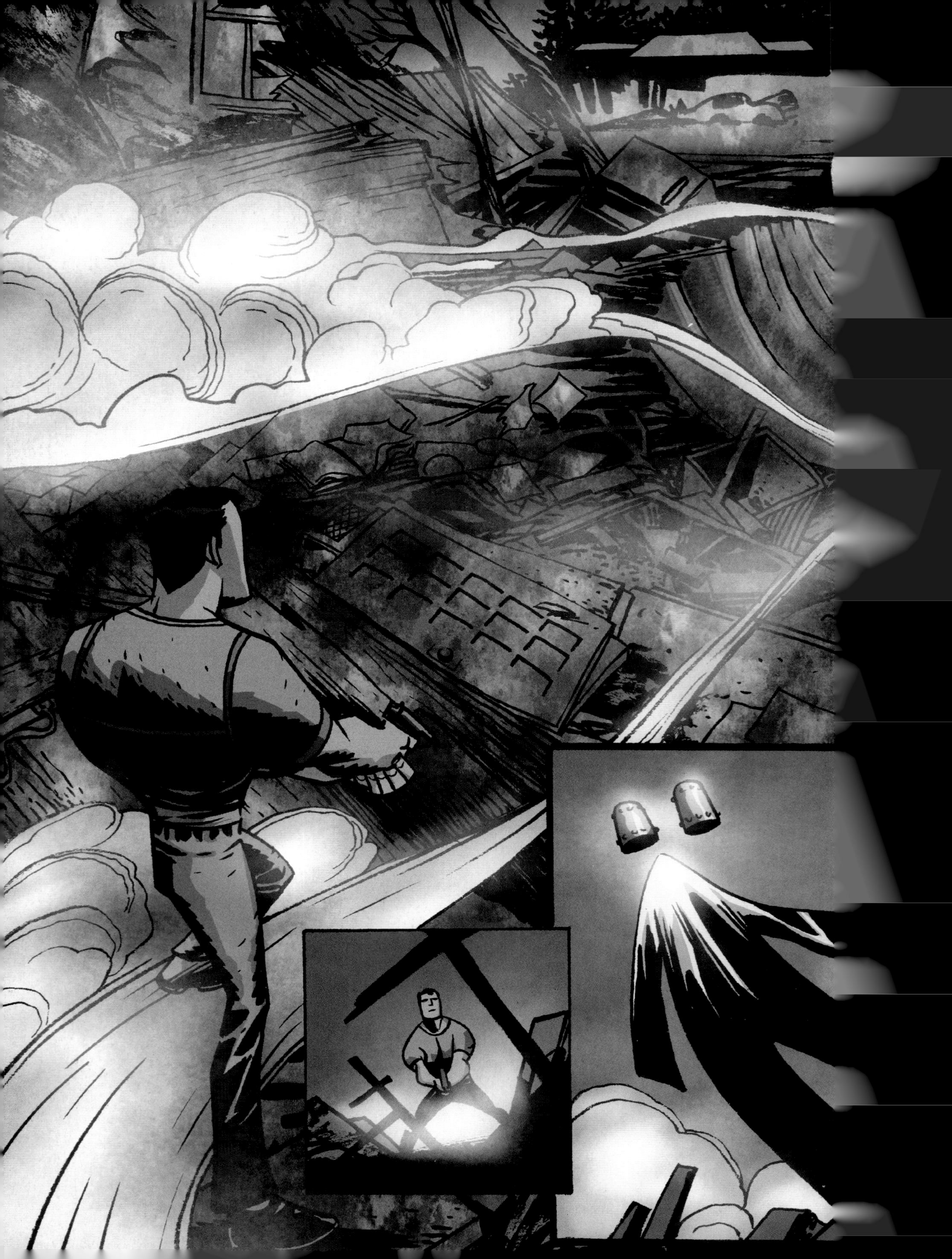

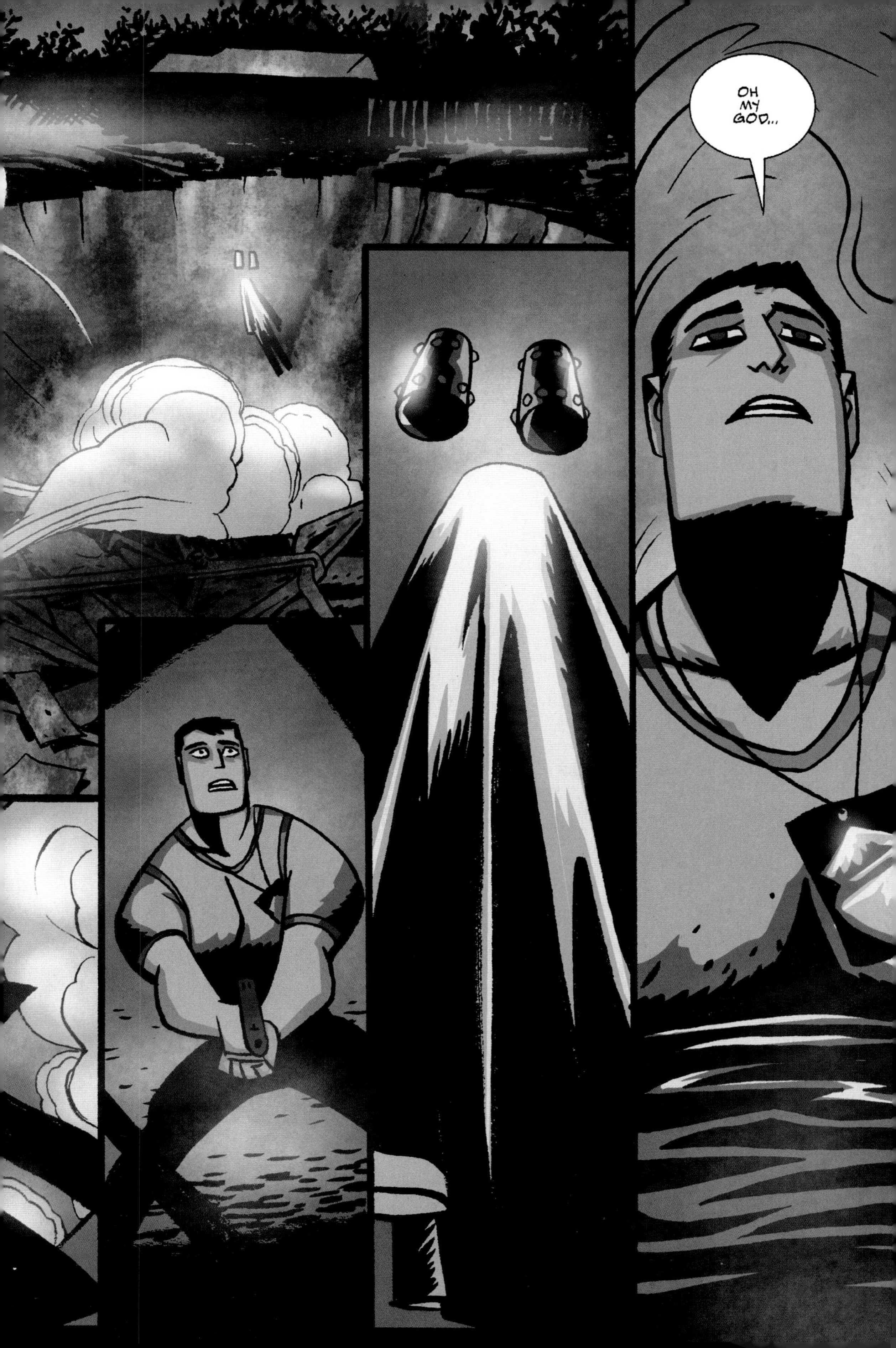
OH MY GOD...

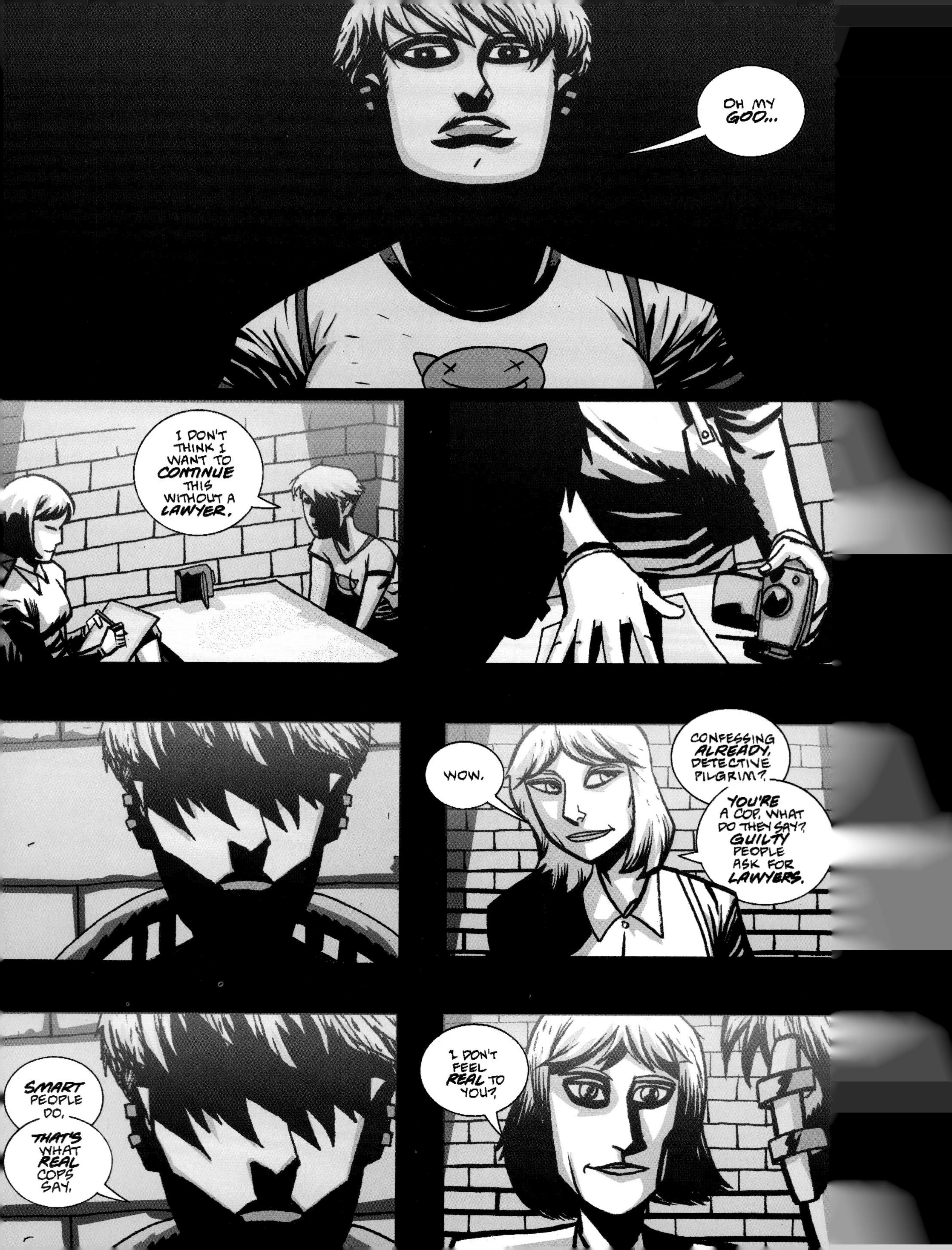
OH MY GOD...
I DON'T THINK I WANT TO CONTINUE THIS WITHOUT A LAWYER.
WOW.
CONFESSING ALREADY, DETECTIVE PILGRIM?
YOU'RE A COP, WHAT DO THEY SAY? GUILTY PEOPLE ASK FOR LAWYERS.
SMART PEOPLE DO.
THAT'S WHAT REAL COPS SAY.
I DON'T FEEL REAL TO YOU?

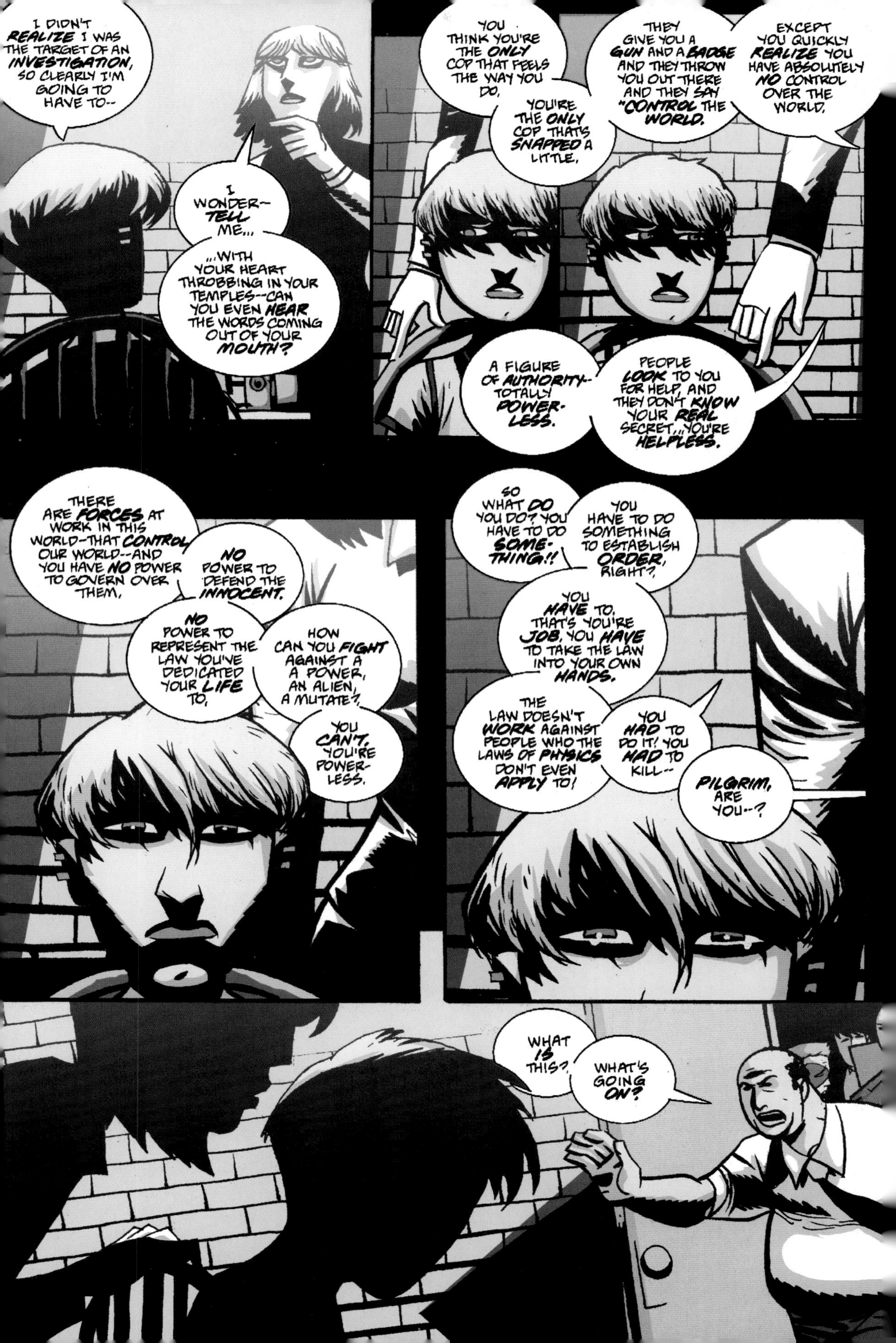
I DIDN'T REALIZE I WAS THE TARGET OF AN INVESTIGATION, SO CLEARLY I'M GOING TO HAVE TO--
I WONDER-- TELL ME...
...WITH YOUR HEART THROBBING IN YOUR TEMPLES--CAN YOU EVEN HEAR THE WORDS COMING OUT OF YOUR MOUTH?
YOU THINK YOU'RE THE ONLY COP THAT FEELS THE WAY YOU DO.
YOU'RE THE ONLY COP THAT'S SNAPPED A LITTLE.
THEY GIVE YOU A GUN AND A BADGE AND THEY THROW YOU OUT THERE AND THEY SAY "CONTROL THE WORLD."
EXCEPT YOU QUICKLY REALIZE YOU HAVE ABSOLUTELY NO CONTROL OVER THE WORLD.
A FIGURE OF AUTHORITY-- TOTALLY POWER-LESS.
PEOPLE LOOK TO YOU FOR HELP, AND THEY DON'T KNOW YOUR REAL SECRET... YOU'RE HELPLESS.
THERE ARE FORCES AT WORK IN THIS WORLD--THAT CONTROL OUR WORLD--AND YOU HAVE NO POWER TO GOVERN OVER THEM.
NO POWER TO DEFEND THE INNOCENT.
NO POWER TO REPRESENT THE LAW YOU'VE DEDICATED YOUR LIFE TO.
HOW CAN YOU FIGHT AGAINST A POWER, AN ALIEN, A MUTATE?
YOU CAN'T. YOU'RE POWER-LESS.
SO WHAT DO YOU DO? YOU HAVE TO DO SOME-THING!!
YOU HAVE TO DO SOMETHING TO ESTABLISH ORDER, RIGHT?
YOU HAVE TO. THAT'S YOU'RE JOB. YOU HAVE TO TAKE THE LAW INTO YOUR OWN HANDS.
THE LAW DOESN'T WORK AGAINST PEOPLE WHO THE LAWS OF PHYSICS DON'T EVEN APPLY TO!
YOU HAD TO DO IT! YOU HAD TO KILL--
PILGRIM, ARE YOU--?
WHAT IS THIS?
WHAT'S GOING ON?

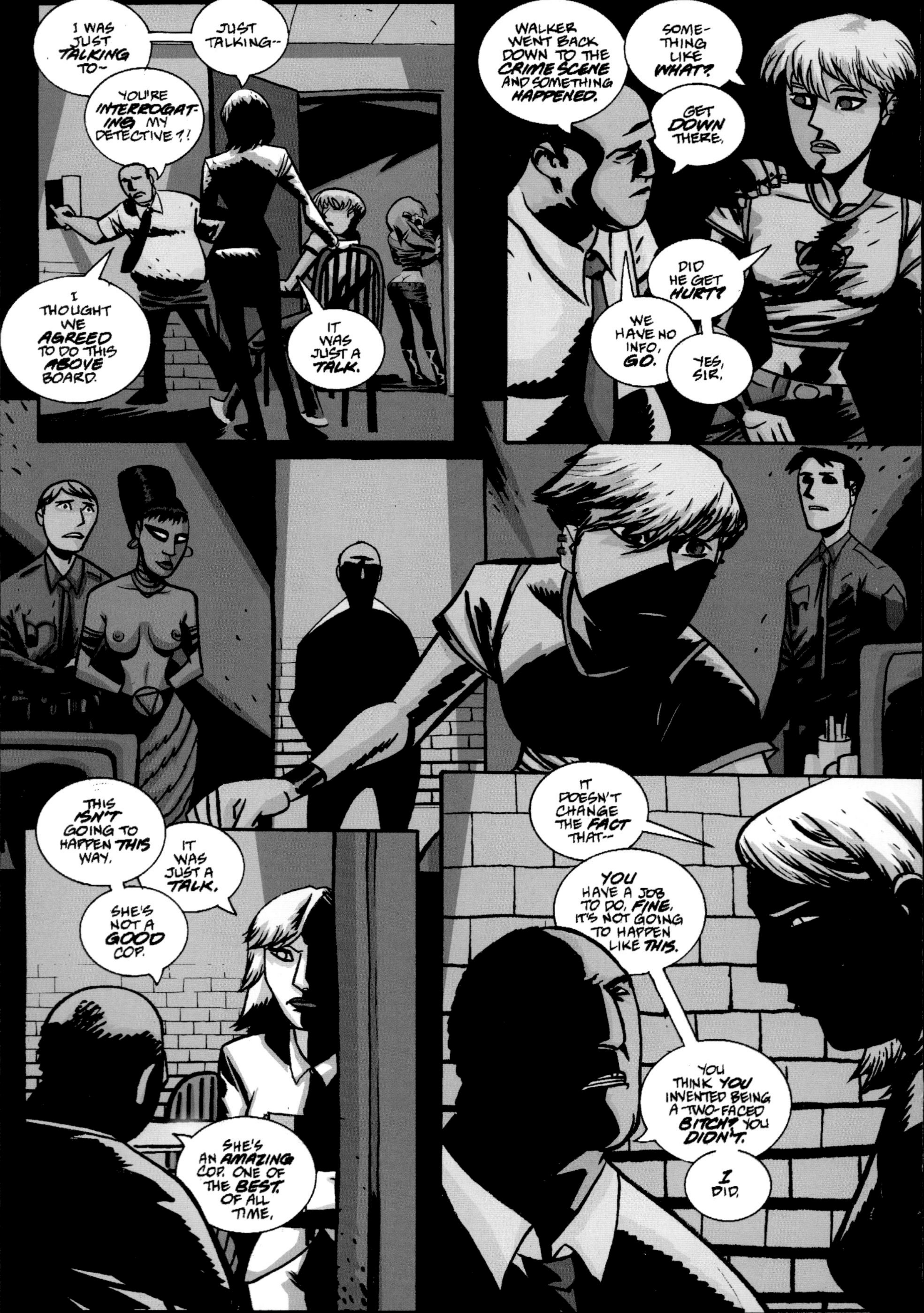
I WAS JUST TALKING TO--
JUST TALKING--
YOU'RE INTERROGATING MY DETECTIVE?!
I THOUGHT WE AGREED TO DO THIS ABOVE BOARD.
IT WAS JUST A TALK.
WALKER WENT BACK DOWN TO THE CRIME SCENE AND SOMETHING HAPPENED.
SOMETHING LIKE WHAT?
GET DOWN THERE.
DID HE GET HURT?
WE HAVE NO INFO. GO.
YES, SIR.
THIS ISN'T GOING TO HAPPEN THIS WAY.
IT WAS JUST A TALK.
SHE'S NOT A GOOD COP.
SHE'S AN AMAZING COP. ONE OF THE BEST OF ALL TIME.
IT DOESN'T CHANGE THE FACT THAT--
YOU HAVE A JOB TO DO, FINE. IT'S NOT GOING TO HAPPEN LIKE THIS.
YOU THINK YOU INVENTED BEING A TWO-FACED BITCH? YOU DIDN'T.
I DID.

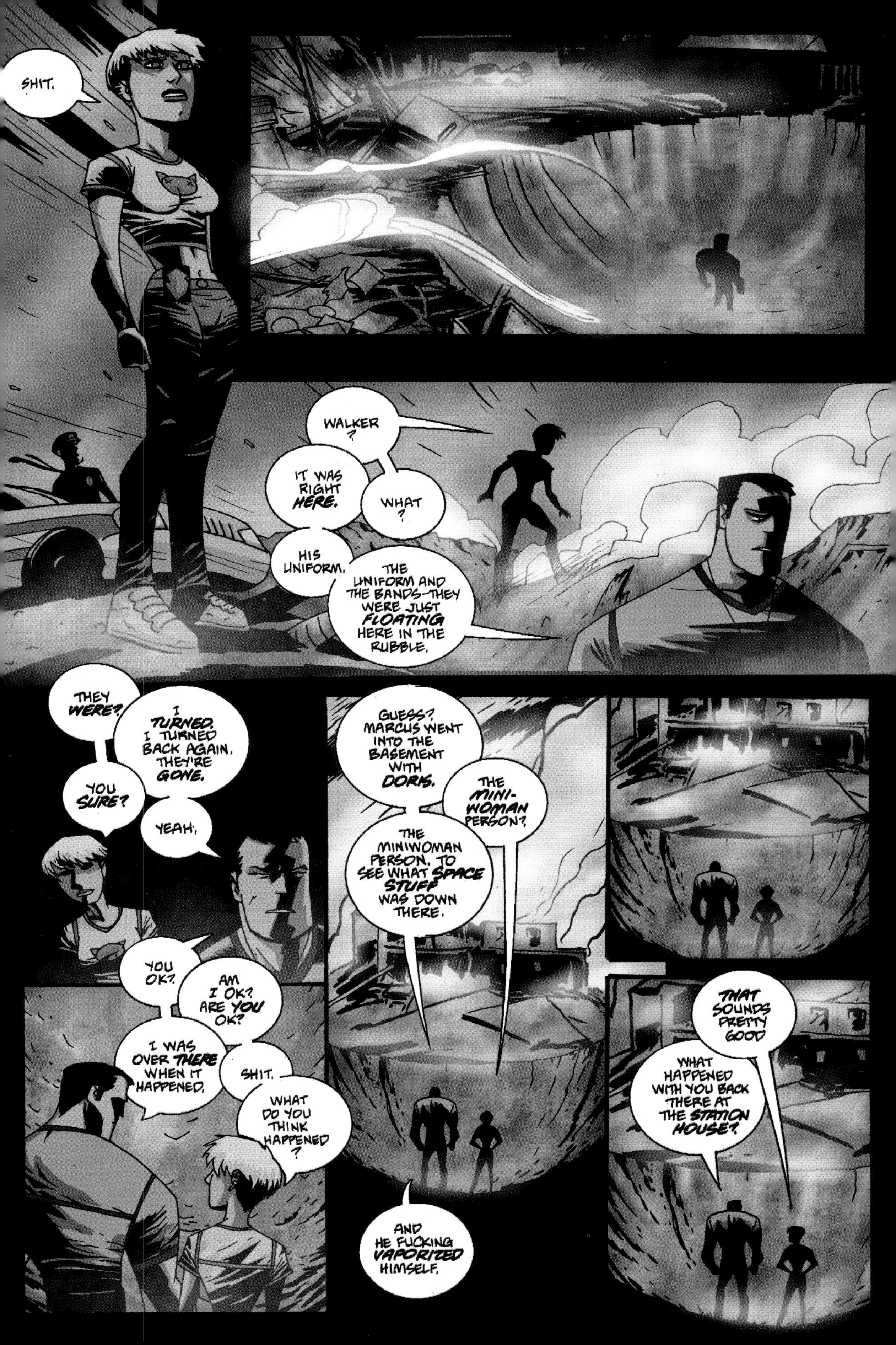
SHIT.
WALKER?
IT WAS RIGHT HERE.
WHAT?
HIS UNIFORM.
THE UNIFORM AND THE BANDS--THEY WERE JUST FLOATING HERE IN THE RUBBLE.
THEY WERE?
I TURNED. I TURNED BACK AGAIN. THEY'RE GONE.
YOU SURE?
YEAH.
YOU OK?
AM I OK? ARE YOU OK?
I WAS OVER THERE WHEN IT HAPPENED.
SHIT.
WHAT DO YOU THINK HAPPENED?
GUESS? MARCUS WENT INTO THE BASEMENT WITH DORIS.
THE MINI-WOMAN PERSON?
THE MINIWOMAN PERSON. TO SEE WHAT SPACE STUFF WAS DOWN THERE.
AND HE FUCKING VAPORIZED HIMSELF.
THAT SOUNDS PRETTY GOOD
WHAT HAPPENED WITH YOU BACK THERE AT THE STATION HOUSE?

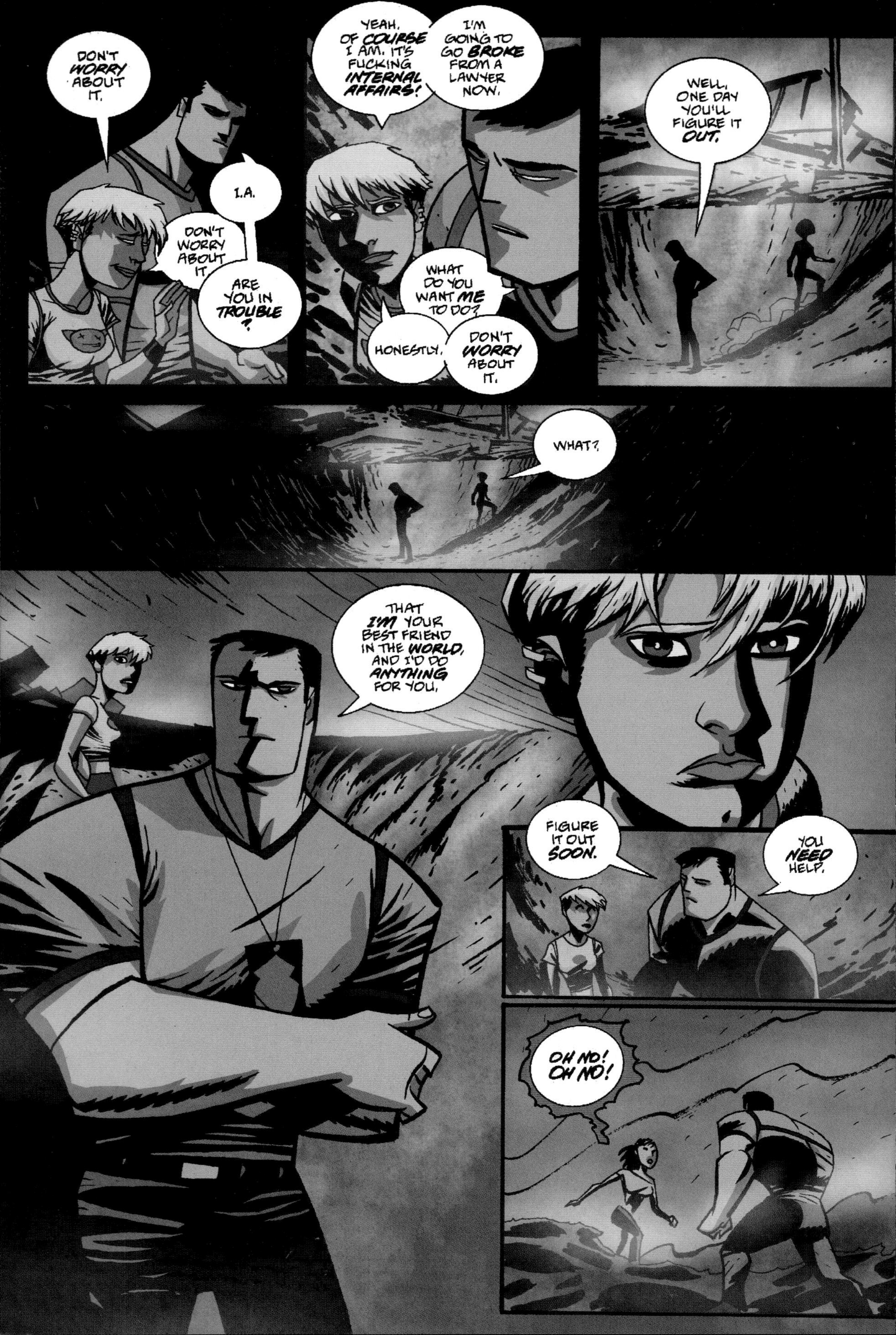

DON'T WORRY ABOUT IT.
I.A.
DON'T WORRY ABOUT IT.
ARE YOU IN TROUBLE?
YEAH, OF COURSE I AM. IT'S FUCKING INTERNAL AFFAIRS!
I'M GOING TO GO BROKE FROM A LAWYER NOW.
WHAT DO YOU WANT ME TO DO?
HONESTLY.
DON'T WORRY ABOUT IT.
WELL, ONE DAY YOU'LL FIGURE IT OUT.
WHAT?
THAT I'M YOUR BEST FRIEND IN THE WORLD, AND I'D DO ANYTHING FOR YOU.
FIGURE IT OUT SOON.
YOU NEED HELP.
OH NO! OH NO!

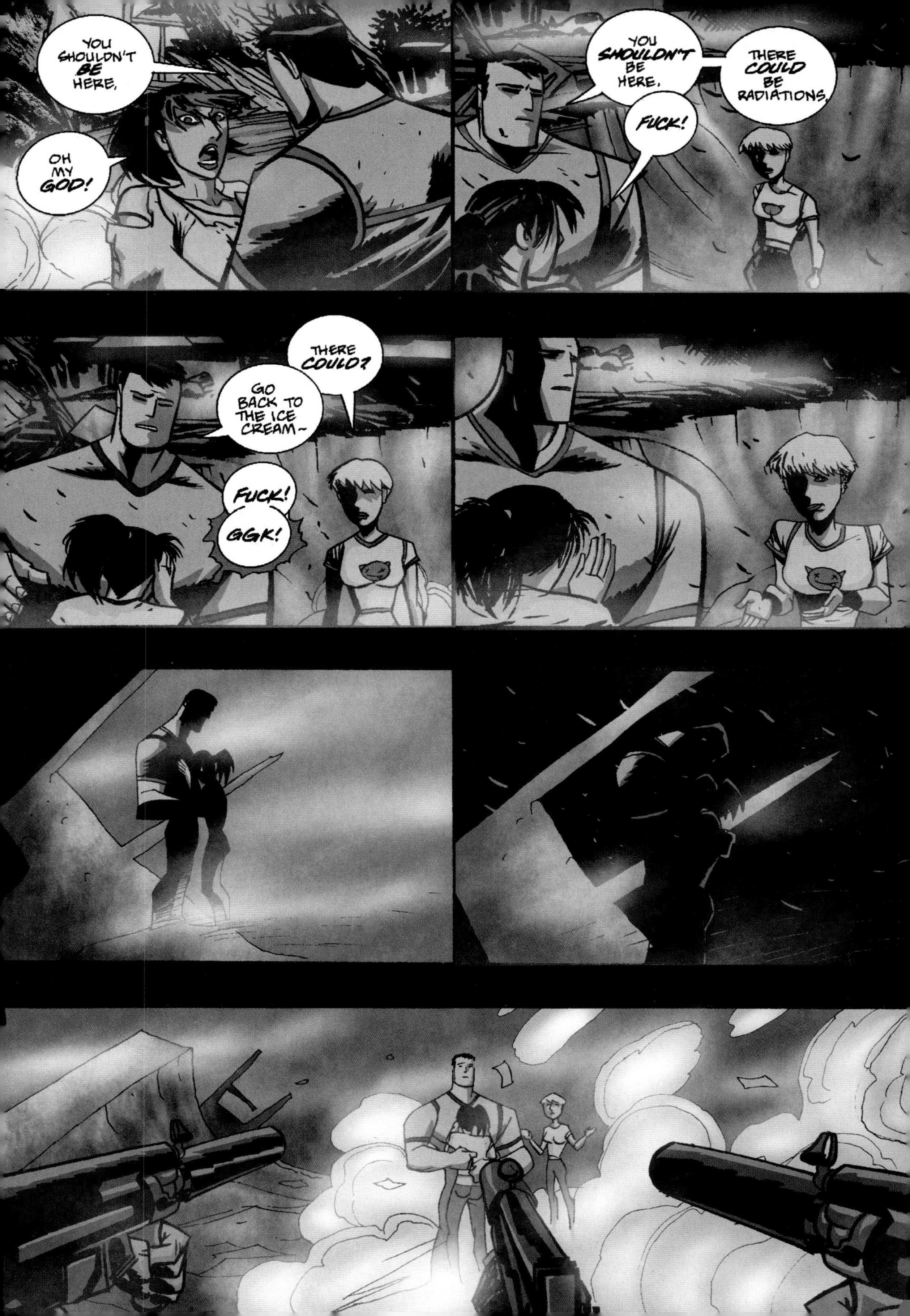
YOU SHOULDN'T BE HERE.
OH MY GOD!
YOU SHOULDN'T BE HERE.
THERE COULD BE RADIATIONS.
FUCK!
THERE COULD?
GO BACK TO THE ICE CREAM~
FUCK!
GGK!

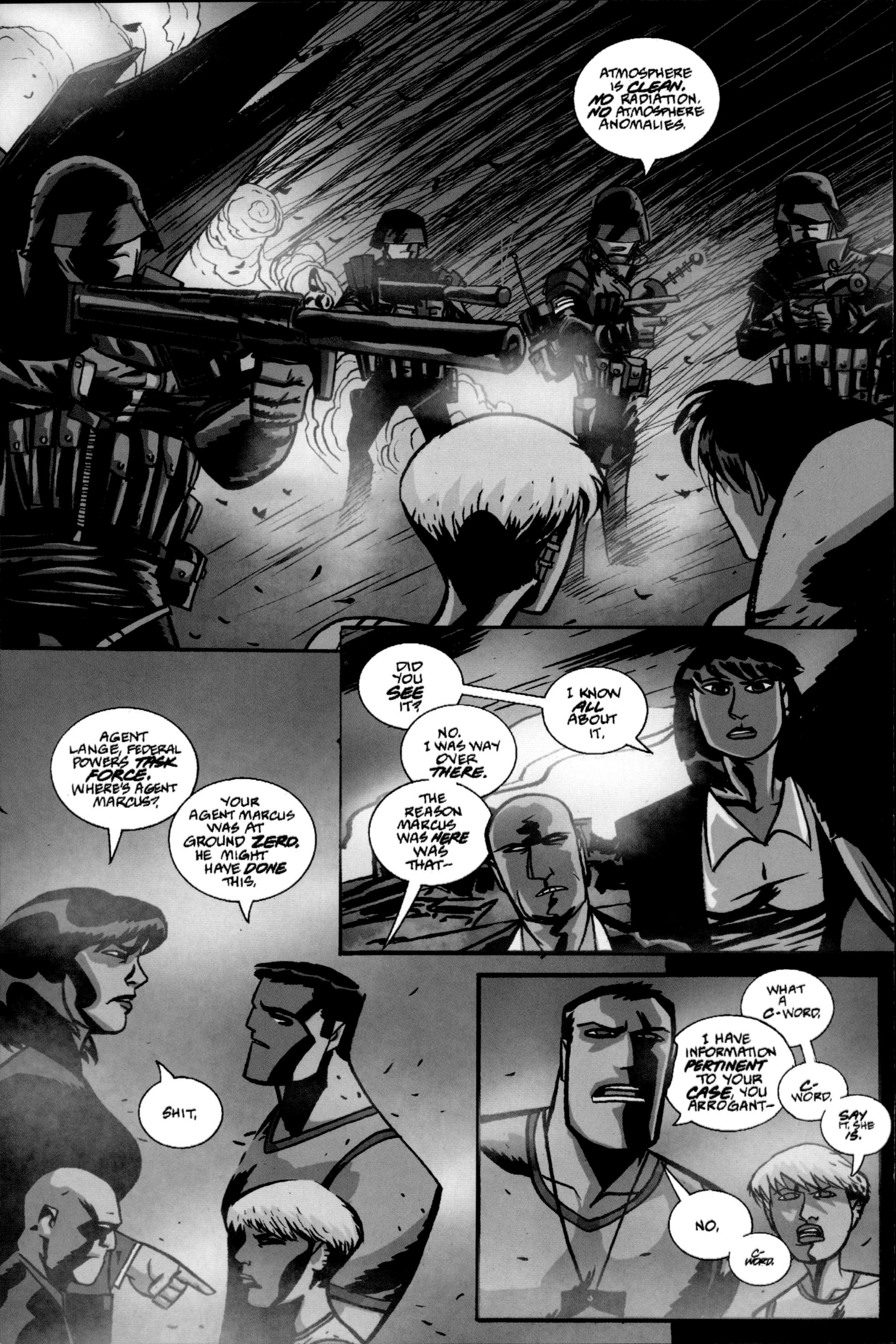
ATMOSPHERE IS CLEAN. NO RADIATION. NO ATMOSPHERE ANOMALIES.
AGENT LANGE, FEDERAL POWERS TASK FORCE. WHERE'S AGENT MARCUS?
YOUR AGENT MARCUS WAS AT GROUND ZERO. HE MIGHT HAVE DONE THIS.
SHIT.
DID YOU SEE IT?
I KNOW ALL ABOUT IT.
NO. I WAS WAY OVER THERE.
THE REASON MARCUS WAS HERE WAS THAT--
I HAVE INFORMATION PERTINENT TO YOUR CASE, YOU ARROGANT--
WHAT A C-WORD.
C-WORD.
SAY IT, SHE IS.
NO.
C-WORD.

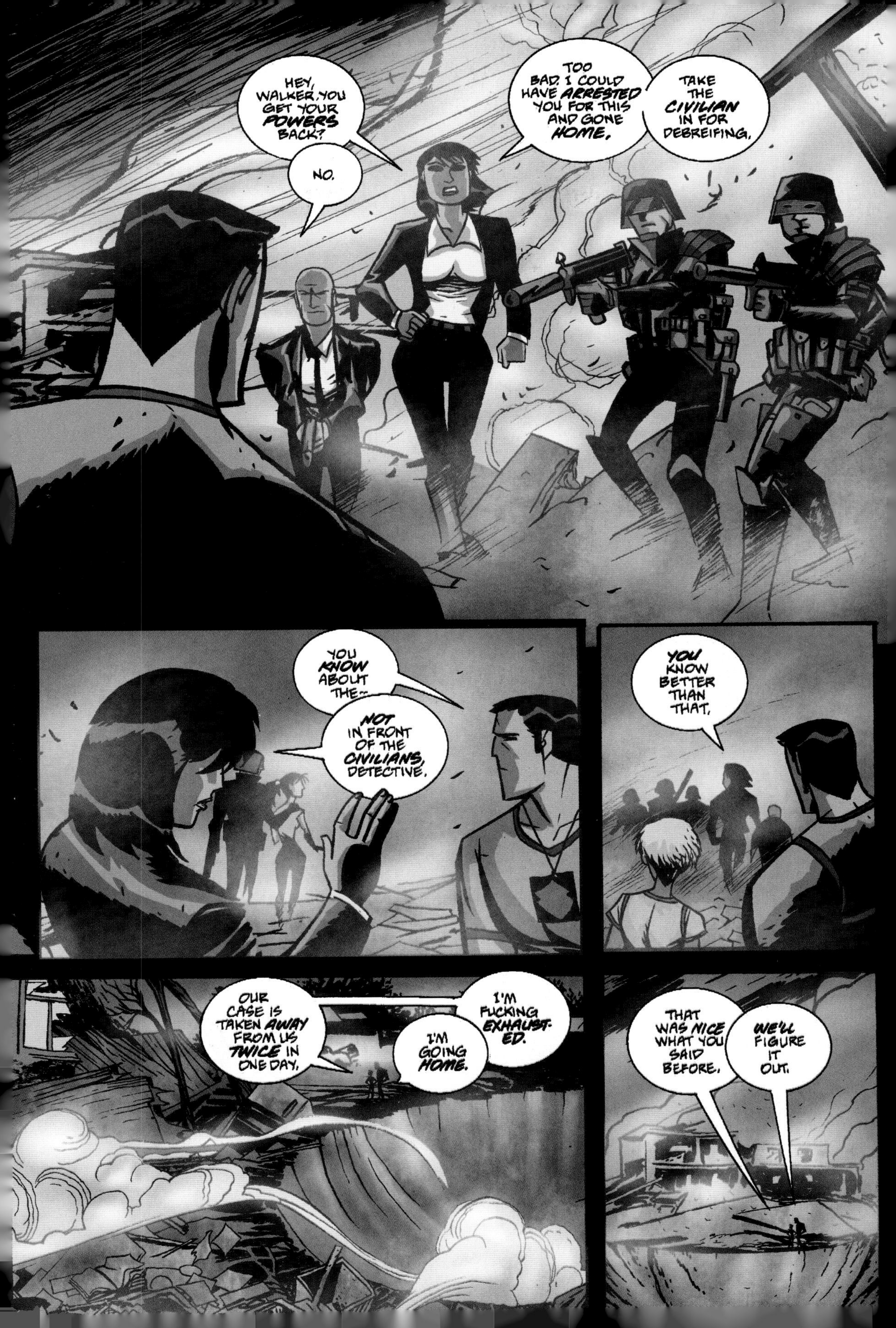
HEY, WALKER, YOU GET YOUR POWERS BACK?
NO.
TOO BAD. I COULD HAVE ARRESTED YOU FOR THIS AND GONE HOME.
TAKE THE CIVILIAN IN FOR DEBREIFING.
YOU KNOW ABOUT THE...
NOT IN FRONT OF THE CIVILIANS, DETECTIVE.
YOU KNOW BETTER THAN THAT.
OUR CASE IS TAKEN AWAY FROM US TWICE IN ONE DAY.
I'M FUCKING EXHAUST-ED.
I'M GOING HOME.
THAT WAS NICE WHAT YOU SAID BEFORE.
WE'LL FIGURE IT OUT.

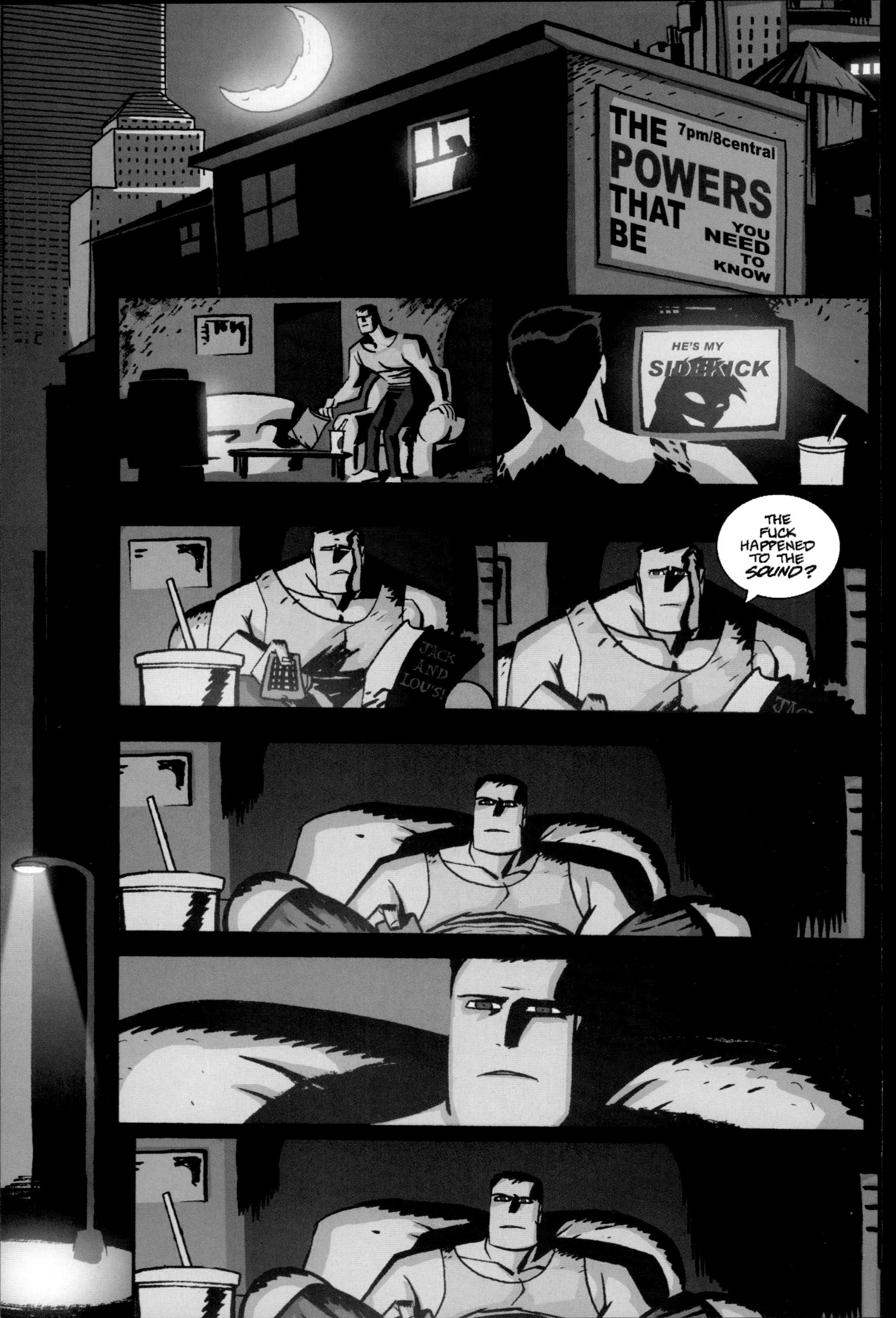
THE POWERS THAT BE
7pm/8central
YOU NEED TO KNOW
HE'S MY SIDEKICK
JACK AND LOU'S!
THE FUCK HAPPENED TO THE SOUND?

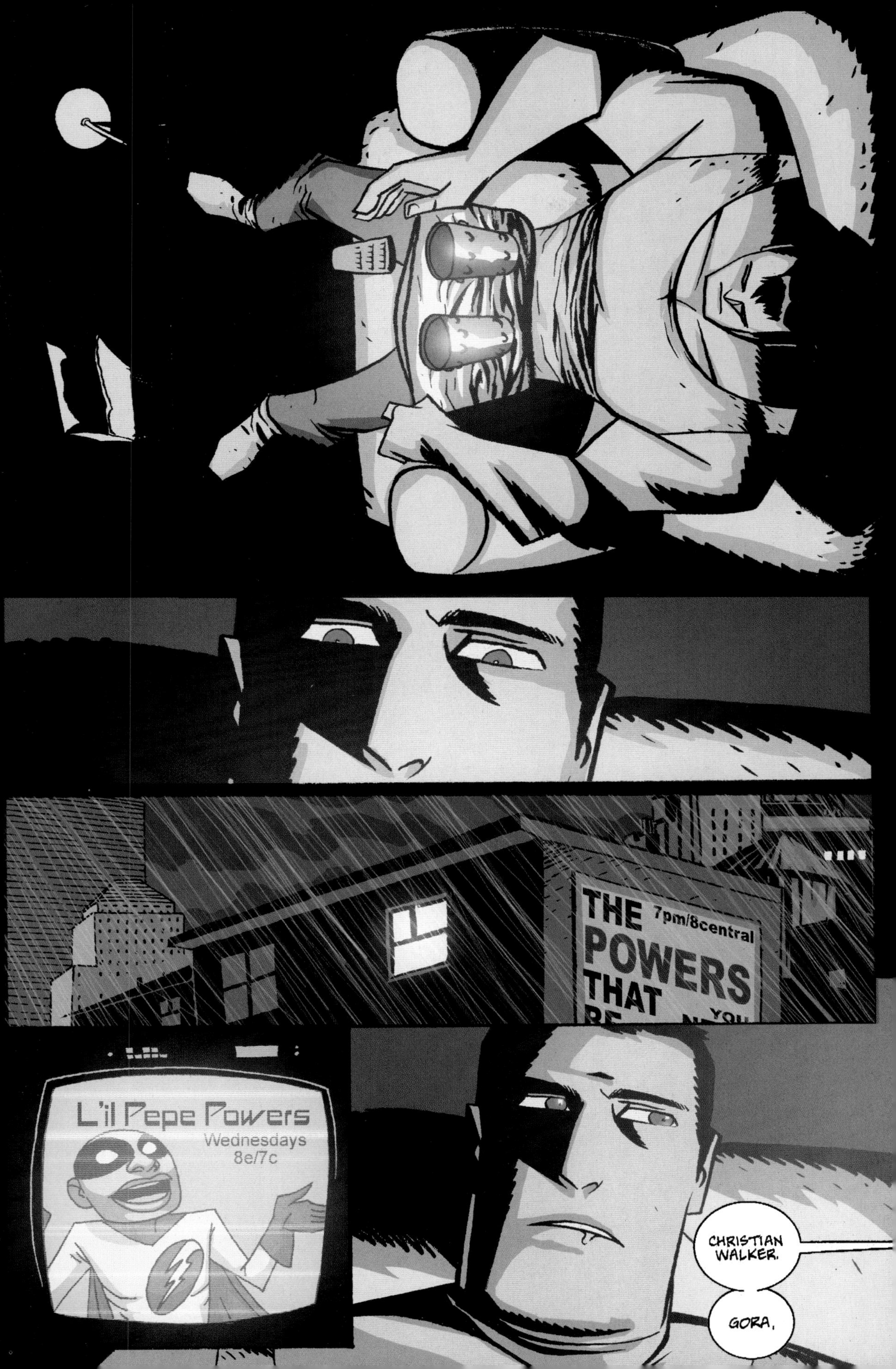
THE
7pm/8central
POWERS
THAT
YOU
L'il Pepe Powers
Wednesdays
8e/7c
CHRISTIAN WALKER.
GORA.

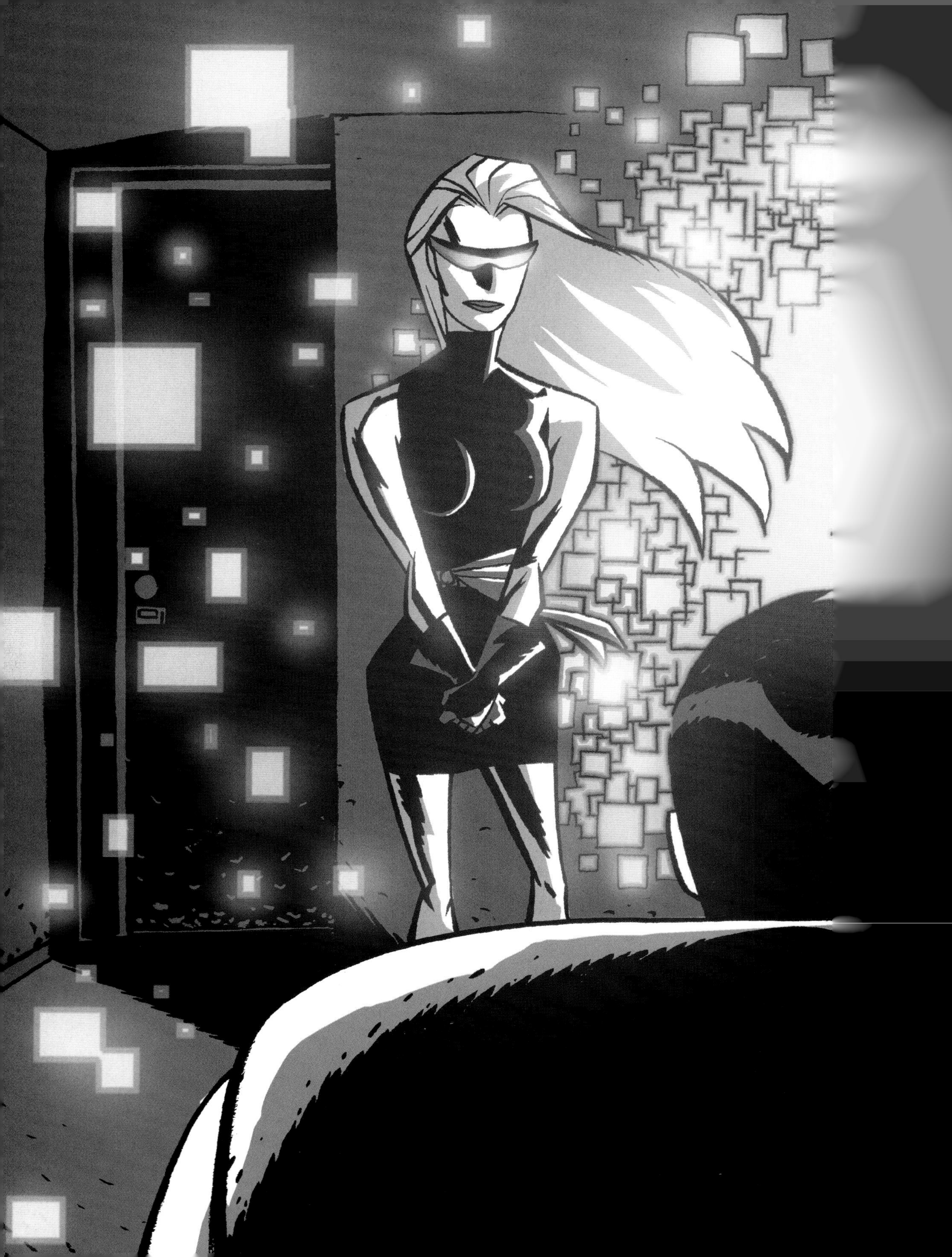

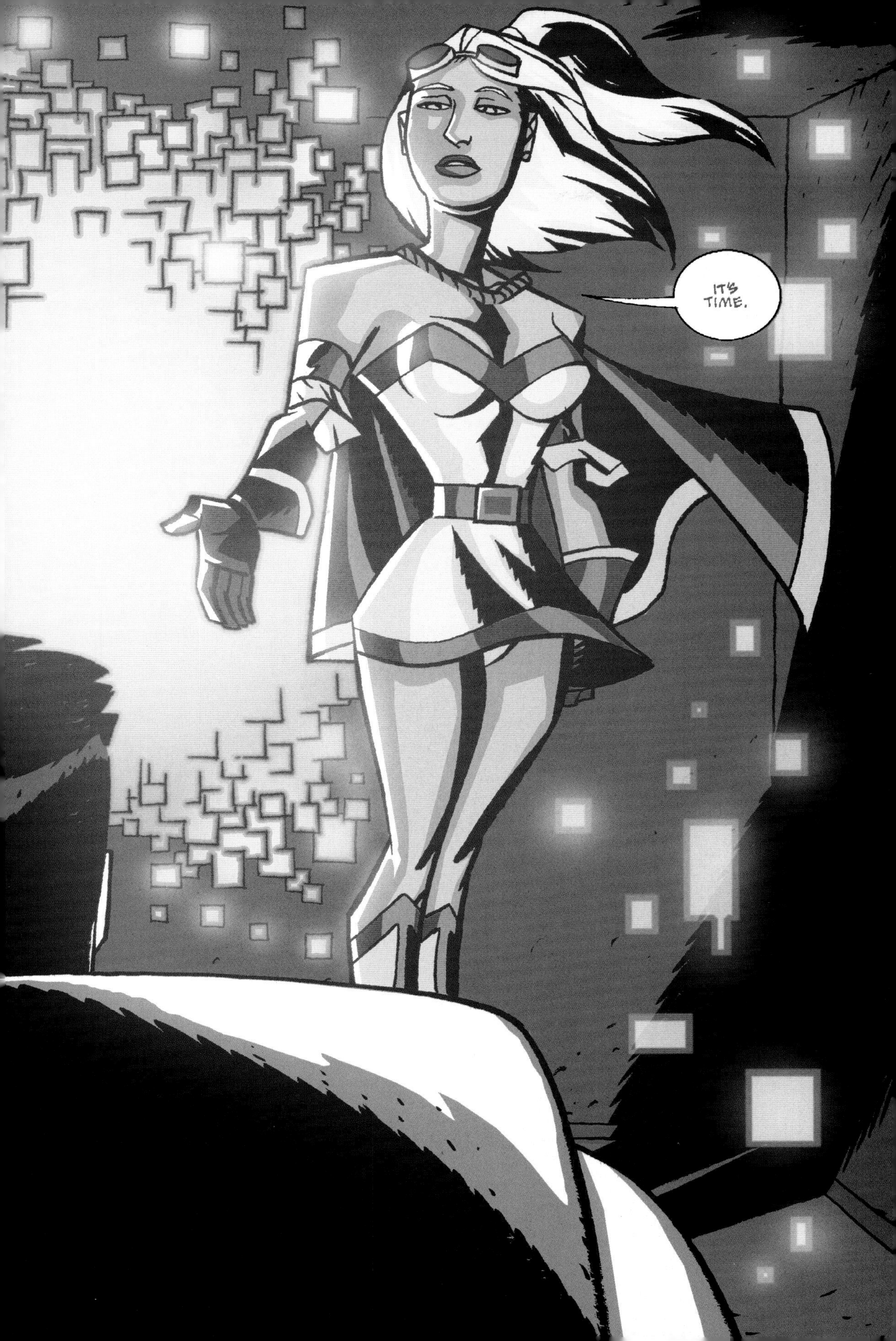
IT'S TIME.

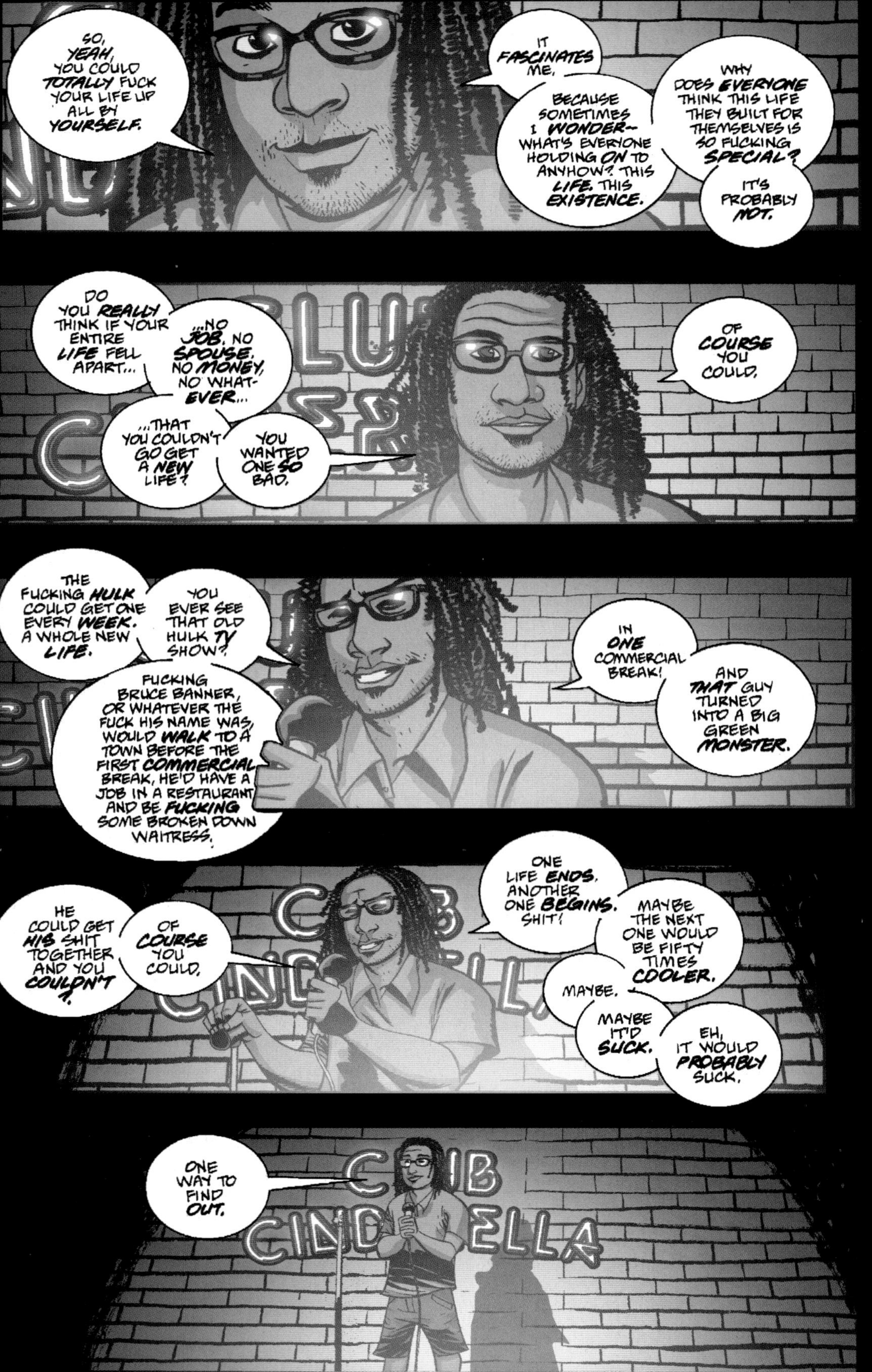
SO, YEAH, YOU COULD TOTALLY FUCK YOUR LIFE UP ALL BY YOURSELF.
IT FASCINATES ME.
BECAUSE SOMETIMES I WONDER-- WHAT'S EVERYONE HOLDING ON TO ANYHOW? THIS LIFE. THIS EXISTENCE.
WHY DOES EVERYONE THINK THIS LIFE THEY BUILT FOR THEMSELVES IS SO FUCKING SPECIAL?
IT'S PROBABLY NOT.
DO YOU REALLY THINK IF YOUR ENTIRE LIFE FELL APART...
...NO JOB, NO SPOUSE, NO MONEY, NO WHATEVER...
...THAT YOU COULDN'T GO GET A NEW LIFE?
YOU WANTED ONE SO BAD.
OF COURSE YOU COULD.
THE FUCKING HULK COULD GET ONE EVERY WEEK. A WHOLE NEW LIFE.
YOU EVER SEE THAT OLD HULK TV SHOW?
FUCKING BRUCE BANNER, OR WHATEVER THE FUCK HIS NAME WAS, WOULD WALK TO A TOWN BEFORE THE FIRST COMMERCIAL BREAK, HE'D HAVE A JOB IN A RESTAURANT AND BE FUCKING SOME BROKEN DOWN WAITRESS.
IN ONE COMMERCIAL BREAK!
AND THAT GUY TURNED INTO A BIG GREEN MONSTER.
HE COULD GET HIS SHIT TOGETHER AND YOU COULDN'T?
OF COURSE YOU COULD.
ONE LIFE ENDS, ANOTHER ONE BEGINS. SHIT!
MAYBE THE NEXT ONE WOULD BE FIFTY TIMES COOLER.
MAYBE.
MAYBE IT'D SUCK.
EH, IT WOULD PROBABLY SUCK.
ONE WAY TO FIND OUT.

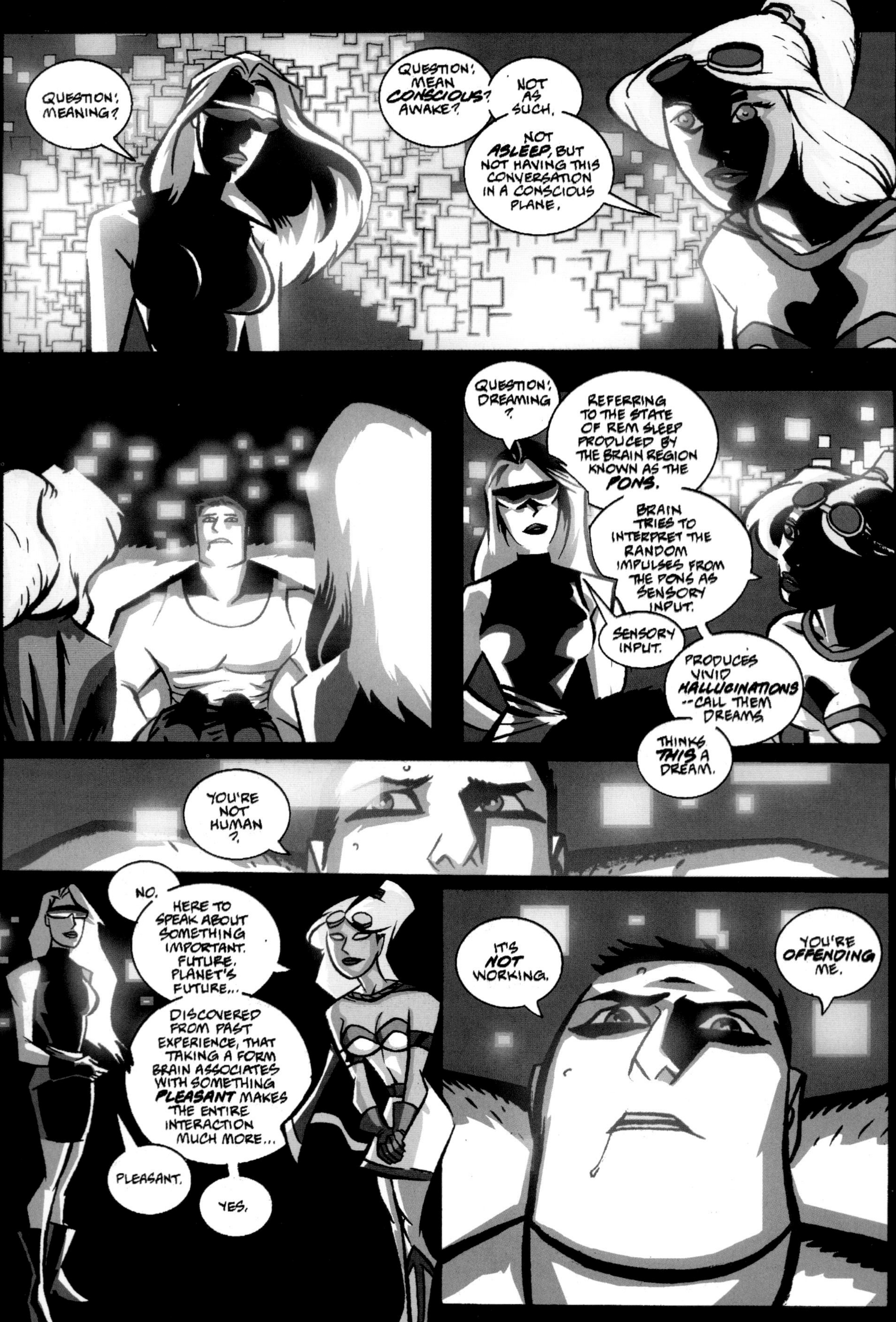
QUESTION: MEANING?
QUESTION: MEAN CONSCIOUS? AWAKE?
NOT AS SUCH.
NOT ASLEEP, BUT NOT HAVING THIS CONVERSATION IN A CONSCIOUS PLANE.
QUESTION: DREAMING?
REFERRING TO THE STATE OF REM SLEEP PRODUCED BY THE BRAIN REGION KNOWN AS THE PONS.
BRAIN TRIES TO INTERPRET THE RANDOM IMPULSES FROM THE PONS AS SENSORY INPUT.
SENSORY INPUT.
PRODUCES VIVID HALLUCINATIONS --CALL THEM DREAMS.
THINKS THIS A DREAM.
YOU'RE NOT HUMAN?
NO.
HERE TO SPEAK ABOUT SOMETHING IMPORTANT. FUTURE. PLANET'S FUTURE...
DISCOVERED FROM PAST EXPERIENCE, THAT TAKING A FORM BRAIN ASSOCIATES WITH SOMETHING PLEASANT MAKES THE ENTIRE INTERACTION MUCH MORE...
PLEASANT.
YES.
IT'S NOT WORKING.
YOU'RE OFFENDING ME.

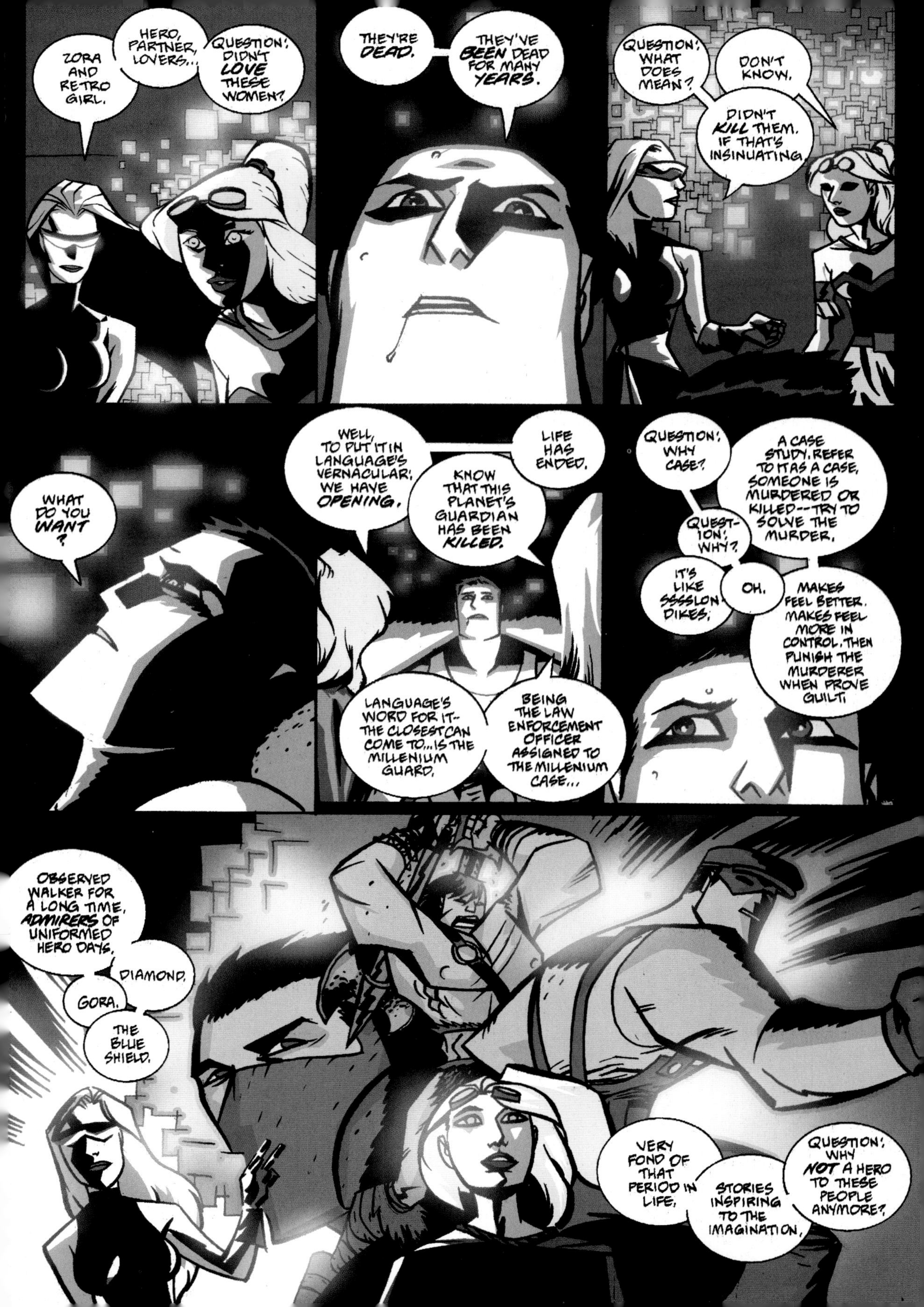

ZORA AND RETRO GIRL.
HERO, PARTNER, LOVERS...
QUESTION: DIDN'T LOVE THESE WOMEN?
THEY'RE DEAD.
THEY'VE BEEN DEAD FOR MANY YEARS.
QUESTION: WHAT DOES MEAN?
DON'T KNOW.
DIDN'T KILL THEM. IF THAT'S INSINUATING.
WHAT DO YOU WANT?
WELL, TO PUT IT IN LANGUAGE'S VERNACULAR: WE HAVE OPENING.
LIFE HAS ENDED.
KNOW THAT THIS PLANET'S GUARDIAN HAS BEEN KILLED.
LANGUAGE'S WORD FOR IT-- THE CLOSEST CAN COME TO... IS THE MILLENIUM GUARD.
BEING THE LAW ENFORCEMENT OFFICER ASSIGNED TO THE MILLENIUM CASE...
QUESTION: WHY CASE?
A CASE STUDY. REFER TO IT AS A CASE. SOMEONE IS MURDERED OR KILLED--TRY TO SOLVE THE MURDER.
QUEST-ION: WHY?
IT'S LIKE SSSSLONDIKES.
OH.
MAKES FEEL BETTER. MAKES FEEL MORE IN CONTROL. THEN PUNISH THE MURDERER WHEN PROVE GUILT.
OBSERVED WALKER FOR A LONG TIME. ADMIRERS OF UNIFORMED HERO DAYS.
DIAMOND.
GORA.
THE BLUE SHIELD.
VERY FOND OF THAT PERIOD IN LIFE.
STORIES INSPIRING TO THE IMAGINATION.
QUESTION: WHY NOT A HERO TO THESE PEOPLE ANYMORE?

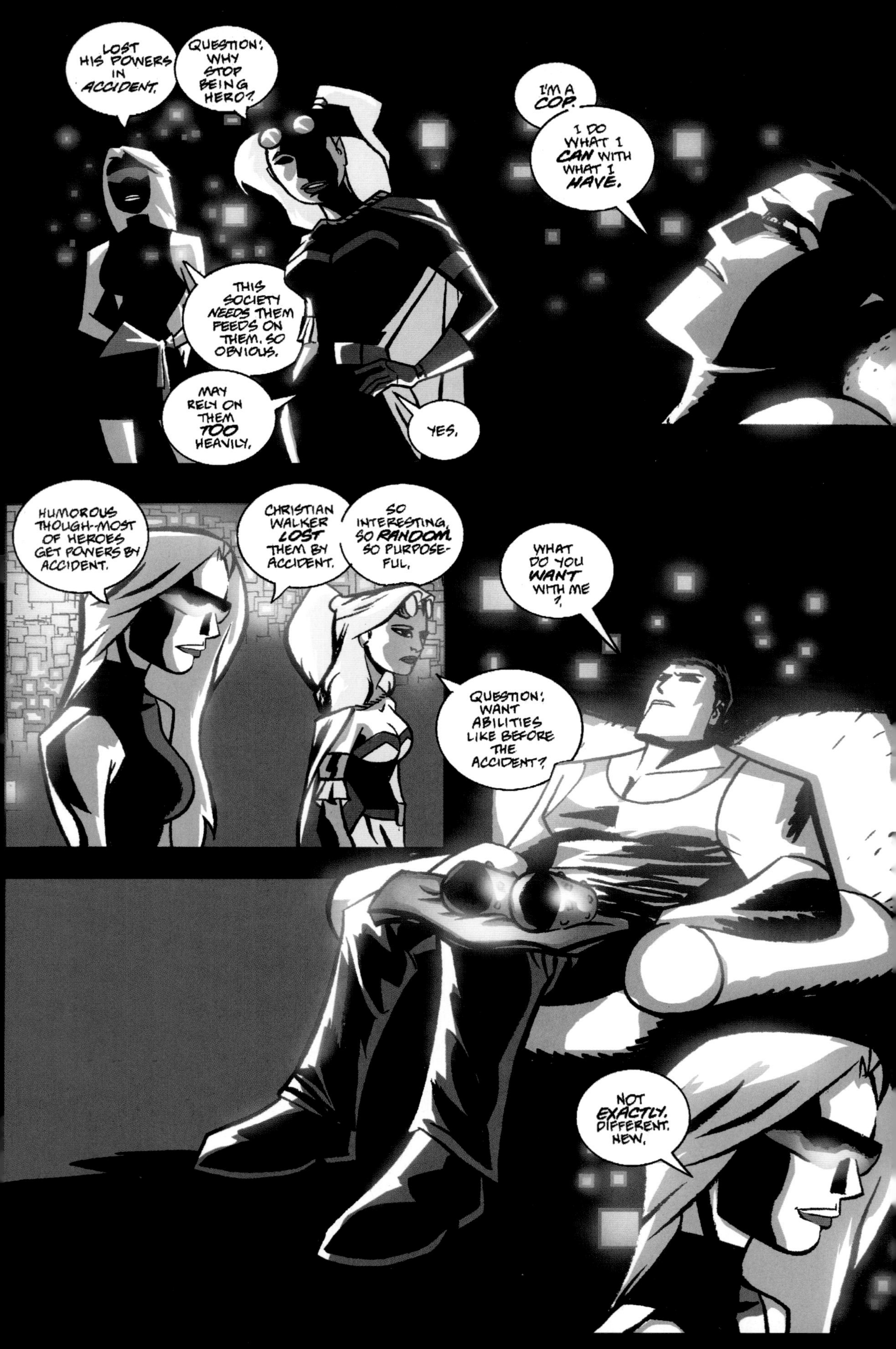
LOST HIS POWERS IN ACCIDENT.
QUESTION: WHY STOP BEING HERO?
I'M A COP.
I DO WHAT I CAN WITH WHAT I HAVE.
THIS SOCIETY NEEDS THEM FEEDS ON THEM. SO OBVIOUS.
MAY RELY ON THEM TOO HEAVILY.
YES.
HUMOROUS THOUGH-MOST OF HEROES GET POWERS BY ACCIDENT.
CHRISTIAN WALKER LOST THEM BY ACCIDENT.
SO INTERESTING, SO RANDOM SO PURPOSE-FUL.
WHAT DO YOU WANT WITH ME ?
QUESTION: WANT ABILITIES LIKE BEFORE THE ACCIDENT?
NOT EXACTLY. DIFFERENT. NEW.

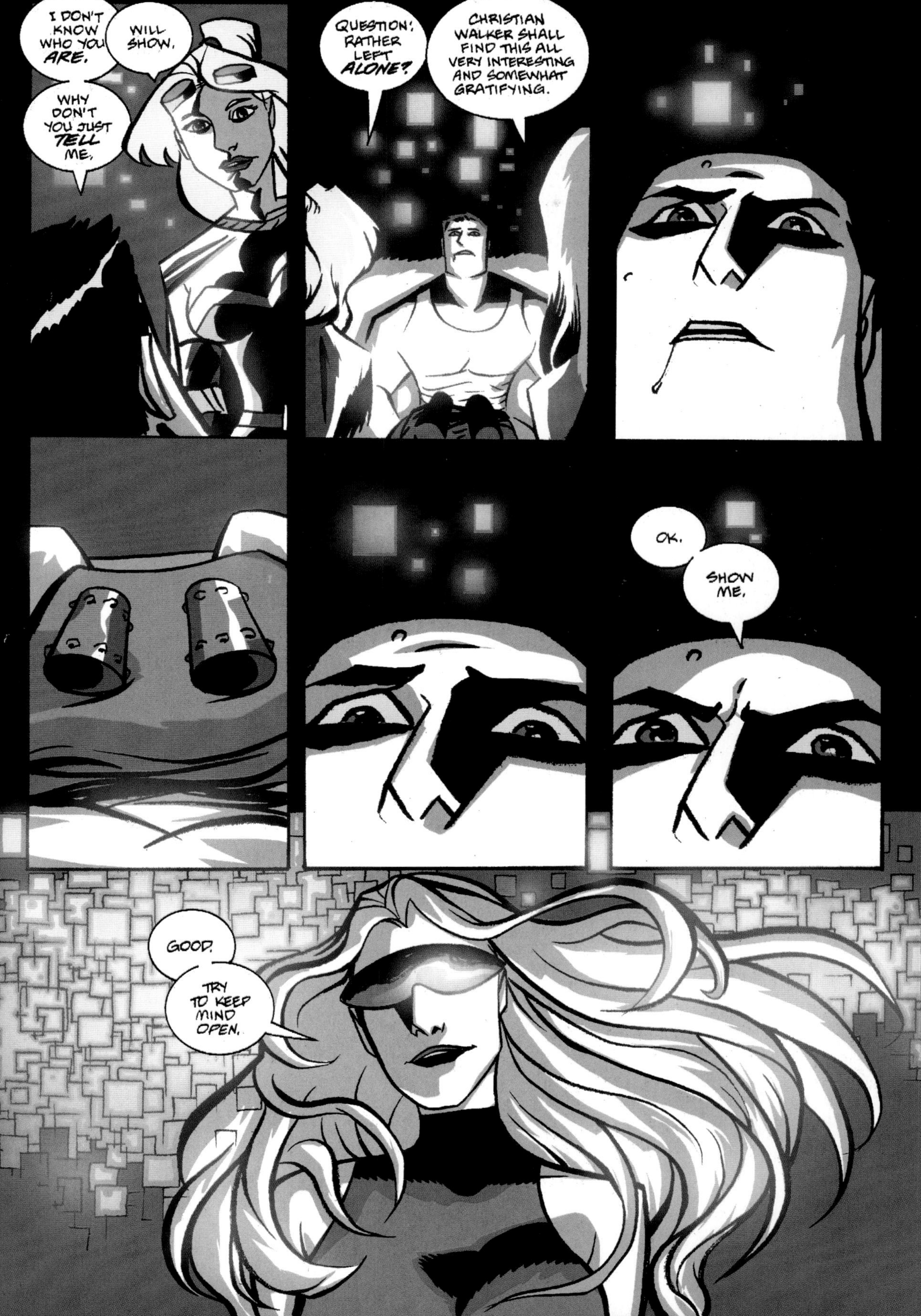
I DON'T KNOW WHO YOU ARE.
WILL SHOW.
WHY DON'T YOU JUST TELL ME.
QUESTION: RATHER LEFT ALONE?
CHRISTIAN WALKER SHALL FIND THIS ALL VERY INTERESTING AND SOMEWHAT GRATIFYING.
OK.
SHOW ME.
GOOD.
TRY TO KEEP MIND OPEN.

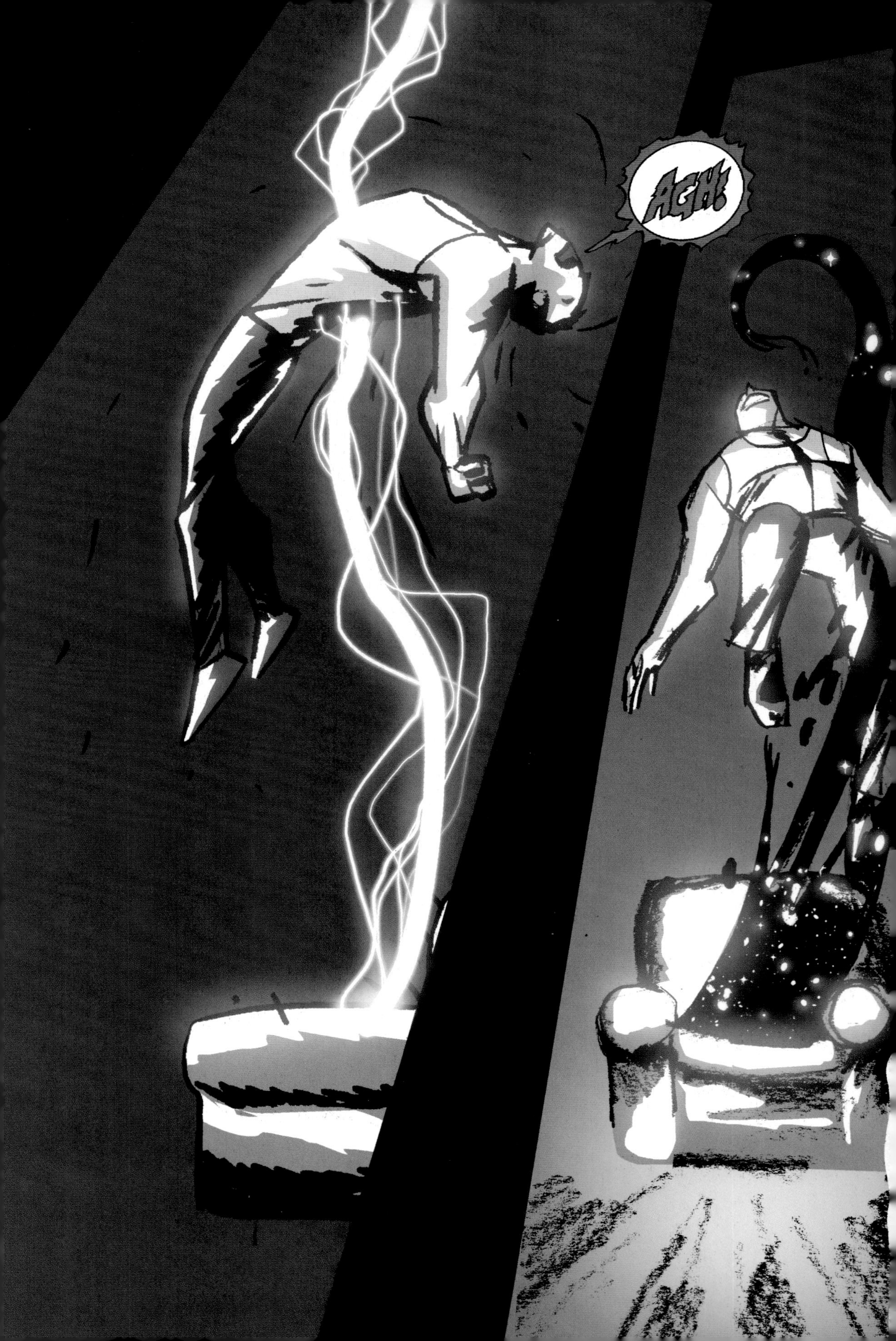
AGH!

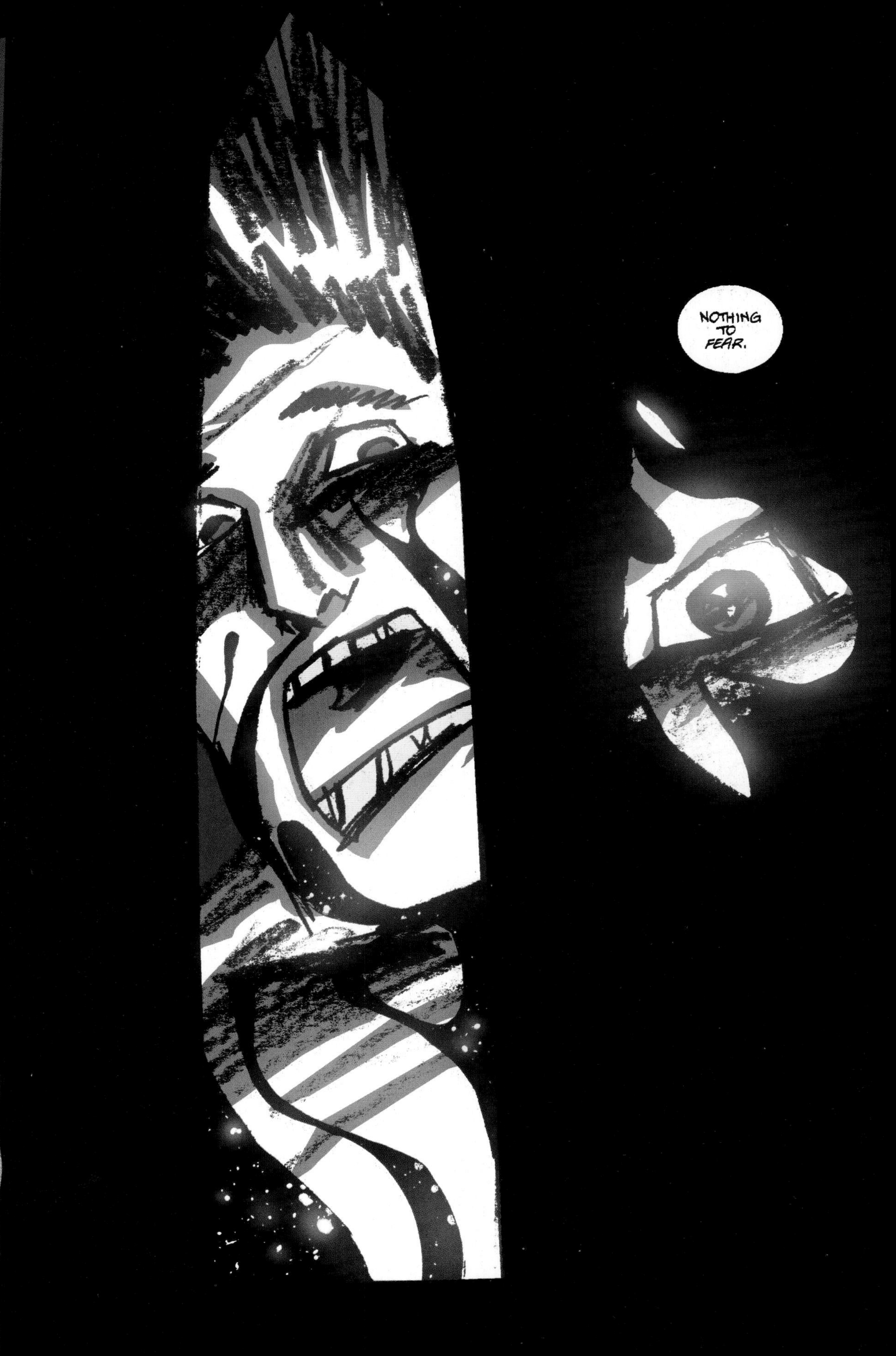
NOTHING TO FEAR.

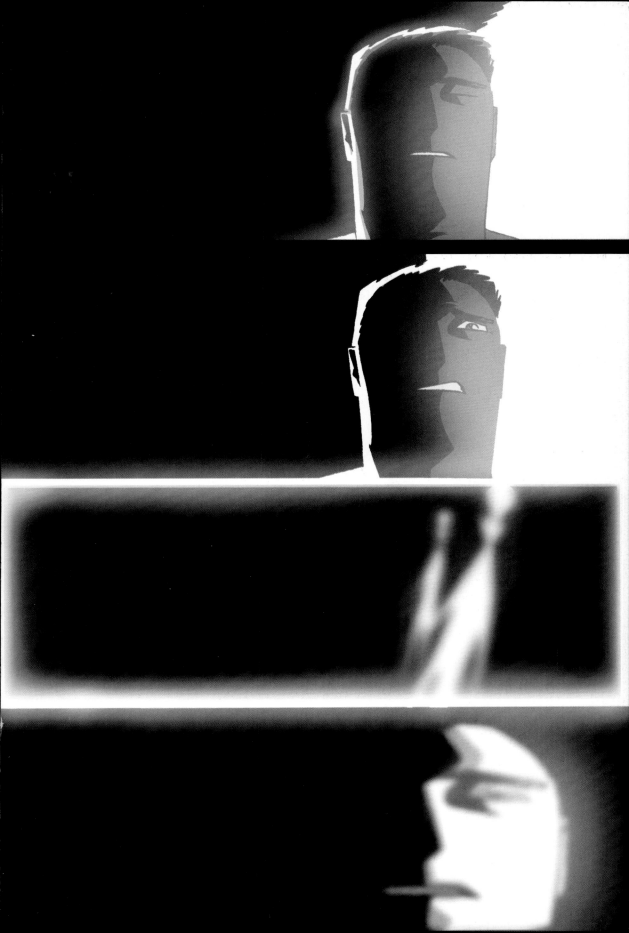

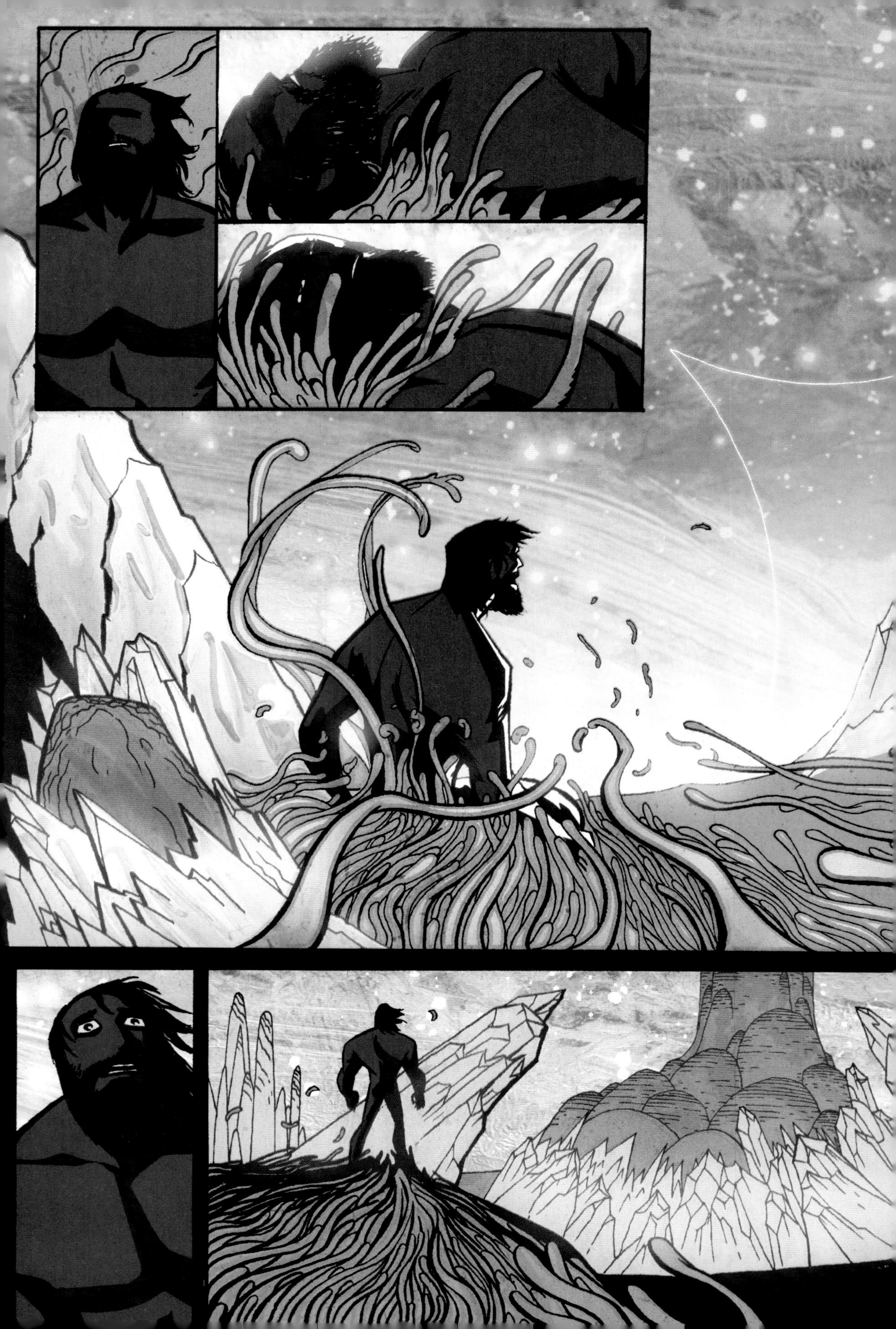

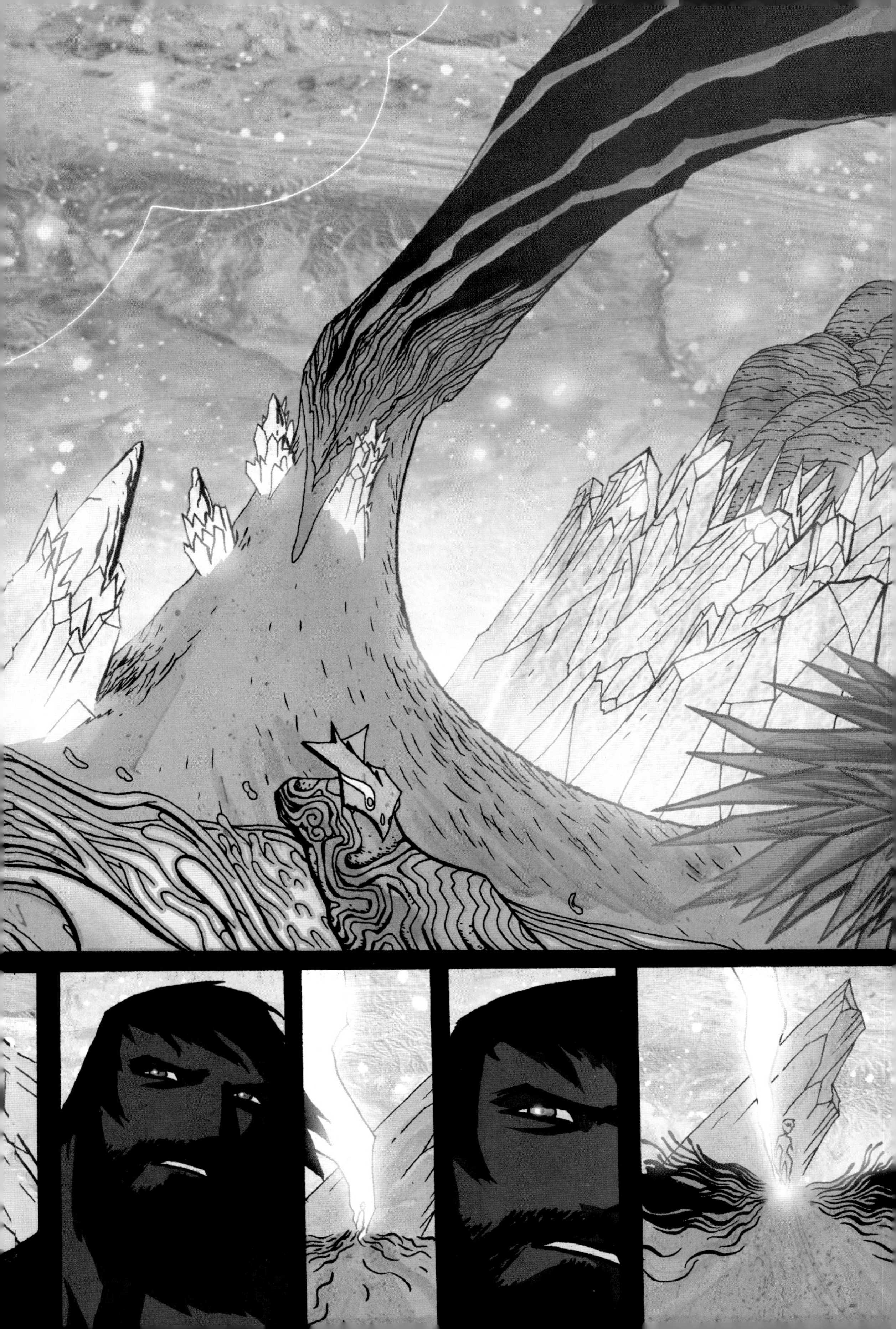

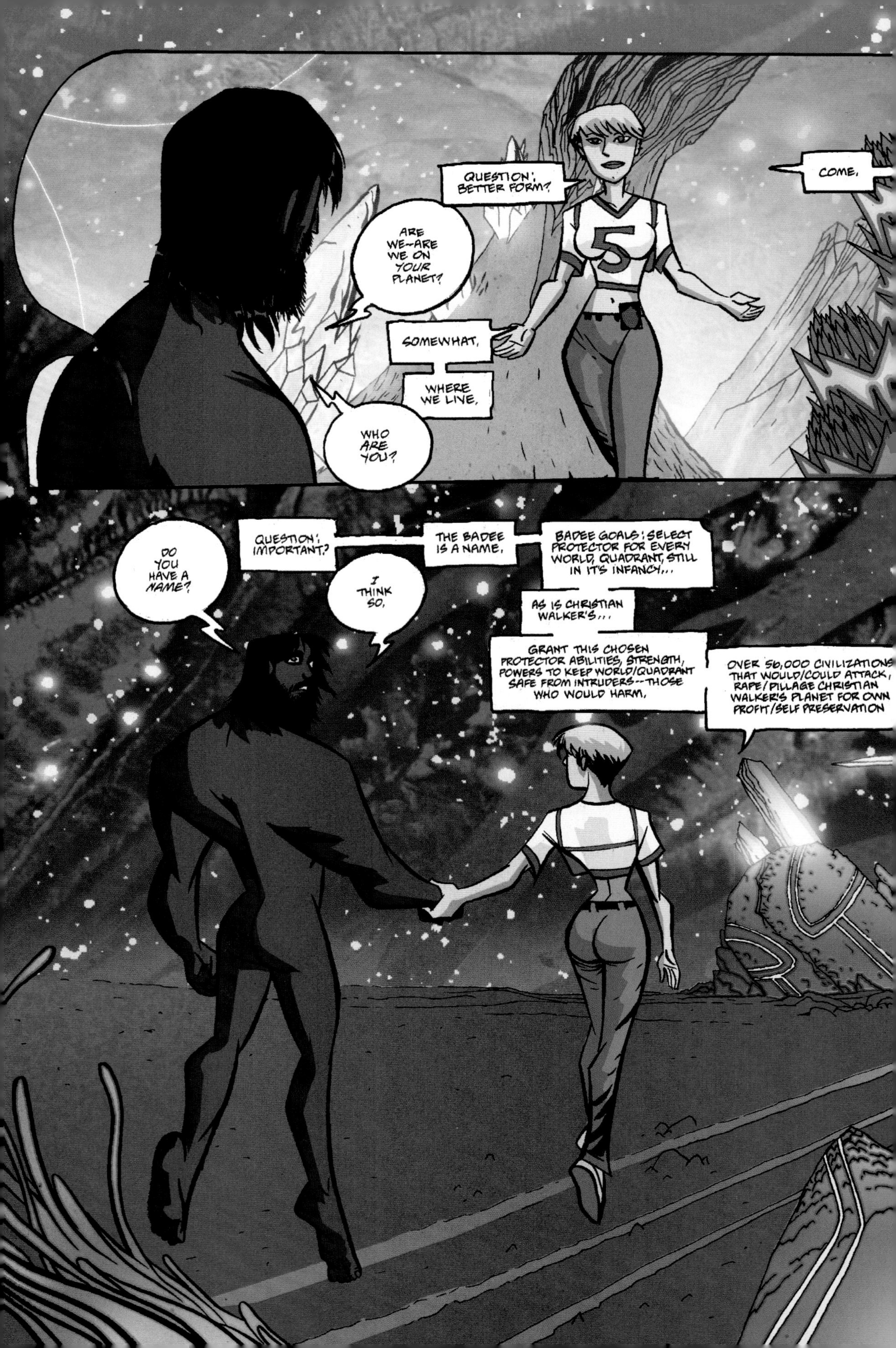
QUESTION: BETTER FORM?
COME.
ARE WE--ARE WE ON YOUR PLANET?
SOMEWHAT.
WHERE WE LIVE.
WHO ARE YOU?
QUESTION: IMPORTANT?
THE BADEE IS A NAME.
BADEE GOALS: SELECT PROTECTOR FOR EVERY WORLD, QUADRANT, STILL IN IT'S INFANCY...
AS IS CHRISTIAN WALKER'S...
GRANT THIS CHOSEN PROTECTOR ABILITIES, STRENGTH, POWERS TO KEEP WORLD/QUADRANT SAFE FROM INTRUDERS--THOSE WHO WOULD HARM.
OVER 56,000 CIVILIZATIONS THAT WOULD/COULD ATTACK, RAPE/PILLAGE CHRISTIAN WALKER'S PLANET FOR OWN PROFIT/SELF PRESERVATION
DO YOU HAVE A NAME?
I THINK SO.

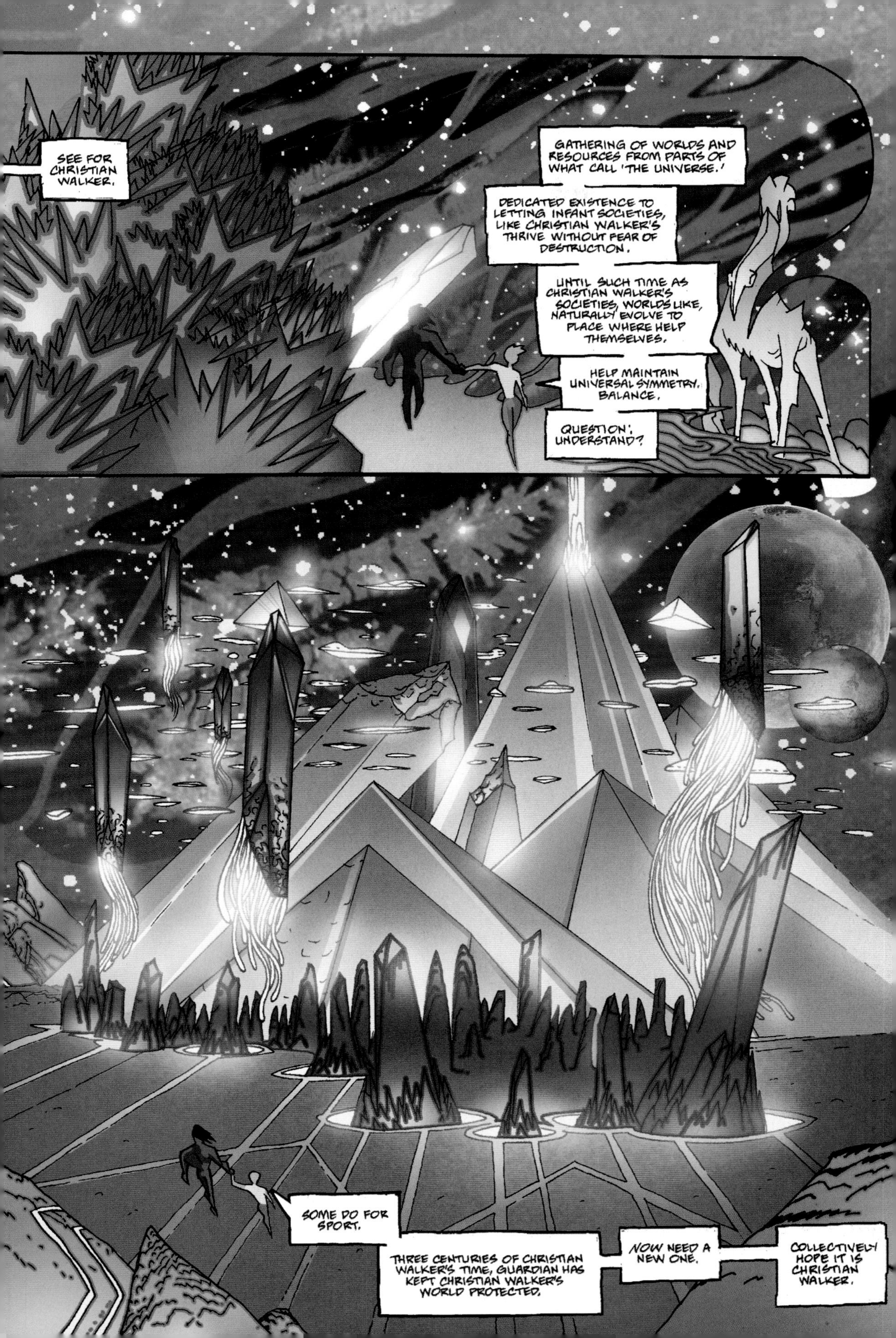
SEE FOR CHRISTIAN WALKER.
GATHERING OF WORLDS AND RESOURCES FROM PARTS OF WHAT CALL 'THE UNIVERSE.'
DEDICATED EXISTENCE TO LETTING INFANT SOCIETIES, LIKE CHRISTIAN WALKER'S THRIVE WITHOUT FEAR OF DESTRUCTION.
UNTIL SUCH TIME AS CHRISTIAN WALKER'S SOCIETIES, WORLDS LIKE, NATURALLY EVOLVE TO PLACE WHERE HELP THEMSELVES.
HELP MAINTAIN UNIVERSAL SYMMETRY. BALANCE.
QUESTION'. UNDERSTAND?
SOME DO FOR SPORT.
THREE CENTURIES OF CHRISTIAN WALKER'S TIME, GUARDIAN HAS KEPT CHRISTIAN WALKER'S WORLD PROTECTED.
NOW NEED A NEW ONE.
COLLECTIVELY HOPE IT IS CHRISTIAN WALKER.

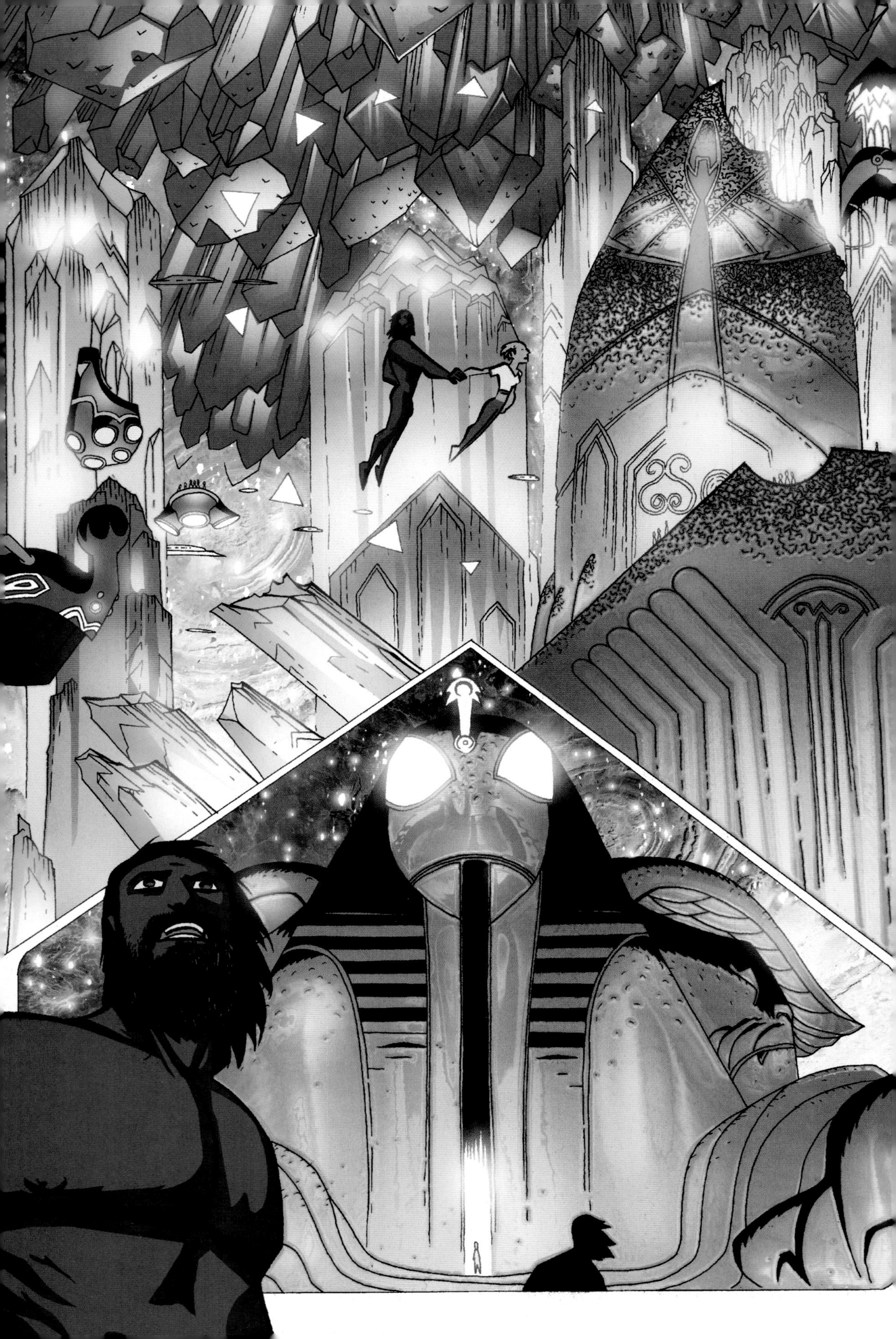

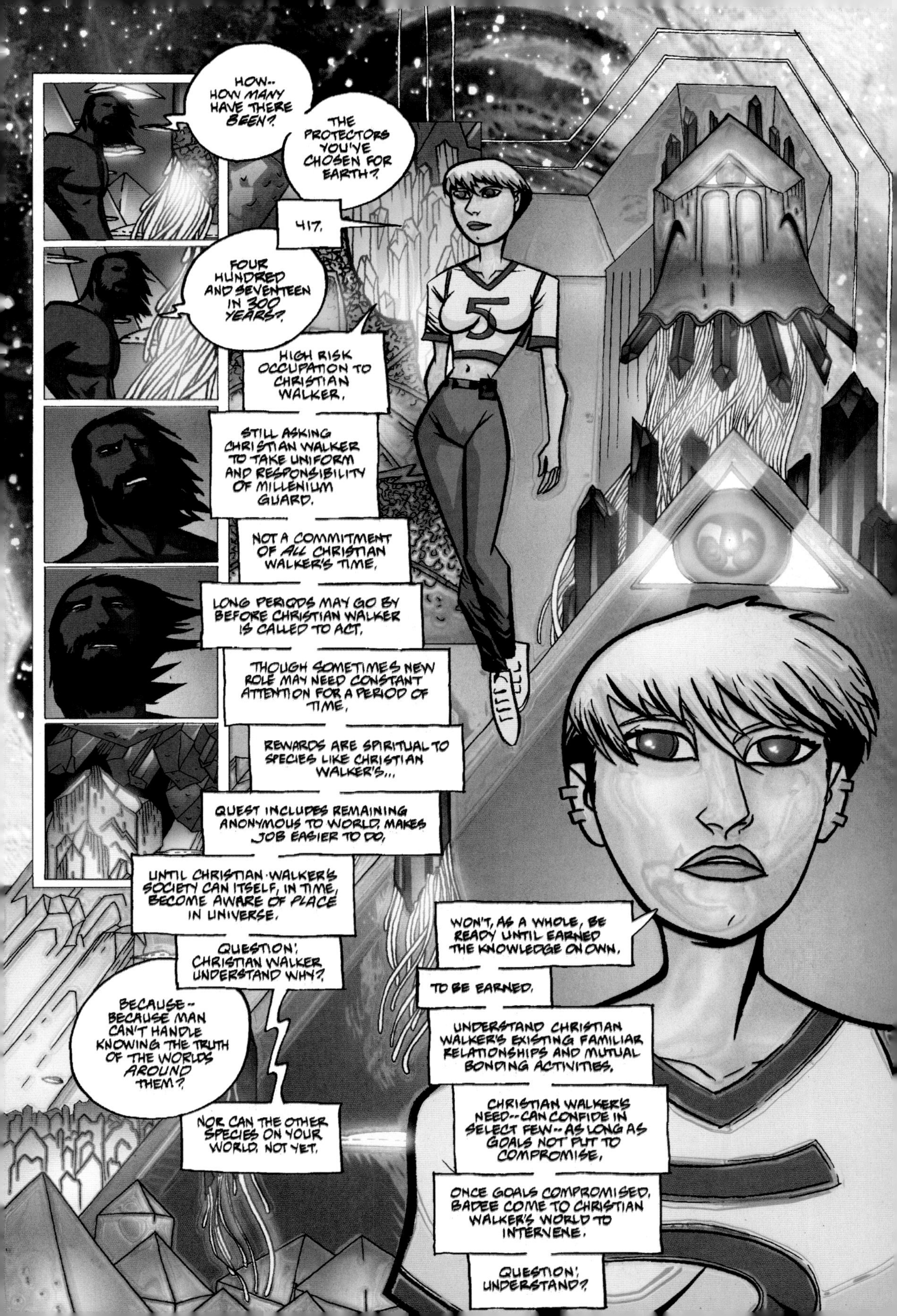
HOW.. HOW MANY HAVE THERE BEEN?
THE PROTECTORS YOU'VE CHOSEN FOR EARTH?
417.
FOUR HUNDRED AND SEVENTEEN IN 300 YEARS?
HIGH RISK OCCUPATION TO CHRISTIAN WALKER.
STILL ASKING CHRISTIAN WALKER TO TAKE UNIFORM AND RESPONSIBILITY OF MILLENIUM GUARD.
NOT A COMMITMENT OF ALL CHRISTIAN WALKER'S TIME.
LONG PERIODS MAY GO BY BEFORE CHRISTIAN WALKER IS CALLED TO ACT.
THOUGH SOMETIMES NEW ROLE MAY NEED CONSTANT ATTENTION FOR A PERIOD OF TIME.
REWARDS ARE SPIRITUAL TO SPECIES LIKE CHRISTIAN WALKER'S...
QUEST INCLUDES REMAINING ANONYMOUS TO WORLD, MAKES JOB EASIER TO DO.
UNTIL CHRISTIAN WALKER'S SOCIETY CAN ITSELF, IN TIME, BECOME AWARE OF PLACE IN UNIVERSE.
QUESTION: CHRISTIAN WALKER UNDERSTAND WHY?
BECAUSE-- BECAUSE MAN CAN'T HANDLE KNOWING THE TRUTH OF THE WORLDS AROUND THEM?
NOR CAN THE OTHER SPECIES ON YOUR WORLD. NOT YET.
WON'T, AS A WHOLE, BE READY UNTIL EARNED THE KNOWLEDGE ON OWN.
TO BE EARNED.
UNDERSTAND CHRISTIAN WALKER'S EXISTING FAMILIAR RELATIONSHIPS AND MUTUAL BONDING ACTIVITIES.
CHRISTIAN WALKER'S NEED-- CAN CONFIDE IN SELECT FEW-- AS LONG AS GOALS NOT PUT TO COMPROMISE.
ONCE GOALS COMPROMISED, BADEE COME TO CHRISTIAN WALKER'S WORLD TO INTERVENE.
QUESTION: UNDERSTAND?

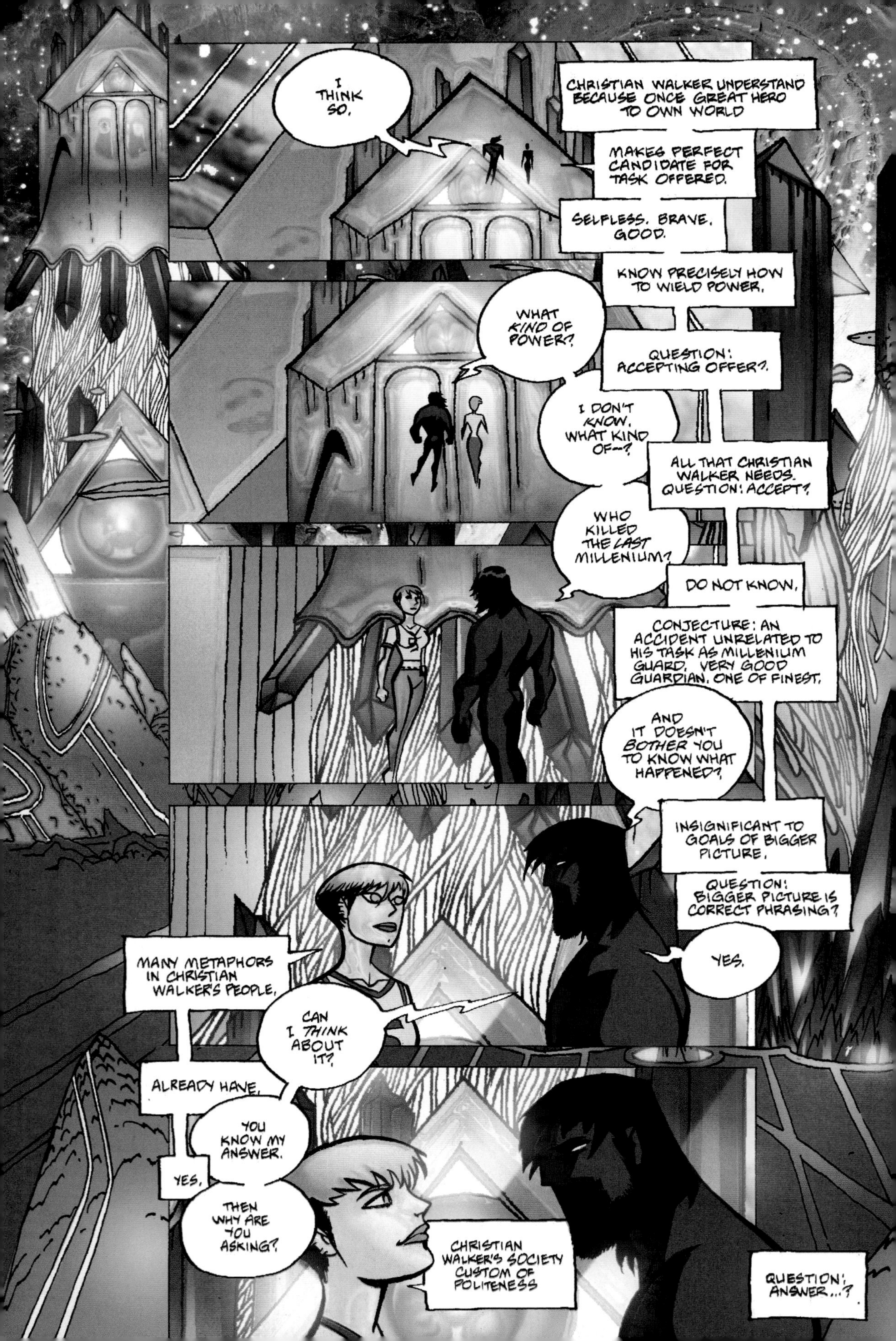
I THINK SO.
CHRISTIAN WALKER UNDERSTAND BECAUSE ONCE GREAT HERO TO OWN WORLD
MAKES PERFECT CANDIDATE FOR TASK OFFERED.
SELFLESS. BRAVE. GOOD.
KNOW PRECISELY HOW TO WIELD POWER.
WHAT KIND OF POWER?
QUESTION: ACCEPTING OFFER?
I DON'T KNOW. WHAT KIND OF--?
ALL THAT CHRISTIAN WALKER NEEDS. QUESTION: ACCEPT?
WHO KILLED THE LAST MILLENIUM?
DO NOT KNOW.
CONJECTURE: AN ACCIDENT UNRELATED TO HIS TASK AS MILLENIUM GUARD. VERY GOOD GUARDIAN. ONE OF FINEST.
AND IT DOESN'T BOTHER YOU TO KNOW WHAT HAPPENED?
INSIGNIFICANT TO GOALS OF BIGGER PICTURE.
QUESTION: BIGGER PICTURE IS CORRECT PHRASING?
YES.
MANY METAPHORS IN CHRISTIAN WALKER'S PEOPLE.
CAN I THINK ABOUT IT?
ALREADY HAVE.
YOU KNOW MY ANSWER.
YES.
THEN WHY ARE YOU ASKING?
CHRISTIAN WALKER'S SOCIETY CUSTOM OF POLITENESS
QUESTION: ANSWER...?

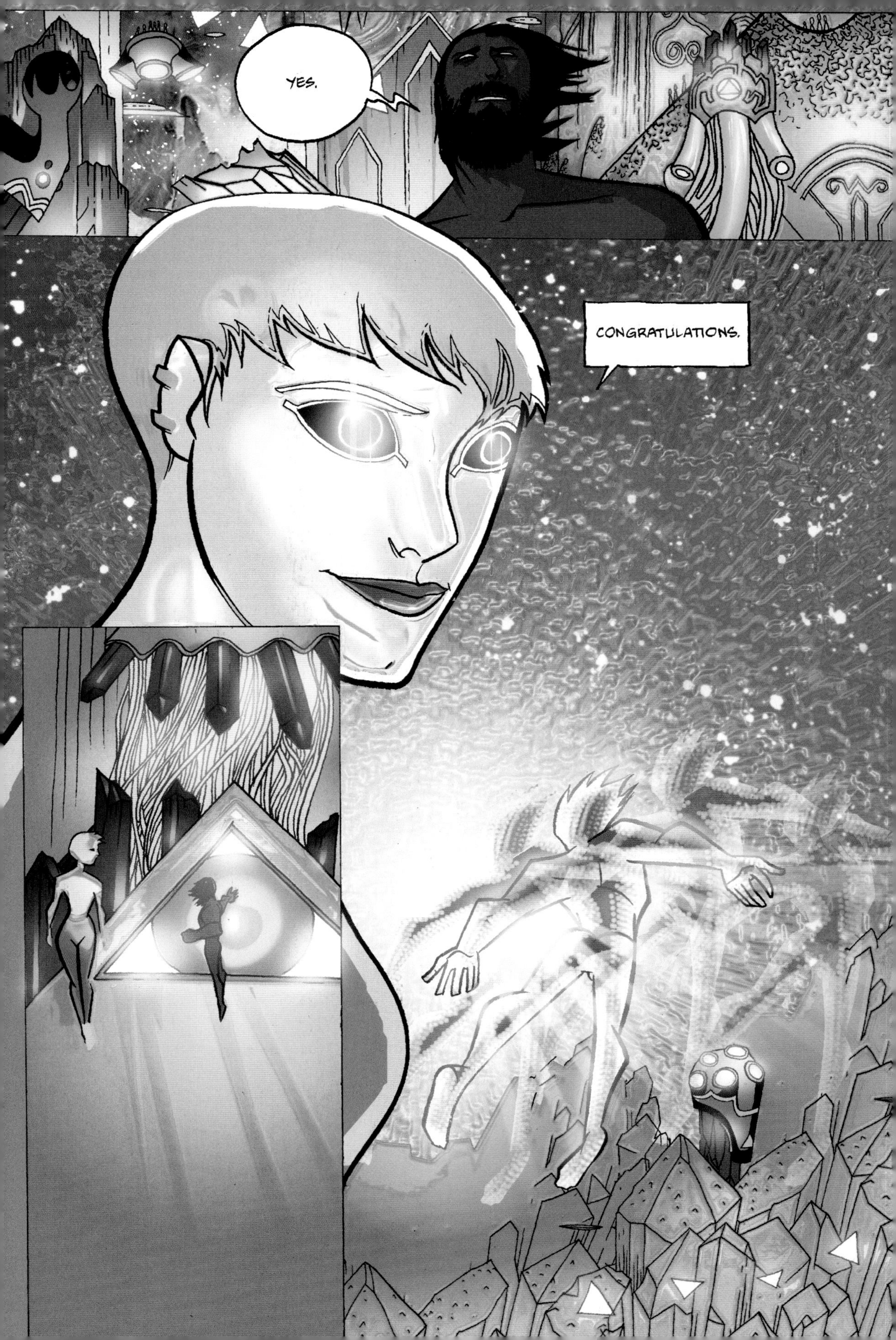
YES.
CONGRATULATIONS.

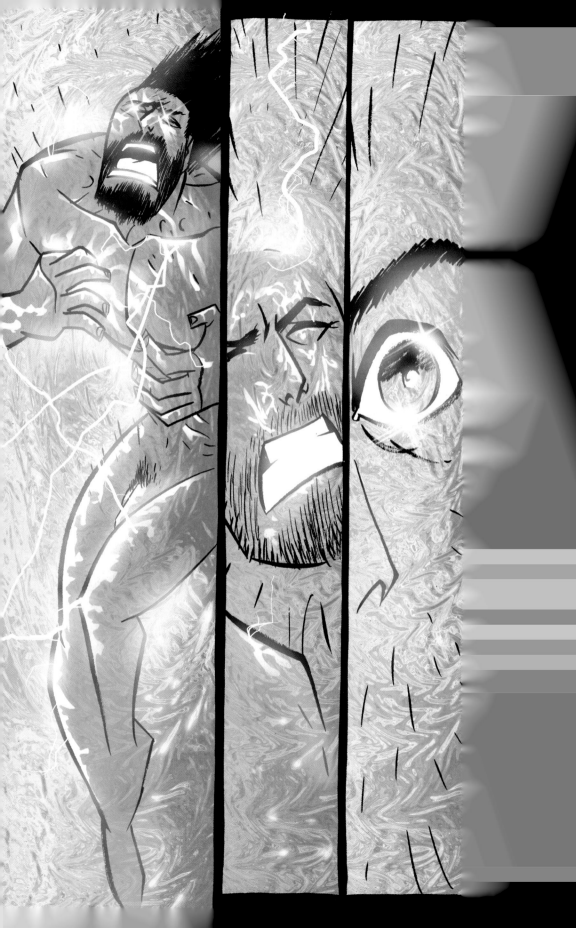

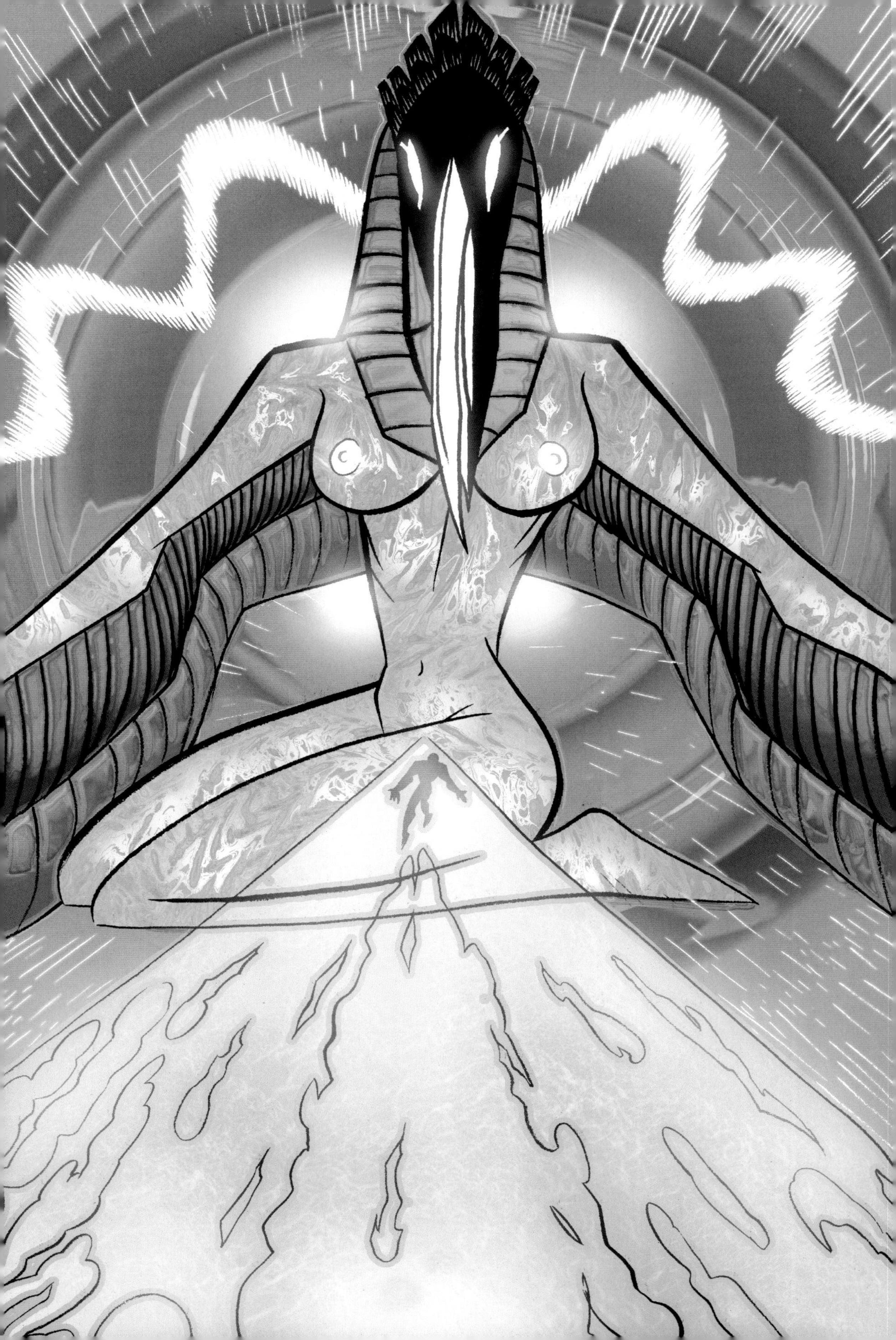

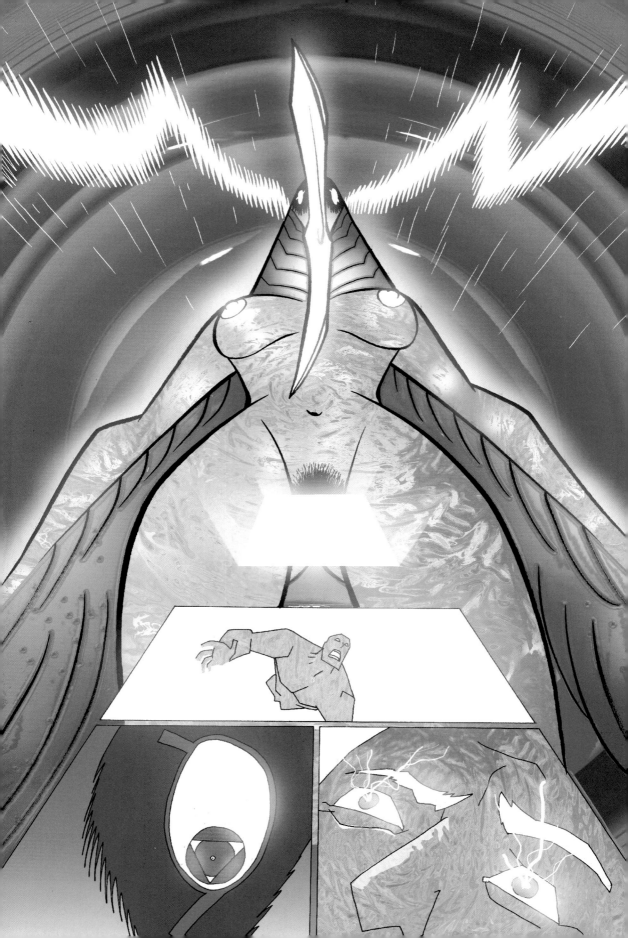

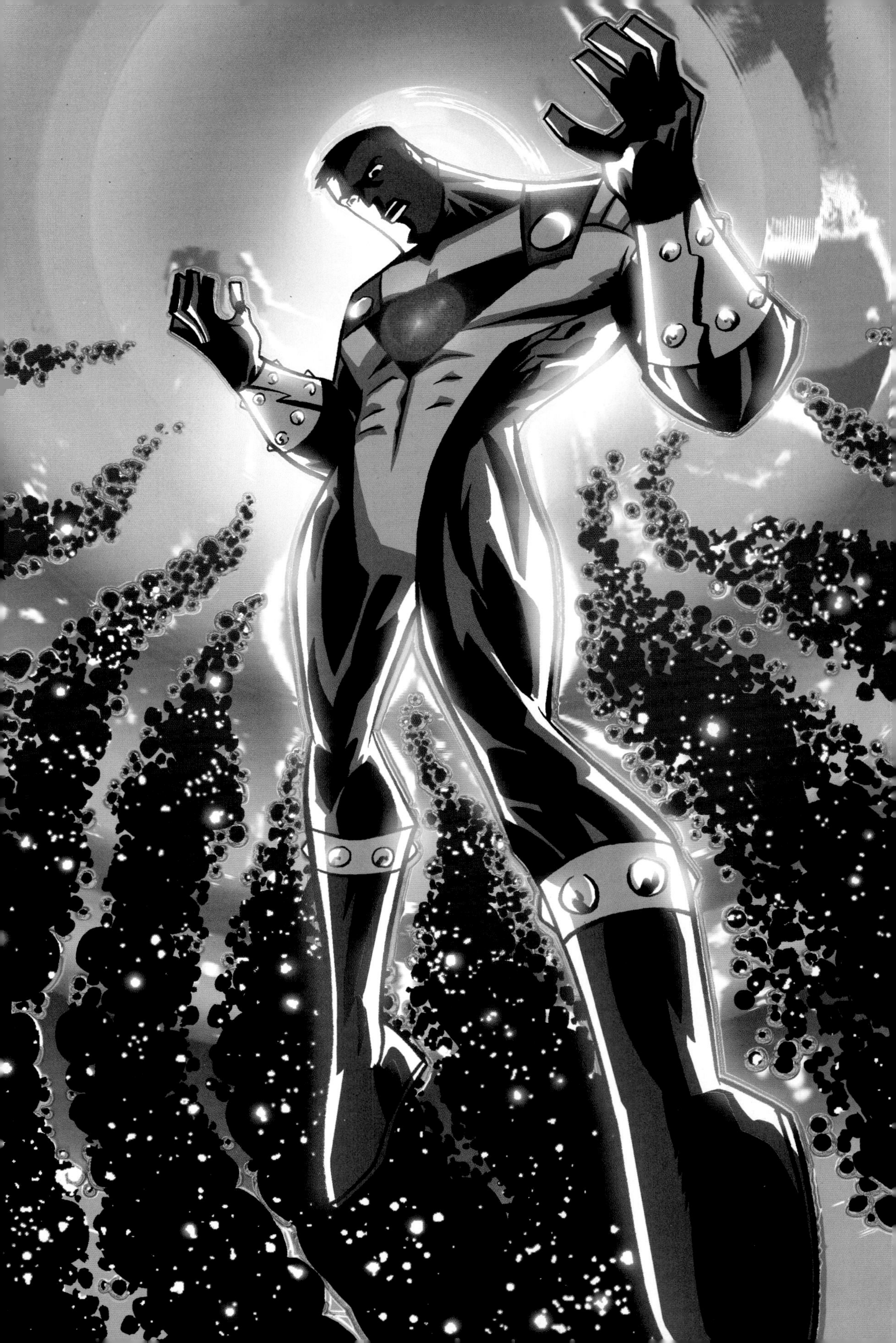

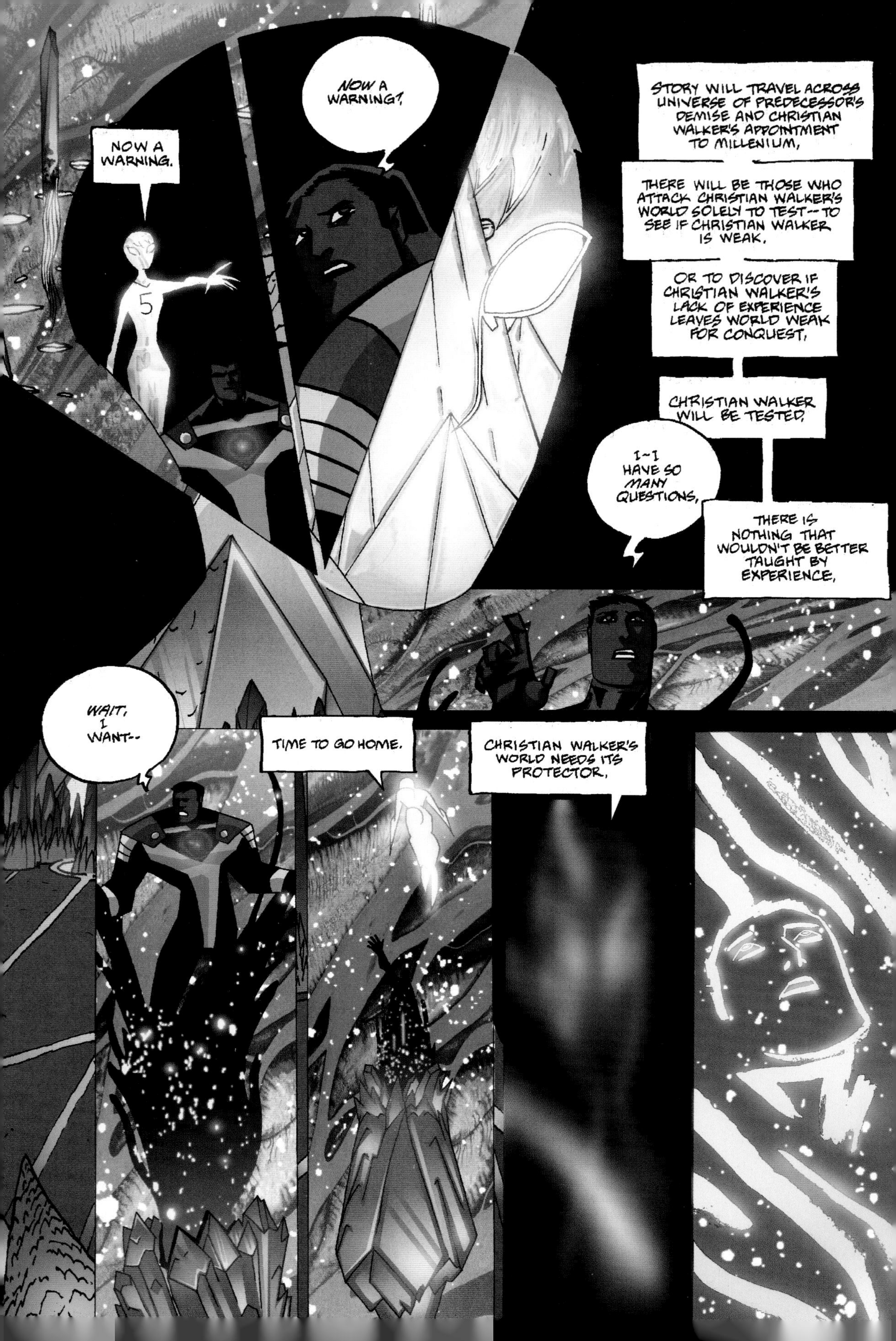
NOW A WARNING.
NOW A WARNING?
STORY WILL TRAVEL ACROSS UNIVERSE OF PREDECESSOR'S DEMISE AND CHRISTIAN WALKER'S APPOINTMENT TO MILLENIUM.
THERE WILL BE THOSE WHO ATTACK CHRISTIAN WALKER'S WORLD SOLELY TO TEST-- TO SEE IF CHRISTIAN WALKER IS WEAK.
OR TO DISCOVER IF CHRISTIAN WALKER'S LACK OF EXPERIENCE LEAVES WORLD WEAK FOR CONQUEST.
CHRISTIAN WALKER WILL BE TESTED.
I-I HAVE SO MANY QUESTIONS.
THERE IS NOTHING THAT WOULDN'T BE BETTER TAUGHT BY EXPERIENCE.
WAIT, I WANT--
TIME TO GO HOME.
CHRISTIAN WALKER'S WORLD NEEDS ITS PROTECTOR.

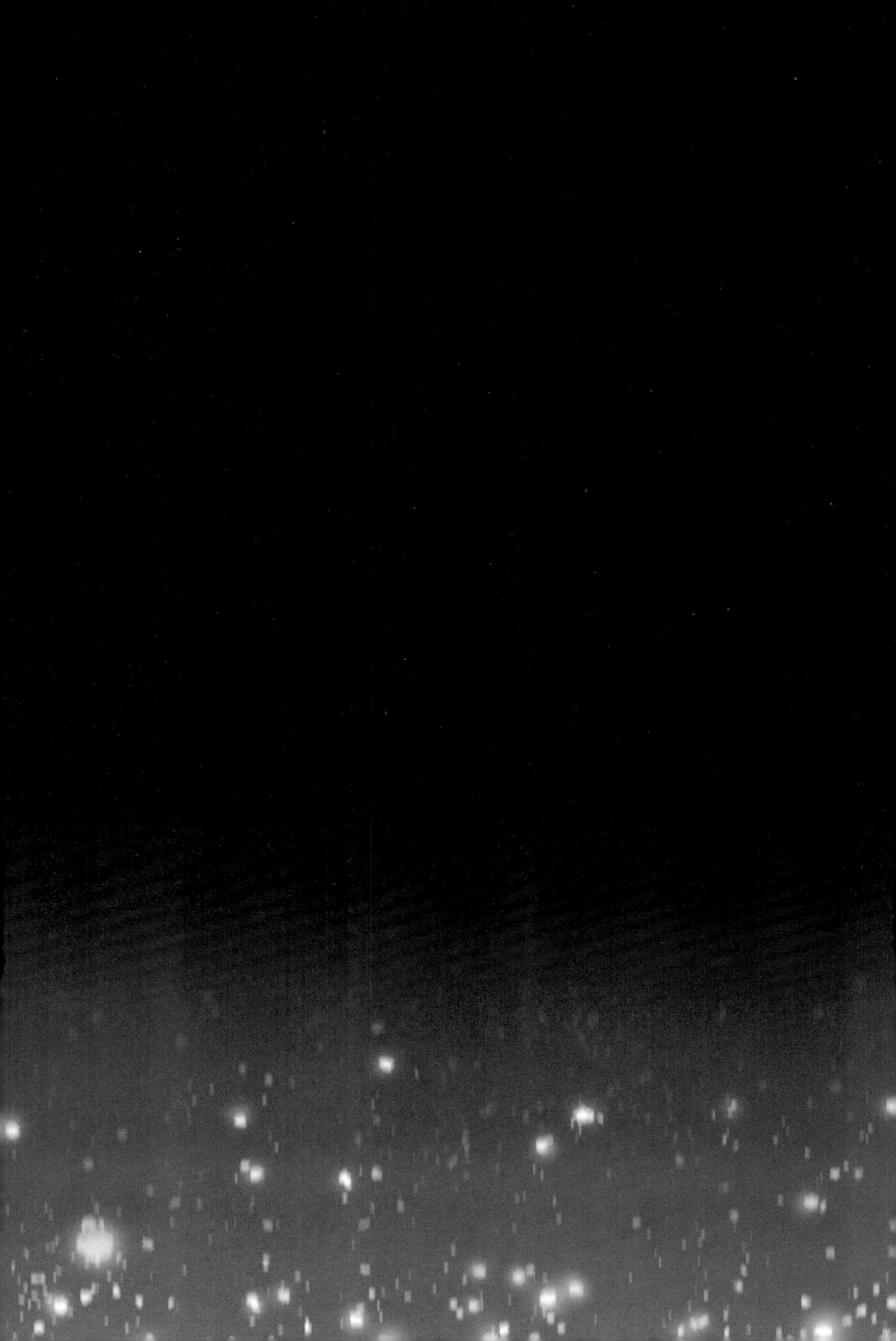

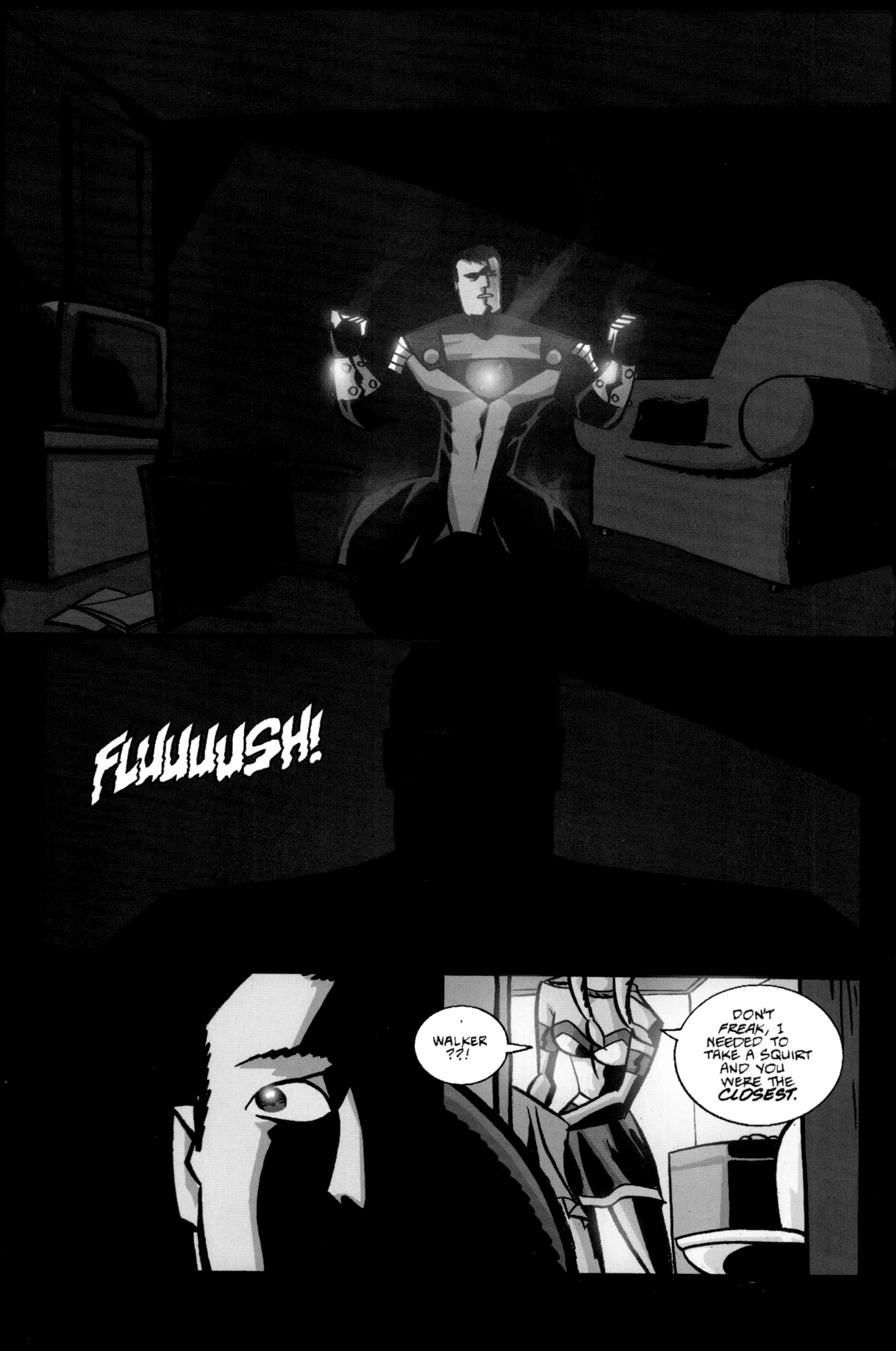
FLUUUUSH!
WALKER ??!
DON'T FREAK, I NEEDED TO TAKE A SQUIRT AND YOU WERE THE CLOSEST.

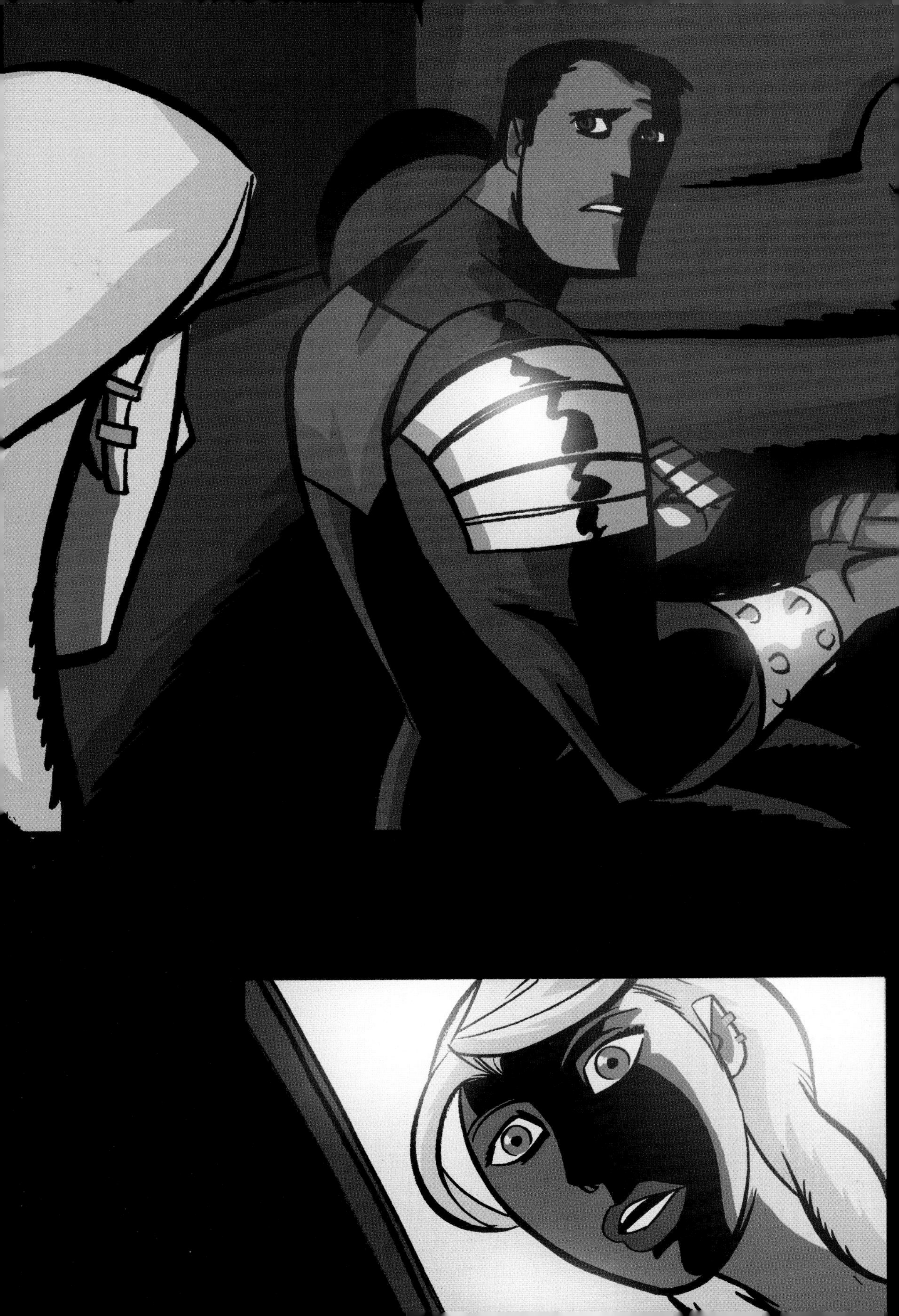

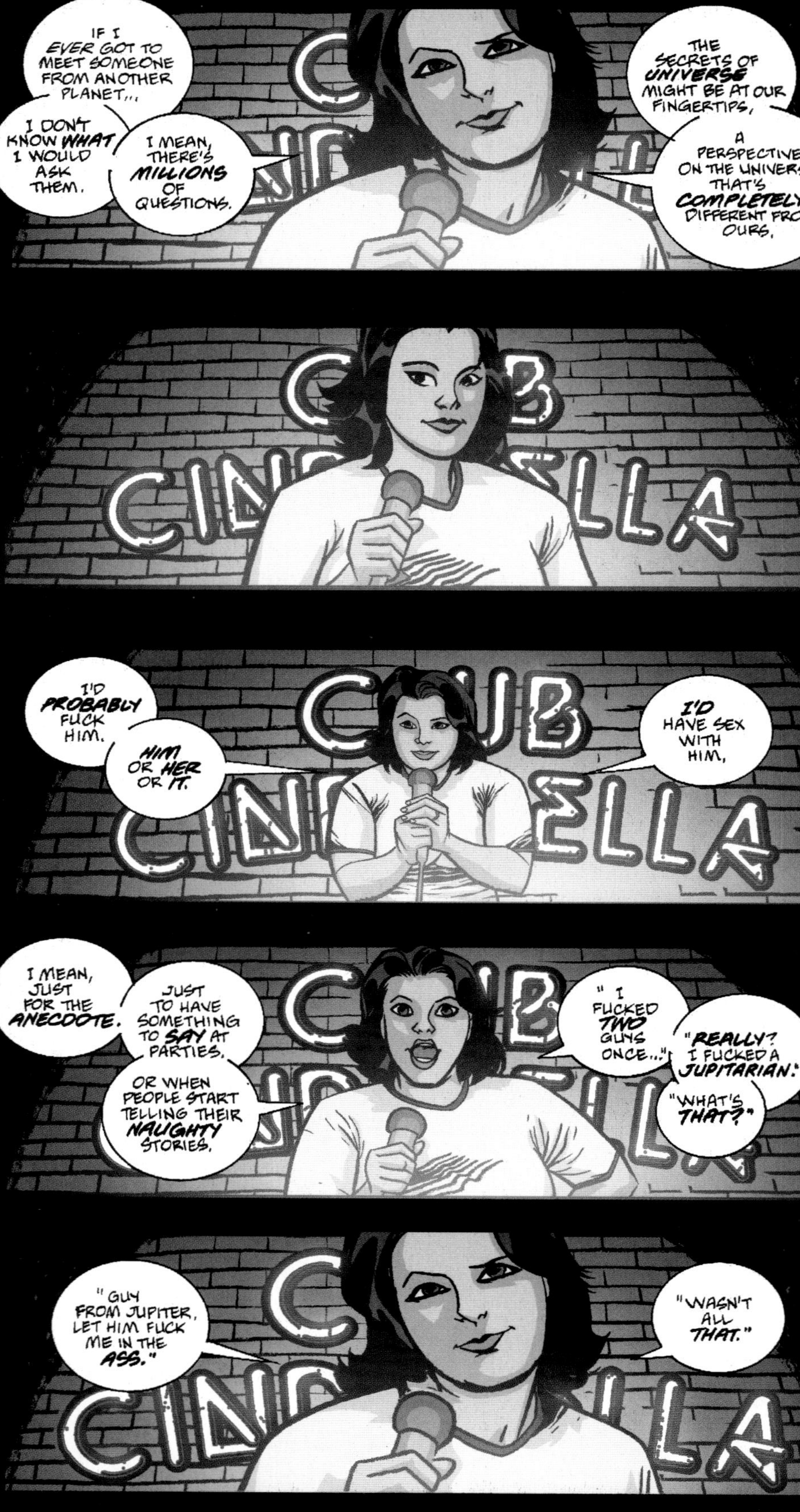
CLUB CINDERELLA
IF I EVER GOT TO MEET SOMEONE FROM ANOTHER PLANET...
I DON'T KNOW WHAT I WOULD ASK THEM.
I MEAN, THERE'S MILLIONS OF QUESTIONS.
THE SECRETS OF UNIVERSE MIGHT BE AT OUR FINGERTIPS,
A PERSPECTIVE ON THE UNIVERSE THAT'S COMPLETELY DIFFERENT FROM OURS.
I'D PROBABLY FUCK HIM.
HIM OR HER OR IT.
I'D HAVE SEX WITH HIM.
I MEAN, JUST FOR THE ANECDOTE.
JUST TO HAVE SOMETHING TO SAY AT PARTIES.
OR WHEN PEOPLE START TELLING THEIR NAUGHTY STORIES.
"I FUCKED TWO GUYS ONCE..."
"REALLY? I FUCKED A JUPITARIAN."
"WHAT'S THAT?"
"GUY FROM JUPITER. LET HIM FUCK ME IN THE ASS."
"WASN'T ALL THAT."

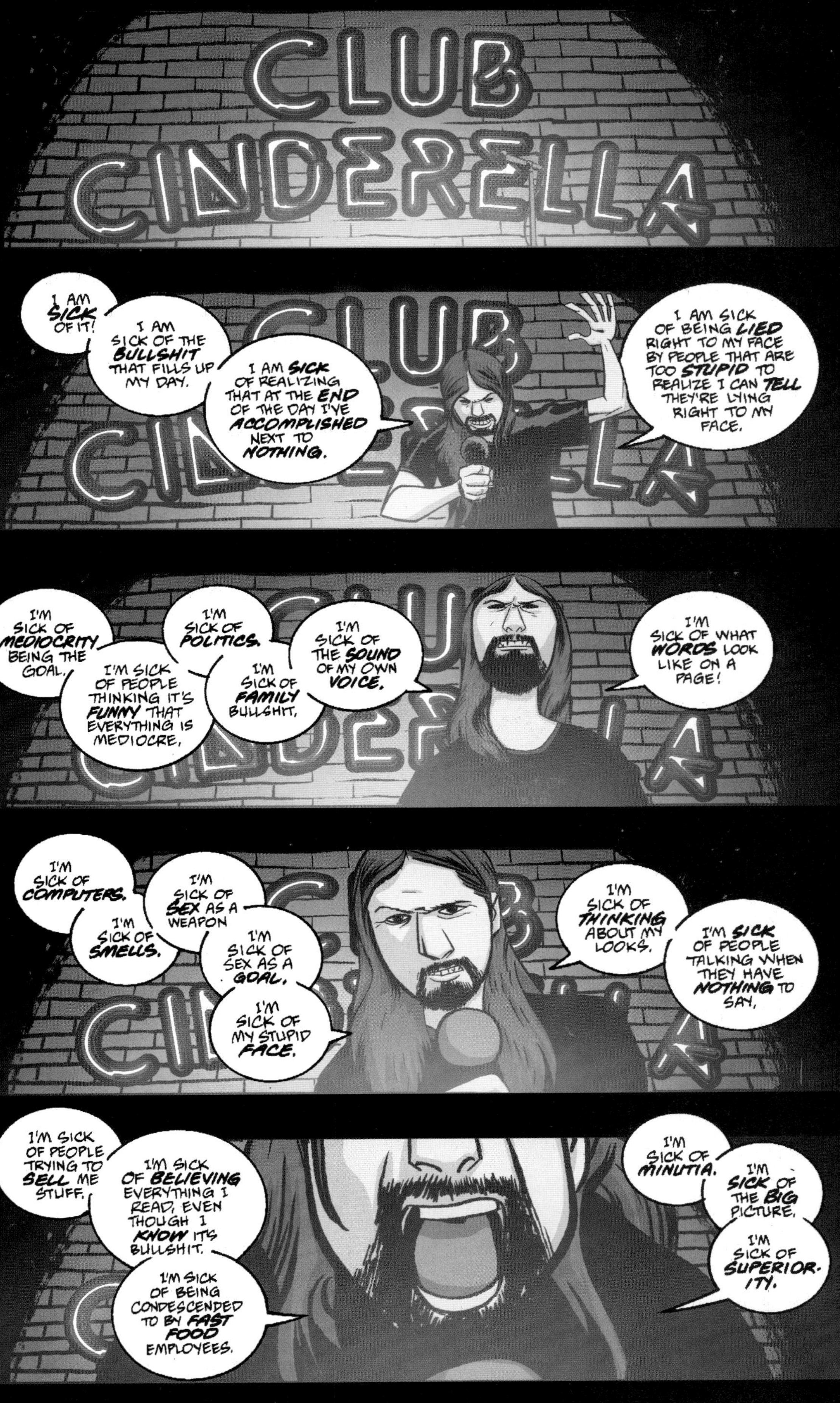
CLUB CINDERELLA
I AM SICK OF IT!
I AM SICK OF THE BULLSHIT THAT FILLS UP MY DAY.
I AM SICK OF REALIZING THAT AT THE END OF THE DAY I'VE ACCOMPLISHED NEXT TO NOTHING.
I AM SICK OF BEING LIED RIGHT TO MY FACE BY PEOPLE THAT ARE TOO STUPID TO REALIZE I CAN TELL THEY'RE LYING RIGHT TO MY FACE.
I'M SICK OF MEDIOCRITY BEING THE GOAL.
I'M SICK OF PEOPLE THINKING IT'S FUNNY THAT EVERYTHING IS MEDIOCRE.
I'M SICK OF POLITICS.
I'M SICK OF FAMILY BULLSHIT.
I'M SICK OF THE SOUND OF MY OWN VOICE.
I'M SICK OF WHAT WORDS LOOK LIKE ON A PAGE!
I'M SICK OF COMPUTERS.
I'M SICK OF SMELLS.
I'M SICK OF SEX AS A WEAPON
I'M SICK OF SEX AS A GOAL.
I'M SICK OF MY STUPID FACE.
I'M SICK OF THINKING ABOUT MY LOOKS.
I'M SICK OF PEOPLE TALKING WHEN THEY HAVE NOTHING TO SAY.
I'M SICK OF PEOPLE TRYING TO SELL ME STUFF.
I'M SICK OF BELIEVING EVERYTHING I READ, EVEN THOUGH I KNOW IT'S BULLSHIT.
I'M SICK OF BEING CONDESCENDED TO BY FAST FOOD EMPLOYEES.
I'M SICK OF MINUTIA.
I'M SICK OF THE BIG PICTURE.
I'M SICK OF SUPERIOR-ITY.

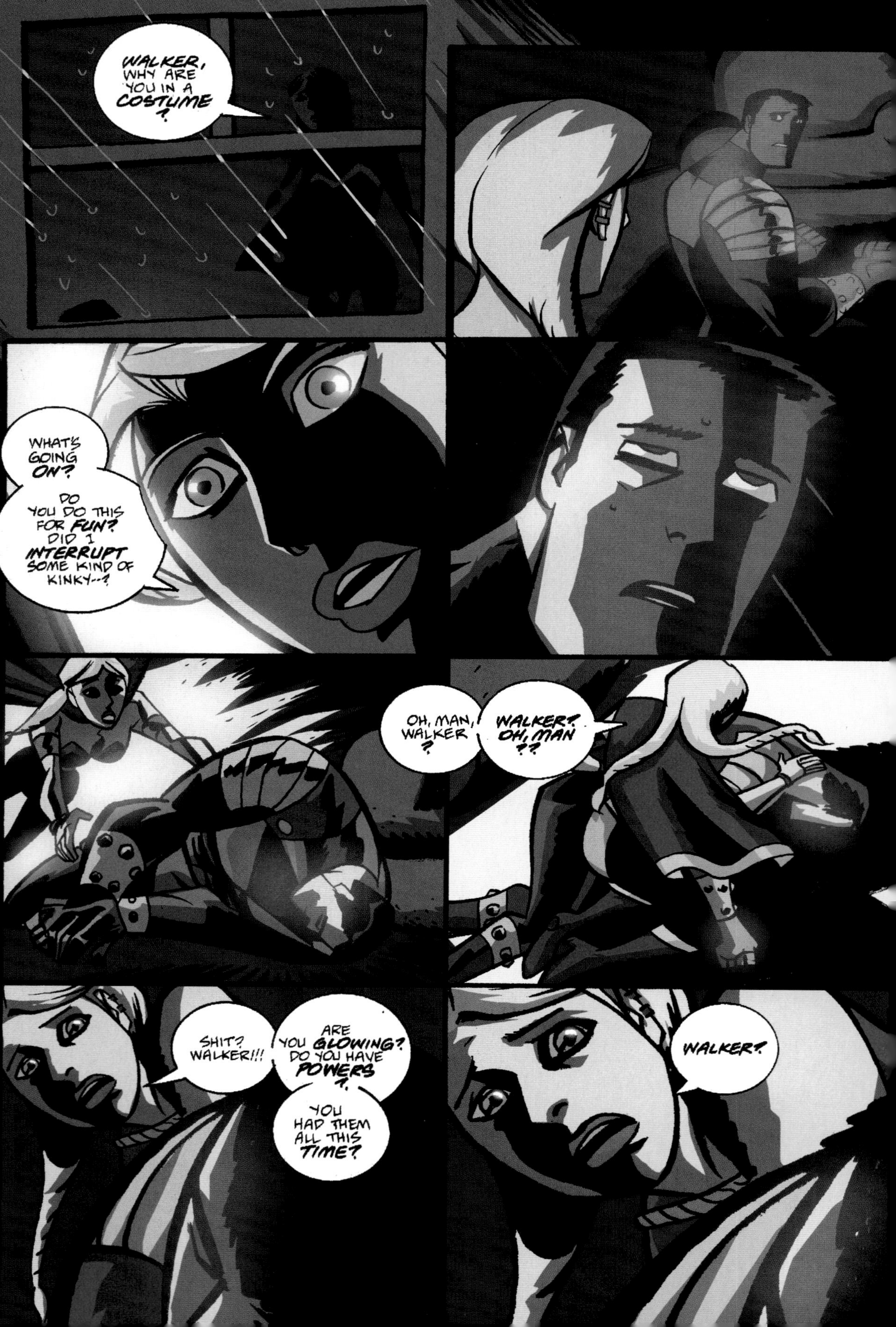
WALKER, WHY ARE YOU IN A COSTUME?
WHAT'S GOING ON?
DO YOU DO THIS FOR FUN? DID I INTERRUPT SOME KIND OF KINKY--?
OH, MAN, WALKER?
WALKER? OH, MAN??
SHIT? WALKER!!!
ARE YOU GLOWING? DO YOU HAVE POWERS?
YOU HAD THEM ALL THIS TIME?
WALKER?

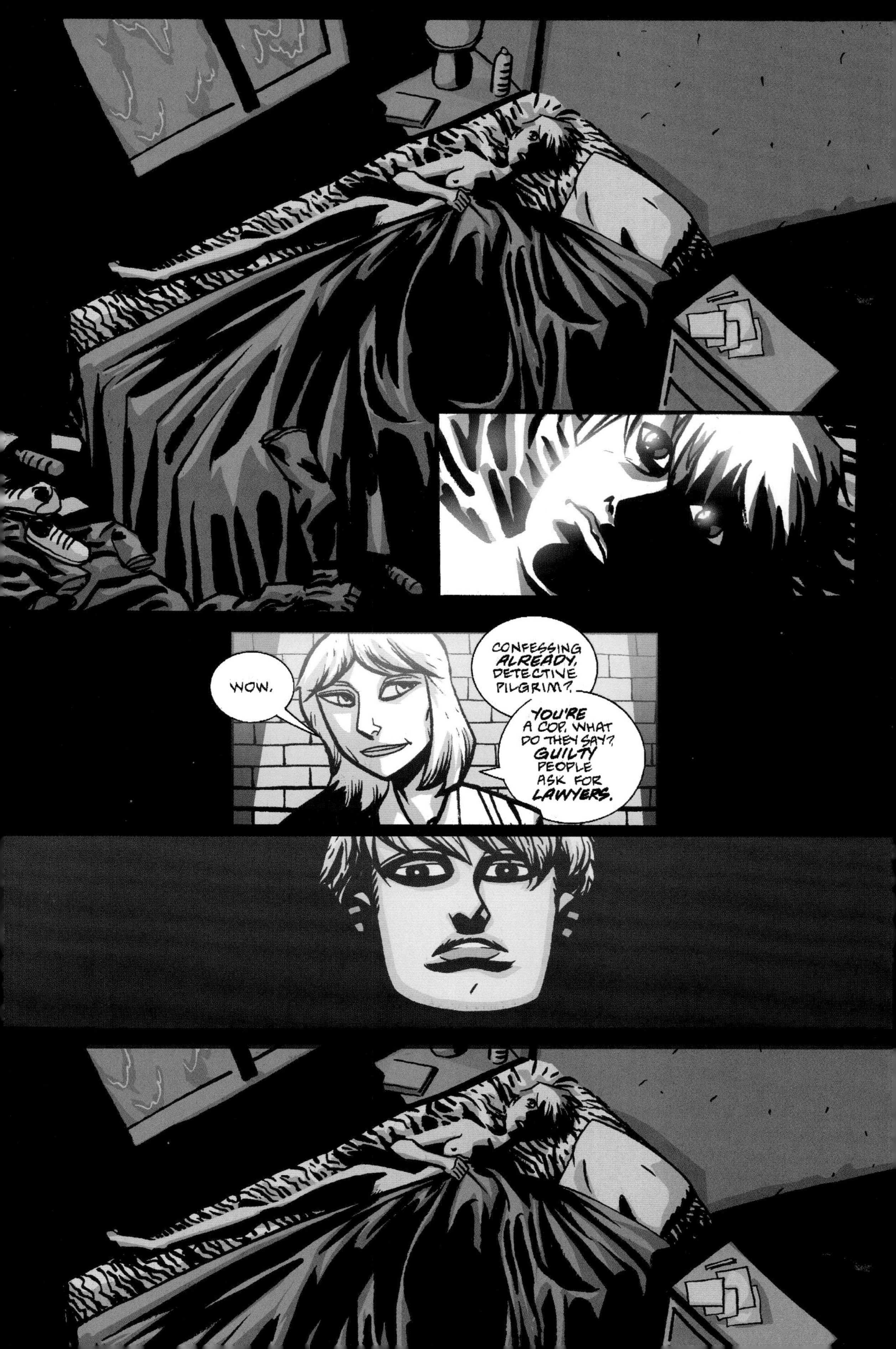
WOW.
CONFESSING ALREADY, DETECTIVE PILGRIM?
YOU'RE A COP. WHAT DO THEY SAY? GUILTY PEOPLE ASK FOR LAWYERS.

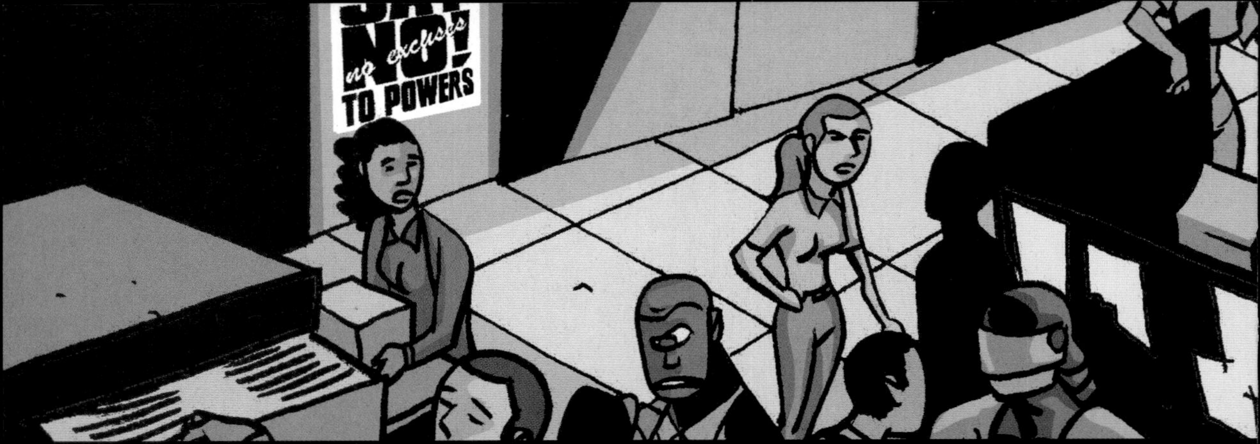
NO!
no excuses
TO POWERS

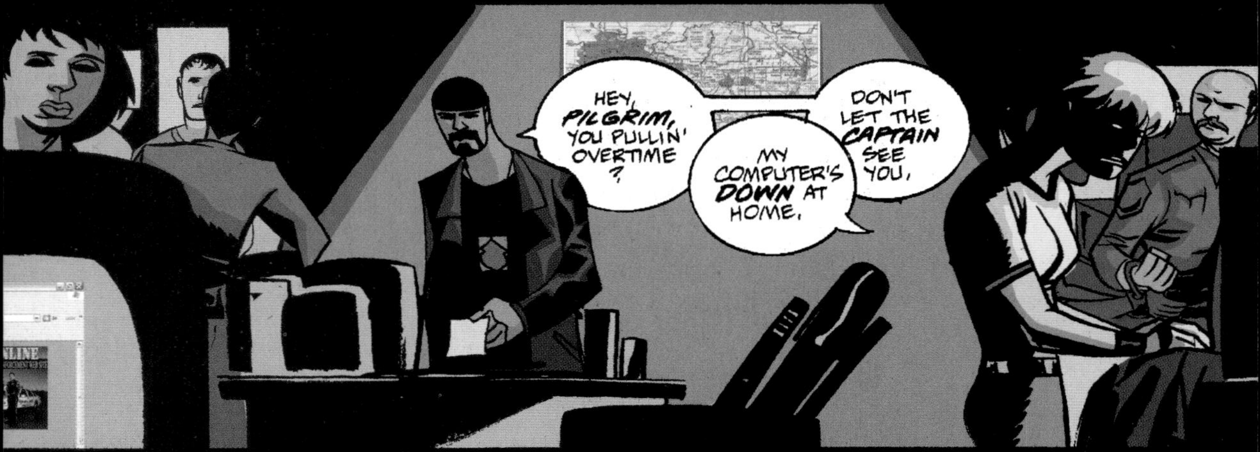
HEY, PILGRIM, YOU PULLIN' OVERTIME?
DON'T LET THE CAPTAIN SEE YOU.
MY COMPUTER'S DOWN AT HOME.

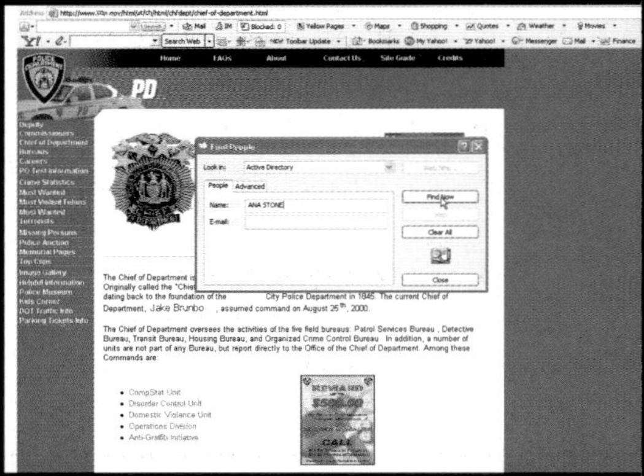
Find People
Look in: Active Directory
People Advanced
Name: ANA STONE
E-mail:
Find Now
Clear All
Close

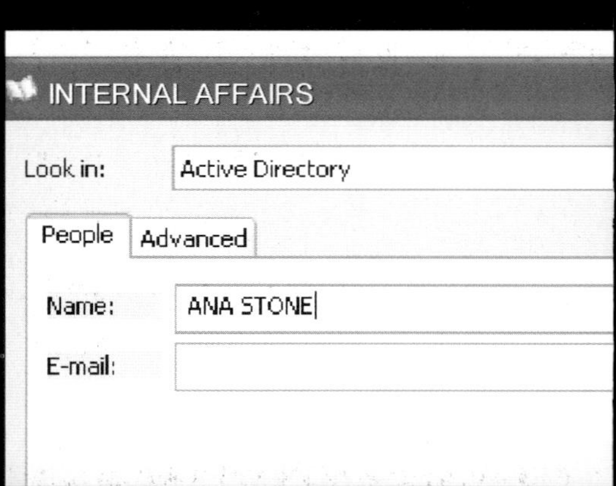
INTERNAL AFFAIRS
Look in: Active Directory
People Advanced
Name: ANA STONE
E-mail:

County Law
Enforcement
Police
Precinct
Personal
Directory

PD

INTERNAL AFFAIRS

Look in: Active Directory   Web Site

People | Advanced

Name: ANA STONE   Find Now

E-mail: Stop

                                    Clear All

                                    Close

hief of Department is
ally called the "Chie
back to the foundation of the   City Police Department in 1845. The current Chief of
tment,   Jake Brunbo   , assumed command on August 25th, 2000.

Properties

ummary | Name | Home | Business | Personal | Othe

Summary of information about this contact

Name: ANA STONE

Address: 1756 SIMONSON

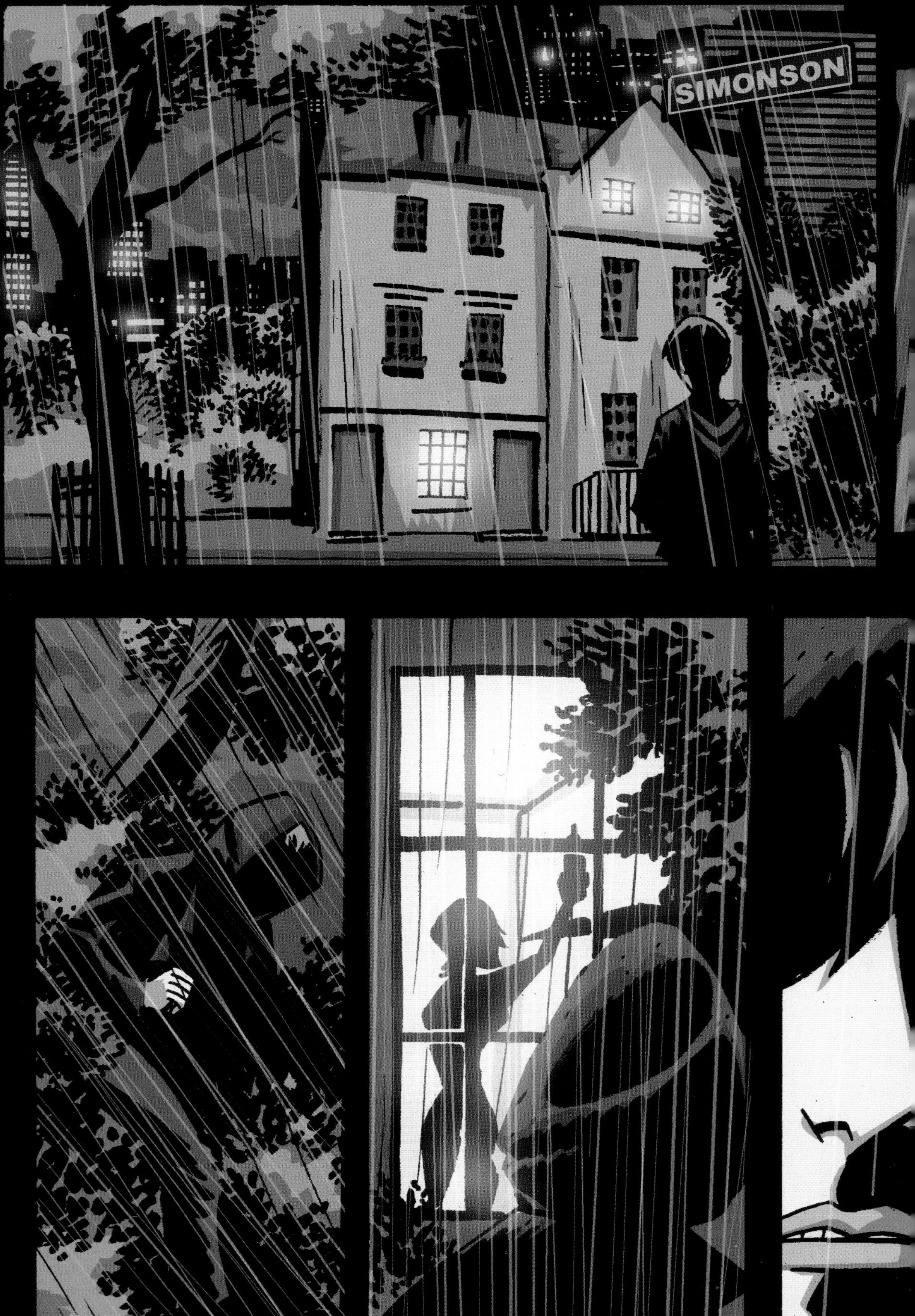
SIMONSON

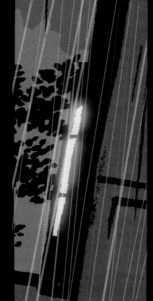

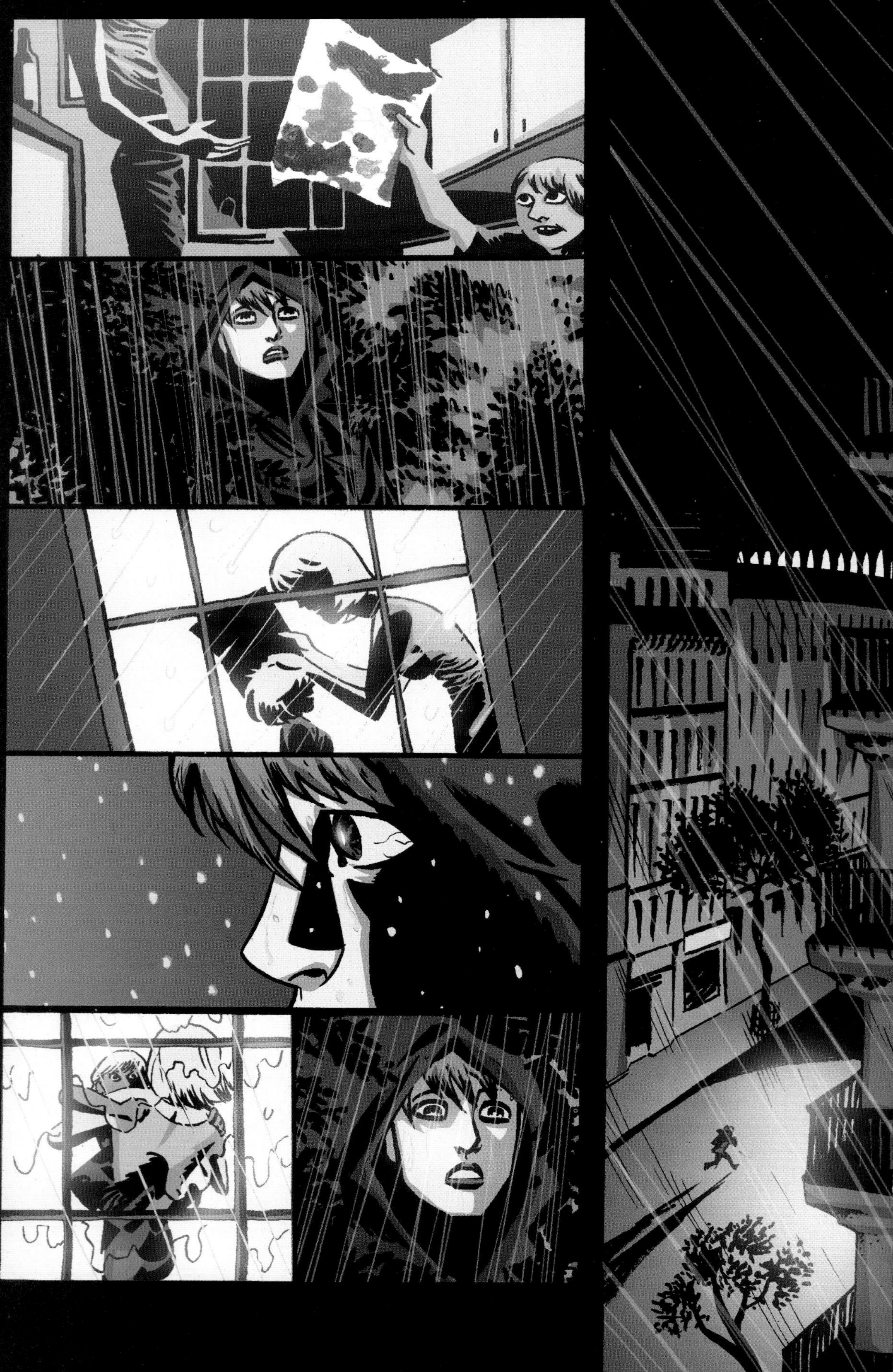

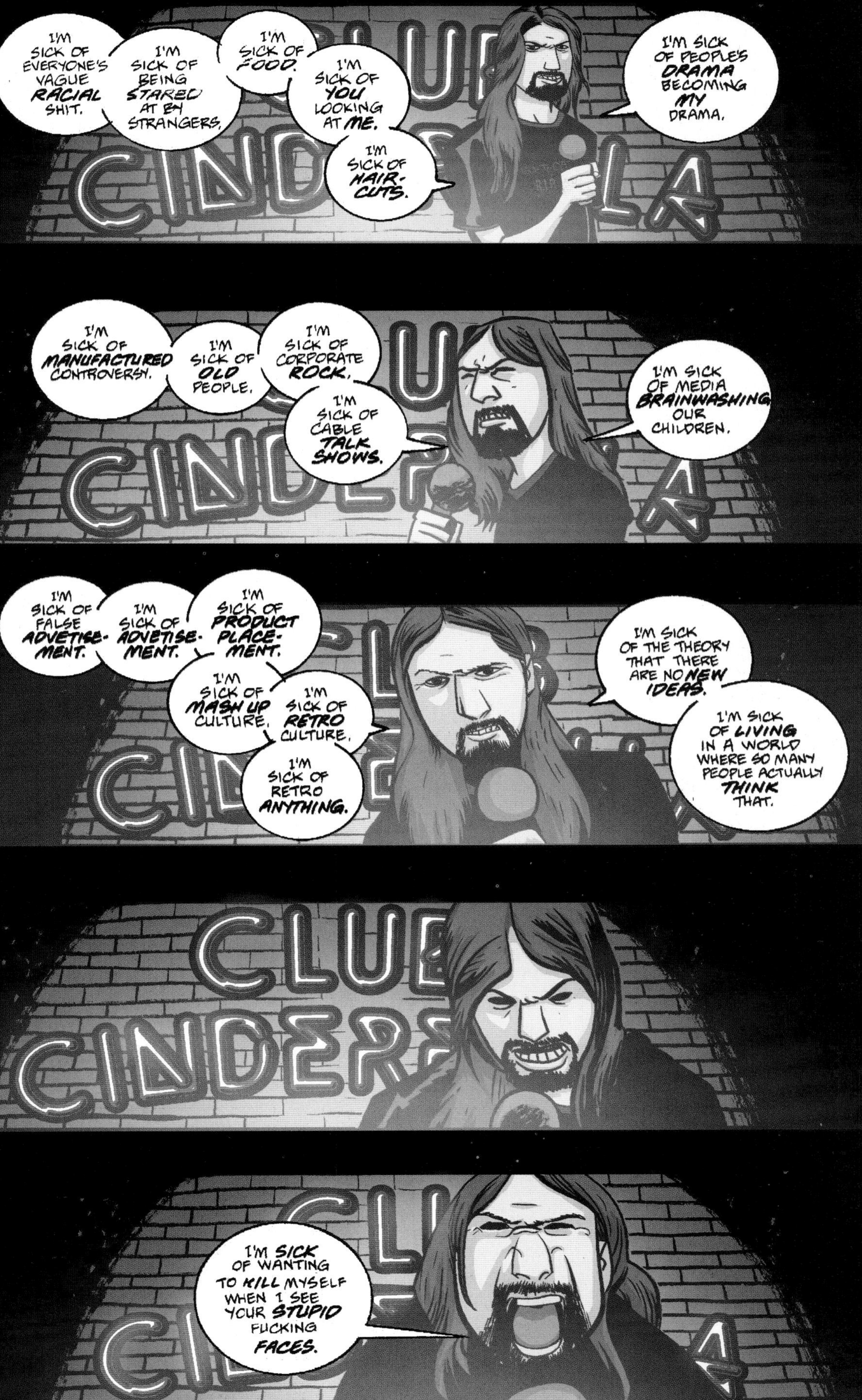
I'M SICK OF EVERYONE'S VAGUE RACIAL SHIT.
I'M SICK OF BEING STARED AT BY STRANGERS.
I'M SICK OF FOOD.
I'M SICK OF YOU LOOKING AT ME.
I'M SICK OF HAIR-CUTS.
I'M SICK OF PEOPLE'S DRAMA BECOMING MY DRAMA.
I'M SICK OF MANUFACTURED CONTROVERSY.
I'M SICK OF OLD PEOPLE.
I'M SICK OF CORPORATE ROCK.
I'M SICK OF CABLE TALK SHOWS.
I'M SICK OF MEDIA BRAINWASHING OUR CHILDREN.
I'M SICK OF FALSE ADVETISE-MENT.
I'M SICK OF ADVETISE-MENT.
I'M SICK OF PRODUCT PLACE-MENT.
I'M SICK OF MASH UP CULTURE.
I'M SICK OF RETRO CULTURE.
I'M SICK OF RETRO ANYTHING.
I'M SICK OF THE THEORY THAT THERE ARE NO NEW IDEAS.
I'M SICK OF LIVING IN A WORLD WHERE SO MANY PEOPLE ACTUALLY THINK THAT.
CLUB CINDERELLA
I'M SICK OF WANTING TO KILL MYSELF WHEN I SEE YOUR STUPID FUCKING FACES.

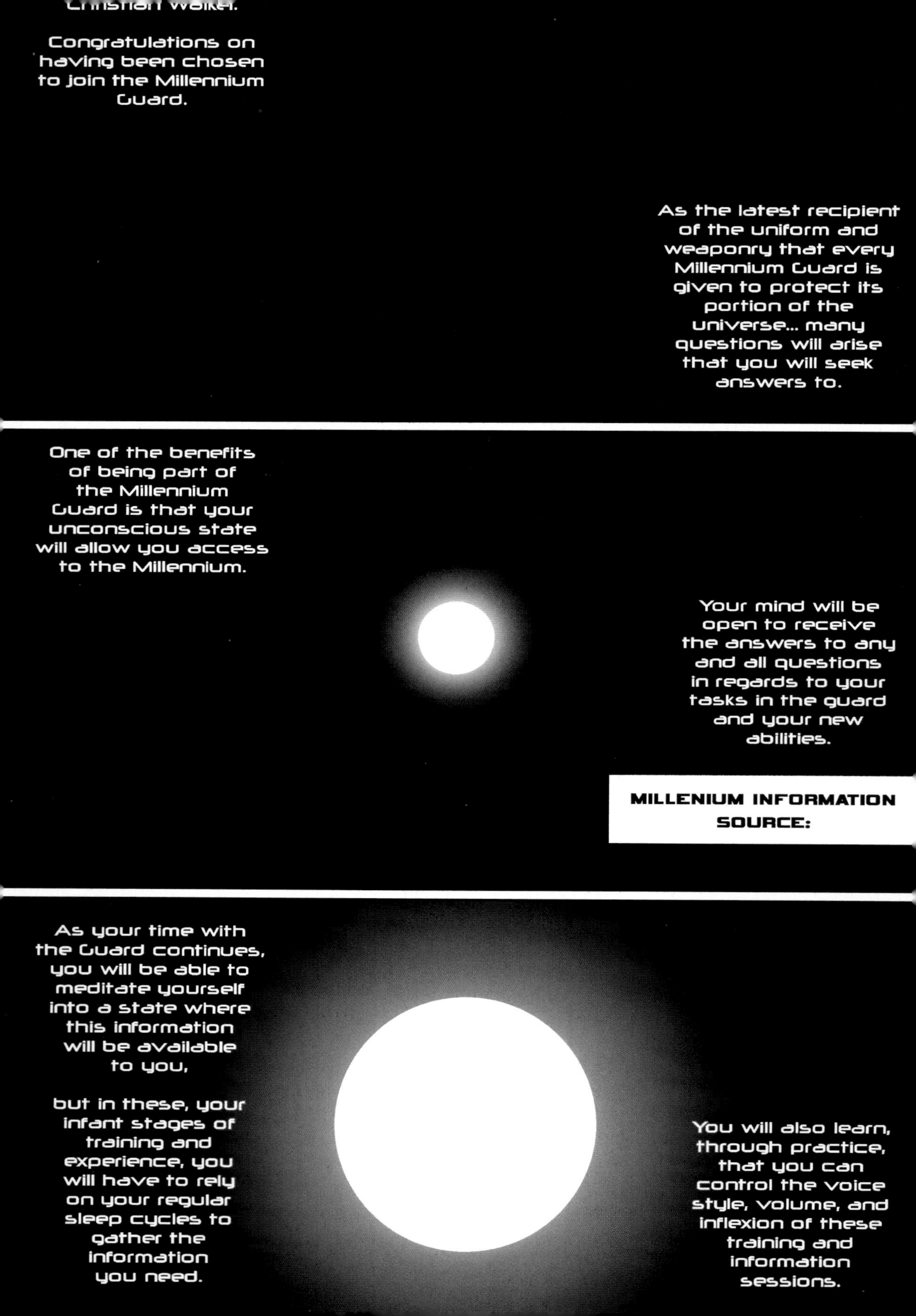
Christian Walker.
Congratulations on having been chosen to join the Millennium Guard.
As the latest recipient of the uniform and weaponry that every Millennium Guard is given to protect its portion of the universe... many questions will arise that you will seek answers to.
One of the benefits of being part of the Millennium Guard is that your unconscious state will allow you access to the Millennium.
Your mind will be open to receive the answers to any and all questions in regards to your tasks in the guard and your new abilities.
MILLENIUM INFORMATION SOURCE:
As your time with the Guard continues, you will be able to meditate yourself into a state where this information will be available to you,
but in these, your infant stages of training and experience, you will have to rely on your regular sleep cycles to gather the information you need.
You will also learn, through practice, that you can control the voice style, volume, and inflexion of these training and information sessions.

How the uniform and its weapons works will be the focus of your next session.

What is of more immediate concern is who you will be protecting your planet from, and why.

There are three major species who pose an immediate threat to your world and now, because of your new responsibilities, to you personally.

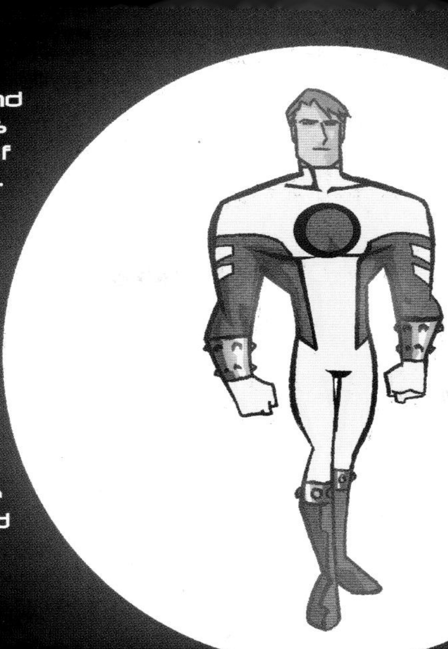

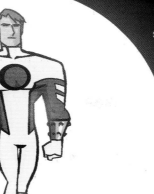

A comprehensive history of these species will be made available to you at a more advanced stage of training.

As you were previously warned, once a new Millennium is chosen, there is a high risk that representatives of any or all of these races will challenge you.

Hoping to use your inexperience as an opening for attack.

MILLENIUM SUIT CAN BE MODIFIED FOR PERSONAL USE BASED ON TECHNIQUE.

KLIKLIT, QUILI, THE CHIRMUT.

There is reason and strong precedent to believe you will be attacked by one or all of them shortly after receiving this information.

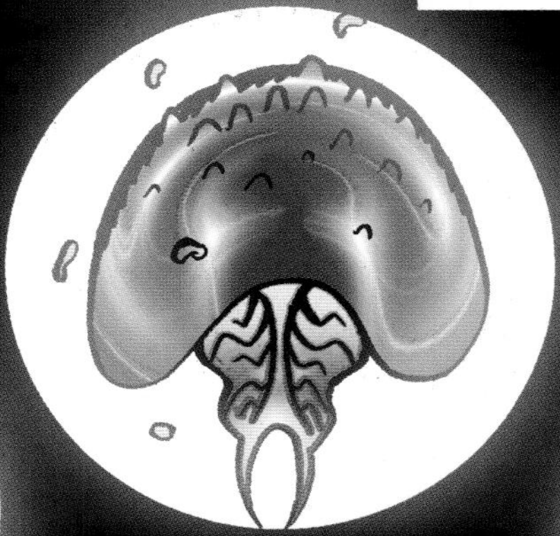

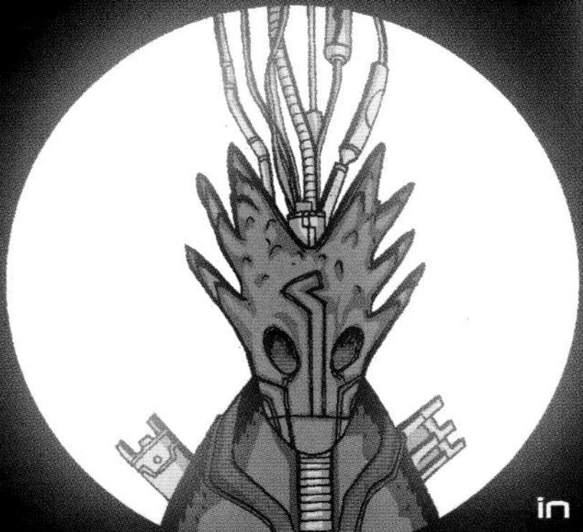

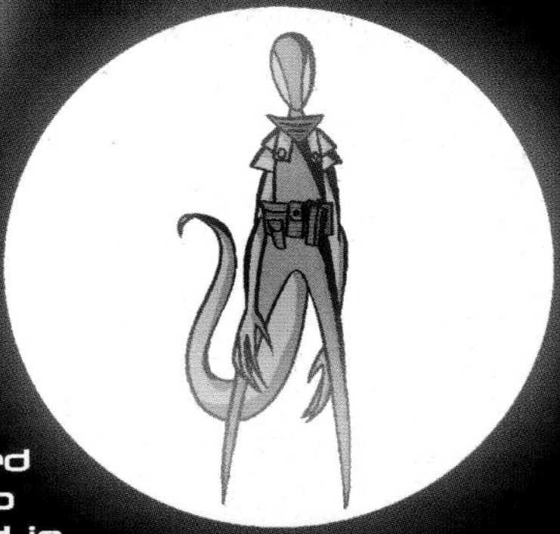

Consider this your training mission.

For if you do not succeed in this unorganized and rushed attack on you there is little to no chance you would succeed in any attack past it.

But the millennium uniform is equipped with a tracking and detection devise that will alarm you of such an attack.

For your specific type of biology this will resemble yellow bands of light.

Yellow haloes that point in perspective towards the incoming attack.

The warning should come within sufficient time to intercept.

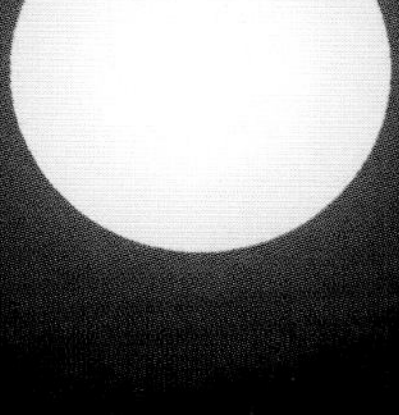

Good fortunes, Christian Walker.

There will be more information coming to you in the near future.

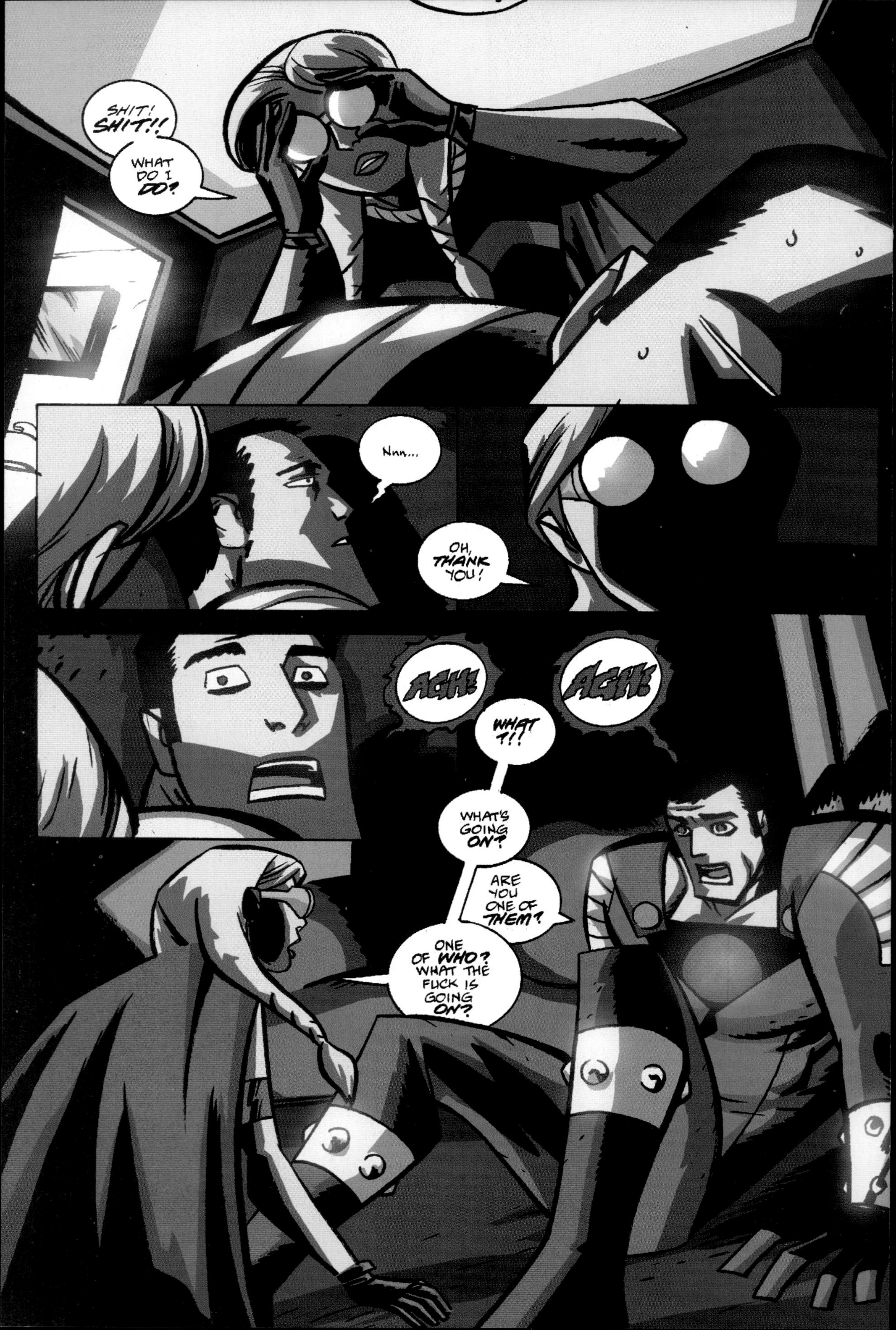

SHIT! SHIT!!
WHAT DO I DO?
Nnn...
OH, THANK YOU!
AGH!
AGH!
WHAT?!!
WHAT'S GOING ON?
ARE YOU ONE OF THEM?
ONE OF WHO? WHAT THE FUCK IS GOING ON?

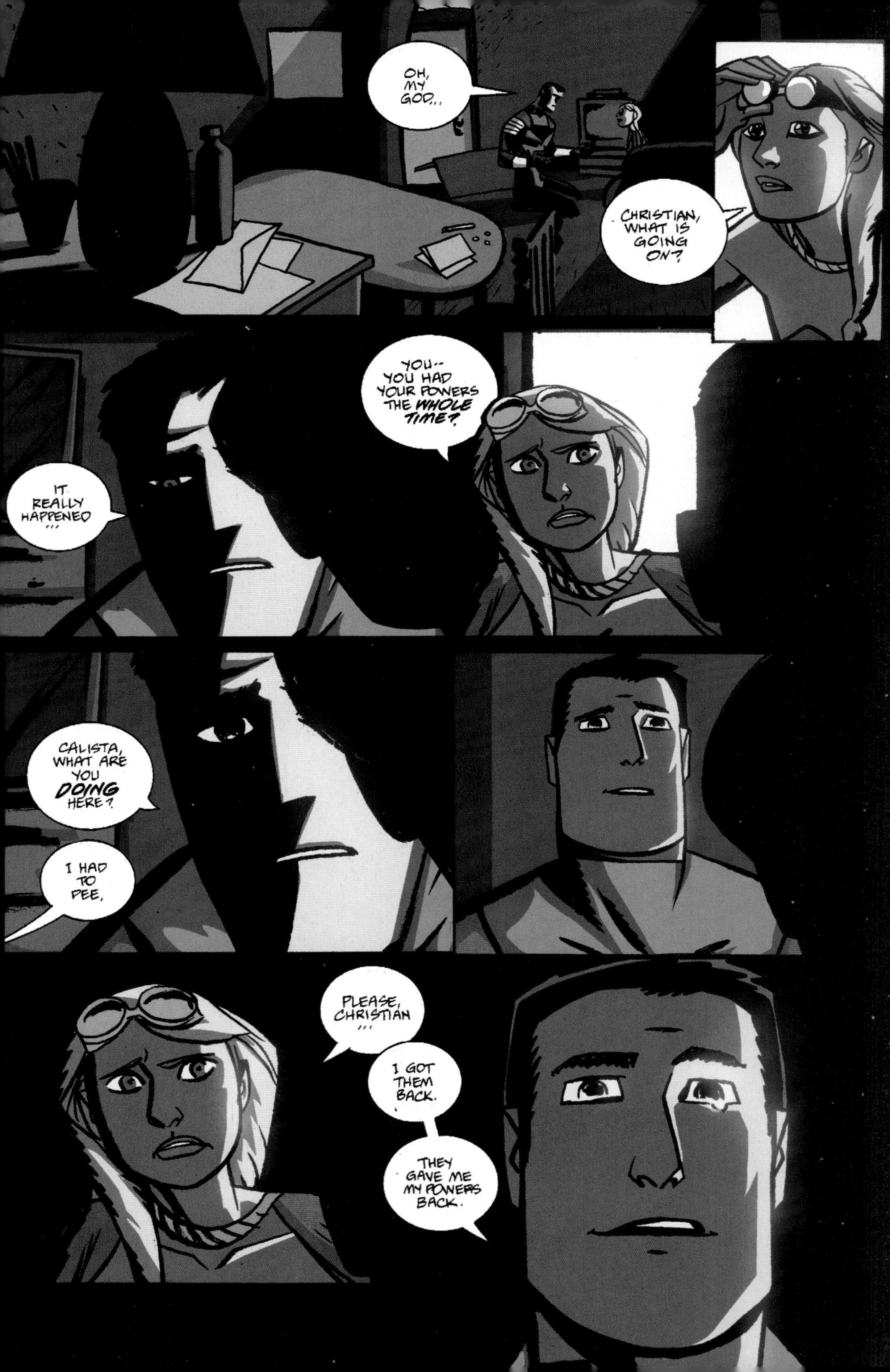
OH, MY GOD...
CHRISTIAN, WHAT IS GOING ON?
YOU-- YOU HAD YOUR POWERS THE WHOLE TIME?
IT REALLY HAPPENED...
CALISTA, WHAT ARE YOU DOING HERE?
I HAD TO PEE.
PLEASE, CHRISTIAN...
I GOT THEM BACK.
THEY GAVE ME MY POWERS BACK.

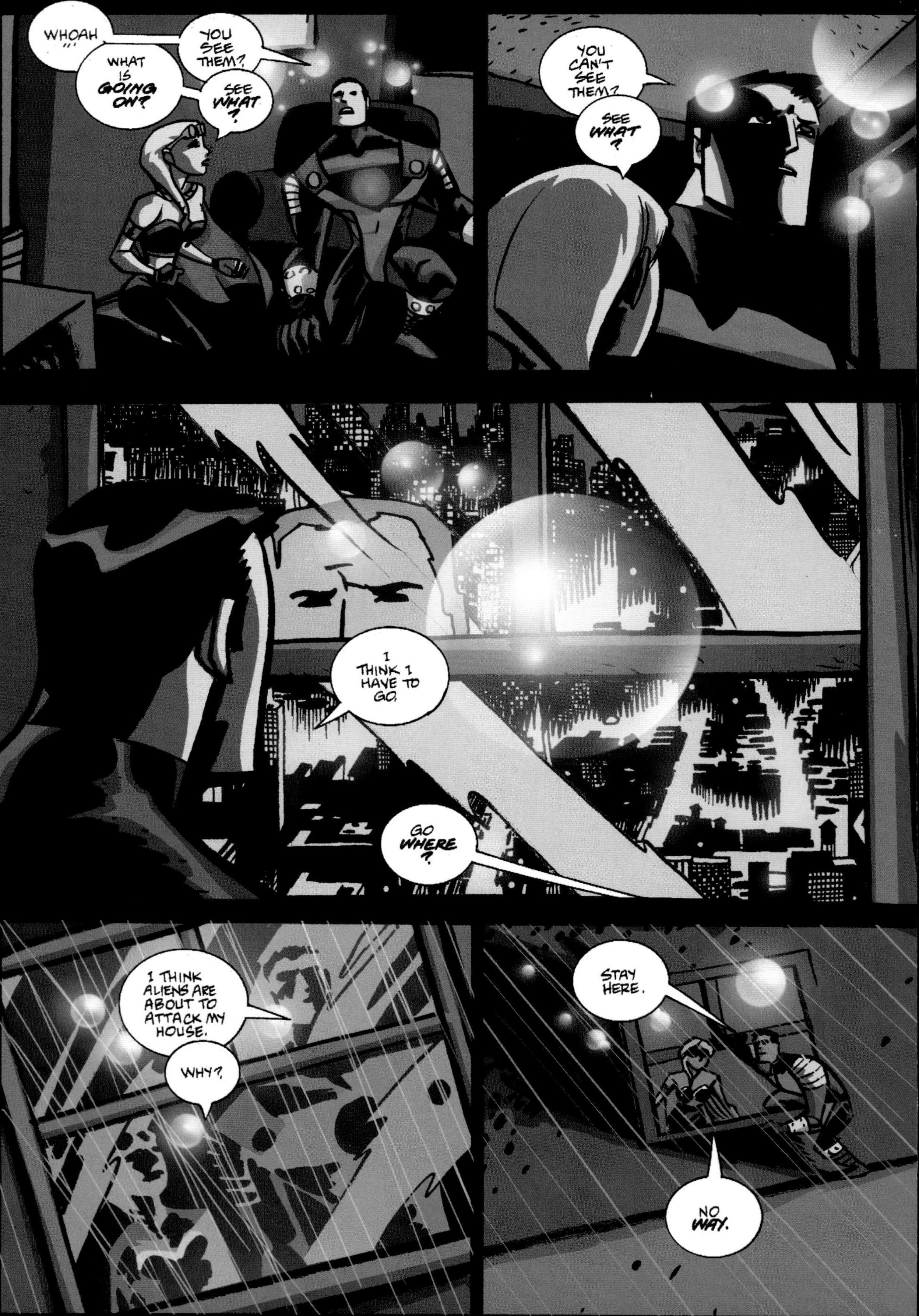
WHOAH ...
YOU SEE THEM?
WHAT IS GOING ON?
SEE WHAT?
YOU CAN'T SEE THEM?
SEE WHAT?
I THINK I HAVE TO GO.
GO WHERE?
I THINK ALIENS ARE ABOUT TO ATTACK MY HOUSE.
WHY?
STAY HERE.
NO WAY.

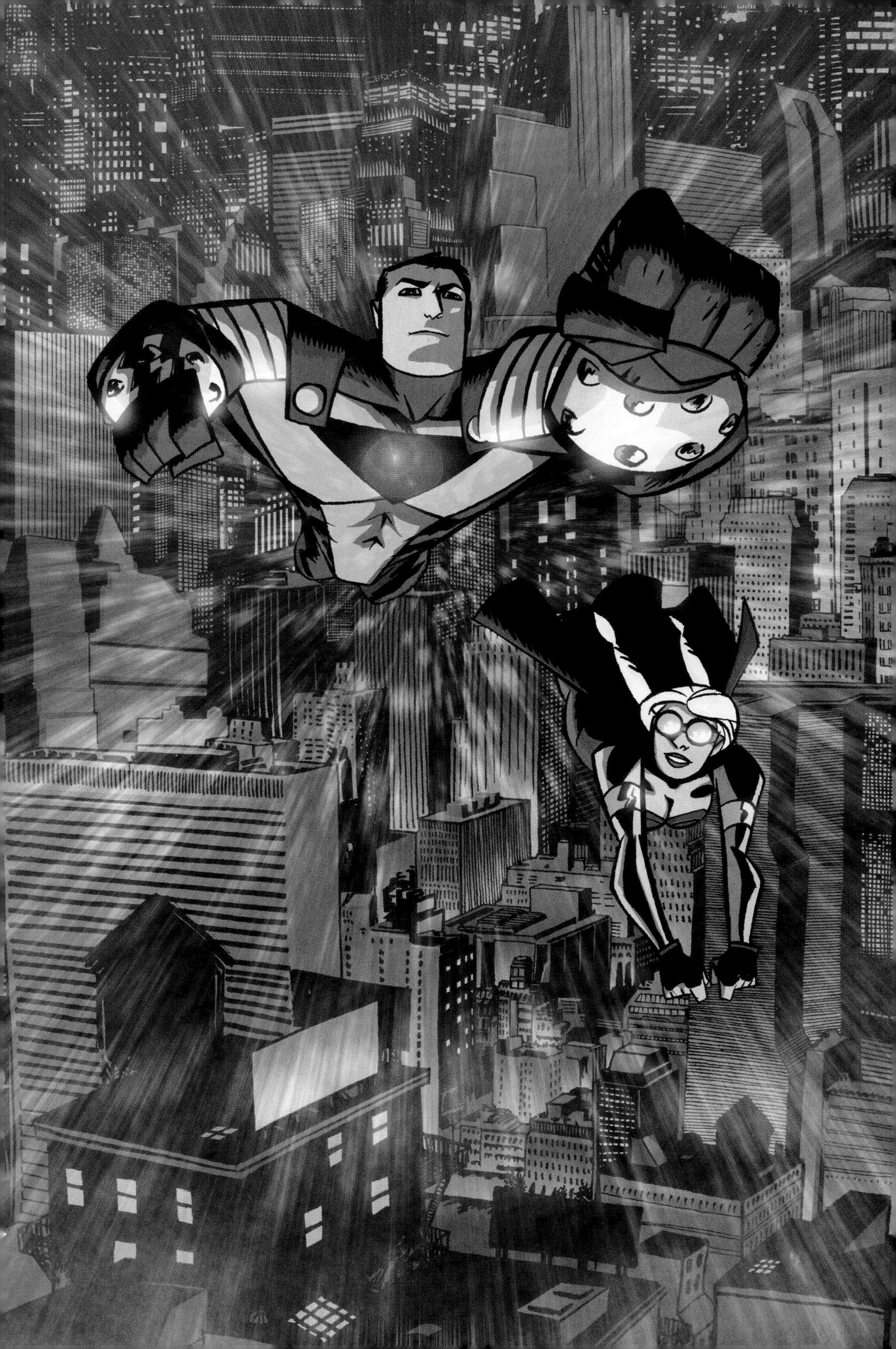

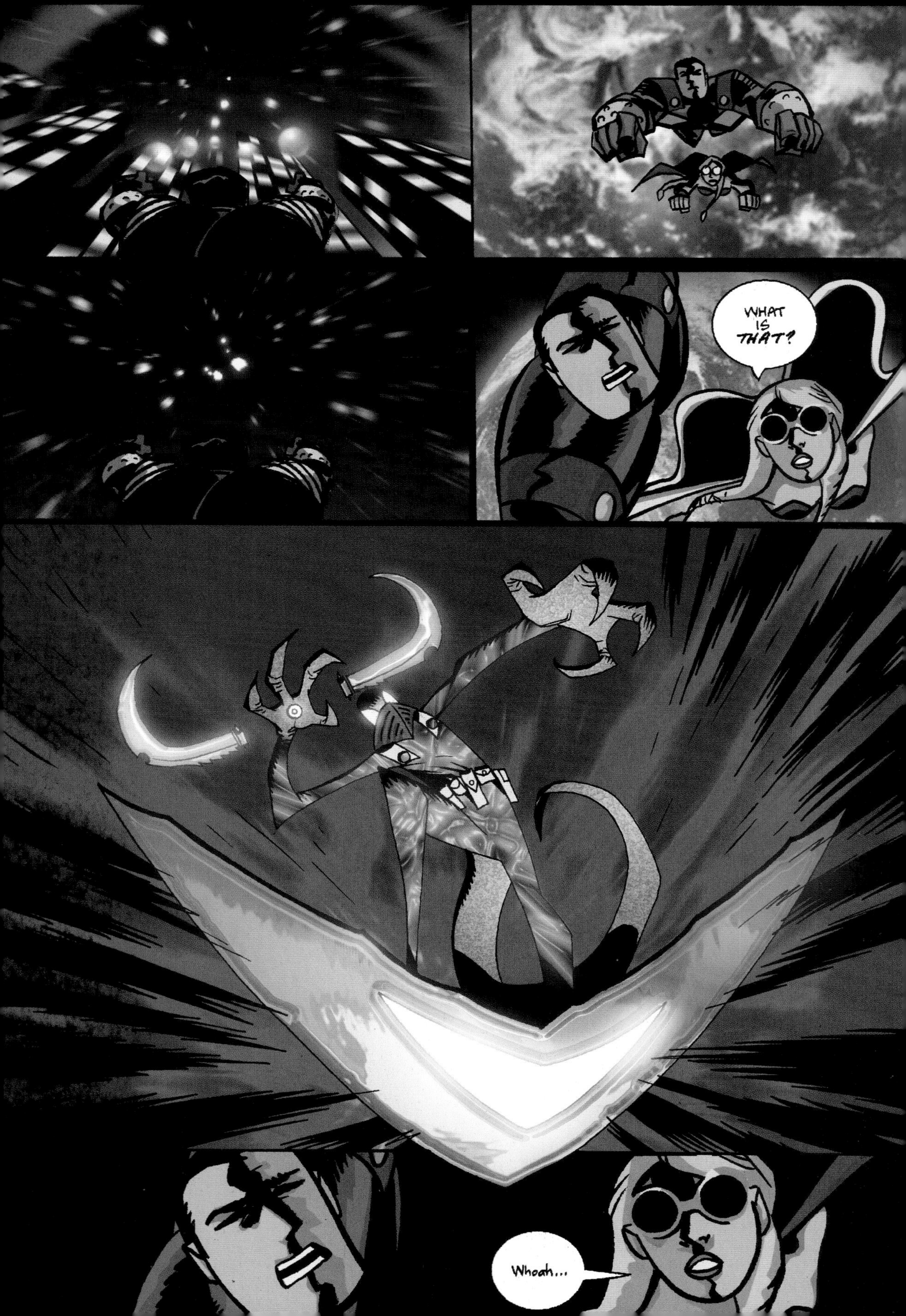
WHAT IS THAT?
Whoah...

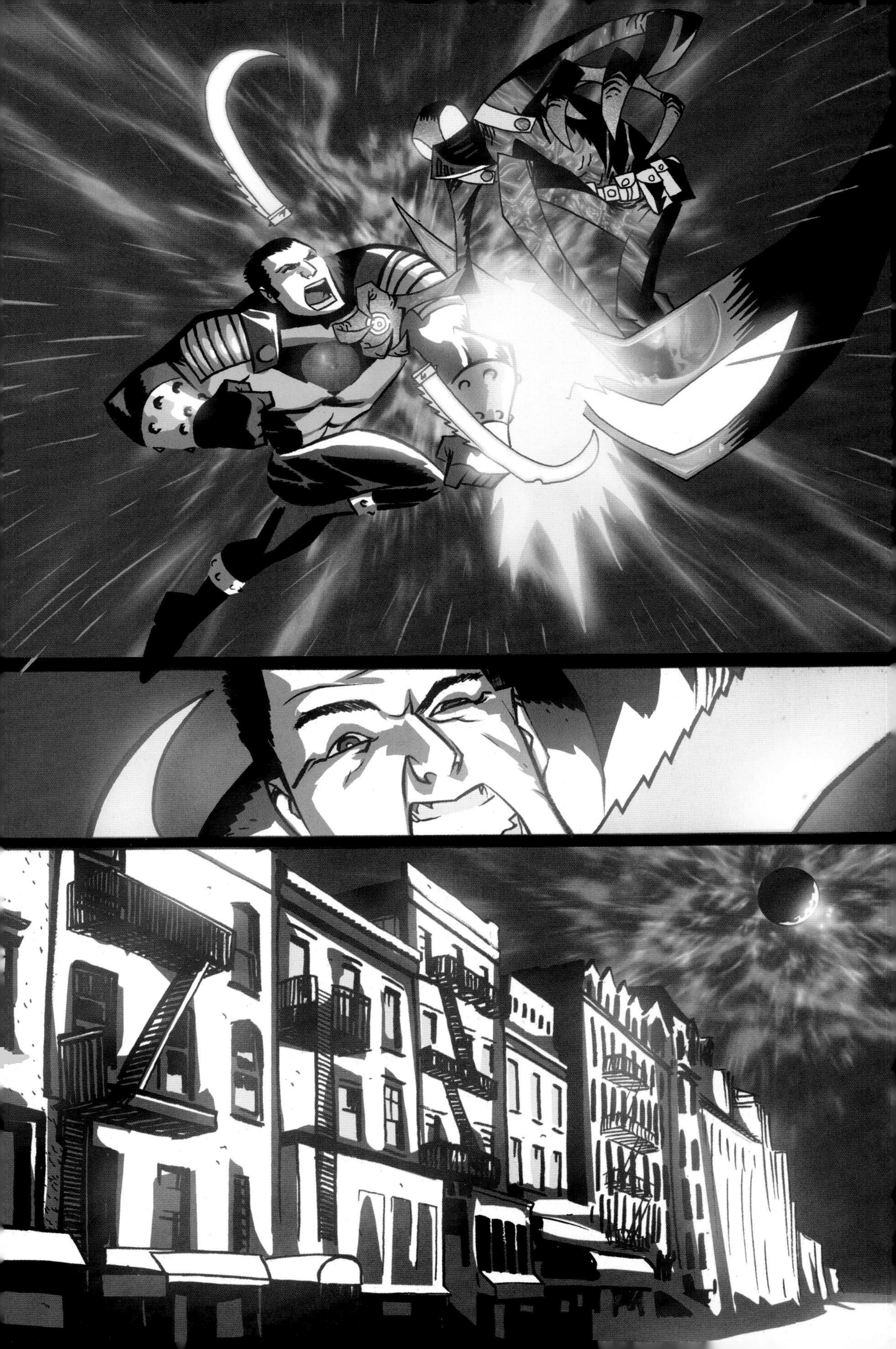

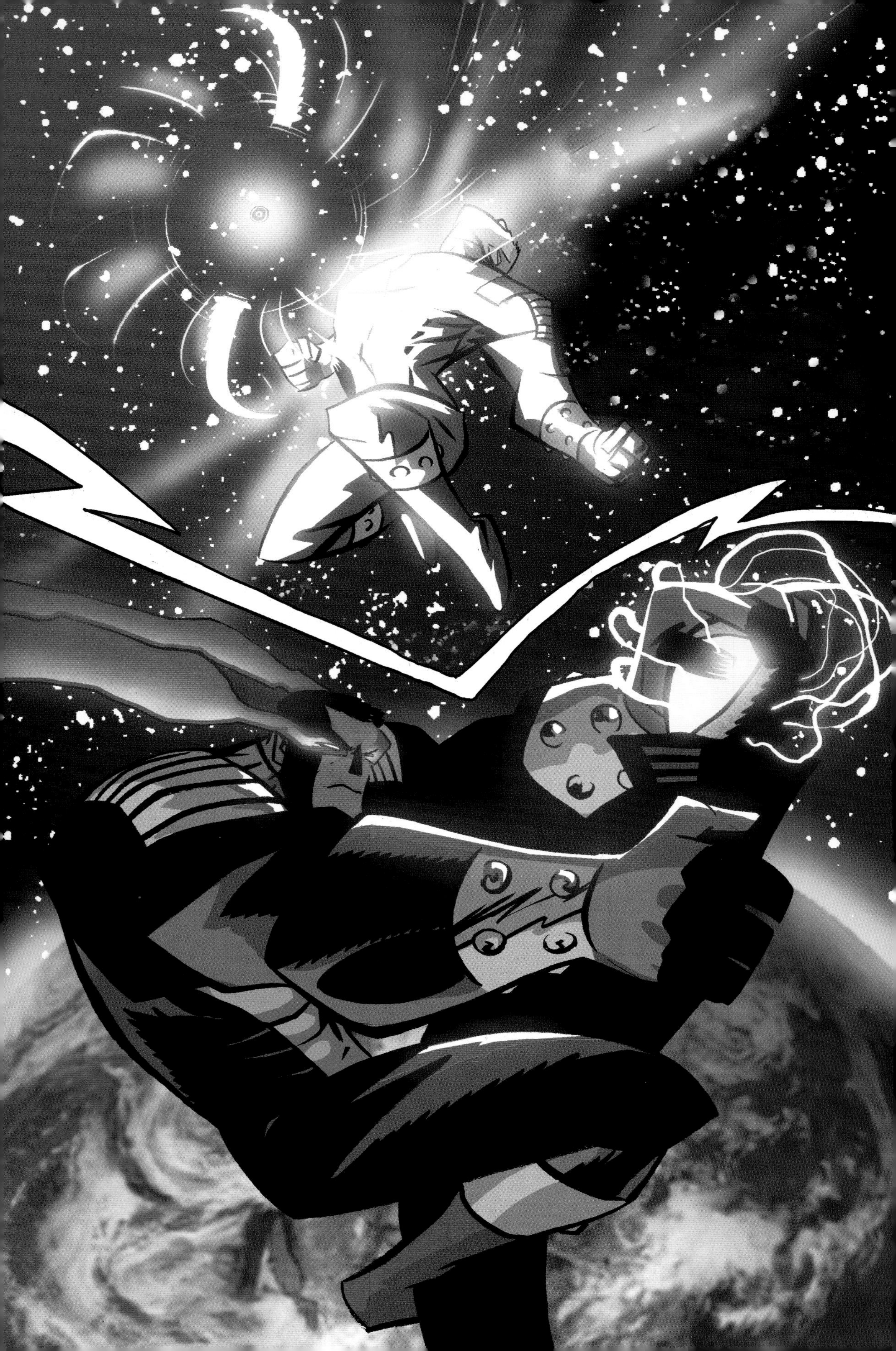

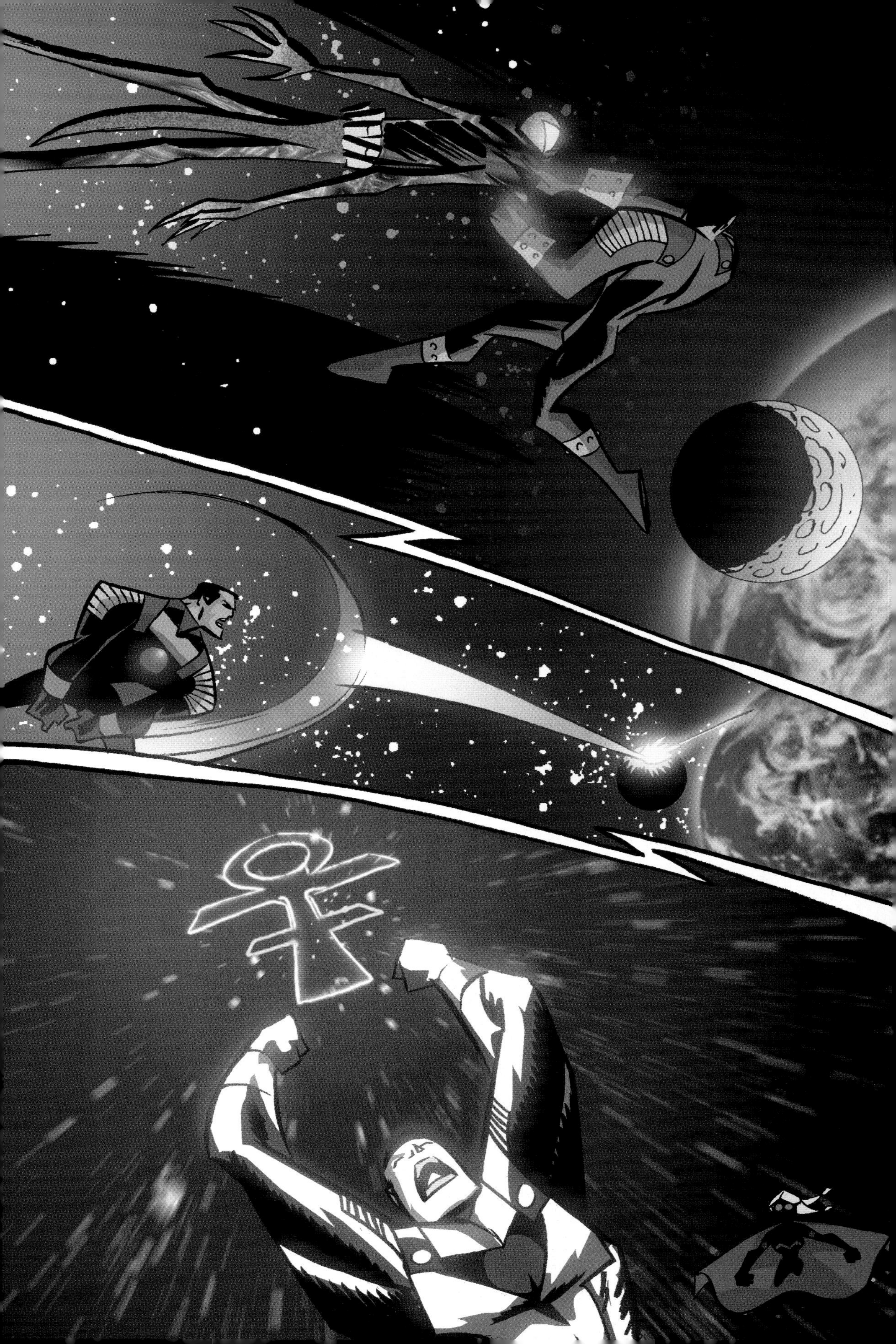

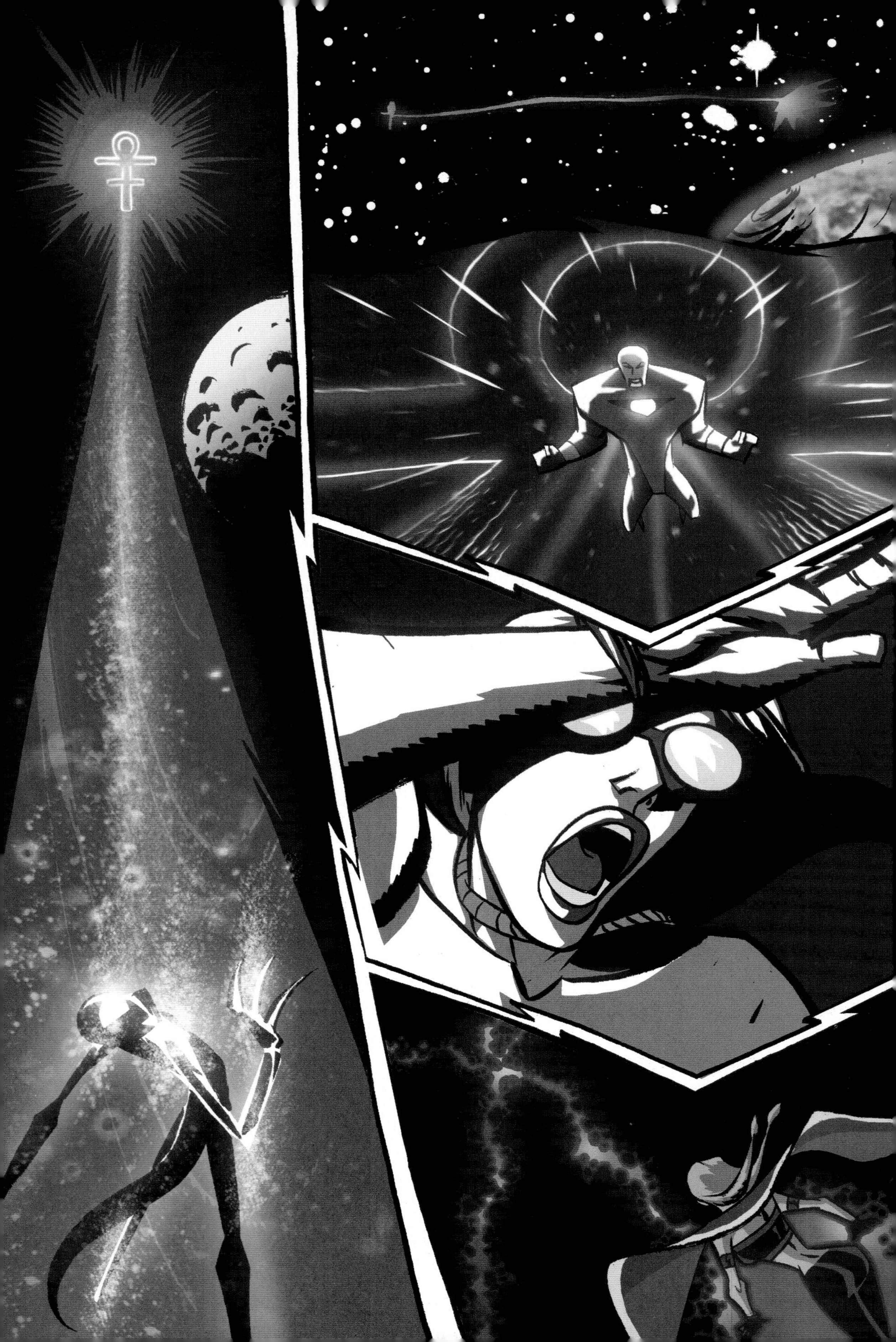

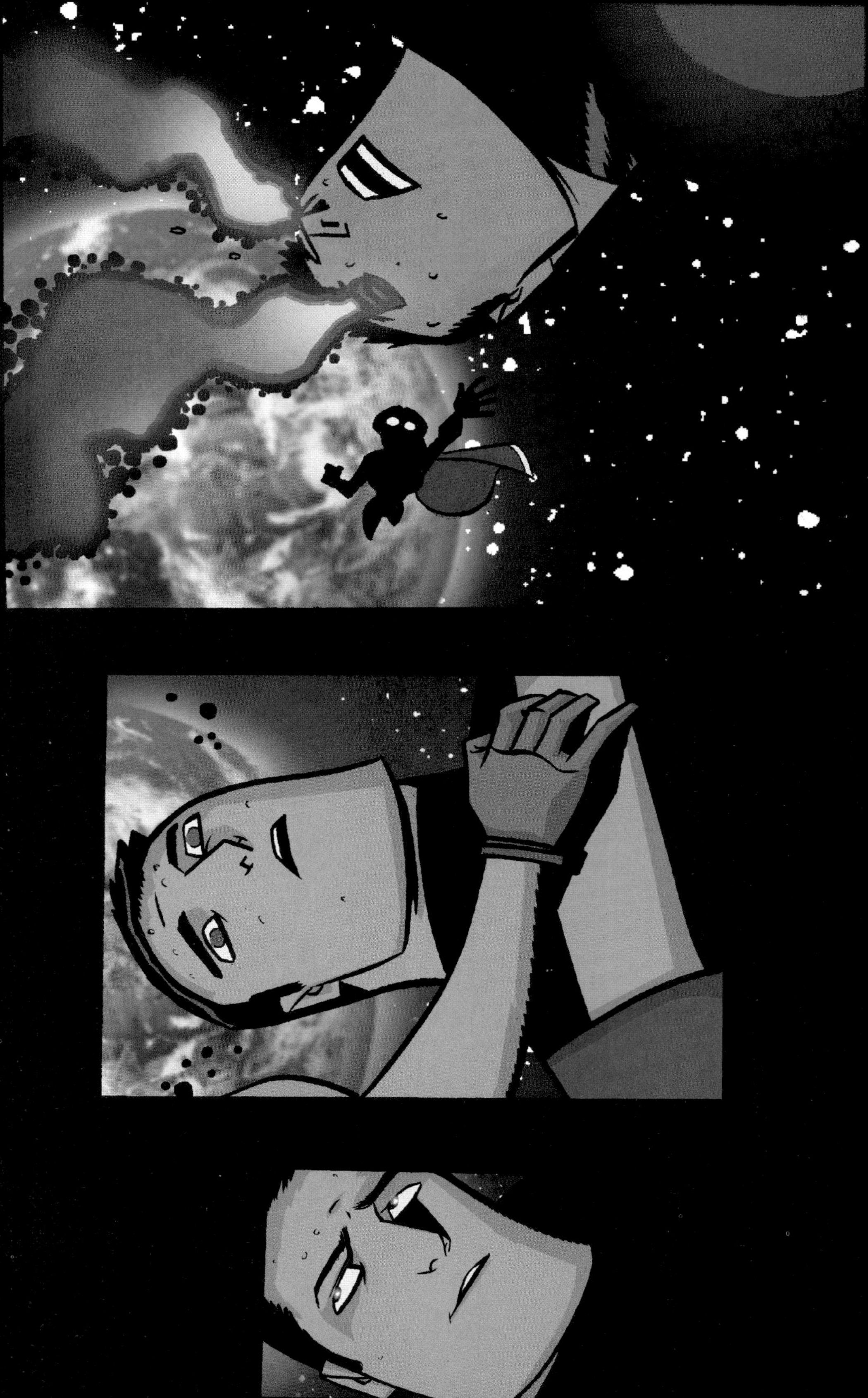

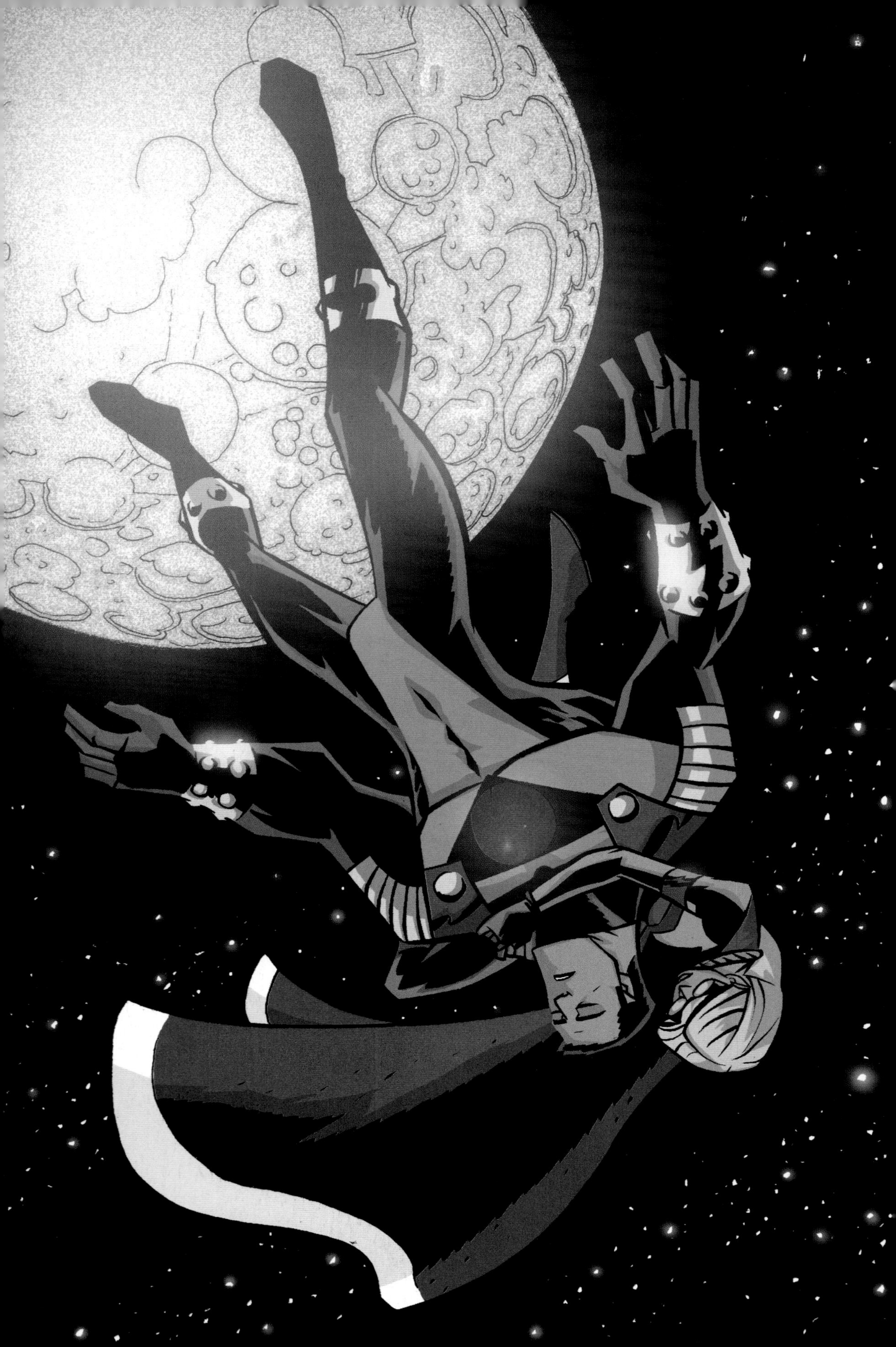

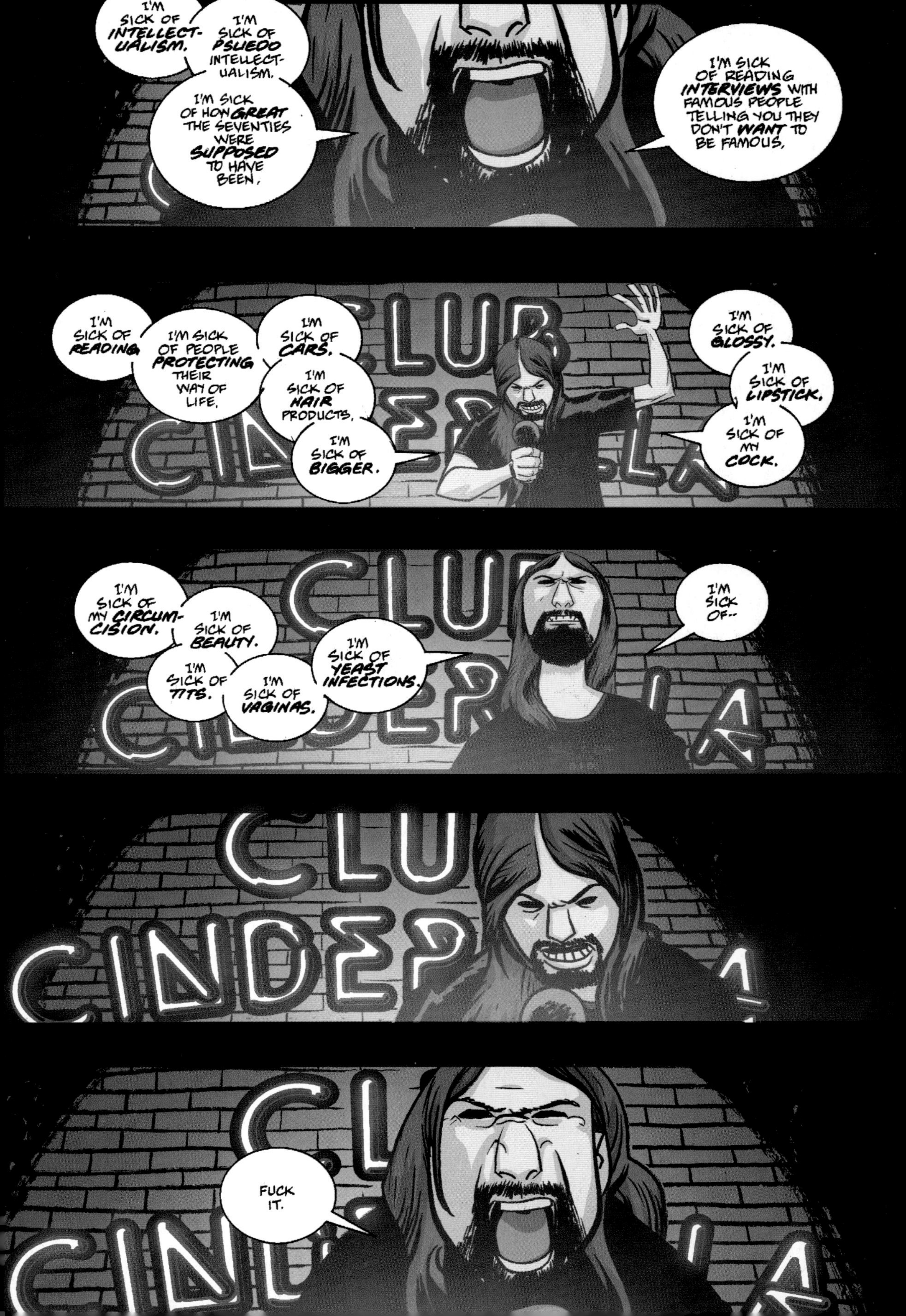
I'M SICK OF **INTELLECT-UALISM.**
I'M SICK OF **PSUEDO** INTELLECT-UALISM.
I'M SICK OF HOW **GREAT** THE SEVENTIES WERE **SUPPOSED** TO HAVE BEEN.
I'M SICK OF READING **INTERVIEWS** WITH FAMOUS PEOPLE TELLING YOU THEY DON'T **WANT** TO BE FAMOUS.
I'M SICK OF **READING.**
I'M SICK OF PEOPLE **PROTECTING** THEIR WAY OF LIFE.
I'M SICK OF **CARS.**
I'M SICK OF **HAIR** PRODUCTS.
I'M SICK OF **BIGGER.**
I'M SICK OF **GLOSSY.**
I'M SICK OF **LIPSTICK.**
I'M SICK OF MY **COCK.**
I'M SICK OF MY **CIRCUM-CISION.**
I'M SICK OF **BEAUTY.**
I'M SICK OF **TITS.**
I'M SICK OF **VAGINAS.**
I'M SICK OF **YEAST INFECTIONS.**
I'M SICK OF--
FUCK IT.

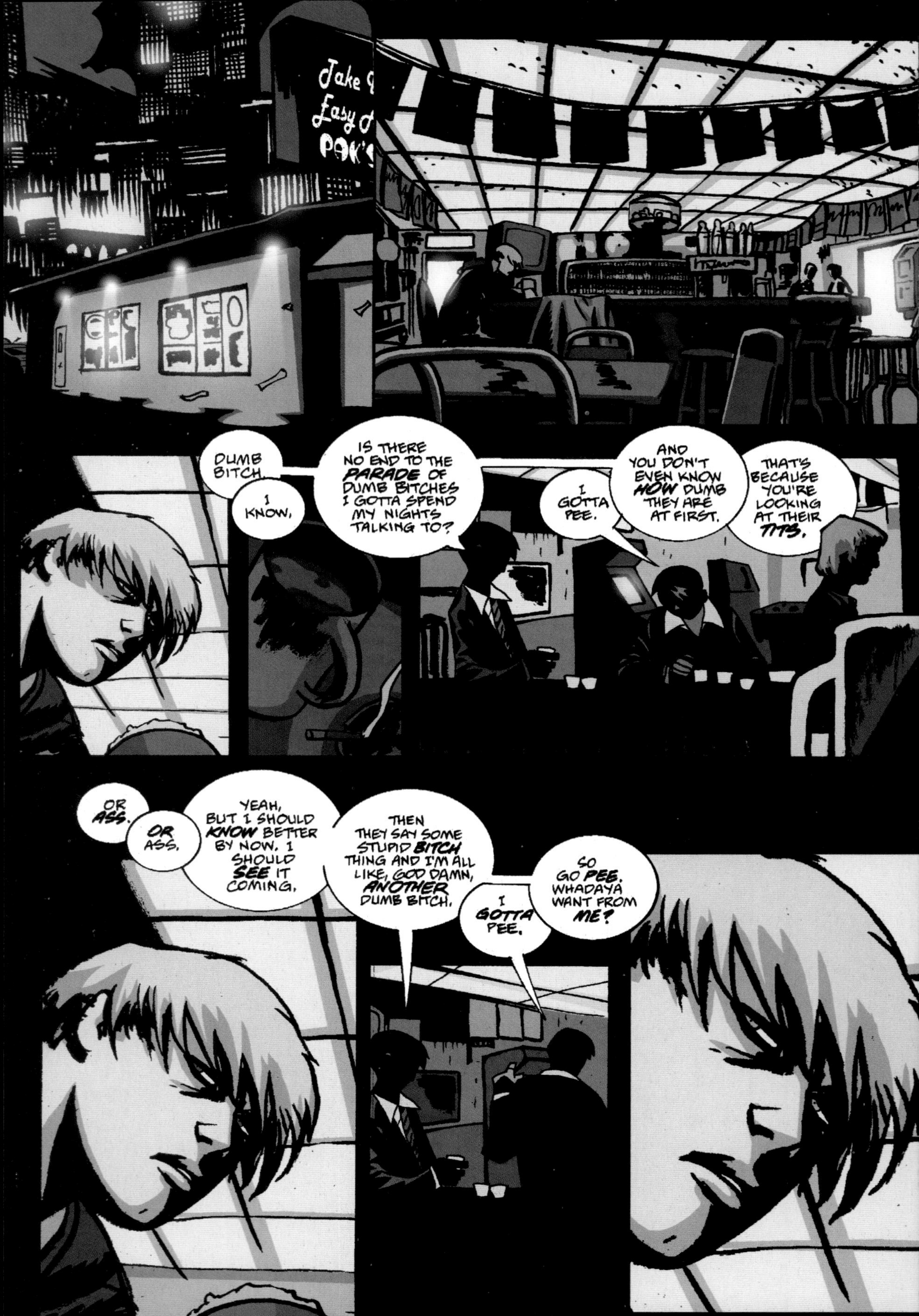
PAK'S
DUMB BITCH.
I KNOW.
IS THERE NO END TO THE PARADE OF DUMB BITCHES I GOTTA SPEND MY NIGHTS TALKING TO?
I GOTTA PEE.
AND YOU DON'T EVEN KNOW HOW DUMB THEY ARE AT FIRST.
THAT'S BECAUSE YOU'RE LOOKING AT THEIR TITS.
OR ASS.
OR ASS.
YEAH, BUT I SHOULD KNOW BETTER BY NOW. I SHOULD SEE IT COMING.
THEN THEY SAY SOME STUPID BITCH THING AND I'M ALL LIKE, GOD DAMN, ANOTHER DUMB BITCH.
I GOTTA PEE.
SO GO PEE. WHADAYA WANT FROM ME?

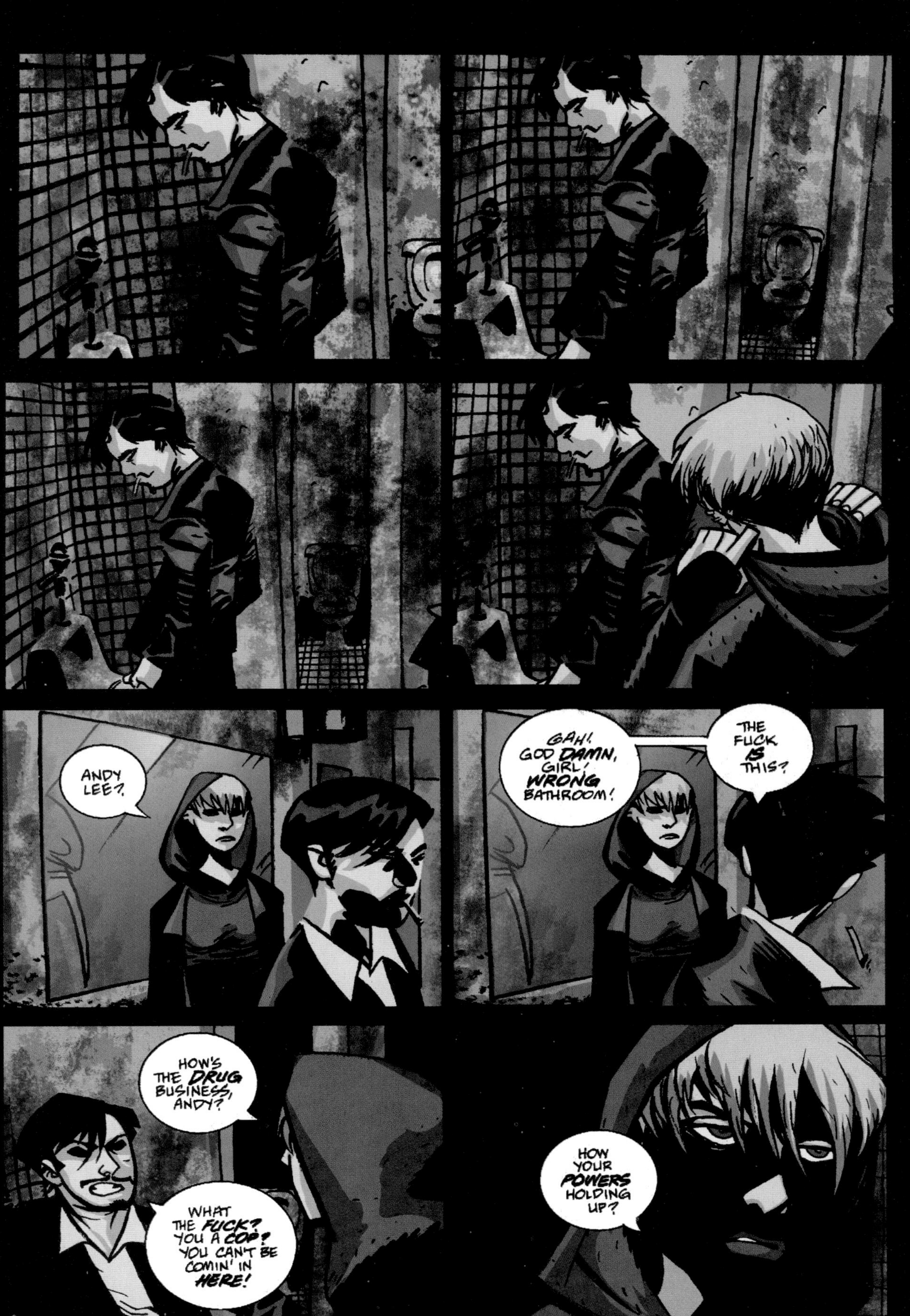
ANDY LEE?
GAH! GOD DAMN, GIRL! WRONG BATHROOM!
THE FUCK IS THIS?
HOW'S THE DRUG BUSINESS, ANDY?
WHAT THE FUCK? YOU A COP? YOU CAN'T BE COMIN' IN HERE!
HOW YOUR POWERS HOLDING UP?

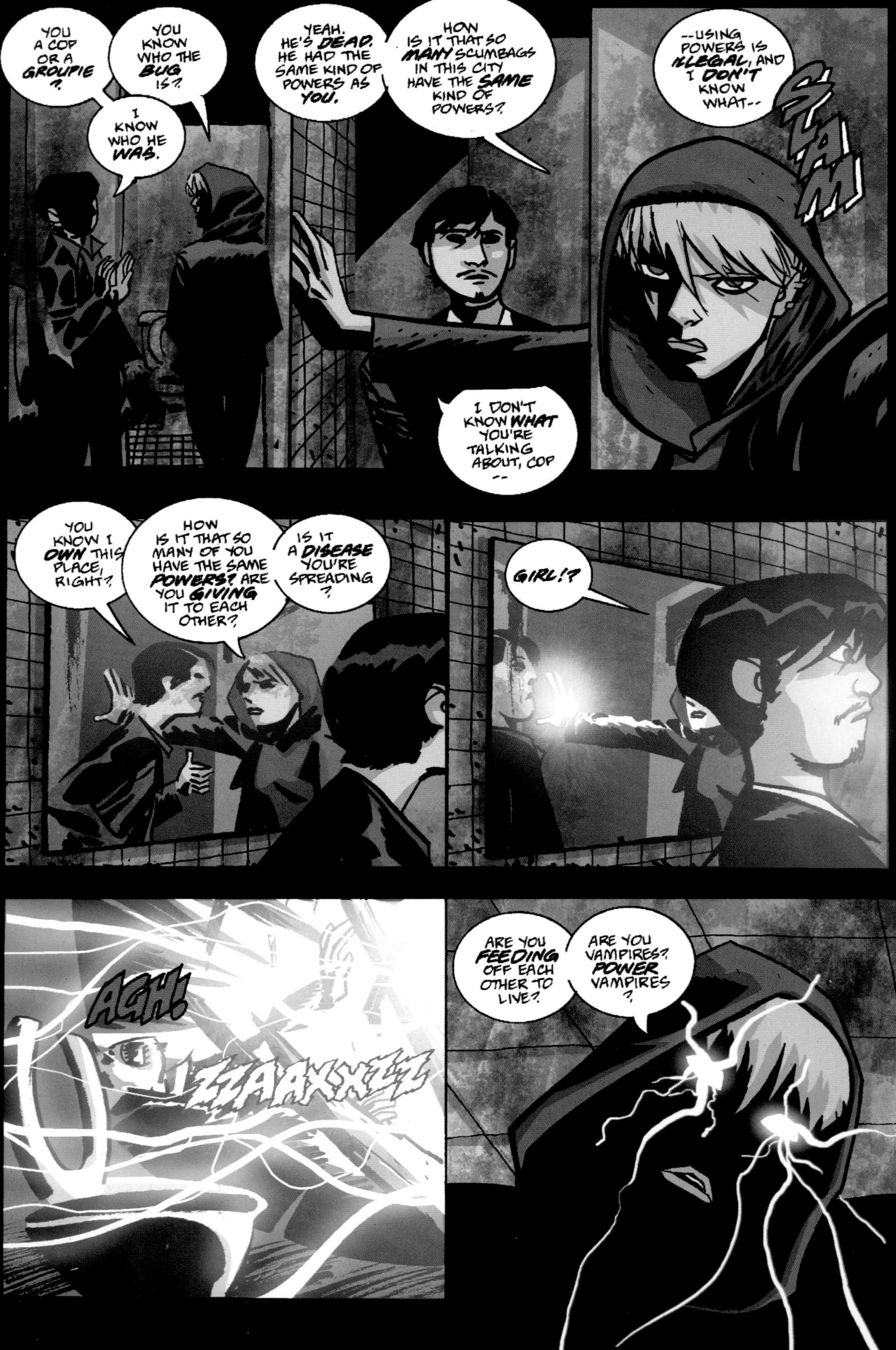
YOU A COP OR A GROUPIE?
YOU KNOW WHO THE BUG IS?
I KNOW WHO HE WAS.
YEAH. HE'S DEAD. HE HAD THE SAME KIND OF POWERS AS YOU.
HOW IS IT THAT SO MANY SCUMBAGS IN THIS CITY HAVE THE SAME KIND OF POWERS?
I DON'T KNOW WHAT YOU'RE TALKING ABOUT, COP--
--USING POWERS IS ILLEGAL, AND I DON'T KNOW WHAT--
SLAM
YOU KNOW I OWN THIS PLACE, RIGHT?
HOW IS IT THAT SO MANY OF YOU HAVE THE SAME POWERS? ARE YOU GIVING IT TO EACH OTHER?
IS IT A DISEASE YOU'RE SPREADING?
GIRL!?
AGH!
ZZAAXXZZ
ARE YOU FEEDING OFF EACH OTHER TO LIVE?
ARE YOU VAMPIRES? POWER VAMPIRES?

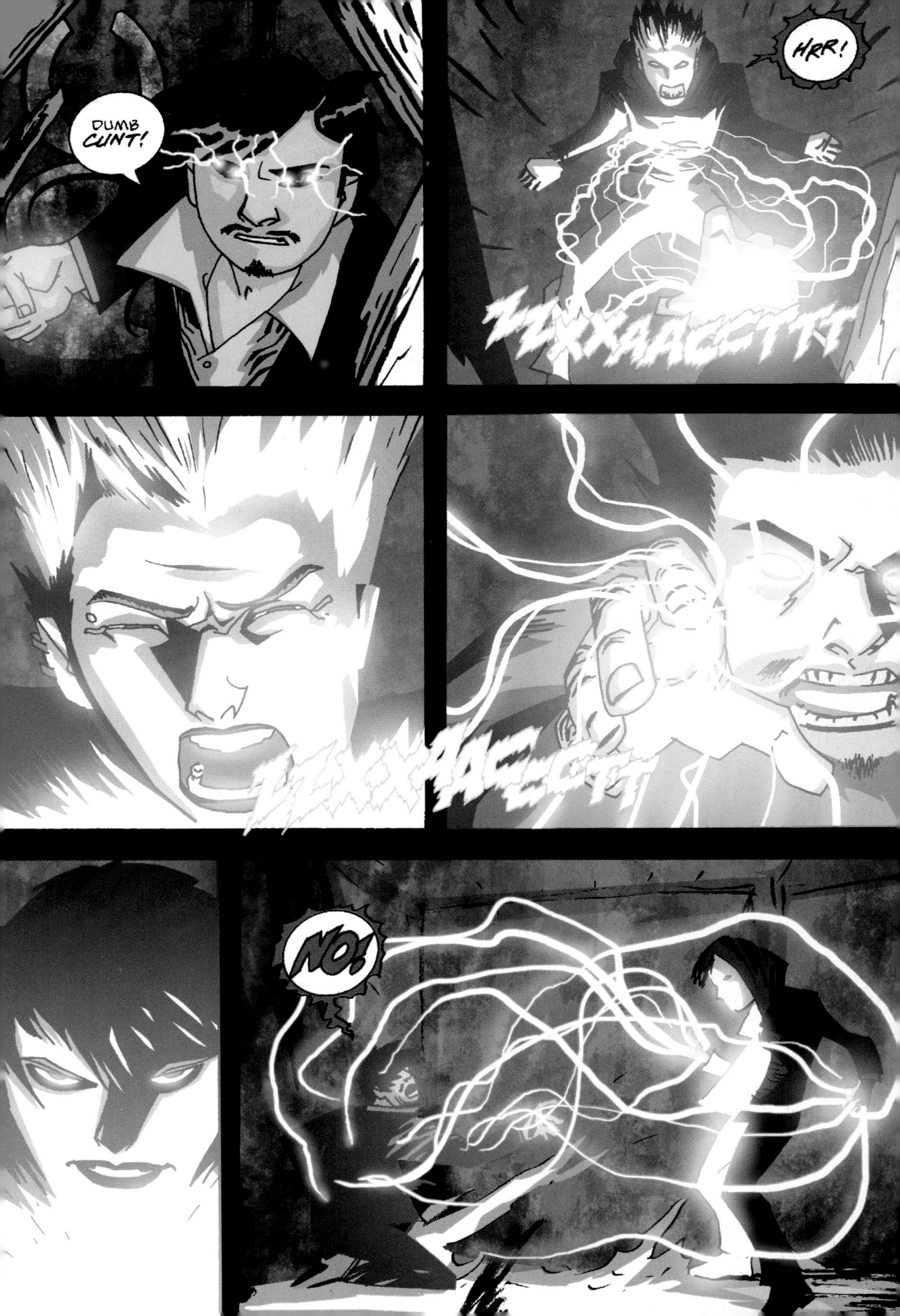
DUMB CUNT!
HRR!
ZZXXAACCTTT
ZZXXAACCTT
NO!

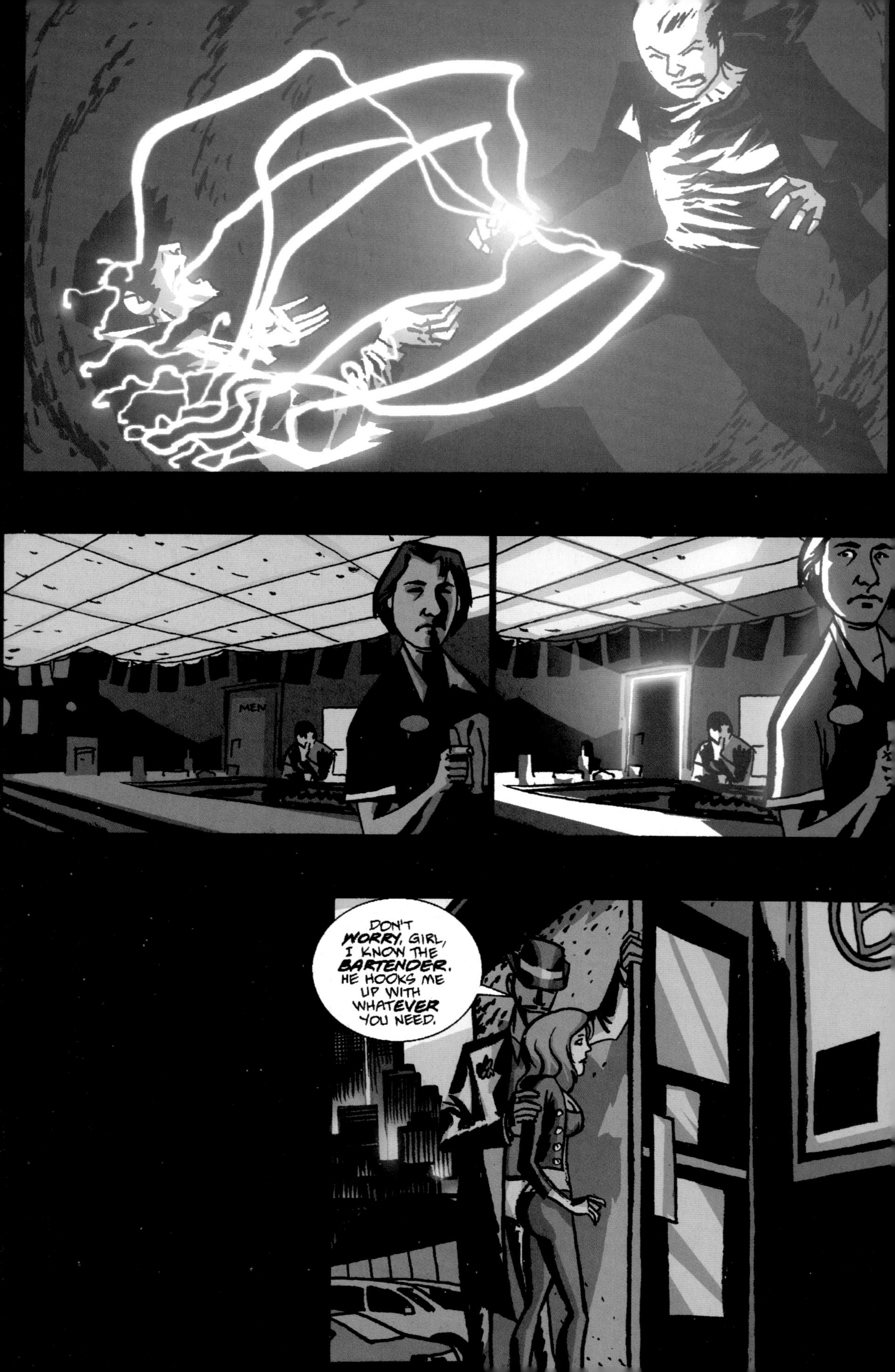
MEN
DON'T **WORRY**, GIRL, I KNOW THE **BARTENDER**. HE HOOKS ME UP WITH WHAT**EVER** YOU NEED.

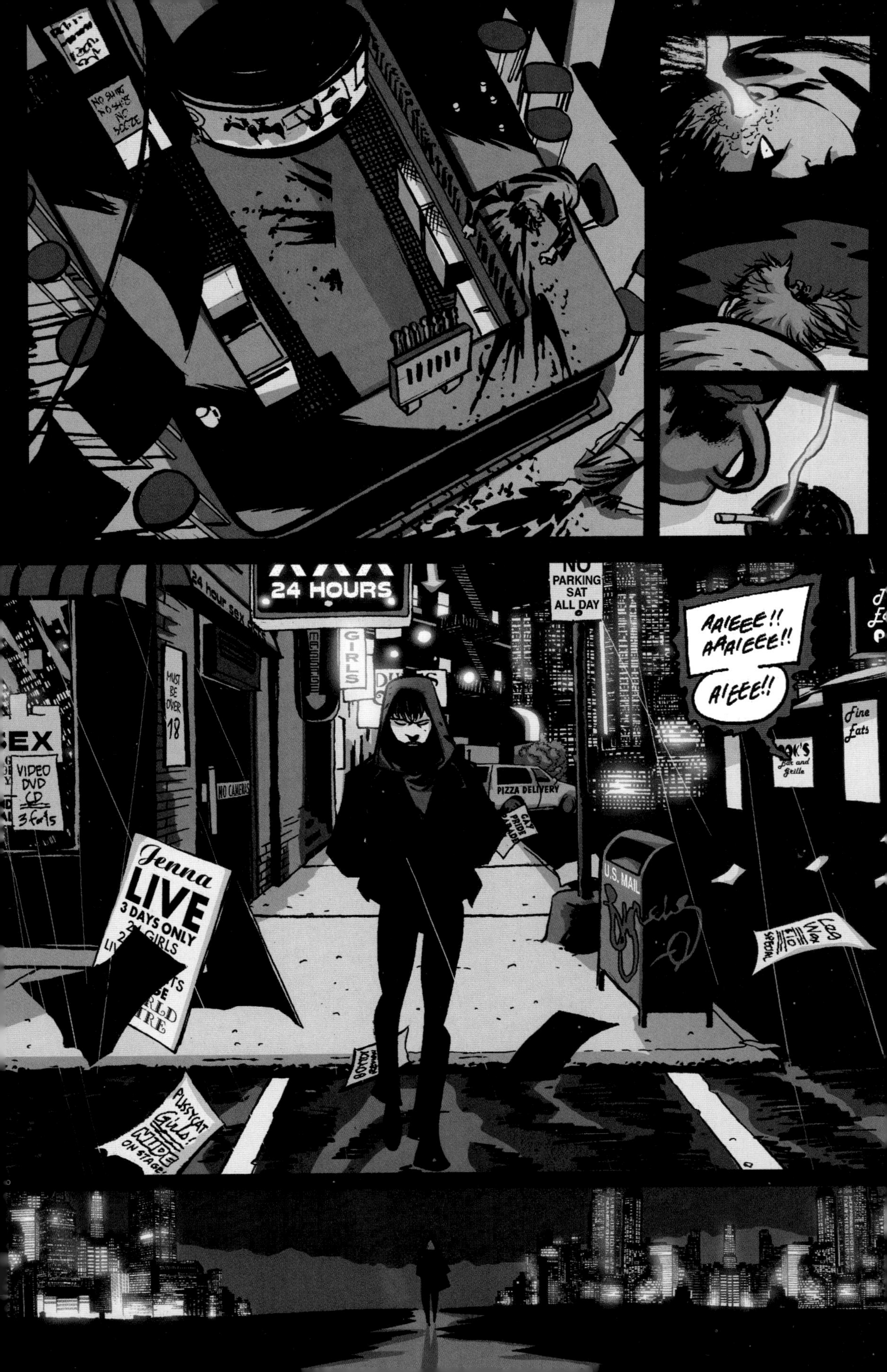
NO SHIRT NO SHOE NO DOOZE
24 HOURS
24 hour sex
NO PARKING SAT ALL DAY
GIRLS
AAIEEE!!
AAAIEEE!!
AIEEE!!
MUST BE OVER 18
SEX
VIDEO DVD CD
NO CAMERAS
PIZZA DELIVERY
GAY PRIDE PARADE
Fine Eats
Bar and Grille
Jenna LIVE 3 DAYS ONLY
U.S. MAIL
PUSSYCAT Girls! NUDE ON STAGE!

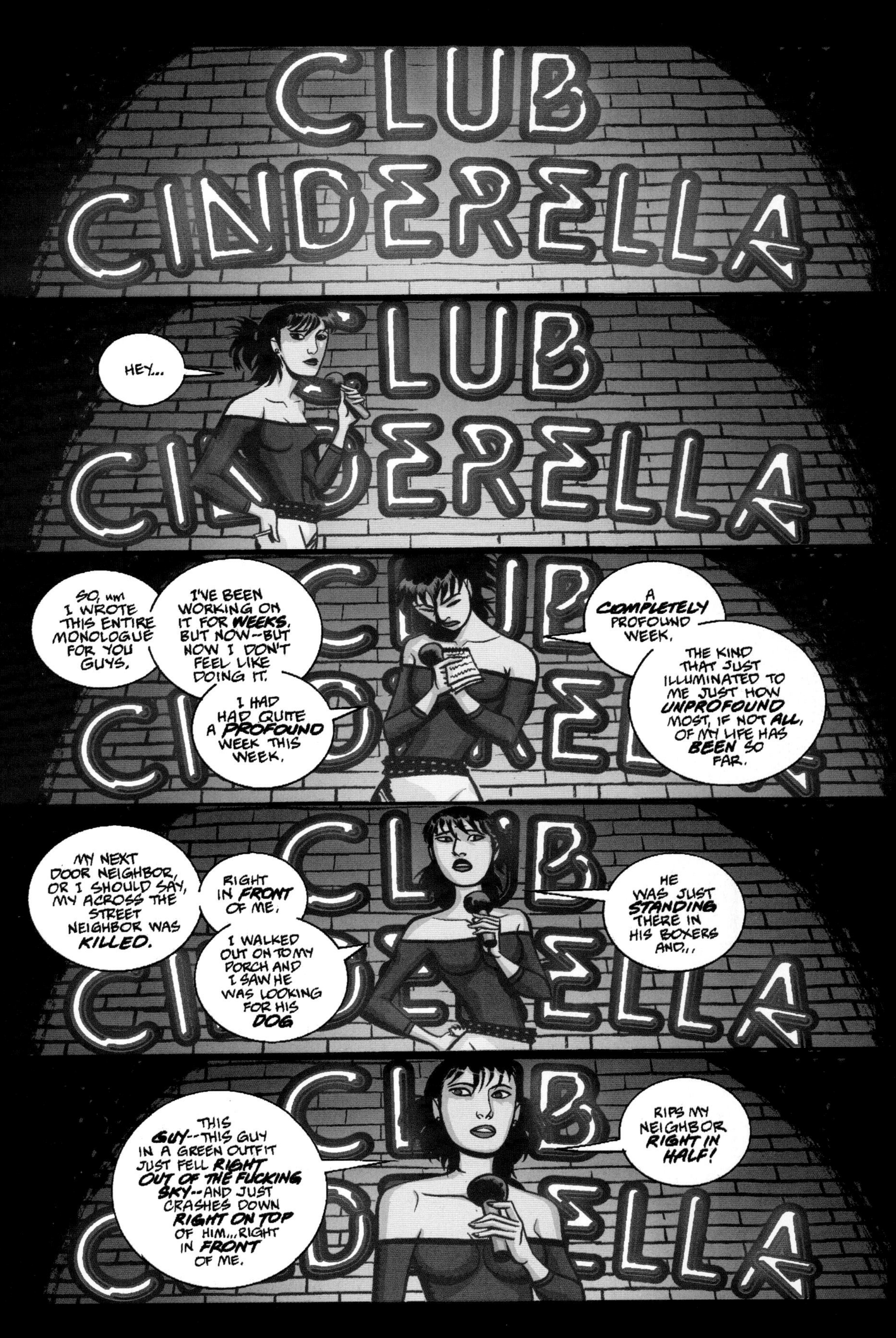
CLUB CINDERELLA
HEY...
SO, UM I WROTE THIS ENTIRE MONOLOGUE FOR YOU GUYS.
I'VE BEEN WORKING ON IT FOR WEEKS, BUT NOW--BUT NOW I DON'T FEEL LIKE DOING IT.
I HAD HAD QUITE A PROFOUND WEEK THIS WEEK.
A COMPLETELY PROFOUND WEEK.
THE KIND THAT JUST ILLUMINATED TO ME JUST HOW UNPROFOUND MOST, IF NOT ALL, OF MY LIFE HAS BEEN SO FAR.
MY NEXT DOOR NEIGHBOR, OR I SHOULD SAY, MY ACROSS THE STREET NEIGHBOR WAS KILLED.
RIGHT IN FRONT OF ME.
I WALKED OUT ON TO MY PORCH AND I SAW HE WAS LOOKING FOR HIS DOG
HE WAS JUST STANDING THERE IN HIS BOXERS AND...
THIS GUY--THIS GUY IN A GREEN OUTFIT JUST FELL RIGHT OUT OF THE FUCKING SKY--AND JUST CRASHES DOWN RIGHT ON TOP OF HIM...RIGHT IN FRONT OF ME.
RIPS MY NEIGHBOR RIGHT IN HALF!

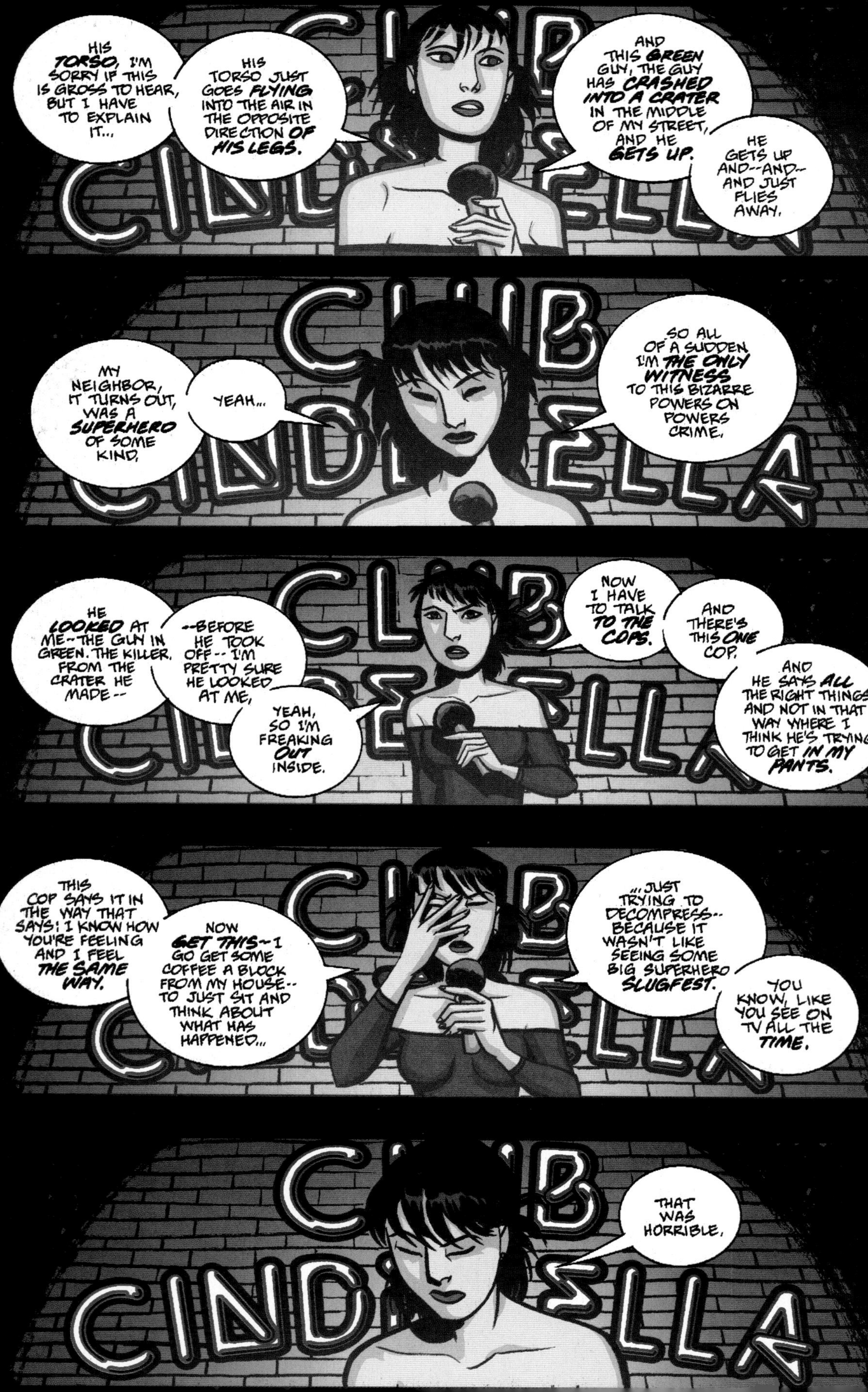

CLUB CINDERELLA
HIS TORSO, I'M SORRY IF THIS IS GROSS TO HEAR, BUT I HAVE TO EXPLAIN IT...
HIS TORSO JUST GOES FLYING INTO THE AIR IN THE OPPOSITE DIRECTION OF HIS LEGS.
AND THIS GREEN GUY, THE GUY HAS CRASHED INTO A CRATER IN THE MIDDLE OF MY STREET, AND HE GETS UP.
HE GETS UP AND--AND--AND JUST FLIES AWAY.
MY NEIGHBOR, IT TURNS OUT, WAS A SUPERHERO OF SOME KIND.
YEAH...
SO ALL OF A SUDDEN, I'M THE ONLY WITNESS TO THIS BIZARRE POWERS ON POWERS CRIME.
HE LOOKED AT ME--THE GUY IN GREEN. THE KILLER. FROM THE CRATER HE MADE--
--BEFORE HE TOOK OFF--I'M PRETTY SURE HE LOOKED AT ME.
YEAH, SO I'M FREAKING OUT INSIDE.
NOW I HAVE TO TALK TO THE COPS.
AND THERE'S THIS ONE COP.
AND HE SAYS ALL THE RIGHT THINGS AND NOT IN THAT WAY WHERE I THINK HE'S TRYING TO GET IN MY PANTS.
THIS COP SAYS IT IN THE WAY THAT SAYS: I KNOW HOW YOU'RE FEELING AND I FEEL THE SAME WAY.
NOW GET THIS--I GO GET SOME COFFEE A BLOCK FROM MY HOUSE--TO JUST SIT AND THINK ABOUT WHAT HAS HAPPENED...
...JUST TRYING TO DECOMPRESS--BECAUSE IT WASN'T LIKE SEEING SOME BIG SUPERHERO SLUGFEST.
YOU KNOW, LIKE YOU SEE ON TV ALL THE TIME.
THAT WAS HORRIBLE.

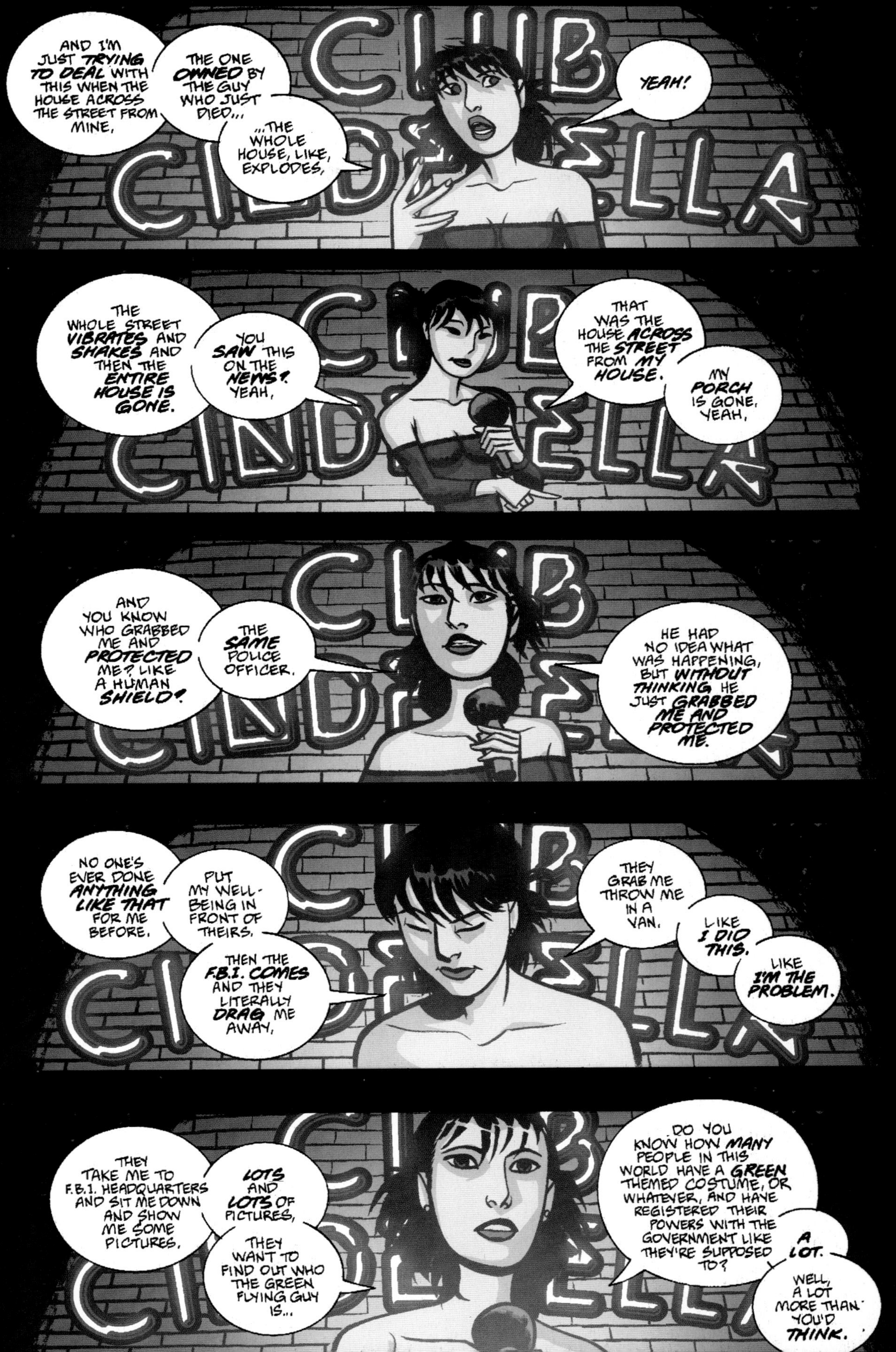
CLUB CINDERELLA
AND I'M JUST TRYING TO DEAL WITH THIS WHEN THE HOUSE ACROSS THE STREET FROM MINE,
THE ONE OWNED BY THE GUY WHO JUST DIED...
...THE WHOLE HOUSE, LIKE, EXPLODES.
YEAH!
THE WHOLE STREET VIBRATES AND SHAKES AND THEN THE ENTIRE HOUSE IS GONE.
YOU SAW THIS ON THE NEWS? YEAH.
THAT WAS THE HOUSE ACROSS THE STREET FROM MY HOUSE.
MY PORCH IS GONE, YEAH.
AND YOU KNOW WHO GRABBED ME AND PROTECTED ME? LIKE A HUMAN SHIELD?
THE SAME POLICE OFFICER.
HE HAD NO IDEA WHAT WAS HAPPENING, BUT WITHOUT THINKING HE JUST GRABBED ME AND PROTECTED ME.
NO ONE'S EVER DONE ANYTHING LIKE THAT FOR ME BEFORE.
PUT MY WELL-BEING IN FRONT OF THEIRS.
THEN THE F.B.I. COMES AND THEY LITERALLY DRAG ME AWAY.
THEY GRAB ME THROW ME IN A VAN.
LIKE I DID THIS.
LIKE I'M THE PROBLEM.
THEY TAKE ME TO F.B.I. HEADQUARTERS AND SIT ME DOWN AND SHOW ME SOME PICTURES.
LOTS AND LOTS OF PICTURES.
THEY WANT TO FIND OUT WHO THE GREEN FLYING GUY IS...
DO YOU KNOW HOW MANY PEOPLE IN THIS WORLD HAVE A GREEN THEMED COSTUME, OR WHATEVER, AND HAVE REGISTERED THEIR POWERS WITH THE GOVERNMENT LIKE THEY'RE SUPPOSED TO?
A LOT.
WELL, A LOT MORE THAN YOU'D THINK.

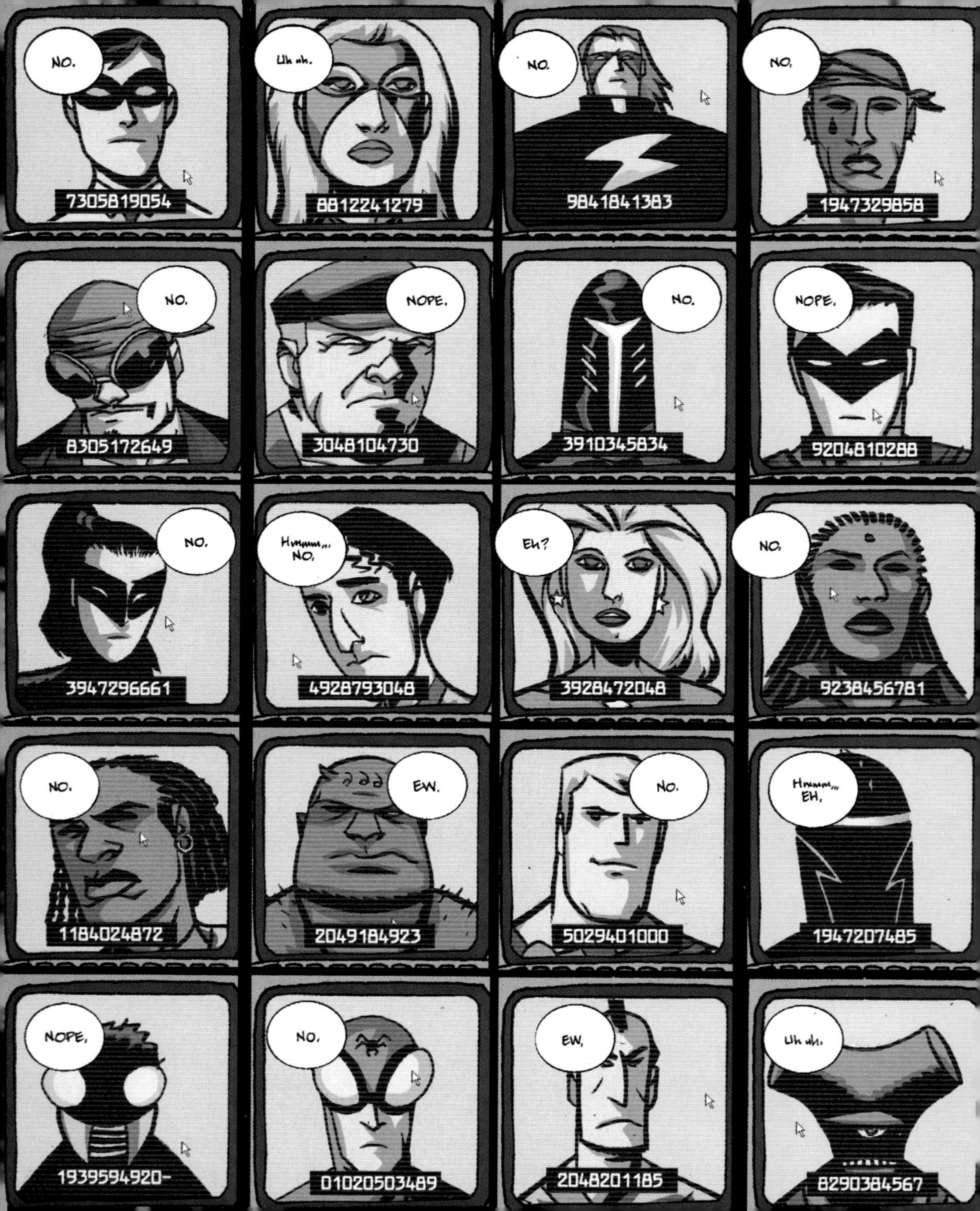
NO.
7305819054
Uh uh.
8812241279
NO.
9841841383
NO.
1947329858
NO.
8305172649
NOPE.
3048104730
NO.
3910345834
NOPE.
9204810288
NO.
3947296661
Hmmm... NO.
4928793048
Eh?
3928472048
NO.
9238456781
NO.
1184024872
EW.
2049184923
NO.
5029401000
Hmmm... EH.
1947207485
NOPE.
1939594920-
NO.
01020503489
EW.
2048201185
Uh uh.
8290384567

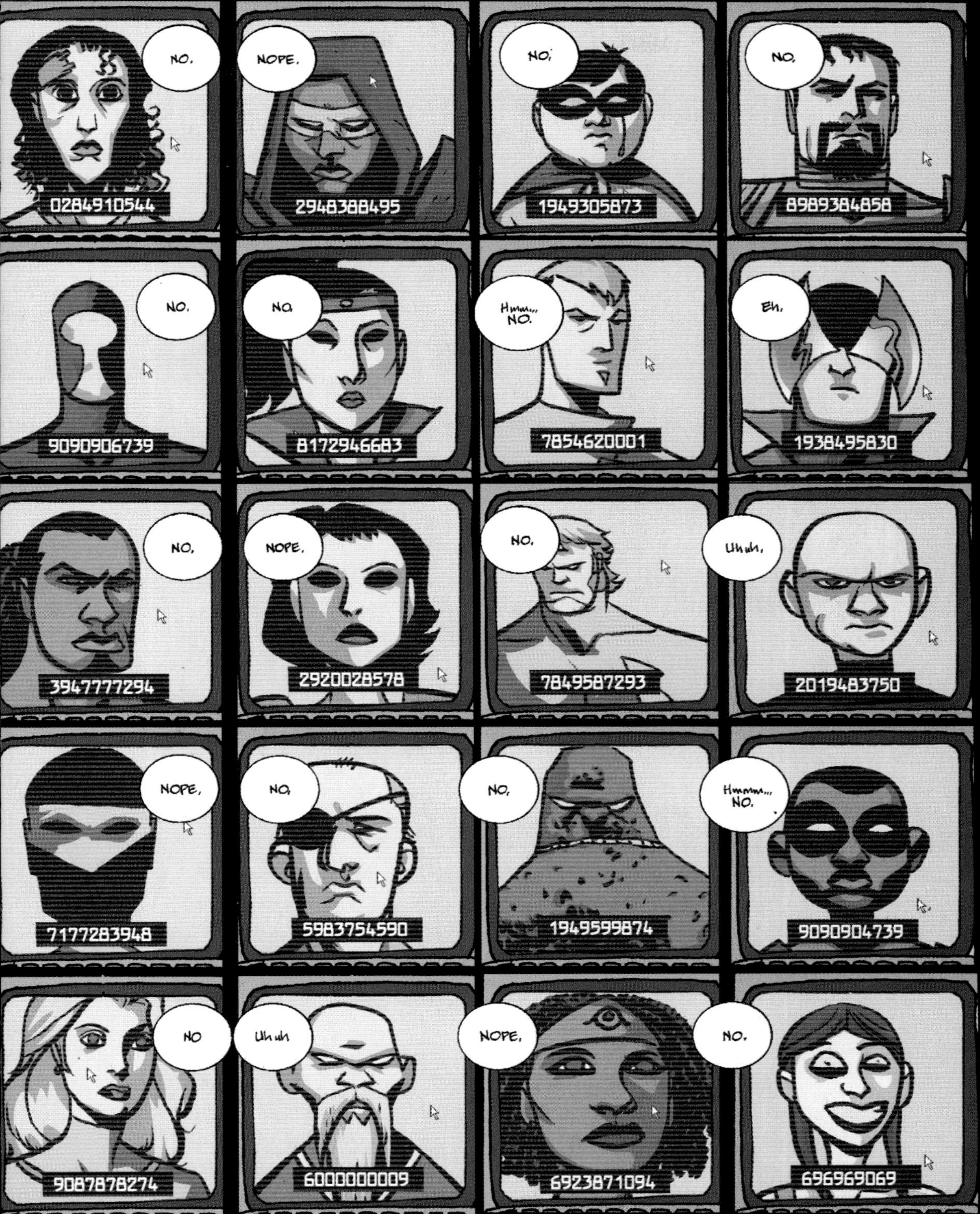
NO.
0284910544
NOPE.
2948388495
NO.
1949305873
NO.
8989384858
NO.
9090906739
NO.
8172946683
Hmm... NO.
7854620001
Eh.
1938495830
NO.
3947777294
NOPE.
2920028578
NO.
7849587293
Uh uh.
2019483750
NOPE.
7177283948
NO.
5983754590
NO.
1949599874
Hmmm... NO.
9090904739
NO
9087878274
Uh uh
6000000009
NOPE.
6923871094
NO.
696969069

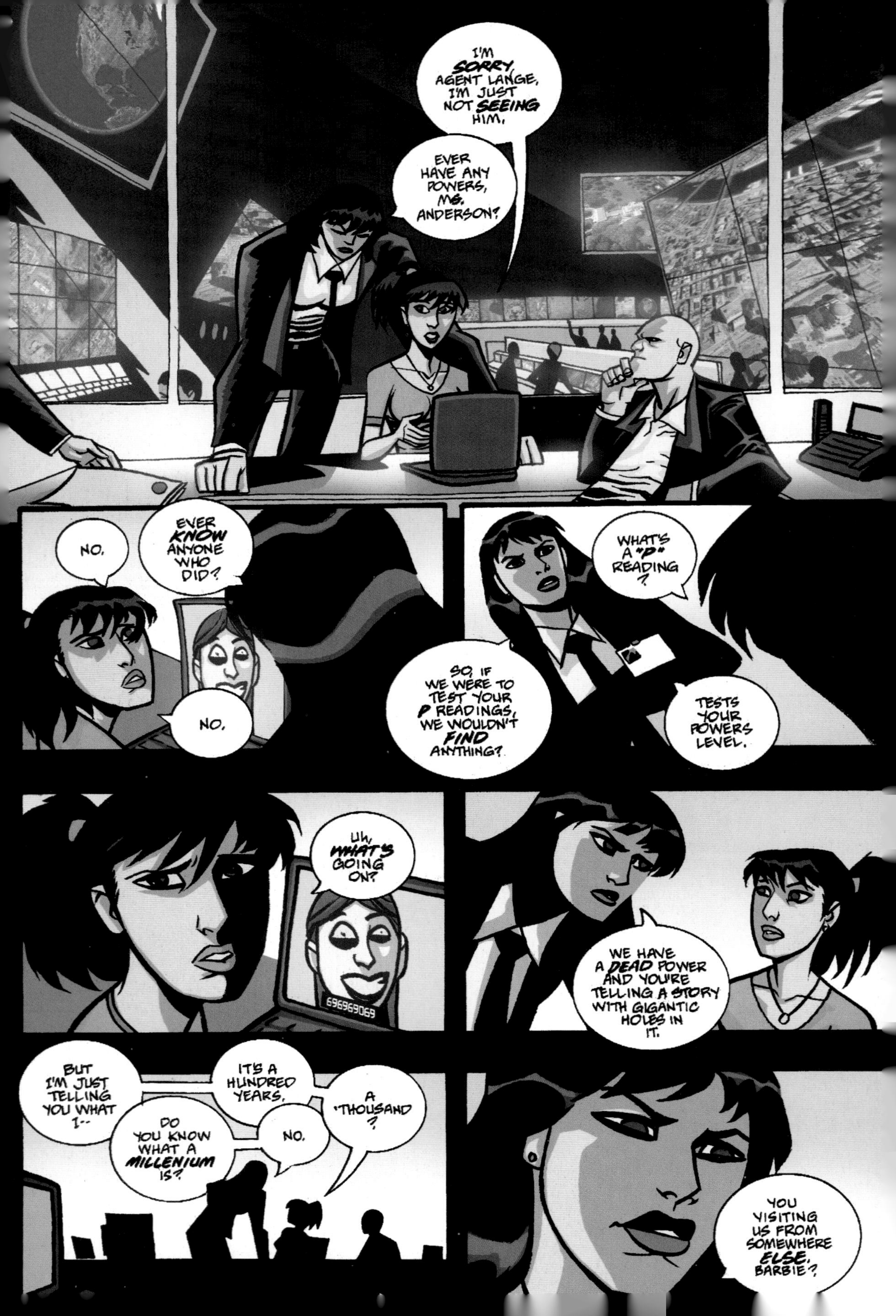
I'M SORRY, AGENT LANGE, I'M JUST NOT SEEING HIM.
EVER HAVE ANY POWERS, MS. ANDERSON?
NO.
EVER KNOW ANYONE WHO DID?
NO.
WHAT'S A "P" READING?
TESTS YOUR POWERS LEVEL.
SO, IF WE WERE TO TEST YOUR P READINGS, WE WOULDN'T FIND ANYTHING?
UH, WHAT'S GOING ON?
696969069
WE HAVE A DEAD POWER AND YOU'RE TELLING A STORY WITH GIGANTIC HOLES IN IT.
BUT I'M JUST TELLING YOU WHAT I--
DO YOU KNOW WHAT A MILLENIUM IS?
IT'S A HUNDRED YEARS.
NO.
A THOUSAND?
YOU VISITING US FROM SOMEWHERE ELSE, BARBIE?

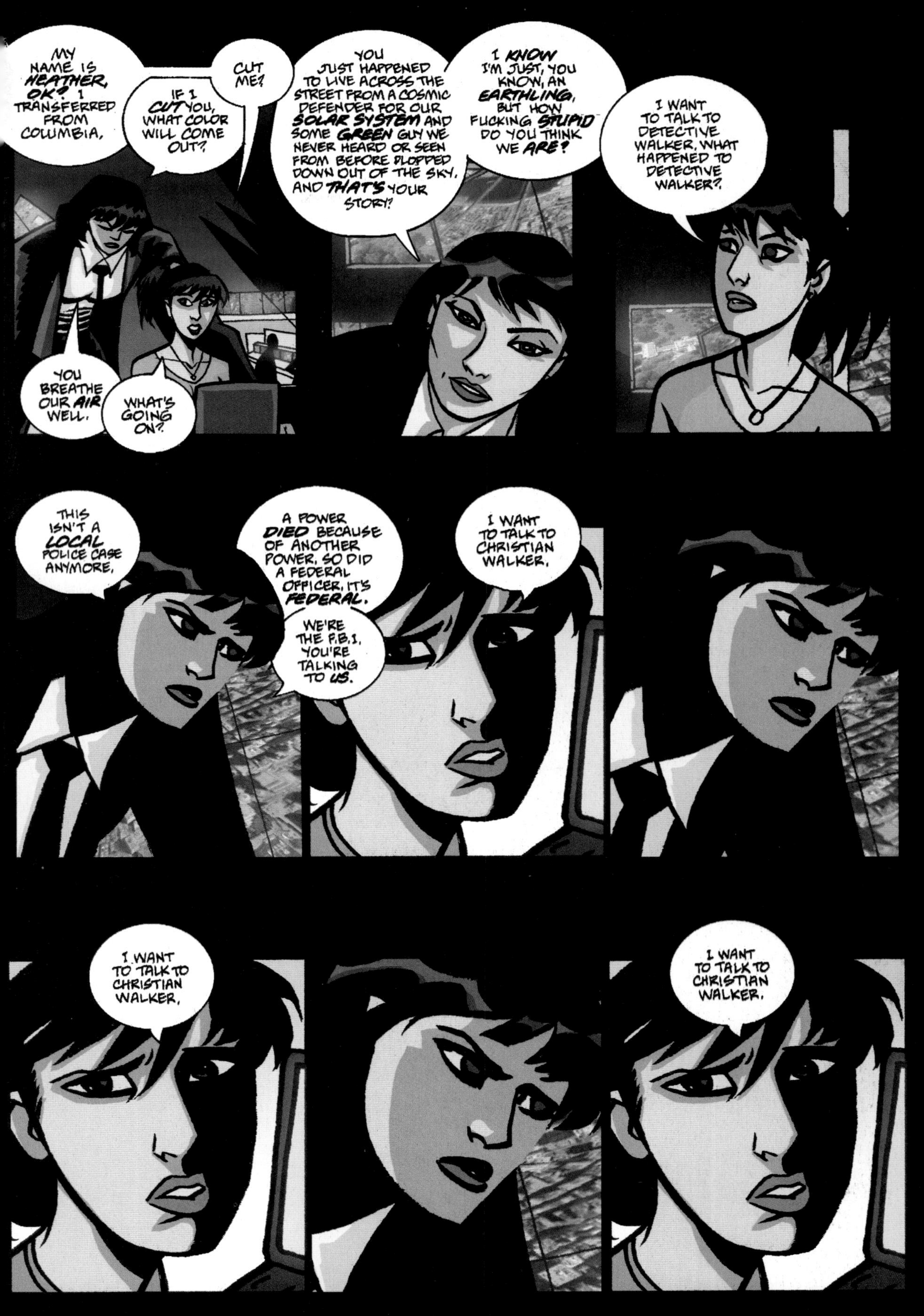
MY NAME IS HEATHER, OK? I TRANSFERRED FROM COLUMBIA.
IF I CUT YOU, WHAT COLOR WILL COME OUT?
CUT ME?
YOU BREATHE OUR AIR WELL.
WHAT'S GOING ON?
YOU JUST HAPPENED TO LIVE ACROSS THE STREET FROM A COSMIC DEFENDER FOR OUR SOLAR SYSTEM AND SOME GREEN GUY WE NEVER HEARD OR SEEN FROM BEFORE PLOPPED DOWN OUT OF THE SKY, AND THAT'S YOUR STORY?
I KNOW I'M JUST, YOU KNOW, AN EARTHLING, BUT HOW FUCKING STUPID DO YOU THINK WE ARE?
I WANT TO TALK TO DETECTIVE WALKER. WHAT HAPPENED TO DETECTIVE WALKER?
THIS ISN'T A LOCAL POLICE CASE ANYMORE.
A POWER DIED BECAUSE OF ANOTHER POWER, SO DID A FEDERAL OFFICER. IT'S FEDERAL.
WE'RE THE F.B.I. YOU'RE TALKING TO US.
I WANT TO TALK TO CHRISTIAN WALKER.
I WANT TO TALK TO CHRISTIAN WALKER.
I WANT TO TALK TO CHRISTIAN WALKER.

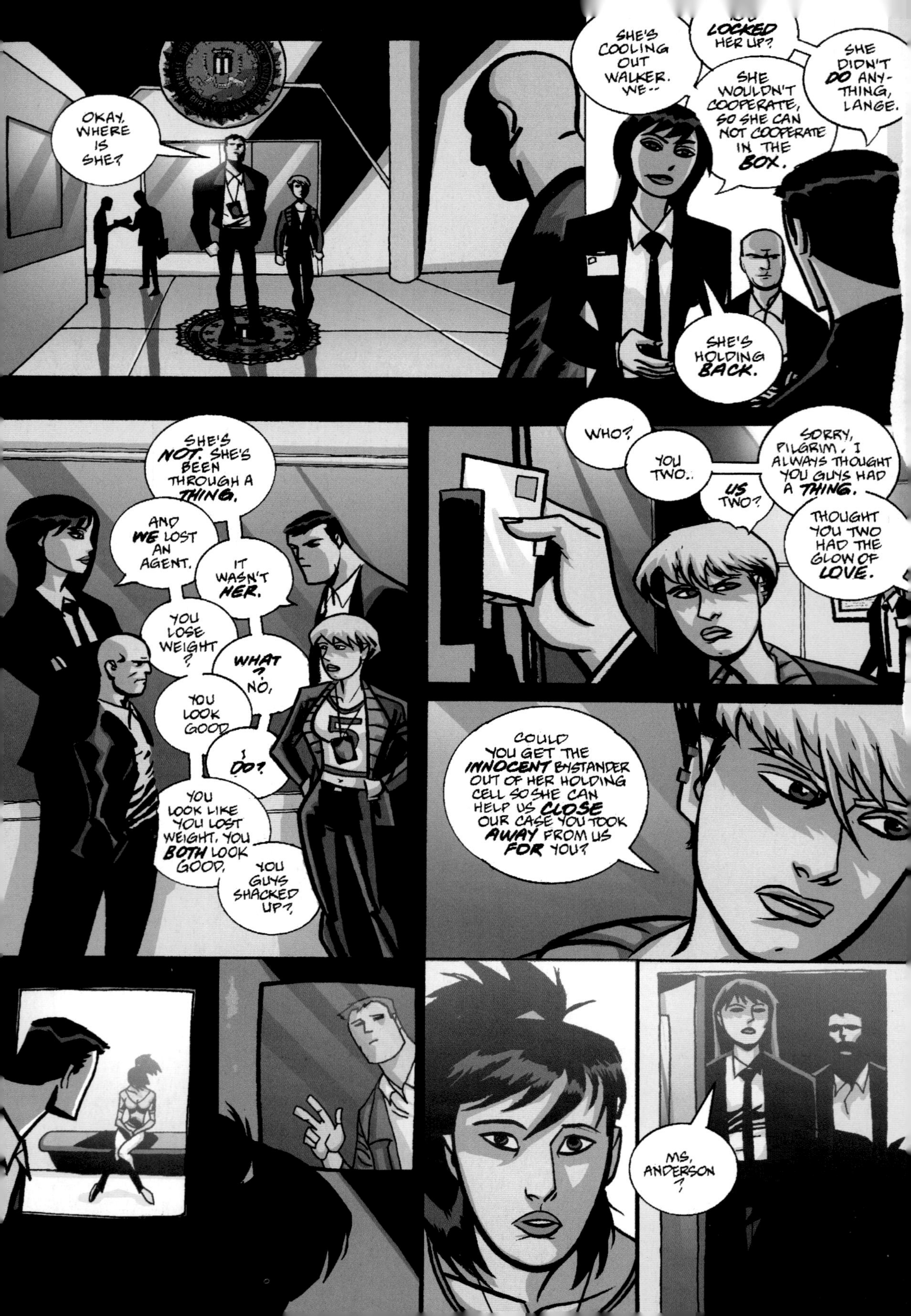

OKAY, WHERE IS SHE?
SHE'S COOLING OUT WALKER. WE--
LOCKED HER UP?
SHE WOULDN'T COOPERATE, SO SHE CAN NOT COOPERATE IN THE BOX.
SHE DIDN'T DO ANY-THING, LANGE.
SHE'S HOLDING BACK.
SHE'S NOT. SHE'S BEEN THROUGH A THING.
AND WE LOST AN AGENT.
IT WASN'T HER.
YOU LOSE WEIGHT?
WHAT? NO,
YOU LOOK GOOD.
I DO?
YOU LOOK LIKE YOU LOST WEIGHT. YOU BOTH LOOK GOOD.
YOU GUYS SHACKED UP?
WHO?
YOU TWO..
US TWO?
SORRY, PILGRIM, I ALWAYS THOUGHT YOU GUYS HAD A THING.
THOUGHT YOU TWO HAD THE GLOW OF LOVE.
COULD YOU GET THE INNOCENT BYSTANDER OUT OF HER HOLDING CELL SO SHE CAN HELP US CLOSE OUR CASE YOU TOOK AWAY FROM US FOR YOU?
MS. ANDERSON?

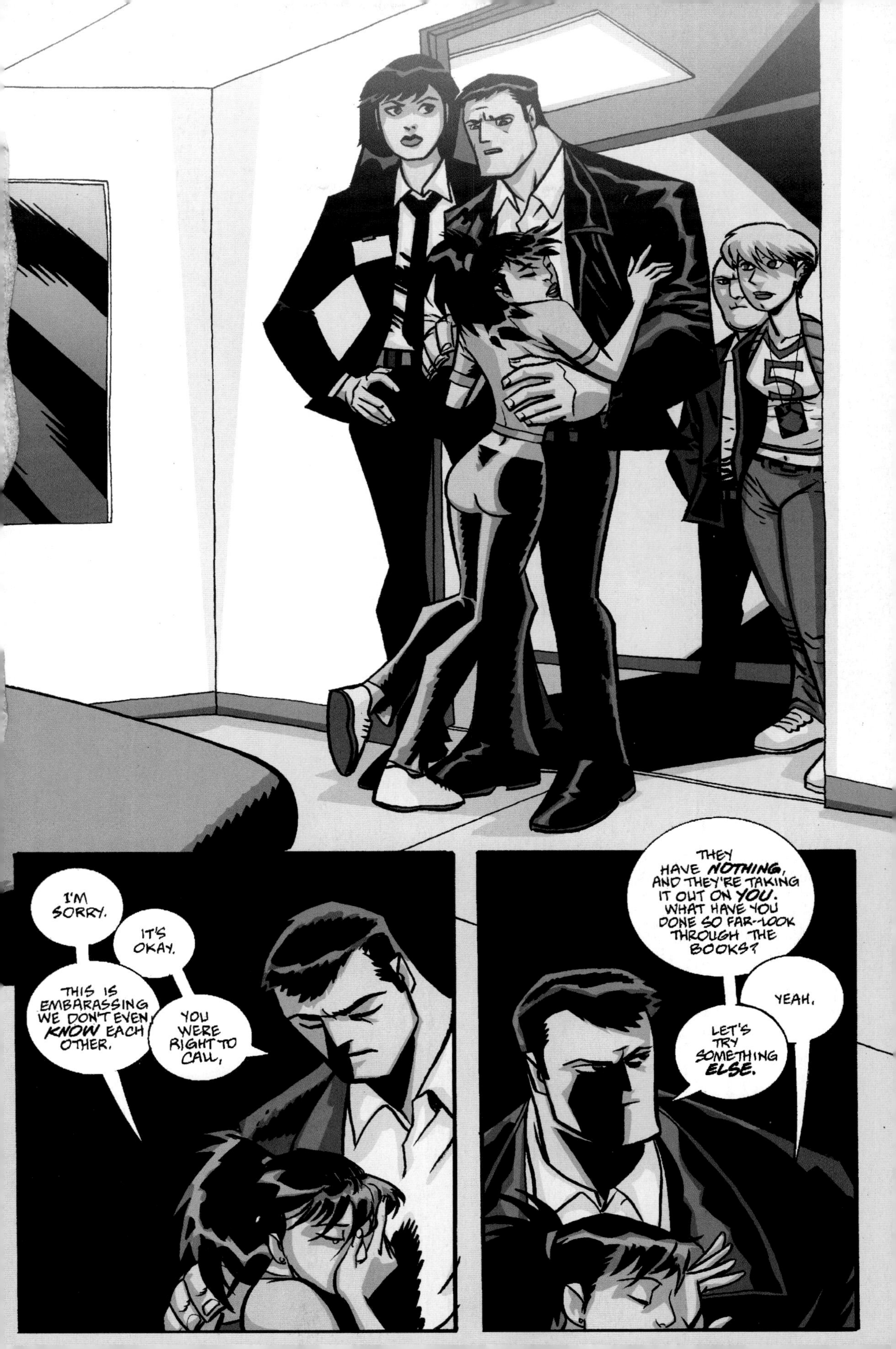
I'M SORRY.
IT'S OKAY.
THIS IS EMBARASSING WE DON'T EVEN KNOW EACH OTHER.
YOU WERE RIGHT TO CALL,
THEY HAVE NOTHING, AND THEY'RE TAKING IT OUT ON YOU. WHAT HAVE YOU DONE SO FAR--LOOK THROUGH THE BOOKS?
YEAH.
LET'S TRY SOMETHING ELSE.

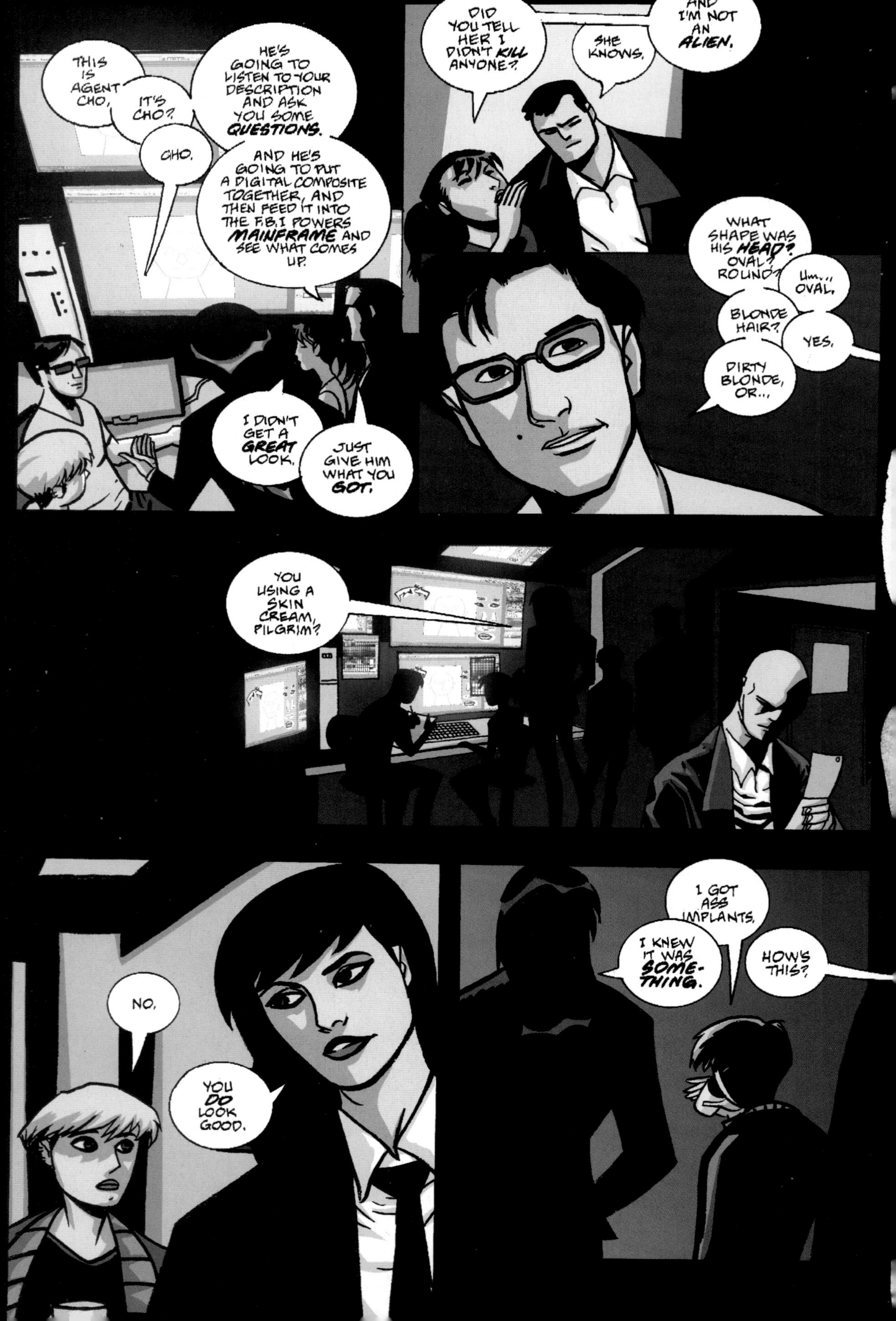
THIS IS AGENT CHO.
IT'S CHO?
CHO.
HE'S GOING TO LISTEN TO YOUR DESCRIPTION AND ASK YOU SOME QUESTIONS.
AND HE'S GOING TO PUT A DIGITAL COMPOSITE TOGETHER, AND THEN FEED IT INTO THE F.B.I POWERS MAINFRAME AND SEE WHAT COMES UP.
I DIDN'T GET A GREAT LOOK.
JUST GIVE HIM WHAT YOU GOT.
DID YOU TELL HER I DIDN'T KILL ANYONE?
SHE KNOWS.
AND I'M NOT AN ALIEN.
WHAT SHAPE WAS HIS HEAD? OVAL? ROUND?
UM... OVAL.
BLONDE HAIR?
YES.
DIRTY BLONDE, OR...
YOU USING A SKIN CREAM, PILGRIM?
NO.
YOU DO LOOK GOOD.
I GOT ASS IMPLANTS.
I KNEW IT WAS SOME-THING.
HOW'S THIS?

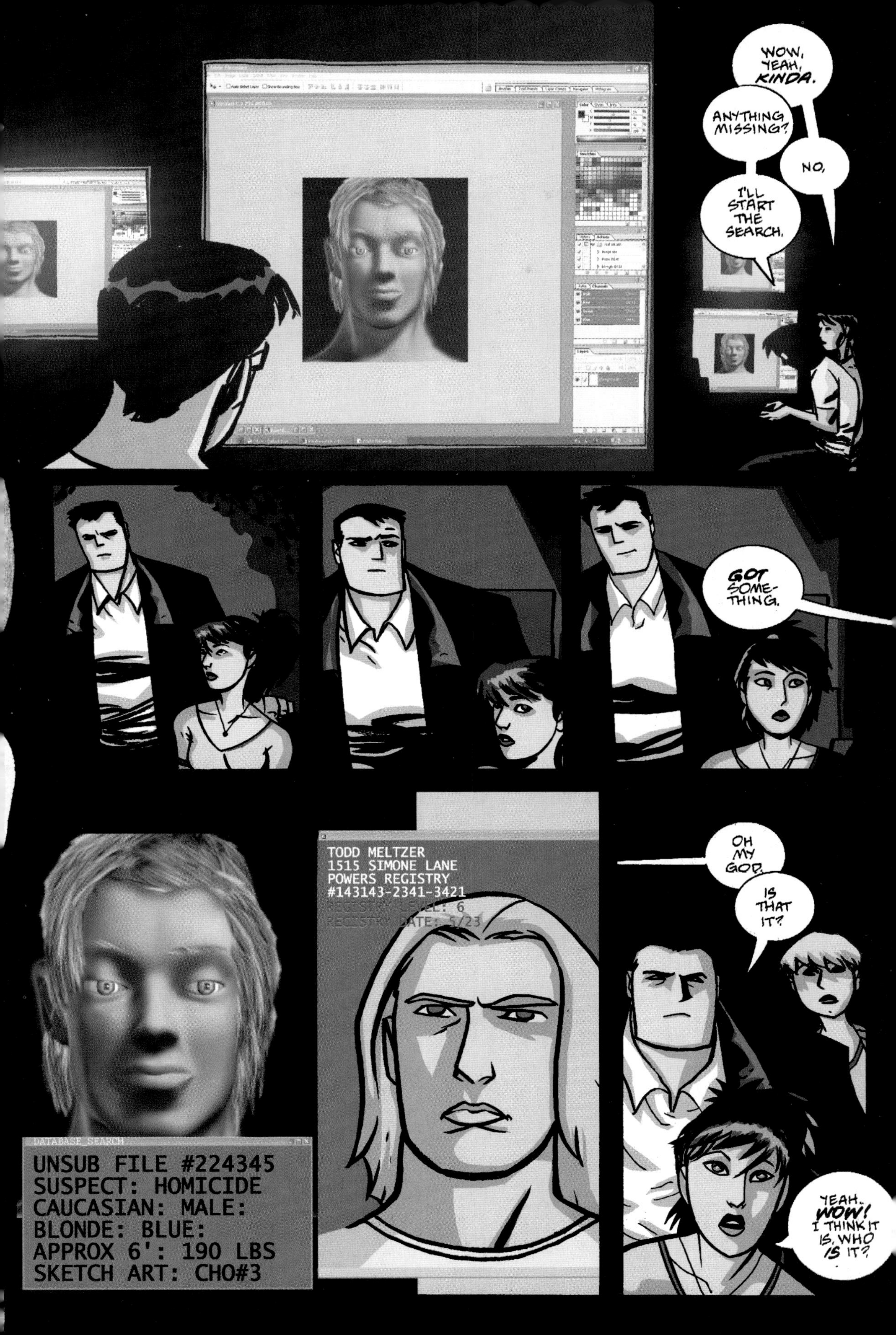
WOW, YEAH, KINDA.
ANYTHING MISSING?
NO,
I'LL START THE SEARCH.
GOT SOME-THING.
DATABASE_SEARCH
UNSUB FILE #224345
SUSPECT: HOMICIDE
CAUCASIAN: MALE:
BLONDE: BLUE:
APPROX 6': 190 LBS
SKETCH ART: CHO#3
TODD MELTZER
1515 SIMONE LANE
POWERS REGISTRY
#143143-2341-3421
REGISTRY LEVEL: 6
REGISTRY DATE: 5/23
OH MY GOD.
IS THAT IT?
YEAH.. WOW! I THINK IT IS. WHO IS IT?

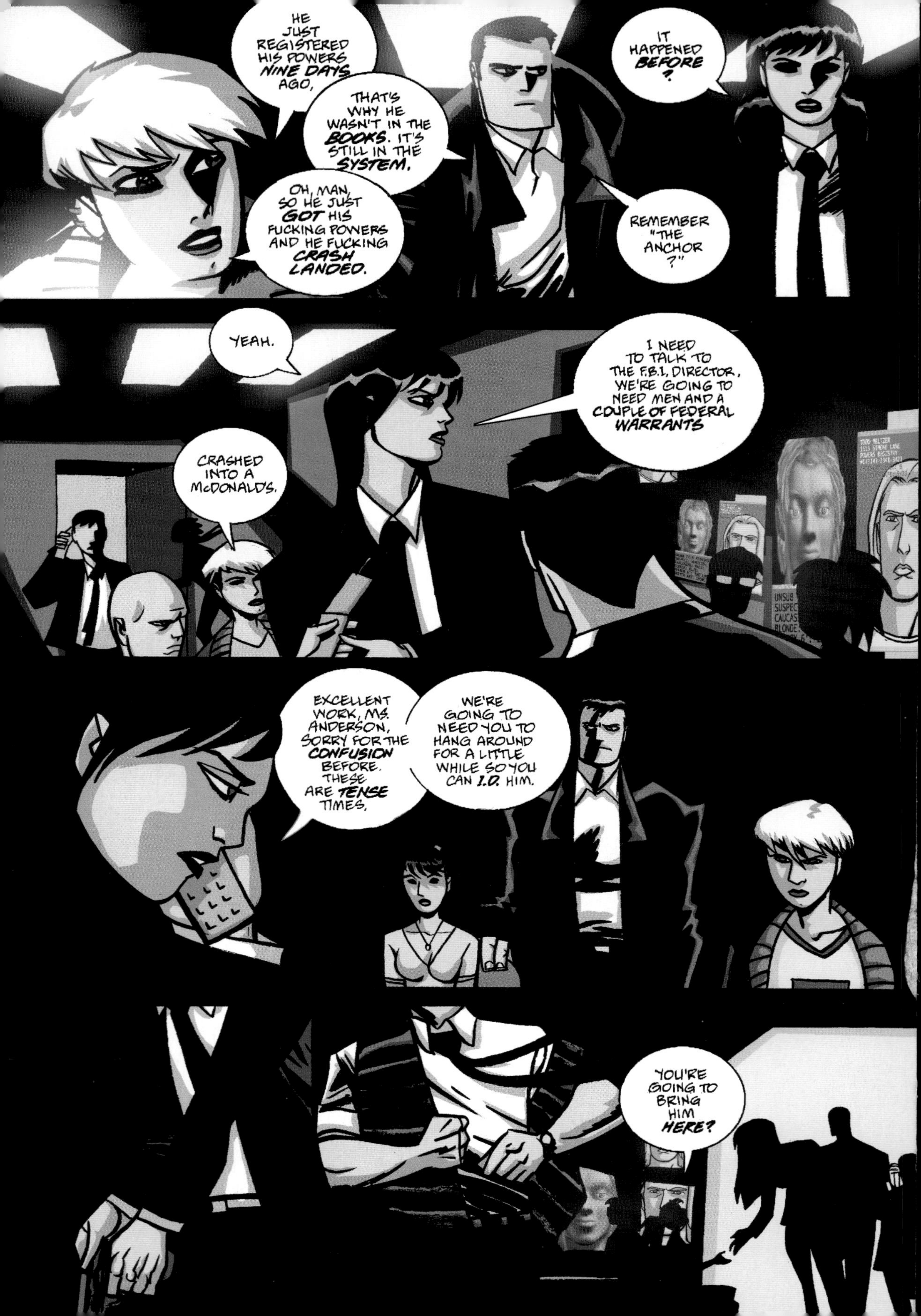
HE JUST REGISTERED HIS POWERS NINE DAYS AGO,
THAT'S WHY HE WASN'T IN THE BOOKS. IT'S STILL IN THE SYSTEM.
OH, MAN, SO HE JUST GOT HIS FUCKING POWERS AND HE FUCKING CRASH LANDED.
IT HAPPENED BEFORE ?
REMEMBER "THE ANCHOR ?"
YEAH.
CRASHED INTO A McDONALD'S.
I NEED TO TALK TO THE F.B.I. DIRECTOR. WE'RE GOING TO NEED MEN AND A COUPLE OF FEDERAL WARRANTS
EXCELLENT WORK, MS. ANDERSON, SORRY FOR THE CONFUSION BEFORE. THESE ARE TENSE TIMES.
WE'RE GOING TO NEED YOU TO HANG AROUND FOR A LITTLE WHILE SO YOU CAN I.D. HIM.
YOU'RE GOING TO BRING HIM HERE?

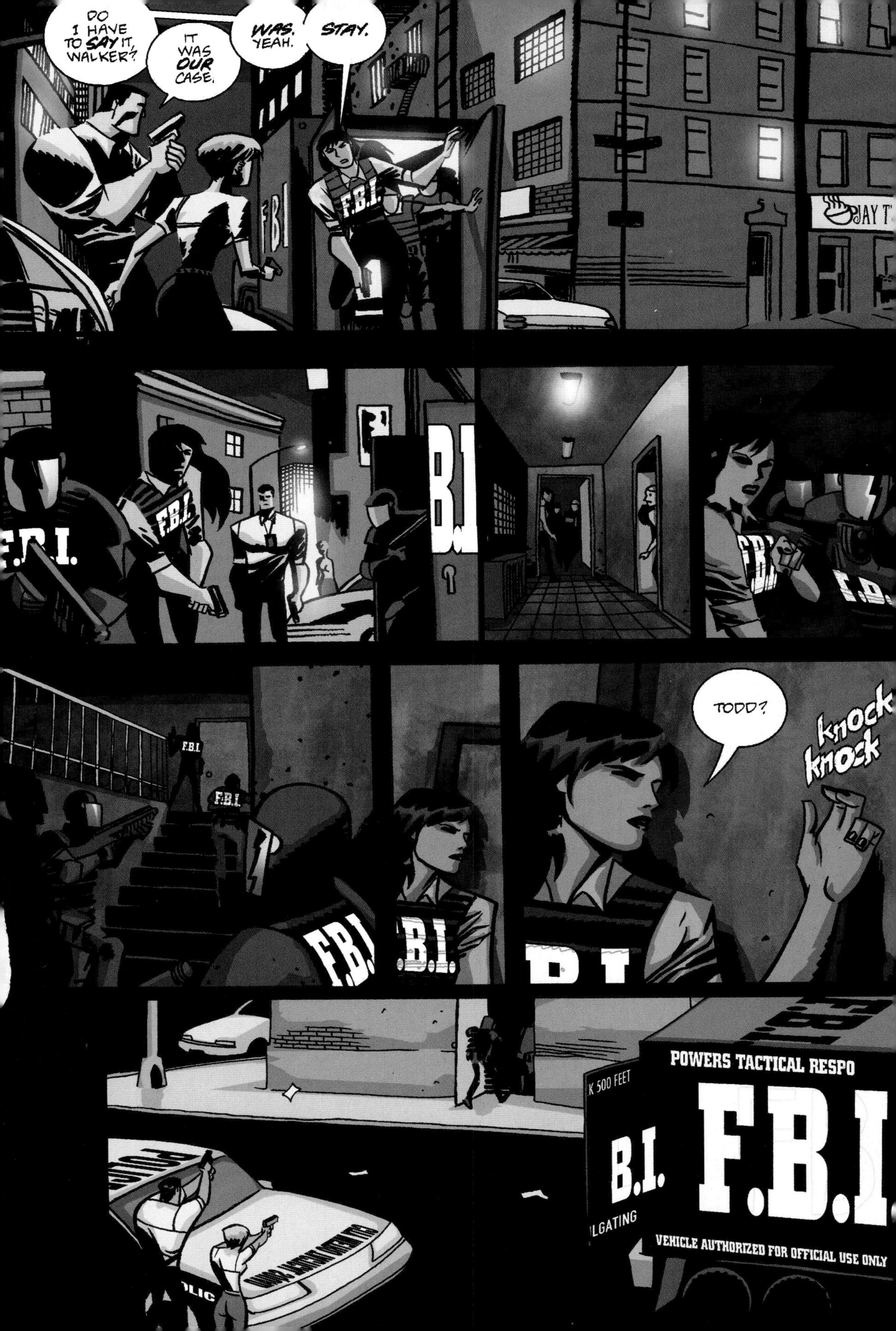
DO I HAVE TO SAY IT, WALKER?
IT WAS OUR CASE.
WAS. YEAH.
STAY.
F.B.I.
JAY T'
TODD?
knock knock
POWERS TACTICAL RESPO
F.B.I.
VEHICLE AUTHORIZED FOR OFFICIAL USE ONLY
K 500 FEET
B.I.
LGATING

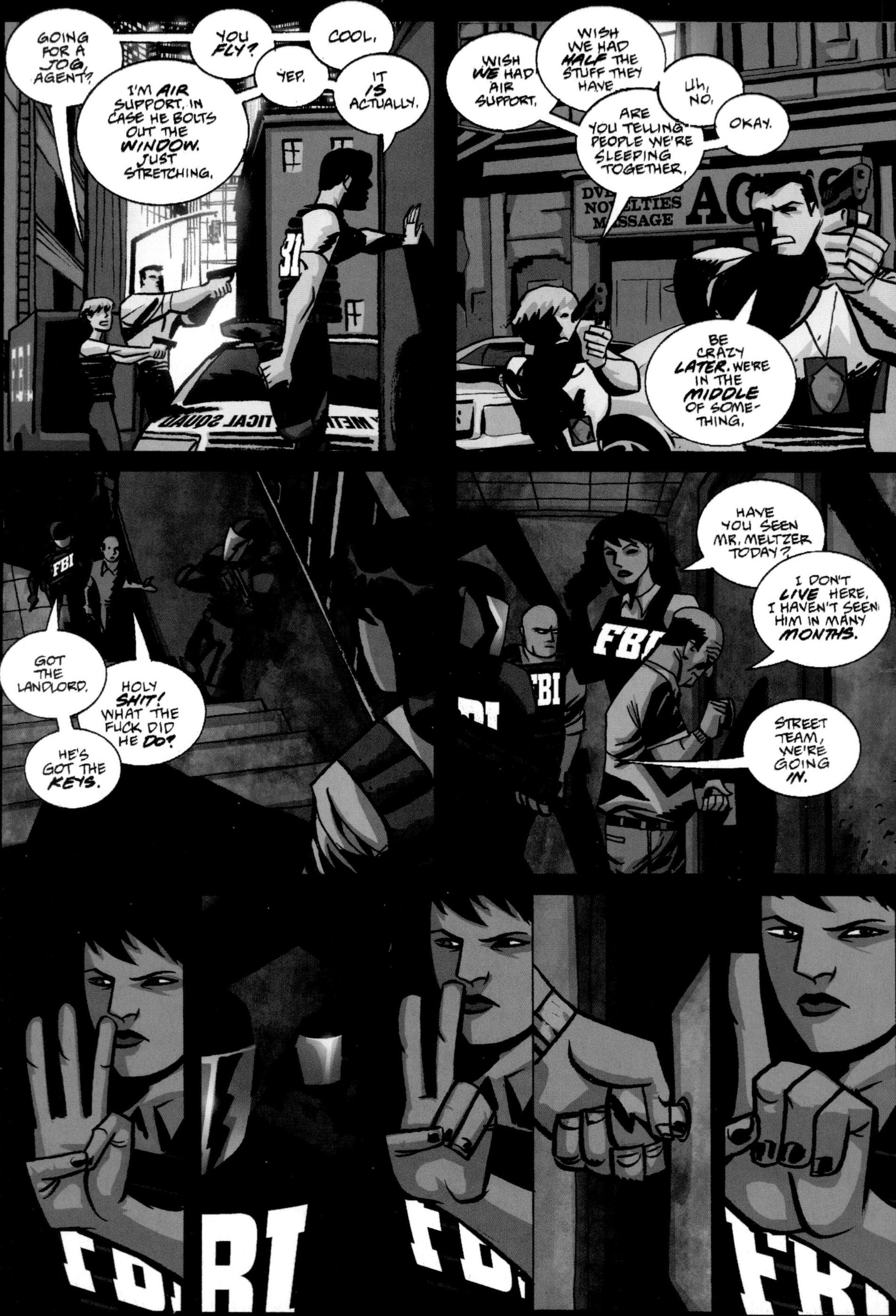
GOING FOR A JOG, AGENT?
I'M AIR SUPPORT, IN CASE HE BOLTS OUT THE WINDOW. JUST STRETCHING.
YOU FLY?
YEP.
COOL.
IT IS ACTUALLY.
WISH WE HAD AIR SUPPORT.
WISH WE HAD HALF THE STUFF THEY HAVE.
ARE YOU TELLING PEOPLE WE'RE SLEEPING TOGETHER.
UH, NO.
OKAY.
DVD NOVELTIES MASSAGE
BE CRAZY LATER. WE'RE IN THE MIDDLE OF SOMETHING.
GOT THE LANDLORD.
HOLY SHIT! WHAT THE FUCK DID HE DO?
HE'S GOT THE KEYS.
HAVE YOU SEEN MR. MELTZER TODAY?
I DON'T LIVE HERE. I HAVEN'T SEEN HIM IN MANY MONTHS.
STREET TEAM, WE'RE GOING IN.

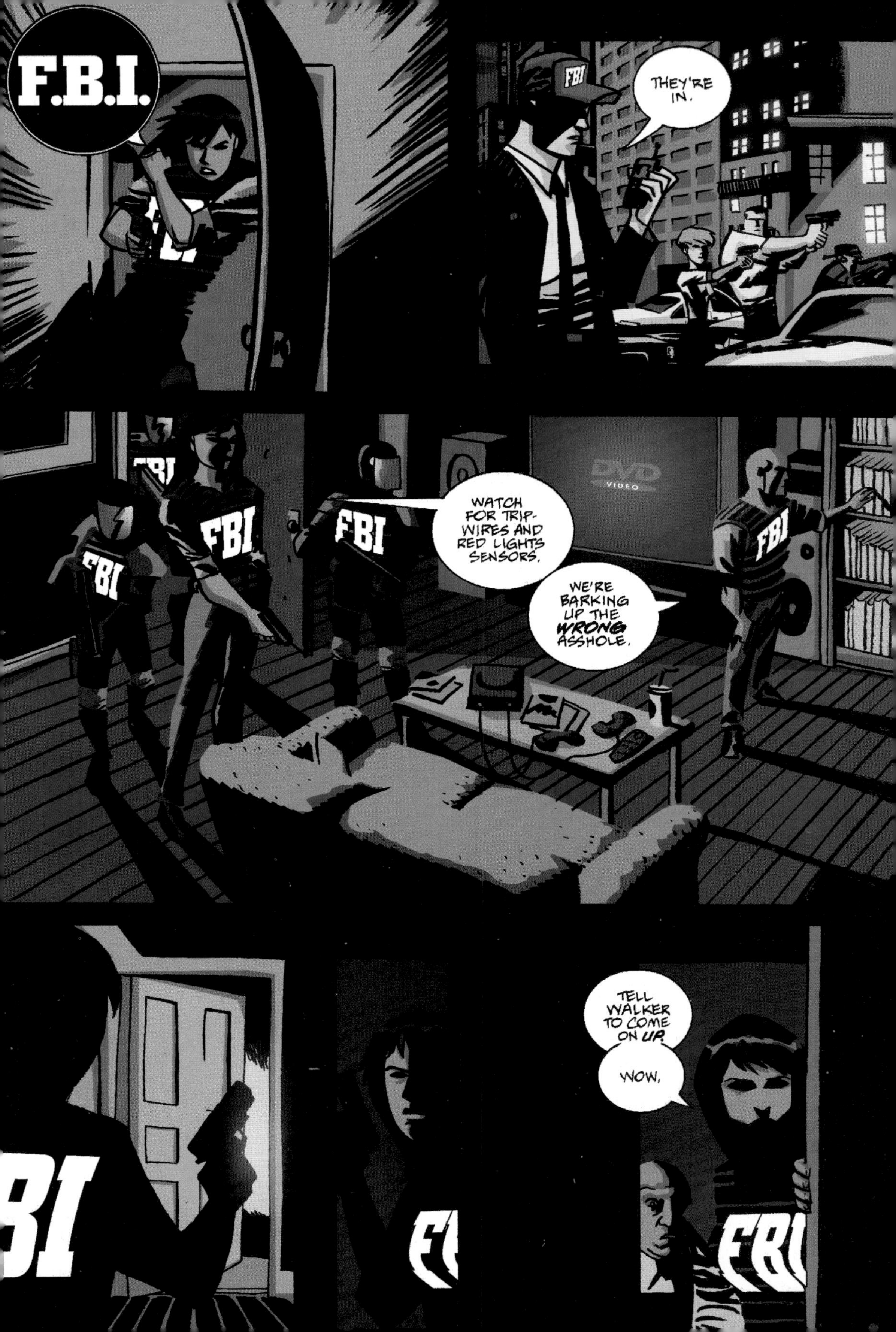
F.B.I.
THEY'RE IN.
FBI
WATCH FOR TRIP-WIRES AND RED LIGHTS SENSORS.
WE'RE BARKING UP THE WRONG ASSHOLE.
DVD VIDEO
TELL WALKER TO COME ON UP.
WOW.

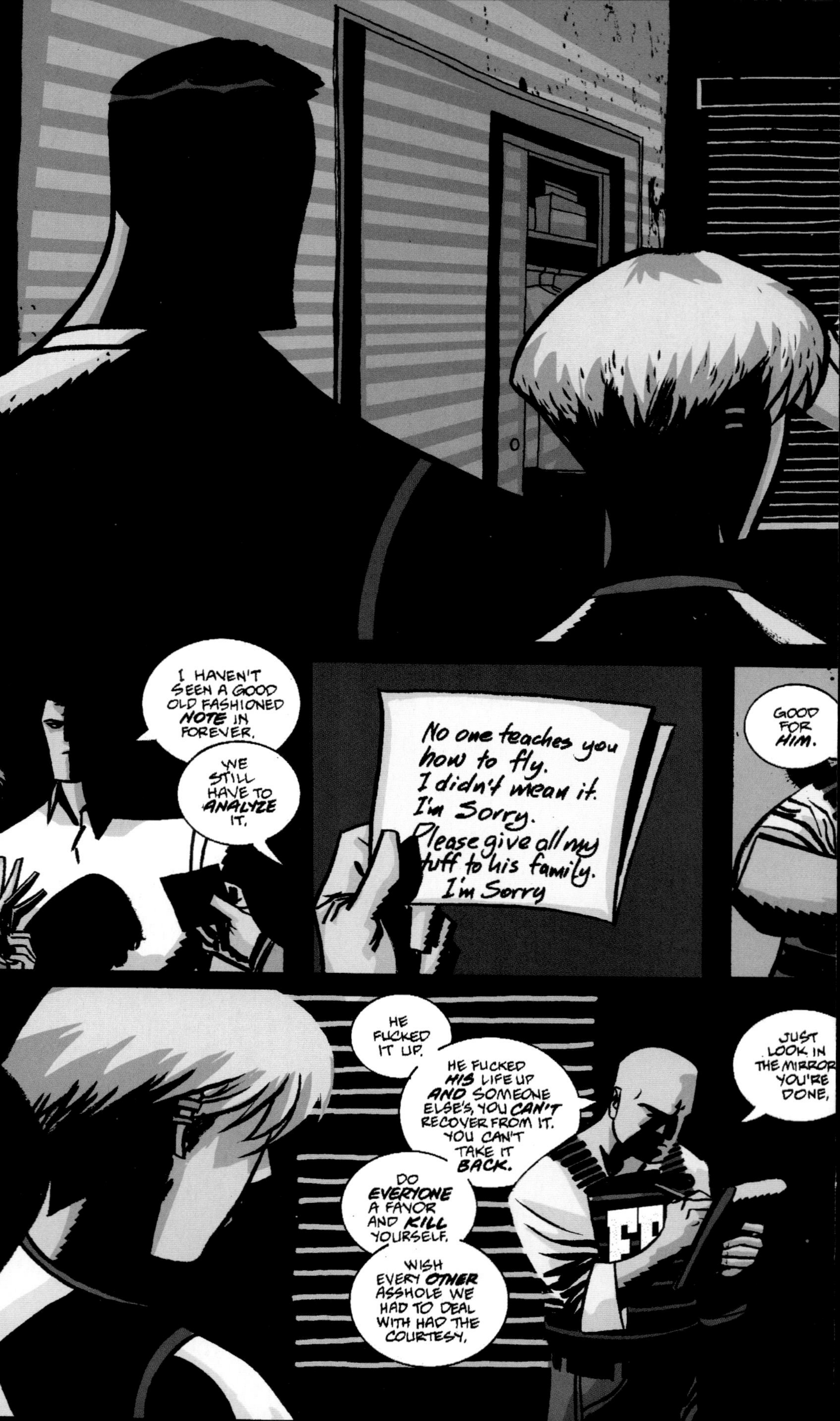
I HAVEN'T SEEN A GOOD OLD FASHIONED NOTE IN FOREVER.
WE STILL HAVE TO ANALYZE IT.
No one teaches you how to fly. I didn't mean it. I'm Sorry. Please give all my stuff to his family. I'm Sorry
GOOD FOR HIM.
HE FUCKED IT UP.
HE FUCKED HIS LIFE UP AND SOMEONE ELSE'S. YOU CAN'T RECOVER FROM IT. YOU CAN'T TAKE IT BACK.
DO EVERYONE A FAVOR AND KILL YOURSELF.
WISH EVERY OTHER ASSHOLE WE HAD TO DEAL WITH HAD THE COURTESY.
JUST LOOK IN THE MIRROR. YOU'RE DONE.

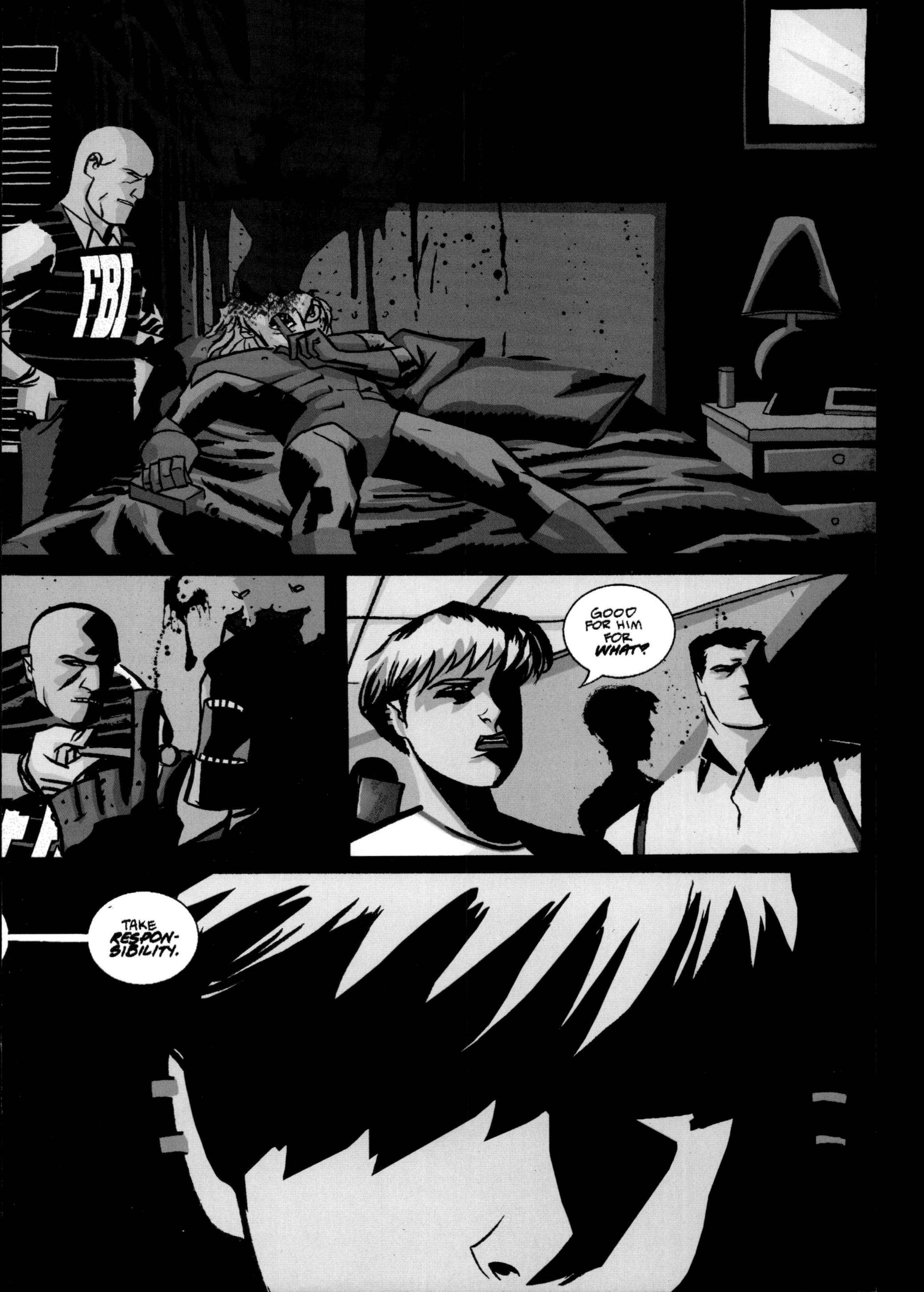
GOOD FOR HIM FOR WHAT?
TAKE RESPON-SIBILITY.

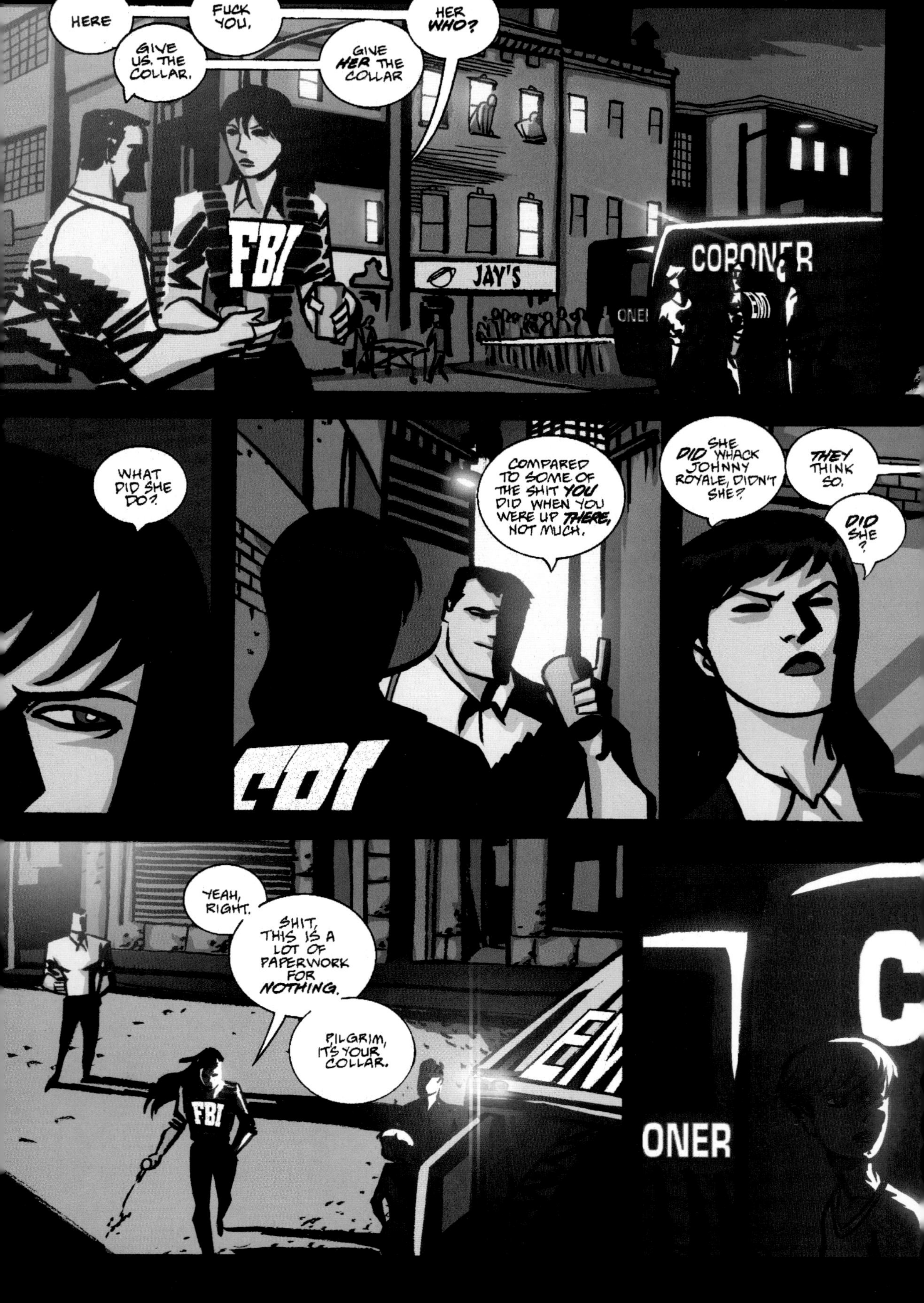
HERE
GIVE US. THE COLLAR.
FUCK YOU.
GIVE HER THE COLLAR
HER WHO?
FBI
JAY'S
CORONER
WHAT DID SHE DO?
COMPARED TO SOME OF THE SHIT YOU DID WHEN YOU WERE UP THERE, NOT MUCH.
SHE DID WHACK JOHNNY ROYALE, DIDN'T SHE?
THEY THINK SO.
DID SHE?
YEAH, RIGHT.
SHIT, THIS IS A LOT OF PAPERWORK FOR NOTHING.
PILGRIM, IT'S YOUR COLLAR.
FBI
ONER

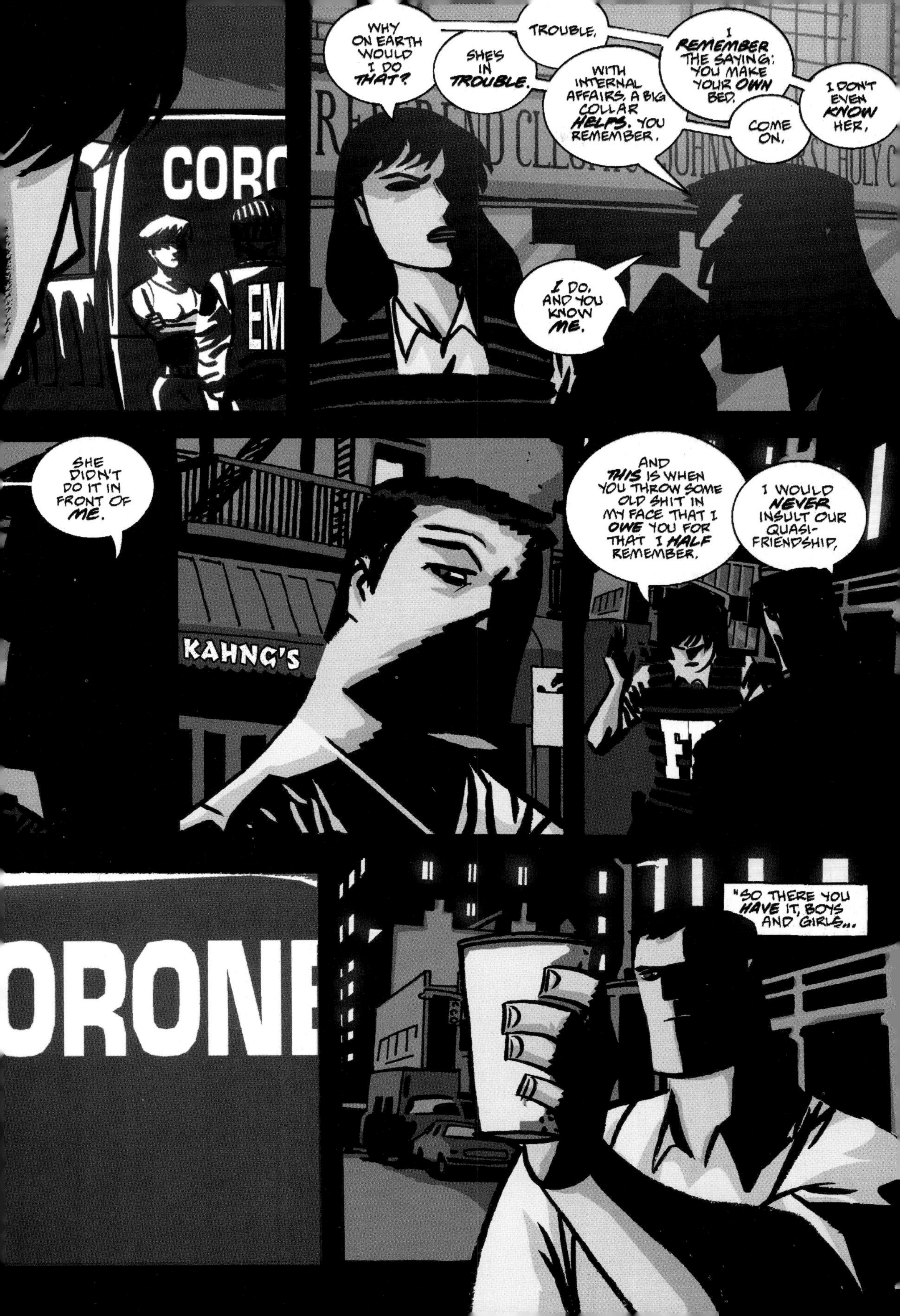

CORO
EM
WHY ON EARTH WOULD I DO THAT?
SHE'S IN TROUBLE.
TROUBLE.
WITH INTERNAL AFFAIRS, A BIG COLLAR HELPS. YOU REMEMBER.
I REMEMBER THE SAYING: YOU MAKE YOUR OWN BED.
COME ON.
I DON'T EVEN KNOW HER.
I DO, AND YOU KNOW ME.
SHE DIDN'T DO IT IN FRONT OF ME.
KAHNG'S
AND THIS IS WHEN YOU THROW SOME OLD SHIT IN MY FACE THAT I OWE YOU FOR THAT I HALF REMEMBER.
I WOULD NEVER INSULT OUR QUASI-FRIENDSHIP.
ORONE
"SO THERE YOU HAVE IT, BOYS AND GIRLS...

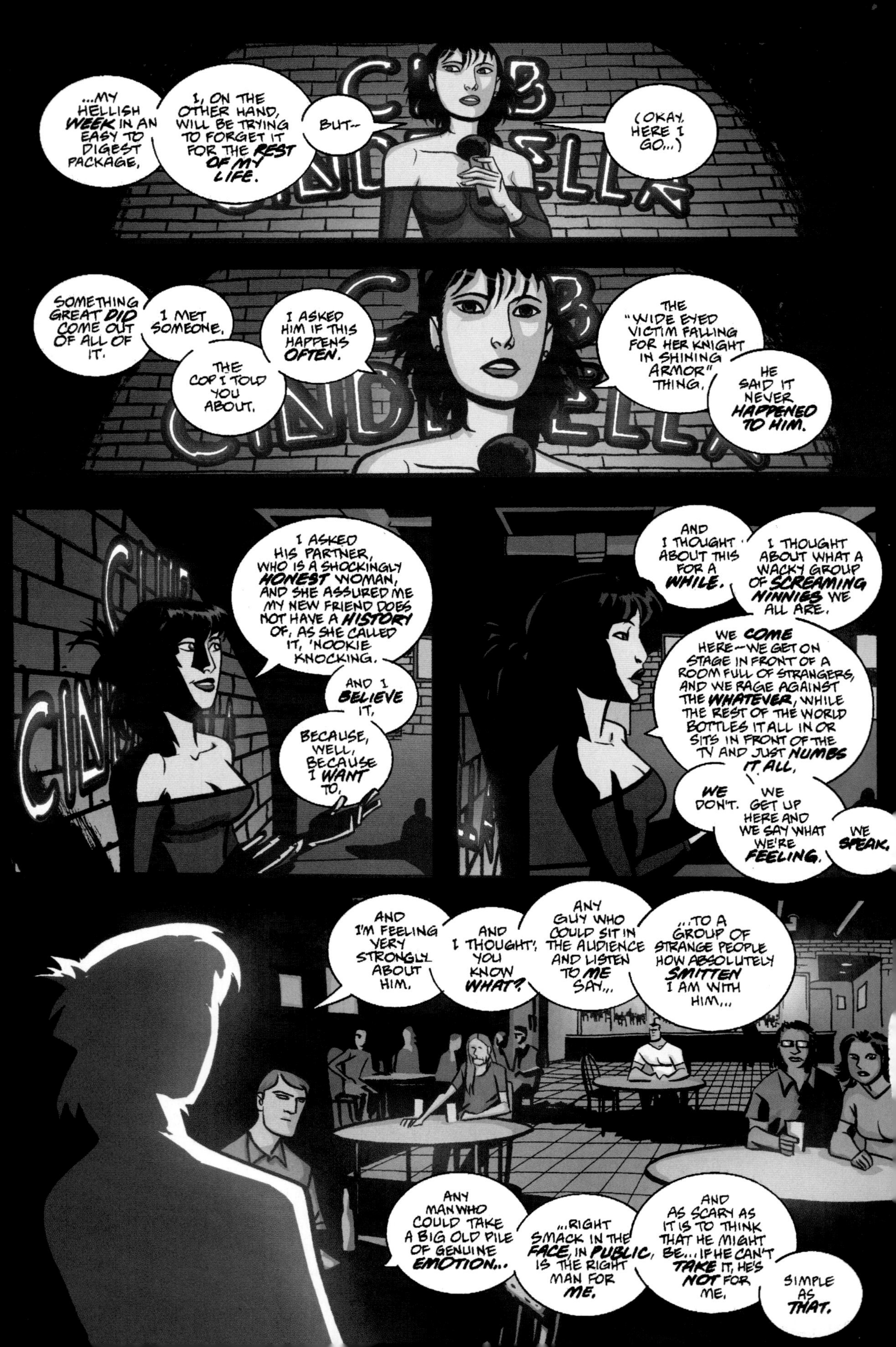

...MY HELLISH WEEK IN AN EASY TO DIGEST PACKAGE,
I, ON THE OTHER HAND, WILL BE TRYING TO FORGET IT FOR THE REST OF MY LIFE.
BUT--
(OKAY, HERE I GO...)
SOMETHING GREAT DID COME OUT OF ALL OF IT.
I MET SOMEONE.
THE COP I TOLD YOU ABOUT.
I ASKED HIM IF THIS HAPPENS OFTEN.
THE "WIDE EYED VICTIM FALLING FOR HER KNIGHT IN SHINING ARMOR" THING.
HE SAID IT NEVER HAPPENED TO HIM.
I ASKED HIS PARTNER, WHO IS A SHOCKINGLY HONEST WOMAN, AND SHE ASSURED ME MY NEW FRIEND DOES NOT HAVE A HISTORY OF, AS SHE CALLED IT, 'NOOKIE KNOCKING.
AND I BELIEVE IT,
BECAUSE, WELL, BECAUSE I WANT TO,
AND I THOUGHT ABOUT THIS FOR A WHILE.
I THOUGHT ABOUT WHAT A WACKY GROUP OF SCREAMING NINNIES WE ALL ARE.
WE COME HERE--WE GET ON STAGE IN FRONT OF A ROOM FULL OF STRANGERS, AND WE RAGE AGAINST THE WHATEVER, WHILE THE REST OF THE WORLD BOTTLES IT ALL IN OR SITS IN FRONT OF THE TV AND JUST NUMBS IT ALL,
WE DON'T.
WE GET UP HERE AND WE SAY WHAT WE'RE FEELING.
WE SPEAK.
AND I'M FEELING VERY STRONGLY ABOUT HIM.
AND I THOUGHT, YOU KNOW WHAT?
ANY GUY WHO COULD SIT IN THE AUDIENCE AND LISTEN TO ME SAY...
...TO A GROUP OF STRANGE PEOPLE HOW ABSOLUTELY SMITTEN I AM WITH HIM...
ANY MAN WHO COULD TAKE A BIG OLD PILE OF GENUINE EMOTION...
...RIGHT SMACK IN THE FACE, IN PUBLIC, IS THE RIGHT MAN FOR ME.
AND AS SCARY AS IT IS TO THINK THAT HE MIGHT BE... IF HE CAN'T TAKE IT, HE'S NOT FOR ME.
SIMPLE AS THAT.

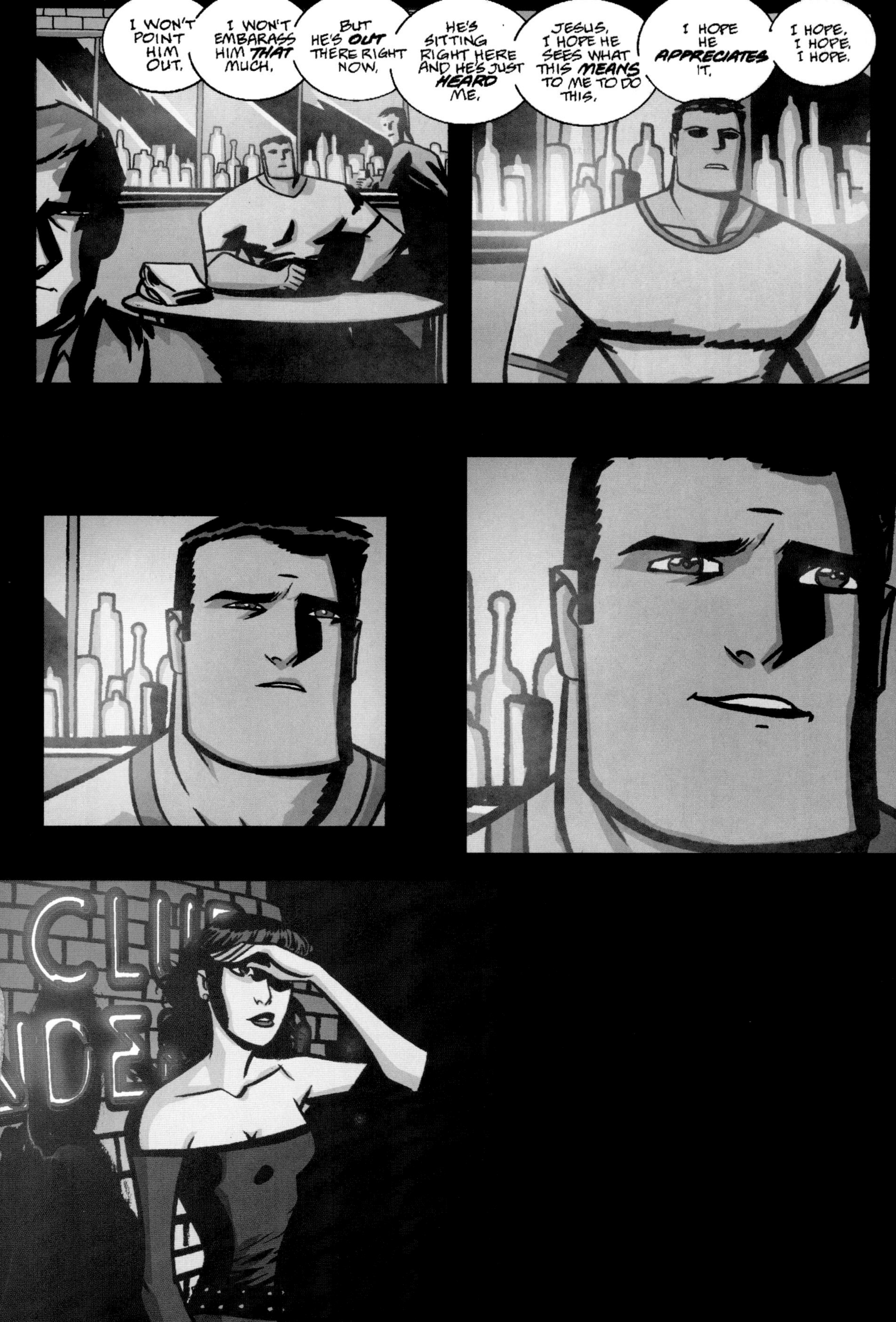
I WON'T POINT HIM OUT.
I WON'T EMBARASS HIM THAT MUCH.
BUT HE'S OUT THERE RIGHT NOW.
HE'S SITTING RIGHT HERE AND HE'S JUST HEARD ME.
JESUS, I HOPE HE SEES WHAT THIS MEANS TO ME TO DO THIS.
I HOPE HE APPRECIATES IT.
I HOPE, I HOPE, I HOPE.
CLU
NDE

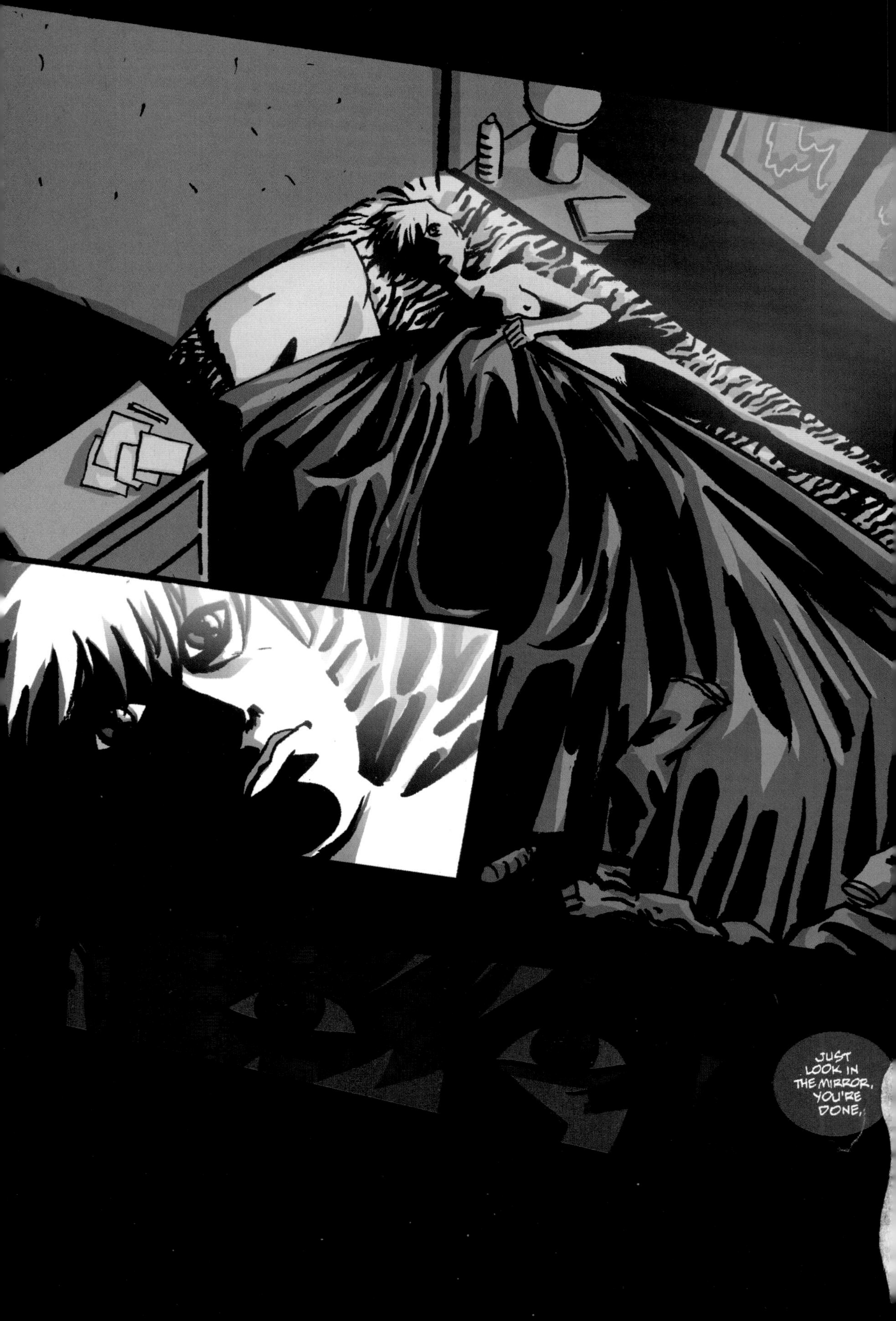
JUST LOOK IN THE MIRROR, YOU'RE DONE,

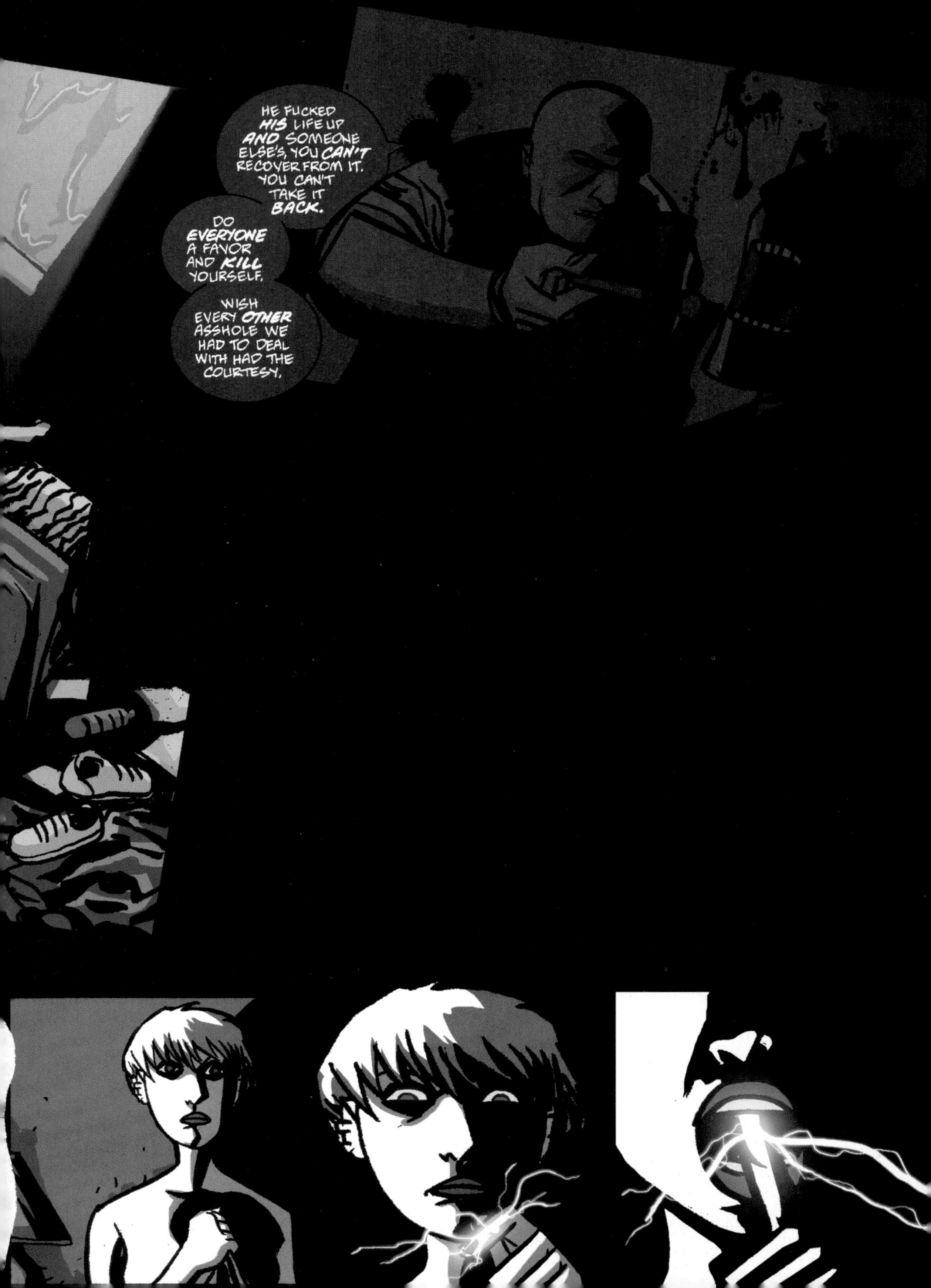
HE FUCKED HIS LIFE UP AND SOMEONE ELSE'S, YOU CAN'T RECOVER FROM IT. YOU CAN'T TAKE IT BACK.
DO EVERYONE A FAVOR AND KILL YOURSELF.
WISH EVERY OTHER ASSHOLE WE HAD TO DEAL WITH HAD THE COURTESY.

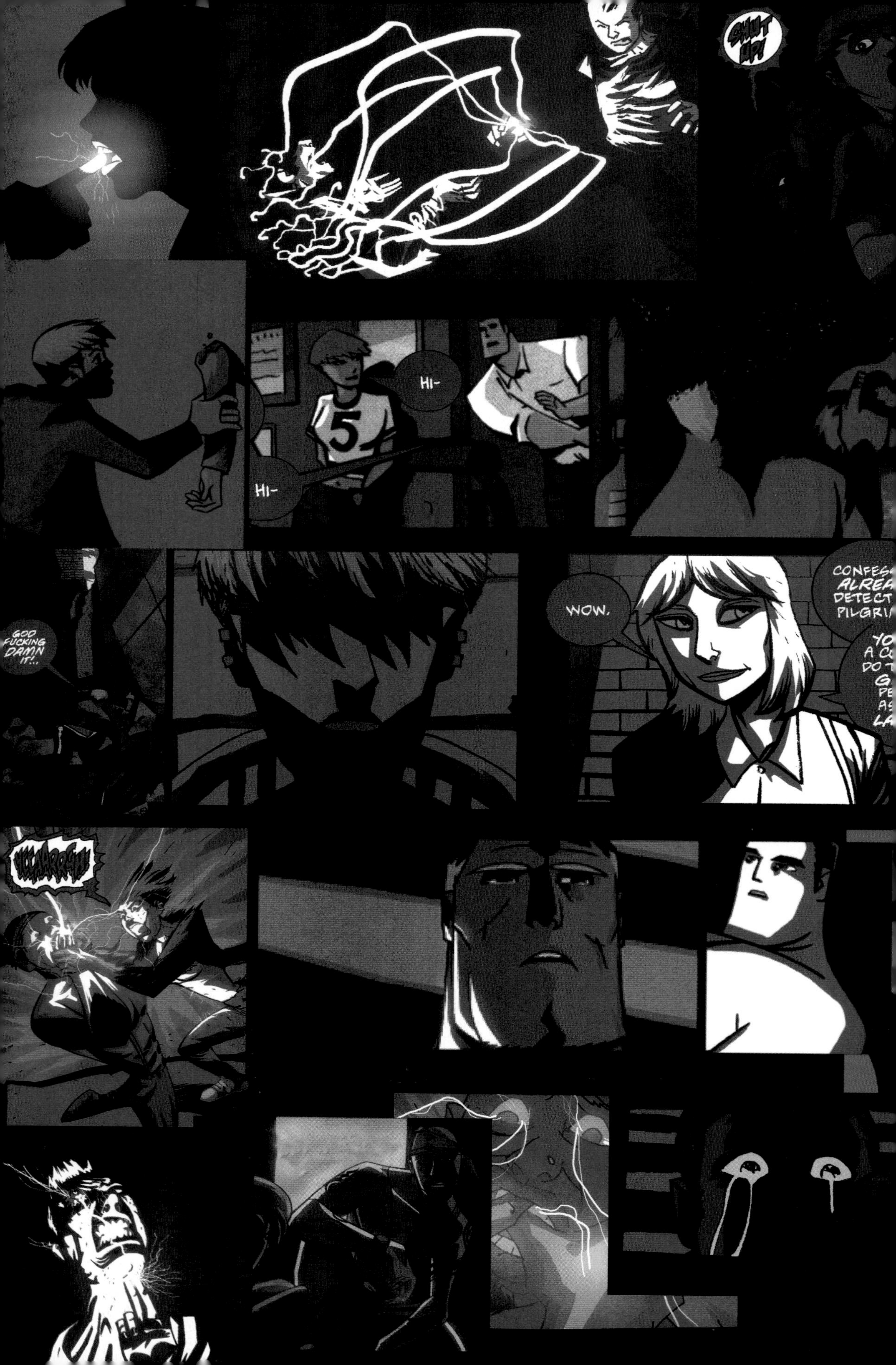

SHUT UP!
HI-
HI-
GOD FUCKING DAMN IT!..
WOW.

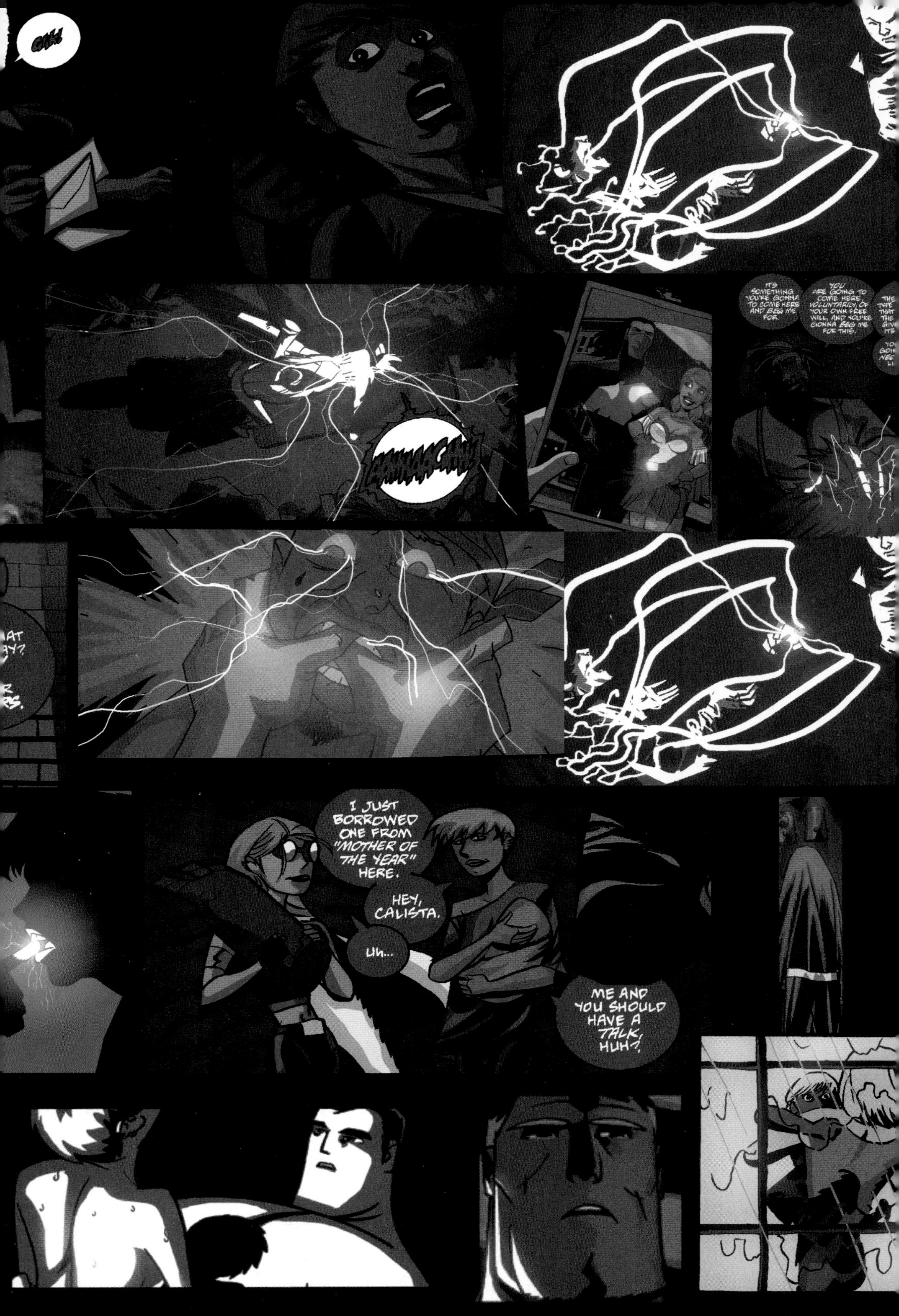

OHH!
IT'S SOMETHING YOU'RE GONNA TO COME HERE AND BEG ME FOR.
YOU ARE GOING TO COME HERE, VOLUNTARILY, OF YOUR OWN FREE WILL, AND YOU'RE GONNA BEG ME FOR THIS.
I JUST BORROWED ONE FROM "MOTHER OF THE YEAR" HERE.
HEY, CALISTA.
UH...
ME AND YOU SHOULD HAVE A TALK, HUH?!

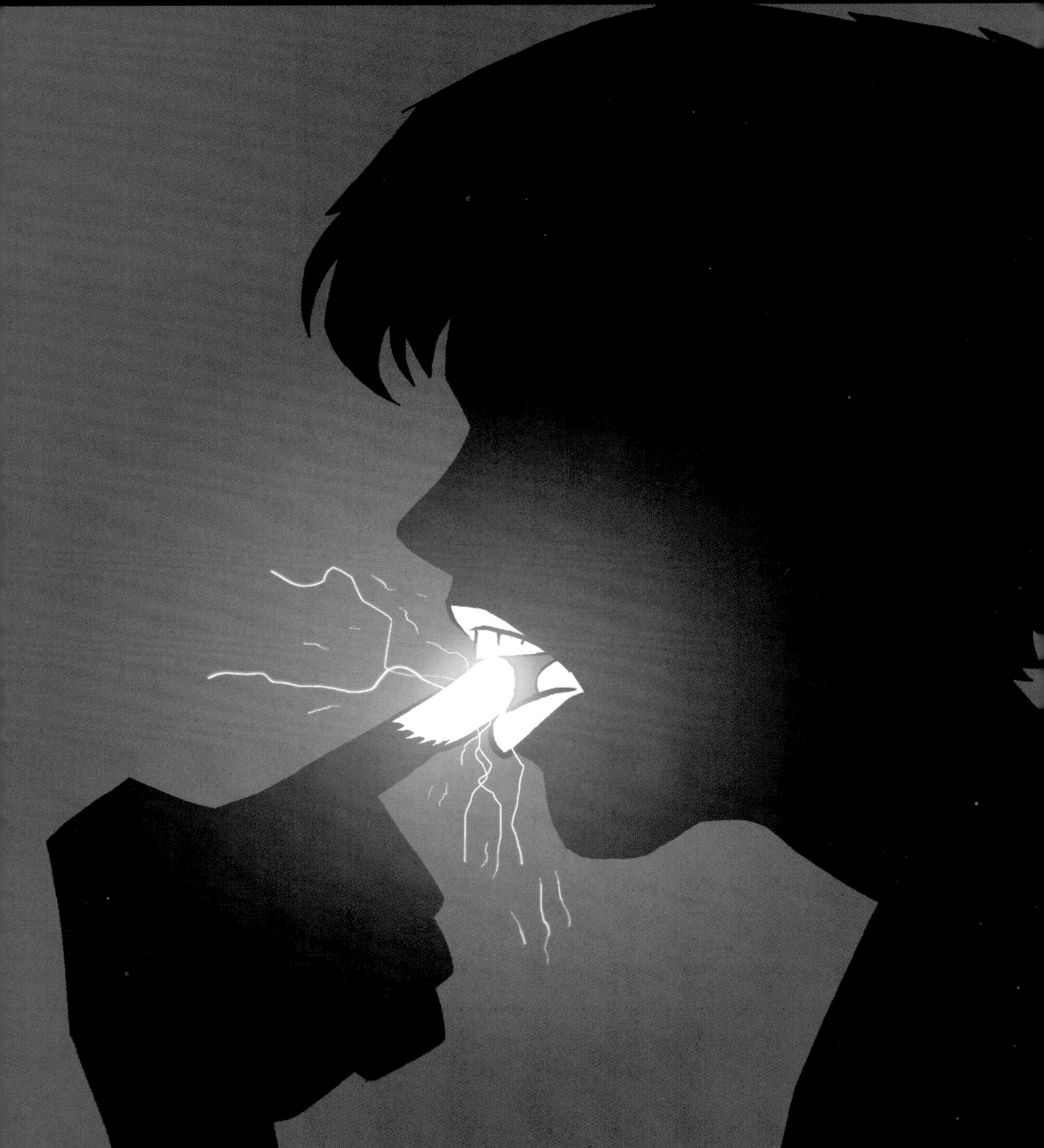

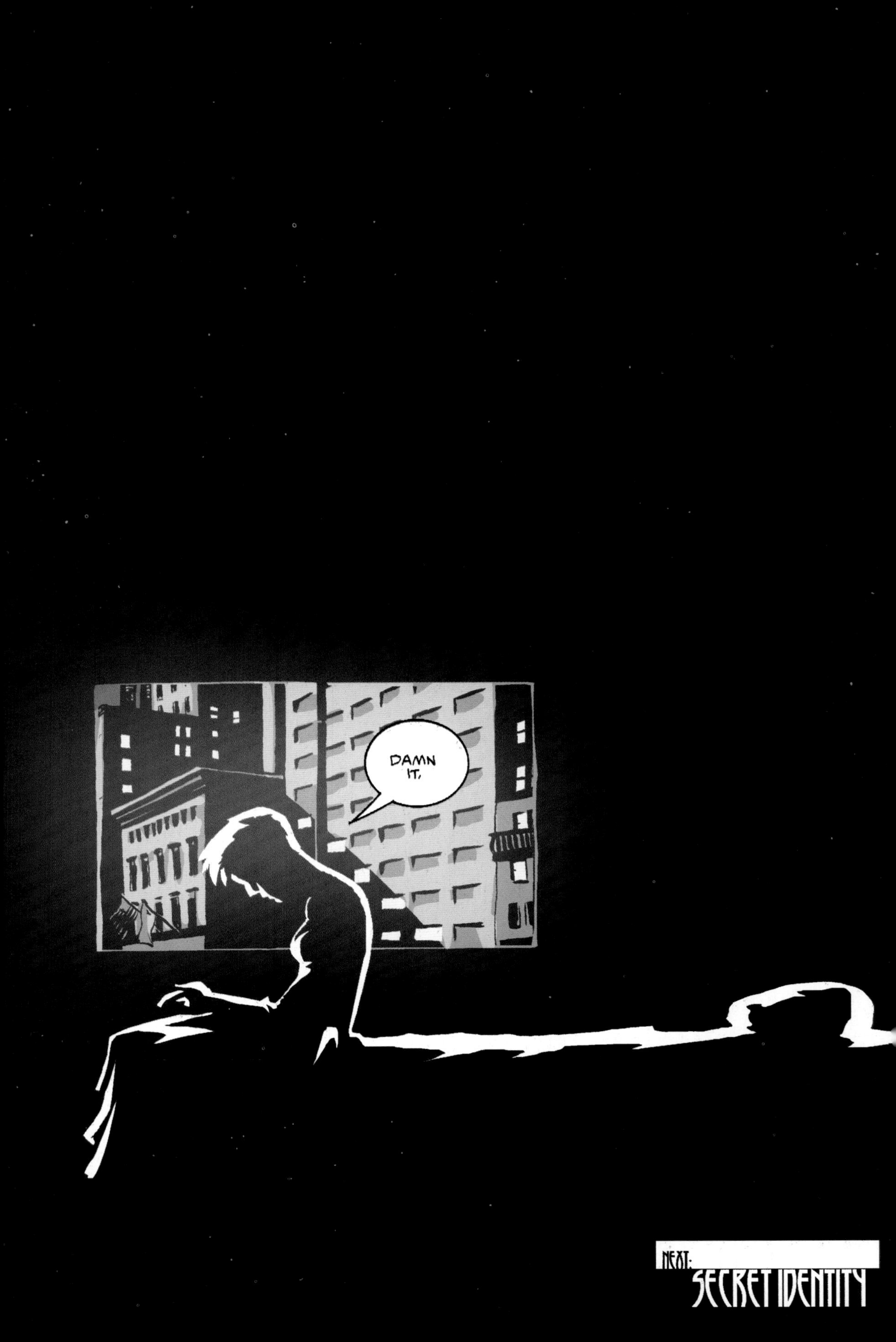
DAMN IT.
NEXT:
SECRET IDENTITY

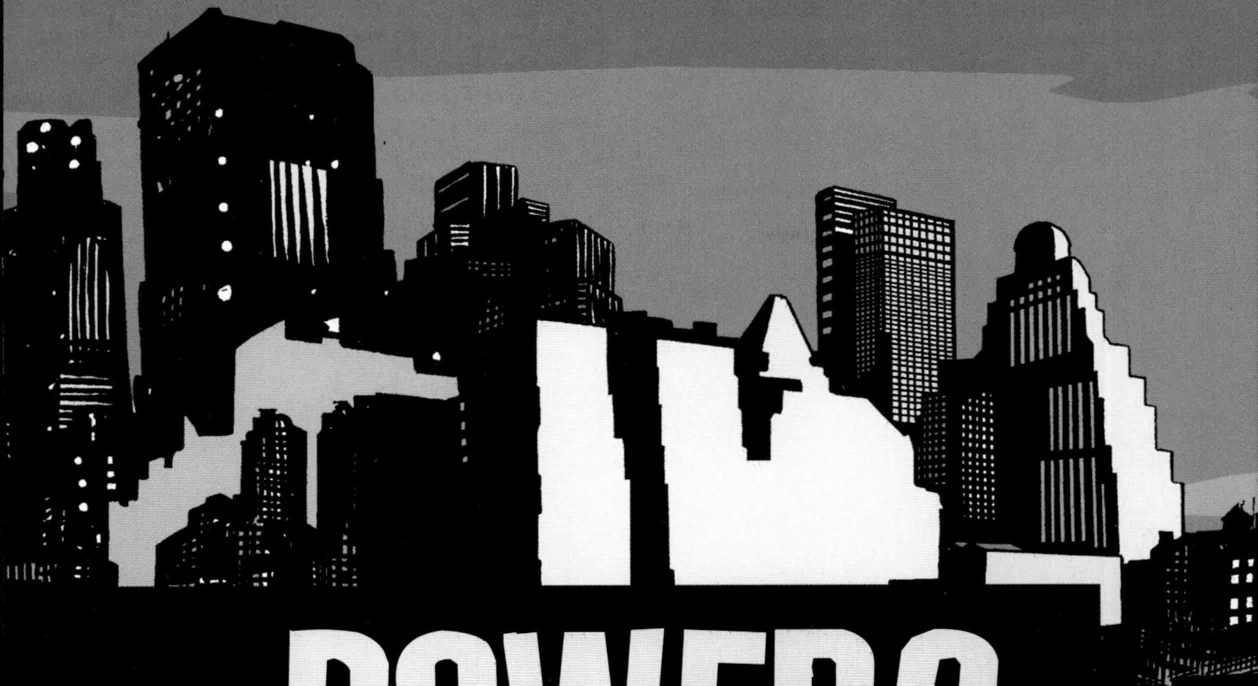

POWERS

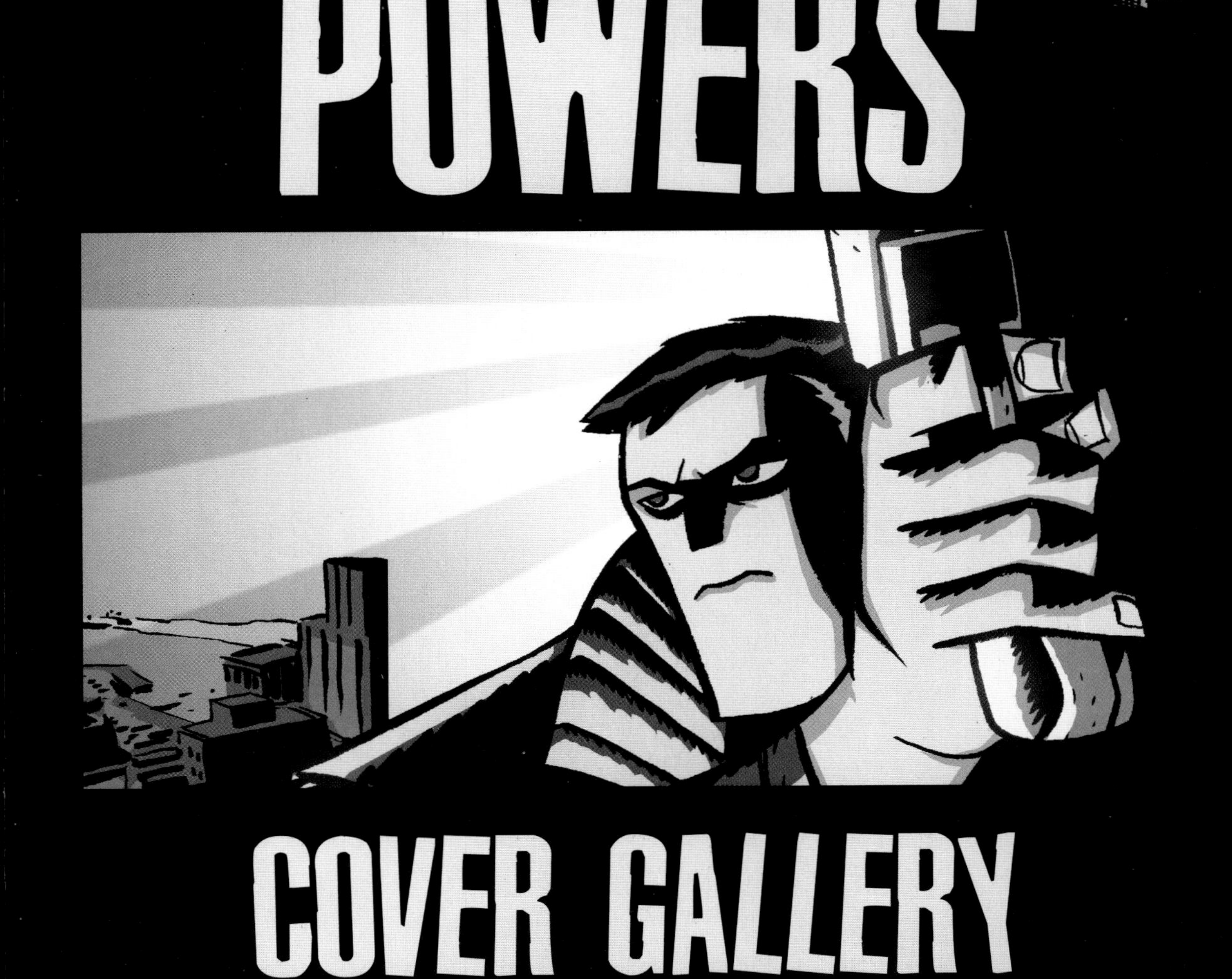

COVER GALLERY

#13

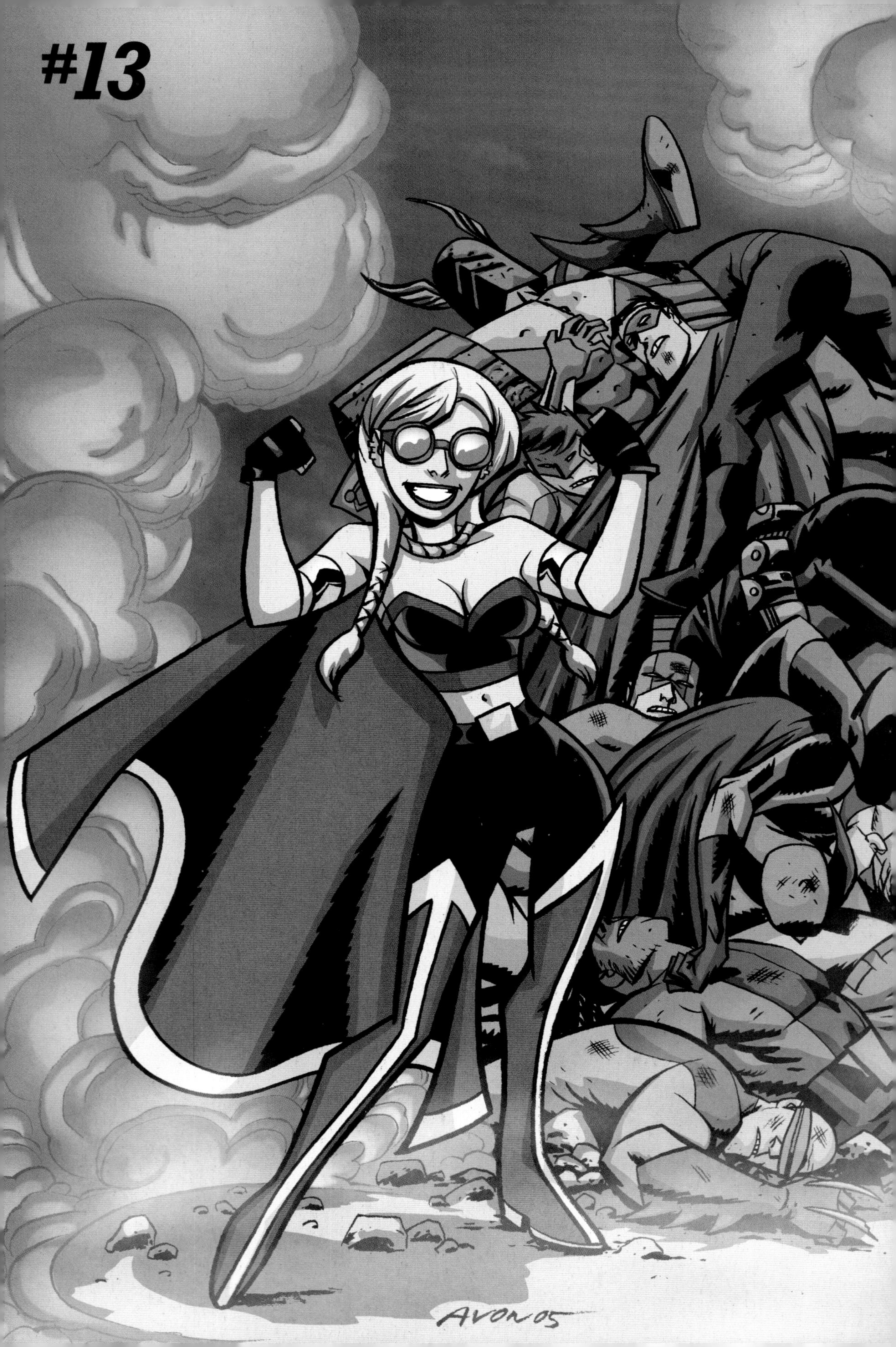
AVON 05

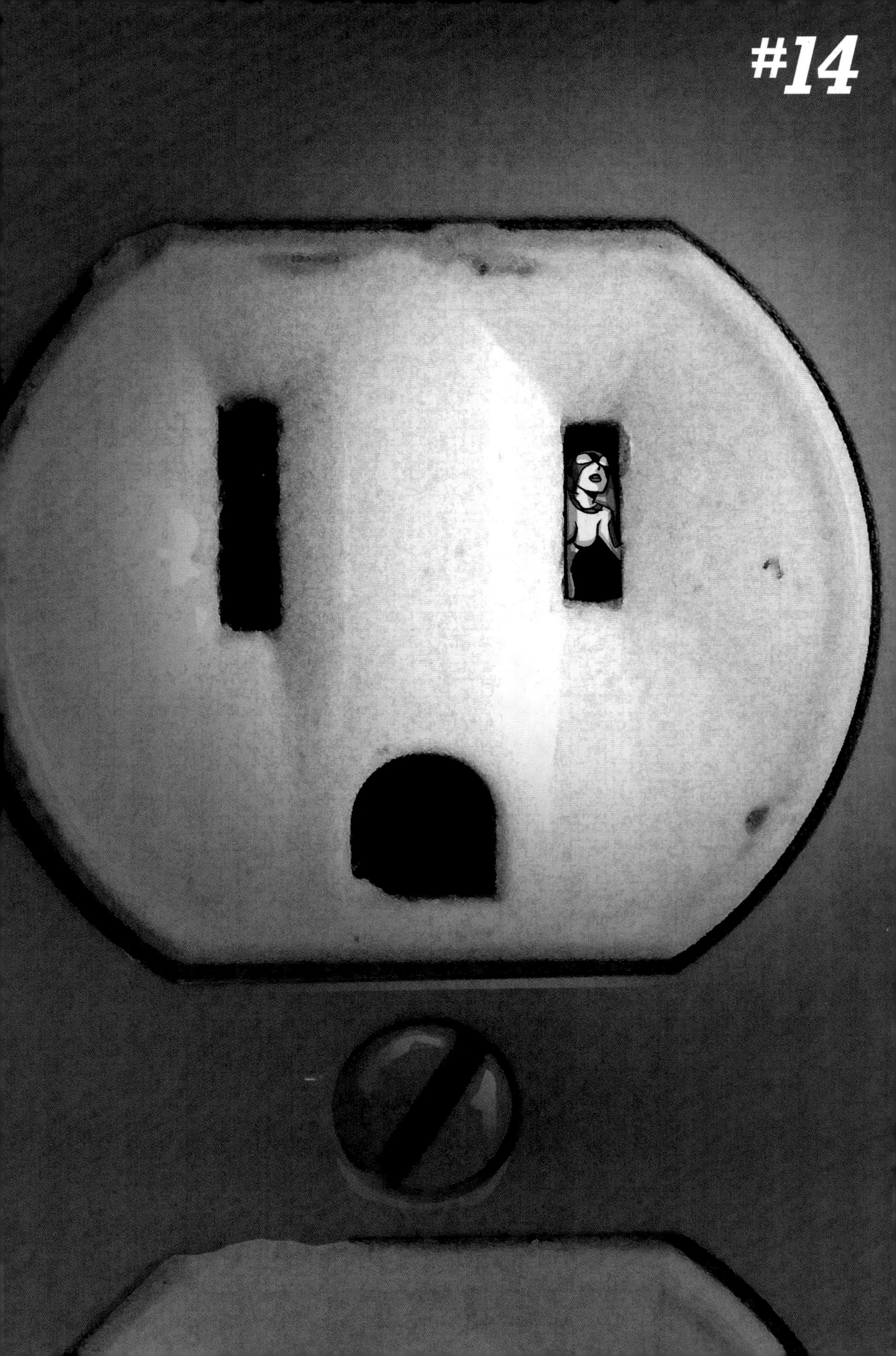
#14

#15

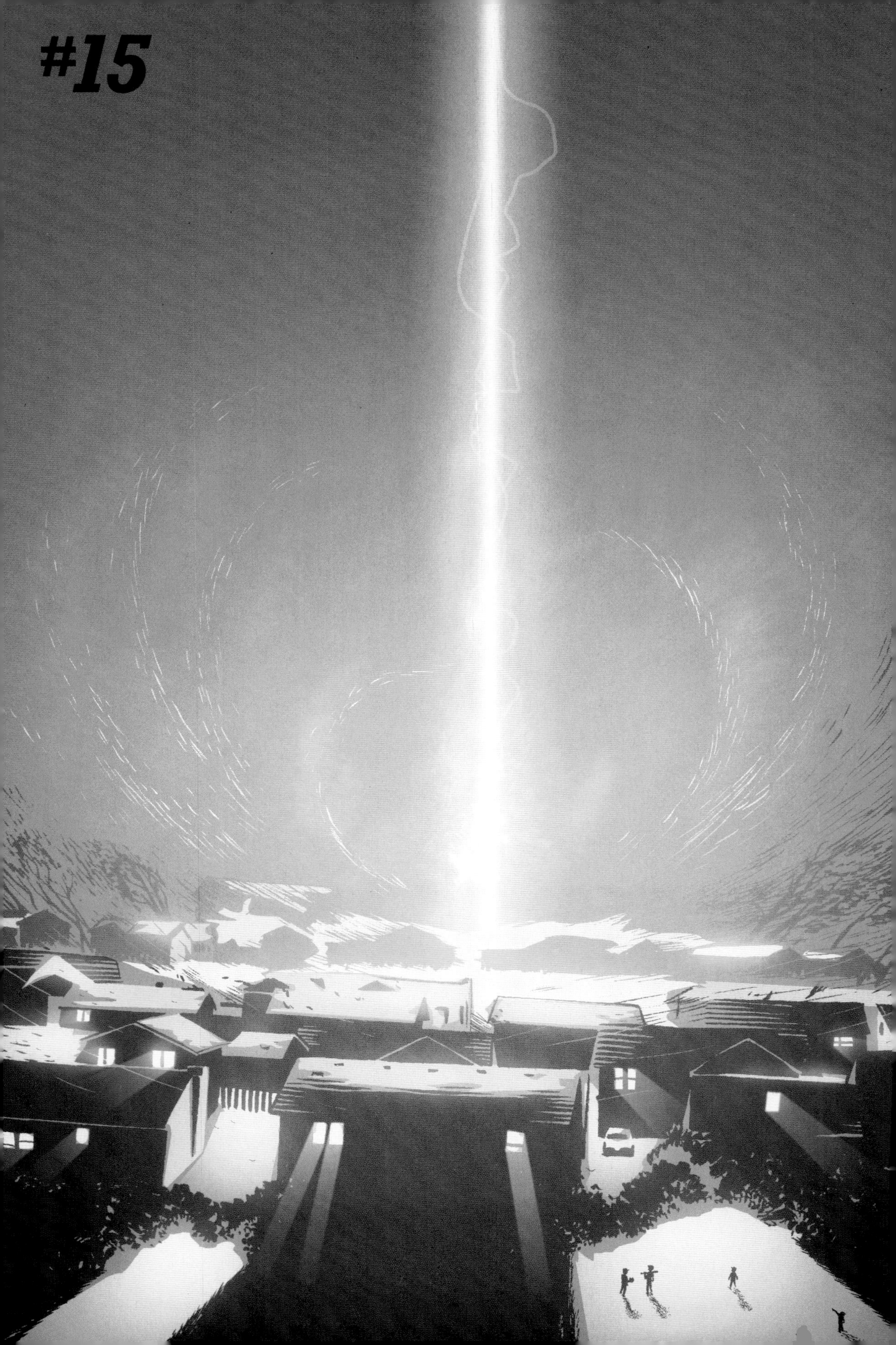

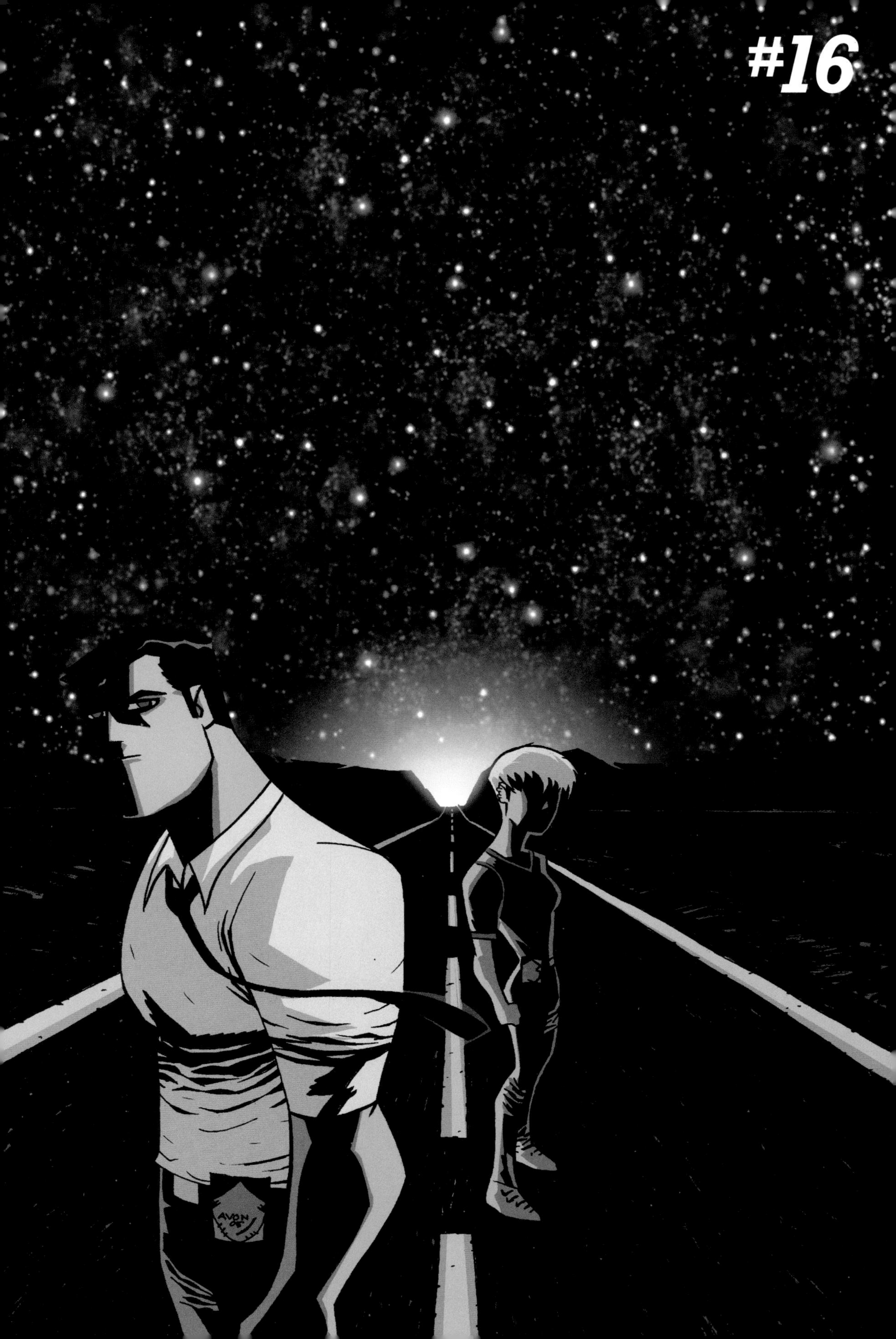
#16

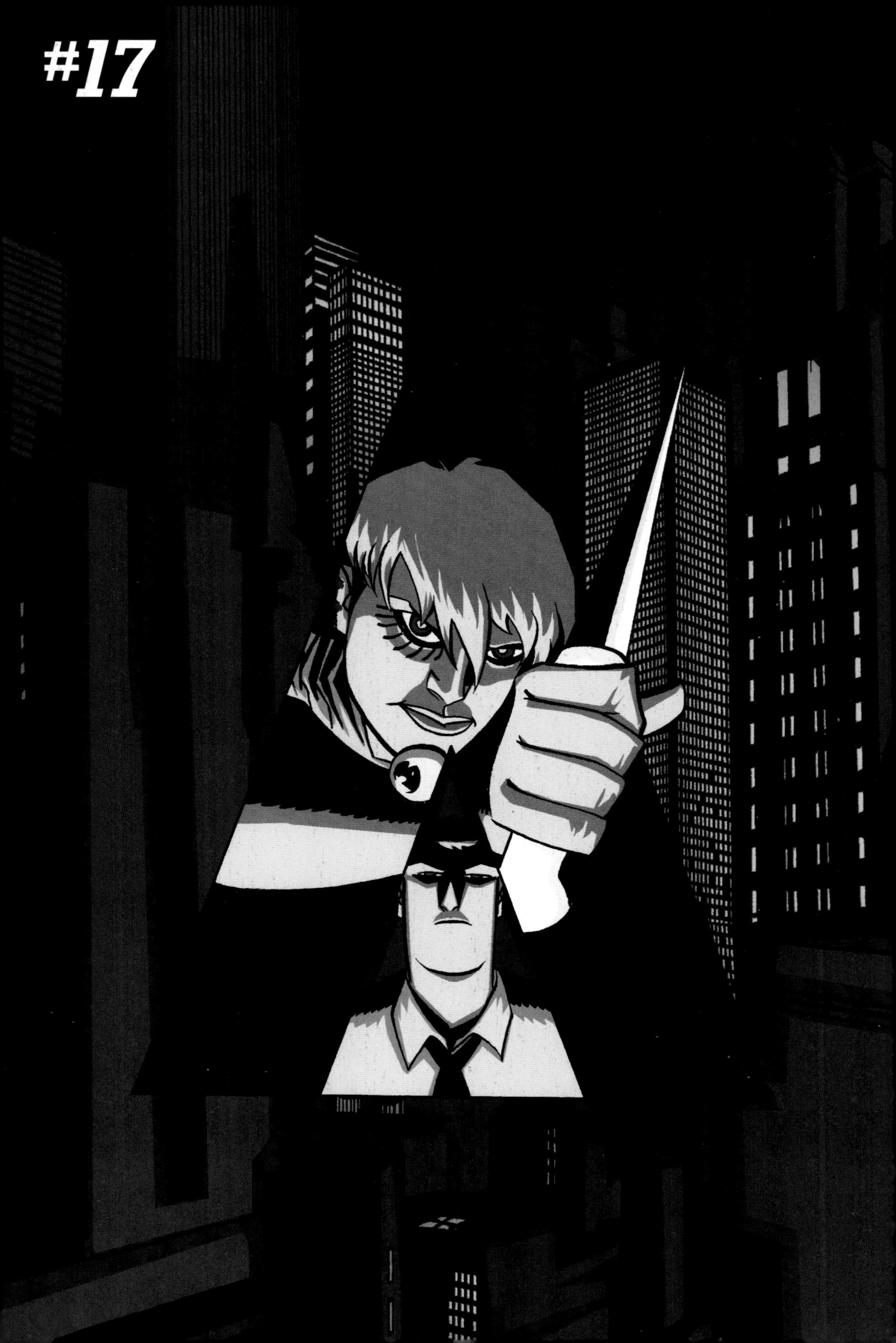
#17

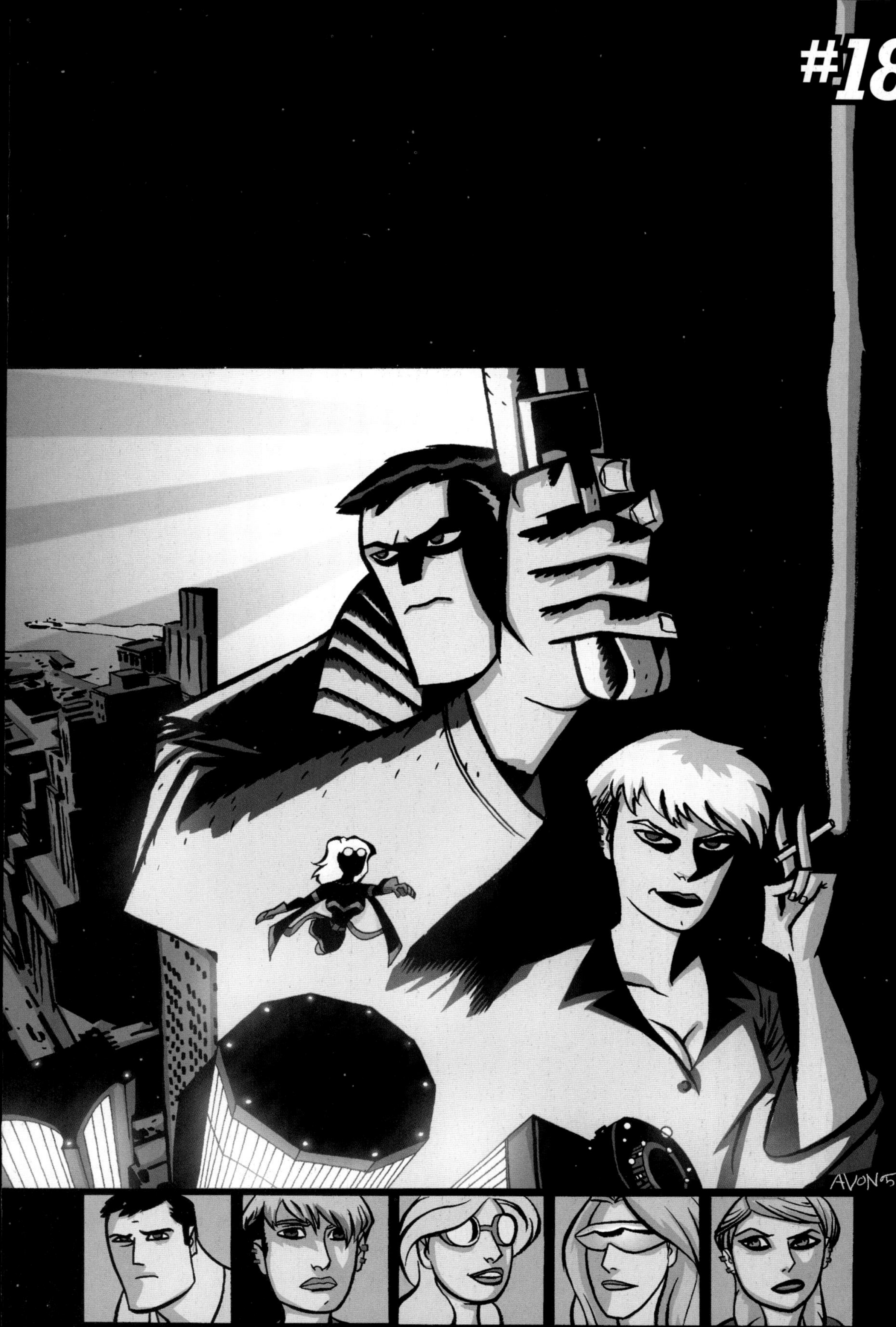
#18
AVON'05

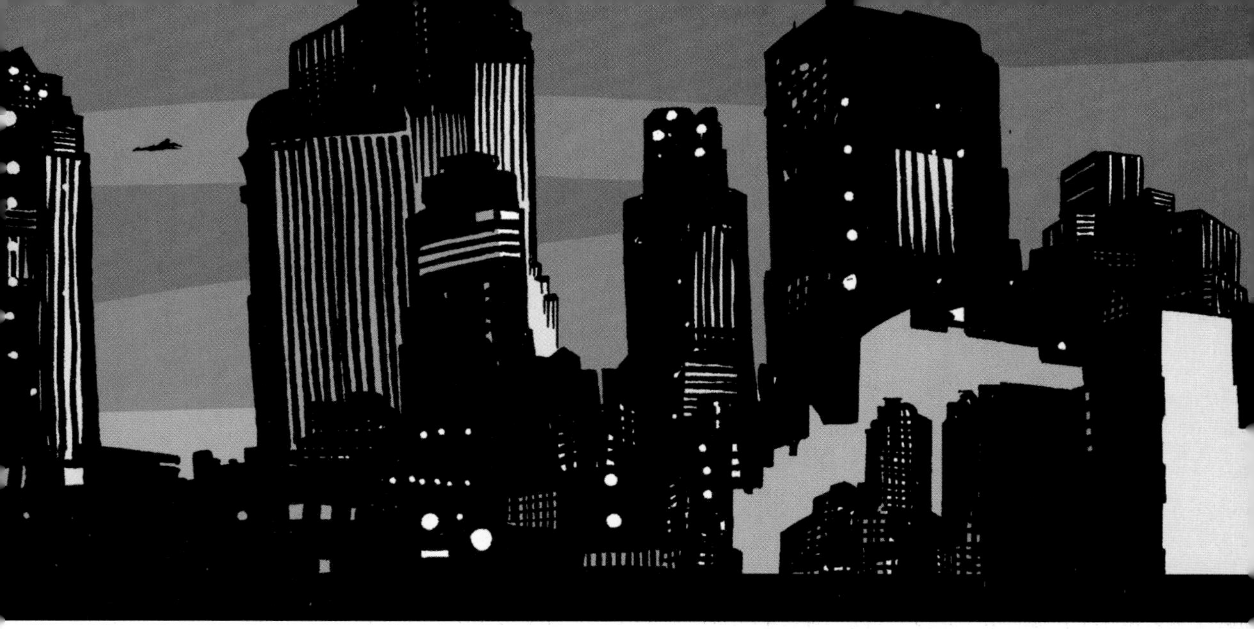

POWERS

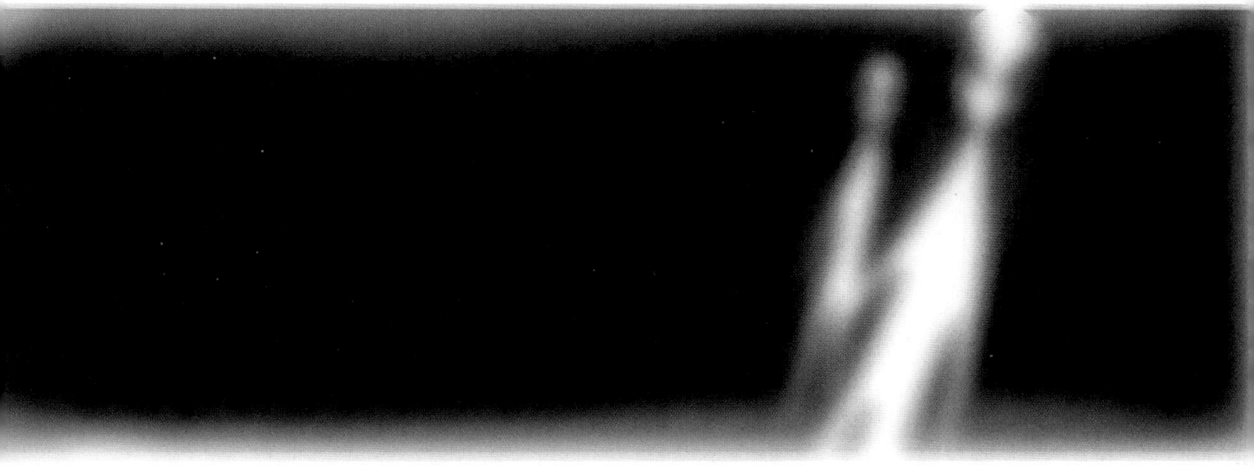

THE SCRIPT

This is one of those issues that is so insanely out of our safety zone and the final product so bizarre that we thought a peek at the script might be of interest. It's very hard to write towards the abstract. You're basically asking the artist to go nuts. And other than writing, "go nuts," what do you do?

Well, in this instant I knew that Mike would go nuts but the imagery I was asking for was fully based on the imagery witnessed by hundreds and hundreds of actual alien abductees. If you study up on this stuff you'll see a lot of the same images and symbols referenced in reports from all over the world.

Check out a great book ALIEN AGENDA by Jim Mars for some really cool background on all this. As far as the glowing alien vagina, that is all Mike working out his issues.

POWERS

COSMIC

PART FOUR

ISSUE 16

BY BRIAN MICHAEL BENDIS FOR MIKE AVON OEMING

Recap page text:

Homicide Detectives Christian Walker and Deena Pilgrim investigate murders specific to superhero cases...

When a seemingly average suburban man is struck by a falling superhero and torn to pieces, Walker and Deena are sent to investigate. When they search the deceased house they discover a hidden uniform.

But their investigation is cut short by a mysterious federal agent Marcus who tells them that the man who died is actually earth's cosmic guardian known as Millennium. A member of a secret order of galactic world protectors. So secret that Walker, with his superhero past, has never heard of him.

But before the detectives can learn anymore, Marcus transports them back to their squad room against their will. Both detectives are shocked to find themselves booted from their murder scene.

Alone in his apartment, relaxing after a long day, walker is visited by ghosts from his past. The heroes retro girl and Zora, long since passed away, have seemingly returned

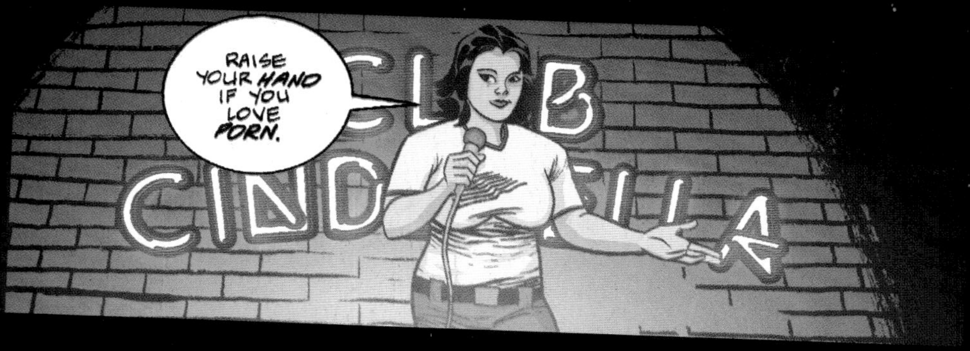
RAISE YOUR HAND IF YOU LOVE PORN.
CLUB
CINDERELLA

PAGE 1-

All widescreen images. All the Same shot.

1- Int. Club Cinderella- main stage - night

A single spotlight pierces the shadows of a brick wall. Like the stage of a comedy club. a microphone stand in the foreground.

2- Same. a rather attractive woman, think actress Jeanne Tripplehorn in basic instinct, with a wild fire in her eyes and wearing all things a three piece men's suit.

She approaches the microphone with purpose. He has a stand up comics swagger and we imagine timing.

JOY

Raise your hand if you love porn.

3- Same. She holds her hand up to her eyebrow to block the light and grabs the microphone with the other and leans forward a bit.

JOY

Oh, ok.

Four kabillion dollar a year industry and me and <u>that</u> guy over there are the only ones that like it.

So, what? Me and you- we spend roughly about 2 billion a <u>piece?</u>

Wow, that makes us <u>freaks</u>.

4- Same. She puts the mike back and straightens her suit and she gleefully expresses herself.

JOY

I <u>love</u> porn. I do.

I love badly <u>made</u> porn.

Not the kind where the girl in the video is obvious on her last legs.

You know... Just one crack pipe away from oblivion.

<u>That's</u> not cool.

That's gross and sad and I can't at all get anywhere <u>near</u> 'off' if the part of my brain that actually has <u>compassion</u> for her fellow man takes over the part of my brain that <u>desperately</u> needs to <u>climax</u>.

5- Same. Joy looks down to someone in the crowd right below her. Someone clearly disgusted with her story, Joy handles it with calm and humor.

JOY

I'm sorry. Am I offending you?

Than you probably <u>should</u> go.

Because I haven't even gotten to the naughty stuff yet.

You're ok? Ok.

PAGE 2-

All widescreen images. All the Same shot.

1- Same. Joy looks down to someone in the crowd right below her.

JOY

As I said, I love porn but most of it <u>does</u> suck very badly, doesn't it?

See, <u>me?</u> I like a little story.

I don't care how fucking <u>stupid</u> the story is- I don't ask for much-

Just a sense of <u>place and purpose</u> for the double anal gangbang.

2- Same. She gestures as if she was putting everyone where they belong.

JOY

Just so I know who everybody is.

I like to think that the director took the time to take the skank aside and give her her 'motivation.'

Makes me happy.

But even with that, the lowest of expectations, I still find myself desperately disappointed by a lot of the erotica I peruse.

I'm not asking for intimate cinematography, or even camera focus... just a <u>little</u> set up.

3- Same, Joy stops herself and gestures to the crowd to stop. She just thought of something.

JOY

Oh, and you know what I hate. I hate <u>jokey</u> porn!!

Ooh!! I <u>hate</u> it!

Wacky porn- <u>ugh!</u> Right?

Guys with these eleven inch dongs that think they're <u>funny.</u>

Or that it <u>makes</u> them funny.

I'm telling you right now, if you have an eleven inch donger... you're <u>not</u> funny.

There's nothing funny about you.

4- Same, Joy is laughing, clearly the crowd is laughing too.

JOY

You might <u>think</u> you're funny because you have a lot of blood that <u>should</u> be going to your brain going down in your eleven inch dong...

But that's <u>light headedness.</u> That's all.

Now, word is that there is more porn titles than there are legit movies and music albums combined.

Did you know that? Wow, huh?

5- Same, Joy puts her hands in her pockets like Letterman and shrugs.

JOY

Can you imagine though- other worlds, like aliens, getting a load of our bad porn.

And maybe not <u>knowing</u> its porn.

Maybe they don't <u>have</u> porn and they don't know what it is?

Maybe they think they're watching our <u>mating rituals.</u>

Maybe that's what the anal probes are about.

They think that's how we say hello or something.

PAGE 3-

Immediate continuation from last issue

2 equal sized panels.

1- Int. Walker's apartment- night

Walker, in the foreground, looking to see the impossible sitting right in his living room.

The original Retro girl and Zora are sitting right there in the room. Zora sitting in the arm chair. Retro girl, the original one, sitting on the arm of the chair.

Both smiling warmly. Both crackling with an unearthly energy. Both look like they absolutely don't belong anywhere in this dank, dark apartment. The lightning crackles outside.

Purple cubes and an unearthly glow.

RETRO GIRL

> Honor to be in your presence, Christian Walker.

2- Over the glowing Retro girl and Zora's shoulder looking to Walker who, just like last issue, is sitting there staring like he's in a trance. The Millennium uniform in his lap.

On the TV. A precocious little kid in a sidekick outfit and mask shrugs his shoulder and smiles at us. Its a shitty different strokes type sitcom. The reception is bad. Something is interfering with the reception.

Walker sits back with a blank stare on his face. Every muscle in his body has gone limp. Walker is drooling a little. He isn't swallowing.

CHRISTIAN WALKER

> Am I dreaming?

PAGE 4-

1- Walker's p.o.v. Zora and Retro girl sit there as pleasant and relaxed as can be. Zora looks to Retro girl. She isn't getting Walker at all.

ZORA

> What does that mean?

RETRO GIRL

> Mean <u>conscious?</u> Awake?
>
> Not as such.
>
> Not asleep, but not having this conversation in conscious plane.

2- Same as 2, last page.

3- Same as 1, Zora is confused, Retro girl casually explains it to her.

ZORA

> Dreaming?

RETRO GIRL

> Referring to the state of REM sleep produced by brain region known as the pons.
>
> Brain tries to interpret the random impulses from the pons as sensory input.

ZORA

> Sensory input.

RETRO GIRL

> Produces vivid <u>hallucinations</u>— call them dreams.
>
> Thinks <u>this</u> a dream.

4- Tight on Walker's stoned face.

CHRISTIAN WALKER

You're not human?

5- Retro girl smiles and gestures her hand. Very pleasant.

RETRO GIRL

No.

Here to speak about something important. Future. Planet's future...

Discovered, from past experience, that taking a form brain associates with something <u>pleasant</u> makes the entire interaction much more...

ZORA

Pleasant.

RETRO GIRL

Yes.

6- Same as 4.

CHRISTIAN WALKER

Its not working.

You're offending me.

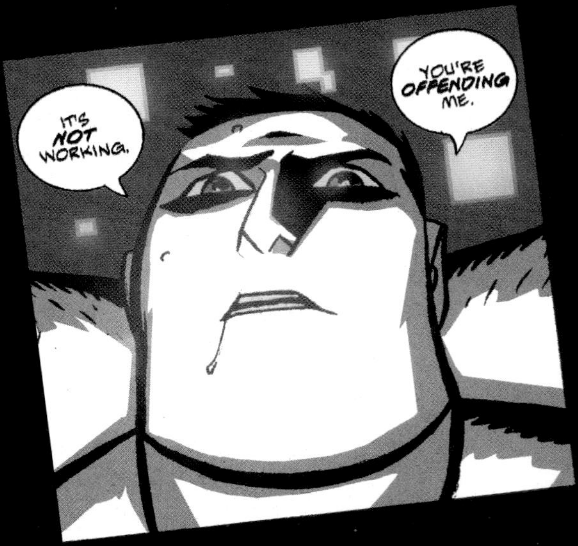
IT'S NOT WORKING.
YOU'RE OFFENDING ME.

PAGE 5-

1- Zora and Retro Girl are both confused. Retro leans in.

ZORA

Zora and Retro Girl.

Hero, partner, lovers...

Didn't <u>love</u> these women?

2- Same as 6, last page.

CHRISTIAN WALKER

They're dead.

They've been dead for many years.

3- Zora looks to an equally confused Retro Girl as to what this means.

ZORA

What does mean?

RETRO GIRL

Don't know.

ZORA

Didn't kill them. If that's insinuating.

4- Same as 2.

CHRISTIAN WALKER

What do you want?

5- Zora and Retro Girl get into their sales pitch. Warmly. Happy to do it proud to do it.

RETRO GIRL

Well, to put it in language's vernacular: we have opening.

ZORA

Know that this planet's guardian has been killed.

RETRO GIRL

Life has ended.

ZORA

He was-

Language's word for it- the closest can come to... is the Millennium guard.

RETRO GIRL

Being the law enforcement officer assigned to the Millennium case...

6- From behind Zora and Retro Girl, Zora turns to Retro girl, Walker watches this insane back and forth.

ZORA

Why call it a case?

RETRO GIRL

A case study. Refer to it as a case. Someone is murdered or killed- try to solve the murder.

ZORA

Why?

RETRO GIRL

Its like Sssssslondikes.

ZORA

OH.

RETRO GIRL

Makes feel better. Makes feel more in control. Then punish the murderer when prove guilt.

ZORA

That's good.

7- Same as 5, Zora and Retro Girl go back to their pitch.

ZORA

Observed Walker for a long time. Admirers of uniformed hero days.

RETRO GIRL

Diamond.

ZORA

Gora.

RETRO GIRL

The Blue Shield.

ZORA

Very fond of that period in life.

Stories inspiring to the imagination.

Why not a hero to these people anymore?

PAGE 6-

1- From behind Walker, Zora and Retro Girl can't help but be sidetracked by their own back and forth.

RETRO GIRL

Lost his powers in accident.

ZORA

Why stop being hero?

This society <u>needs</u> them. Feeds on them. So obvious.

RETRO GIRL

May rely on them too heavily.

2- Walker is just sitting there slumped and dazed. Is he being insulted by Aliens?

CHRISTIAN WALKER

I'm a cop.

I do what I can with what I have.

3- Same as 1.

RETRO GIRL

Yes.

ZORA

Humorous though- Most of heroes get powers by accident.

Christian Walker <u>lost</u> them by accident.

So interesting. So <u>random</u>. So purposeful.

4- Walker is just sitting there slumped and dazed.

CHRISTIAN WALKER

What do you want with me?

5- Zora and Retro Girl continue.

RETRO GIRL

Question: want abilities like before the accident?

ZORA

Not exactly. Different. New.

PAGE 7-

1- Same as 2, last page.

CHRISTIAN WALKER

I don't know who you are.

RETRO GIRL

Will show.

CHRISTIAN WALKER

Why don't you just tell me?

2- Same as 1. Last page

ZORA

Rather left alone?

RETRO GIRL

Christian Walker shall find this all very interesting and somewhat gratifying.

3- Walker stares. Confused. But his face is blank. Only his eyes give any sense of urgency.

4- Walker's p.o.v. Of the Millennium suit on his lap.

5- Walker is looking down at it. This is a life changing decision either way.

6- Walker looks back up. His eyes strong. Determined. Mind made up.

CHRISTIAN WALKER

Ok.

Show me.

7- Zora smiles warmly, we can see the eyes behind the vizor may not exactly be human.

ZORA

Good.

Try to keep mind open.

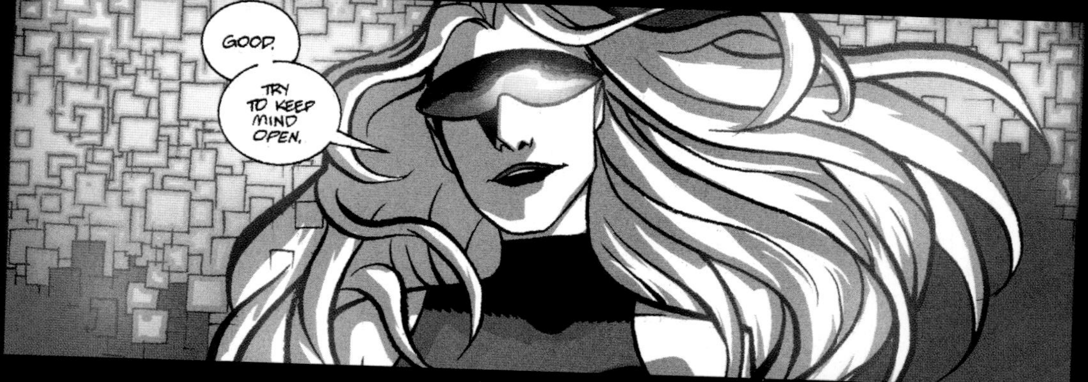
GOOD.
TRY TO KEEP MIND OPEN.

PAGE 8-9

Double page spread

1- Wide of the room. Walker is lifted off the ground. His back pivots. His eyes wide. He clearly is not in control of this. They are preparing him for a life changing event.

Retro girl and Zora smile warmly and watch.

CHRISTIAN WALKER

Agh!

2- Low looking up. Walker looks down at us in shock. Mouth closed. Eyes open.

3- Walker's p.o.v. Looking down. There is a pool of grey and silvery liquid on the floor right under his feet. Perfect circle. A pool of silver. a new kind of liquid effect.

4- The circular pool rises up to enclose his hovering feet and ankles.

5- Walker is shocked as the silvery black liquid is half covering his hovering body.

6- The liquid is at Walker's shoulders. His eyes are wide.

Walker's p.o.v. The girls smile warmly. Zora holds up her hand. Their quiet calm in direct contrast to his calm panic.

RETRO GIRL

Nothing to fear.

7- Walker's mouth is covered. His eyes wide.

8- Walker's p.o.v. Through the silvery liquid. Blurry, liquid images of the two superhero woman, but clearly they aren't woman. They are aliens.

We can barely make out their big grey heads. Is it the liquid distorting them? Or is this a hint of their actual form?

9- Inside the liquid. Walker's eyes roll up in his head.

10- Wide of his room. Similar to panel one. Walker is gone. They are gone. Everything is still and normal. No liquid. No nothing. Just the rain outside and the muted TV.

PAGE 10-

Black page.

PAGE 11-

First half of the page is black. Second half has thin widescreen panels. Hugging the bottom.

1- Int. Room- Same

Tight on Walker. Walker is lying down in a very dark room of some kind. A hint of a white table made of hard liquid under him.

But we are so tight on his sleeping face that we can't see anything but him. Low light. He barely opens his eyes. Fluttering awake. He is naked. We see. Lying down.

2- Walker squints awake. He has no idea where he is or what is going on. Something hurts him awake. A wince.

3- Walker's blurry p.o.v. Silhouette aliens. Very silhouette. Very blurry, very backlit by lights.

Backlit. No lights. Blurred in Photoshop. Are they watching him? Working on him? Examining him?

4- Same as 2. Walker's dreary, dreamy eyes roll back up into his head. He is going back to night night.

PAGE 12-13

Double page spread

From here to the end of the issue is walker on an alien world/ dimension. We have to go all out on this visually. Full out imagination. The colors are bold and flat primary to start. Nothing is the color of our world because this system doesn't have the same sun or atmosphere.

Plus I would love to do a valentine to the euro sci fi comics. Moebius, Bilal, Manara etc.

1- Ext. Garden/ jungle/ alien world- day

Same angle as last page.

Tight on Walker resting peacefully in odd blue and purple hued alien world grass. He is asleep.

A hint of a floral and grass style unlike anything we have ever seen. Colors we have never seen because we're in an atmosphere that is not oxygen and the color of the sun is not yellow and that makes all the colors of the world not what we are used to seeing.

2- Same. Walker's face is being tickled by a long blue blade of grass. The grass has little balls on the top. Balls of dew? Just part of the blade?

3- Same. Walker's eyes flutter open peacefully. This is an easy wake up.

4- Big panel. Half a page across both pages. Wide of the field. An alien world. Peaceful. Beautiful. Blue and purple foliage with green skies in the background.

Walker is naked and just standing up.

The foliage and wildlife is like nothing we have ever seen. Based on an entirely different type of ecosystem.

No animals. Just treelike structure. Grass like ground. Foliage. Some bugs. A couple in the foreground for the reader to ponder. Tall, wild grass.

5- Walker is stunned, looking around. So amazed by his surroundings that he doesn't realize he is naked. His hair blowing gently in the cool breeze.

6- Wider of this field. Walker seems alone in a very huge alien park. a hint of cubist odd insect wildlife.

7- Tight on Walker, he sees something.

8- Over his shoulder, five hundred feet away in the wild grass. In the tall blue grass. There's a silhouette figure waving to him.

9- Walker squints. Who is that?

10- Walker's p.o.v. The figure is walking towards him. Is that Deena?

PAGE 14-15

Double page spread

1- Over Walker's shoulder, Deena warmly holds out her hand to take Walker's, who is suddenly very self conscious that he is naked.

Deena is in the outfit we first saw her in in the first issue. The five shirt. The short hair and badly drawn earrings :) draw her in the original powers style.

This is Walker's mind's eye image of Deena. This is not Deena. Its one of the aliens.

Where we live.

CHRISTIAN WALKER

Who <u>are</u> you?

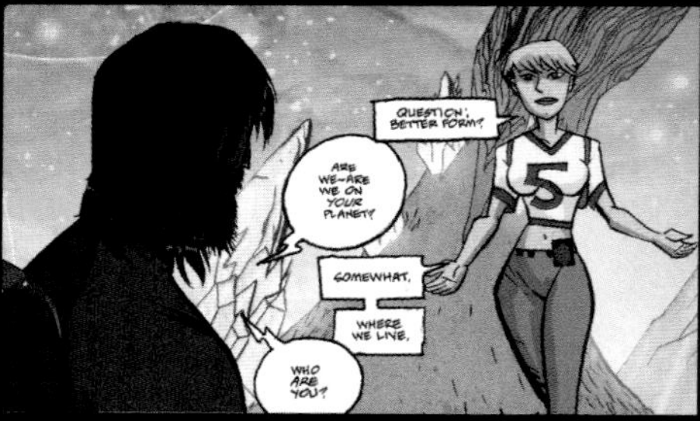
QUESTION: BETTER FORM?
ARE WE—ARE WE ON YOUR PLANET?
SOMEWHAT.
WHERE WE LIVE.
WHO ARE YOU?

2- Deena smiles warmly and takes his hand.

DEENA PILGRIM

Come.

See for Christian Walker.

3- Wide of the field. Christian is following her. They are both slowly floating two feet over the lush purple alien ground-scape. Walker is mesmerized by this. 'Deena' leads the way.

The world is increasingly alien. Maybe some alien animals start crawling around. There is nothing normal about this place. Nothing. Its all alien on every level.

DEENA PILGRIM

Gathering of worlds and resources from parts of what call 'the universe.'

Dedicated existence to letting infant societies, like Christian Walker's, thrive without fear of destruction.

Until such time as Christian Walker's societies, worlds like, naturally evolve to place where help themselves.

Help maintain universal symmetry. Balance.

Question: Understand?

4- Walker and Deena continue to float through this world-scape but its changing. The foliage is not as intense.

Its giving way to an almost desert like, bleached out ground, the sky is very green.

CHRISTIAN WALKER

Do you have a name?

DEENA PILGRIM

Question: Important?

CHRISTIAN WALKER

I think so.

DEENA PILGRIM

The Badee is a name.

Badee goals: select protector for every world, quadrant, still in its infancy...

As is Christian Walker's...

Grant this chosen protector abilities, strength, powers, to keep world/ quadrant safe from intruders- those who would harm.

5- Ext. City- Same

Huge panel. Walker and Deena continue to float through this world-scape but its changing. They are heading away from us and towards a truly vast city made of crystalline and pyramids in the far distance.

Floating crystals on top of perfect skyscraper pyramids as far as the eye can see. Blue and desert colors.

DEENA PILGRIM

Over 56,000 civilizations that would/ could attack, rape/ pillage Christian Walker's planet for own profit/ self preservation.

Some do for sport.

Three centuries of Christian Walker's time, guardian has kept Christian Walker's world protected.

<u>Now</u> need a new one.

Collectively hope it is Christian Walker.

PAGE 16-

1- Huge panel. Inside the city.

Most of page. Walker and Deena continue to float through this alien world scape. They are now deep in the crystalline city-scape. Dwarfed by huge moments of crystalline architecture. The intricate details of the world coming in clear.

Very ornate and a orgasm of other worldly design. See Moebius, Bilal. This is our homage to Eurosci-fi.

Its clean. Not dirty. Its about crystalline and glass. Not dirt and brick. But there is ornate symbolism in all the shapes and carvings. Triangles and pyramids. Not boxes.

Flying transports of some sort buzz around. No advertising or typography of any kind they don't need it.

2- Walker, floating by, mouth hanging open, turns to see...

3- Over Walker's head. One of the huge buildings/ pyramids. A perfect crystalline sphinx head. Perfect. Ornate. Carved into a crystalline pyramid.

Its like our pyramids only perfect, perfected.

PAGE 17-

1- Deena flies in front of Walker and turns back mid flight to address Walker directly as they pass through the denser caverns of the crystal city.

CHRISTIAN WALKER

How- how many have their been?

The protectors you've chosen for earth?

DEENA PILGRIM

417.

2- Walker is shocked. That seems like a lot.

CHRISTIAN WALKER

Four hundred and seventeen in 300 years?

DEENA PILGRIM

High risk occupation to Christian Walker.

Still asking Christian Walker to take uniform and responsibility of Millennium guard.

3- Deena stops and hovers. Behind her is a church like edifice.

A different style of architecture. Made with arcs and grandeur. This is their religious church. Their holiest of holy places.

DEENA PILGRIM

Asking Christian Walker to protect world's entire population.

Not a commitment of all Christian Walker's time.

Long periods may go by before Christian Walker is called to act.

Though sometimes new role may need constant attention for period of time.

4- Tighter on Deena. The background is coming up behind her. The church and its alien symbols. a place of supreme importance to their life and civilization.

A cathedral of power with a giant crystal window. A triangle and a circle combined.

DEENA PILGRIM

Rewards are spiritual to species like Christian Walker's...

Quest includes remaining anonymous to world. Makes job easier to do.

5- Walker is looking up and around. The church is spectacular. He can feel how important it is.

DEENA PILGRIM

Until Christian Walker's society can itself, in time, become aware of place in universe.

Christian Walker understand why?

CHRISTIAN WALKER

Because- because man can't handle knowing the truth of the worlds around them?

6- Deena pleased that Walker understands this fundamentally.

DEENA PILGRIM

Nor can the other species on your world. Not yet.

Won't, as a whole, be ready until earned the knowledge on own.

To be earned.

Understand Christian Walker's existing familiar relationships and mutual bonding activities.

7- Over Deena's glowing shoulder, Walker looks at her. What?

DEENA PILGRIM

Christian Walker's need- can confide in select few- as long as goals not put to compromise.

8- Deena looks at him. This is pretty close to a threat.

DEENA PILGRIM

Once goals compromised. Badee come to Christian Walker's world and intervene.

Question: understand?

PAGE 18-

Widescreen images. Starting wide and pulling tighter.

1- Wide very wide of the church area. The tiny figure floating in front of this church like edifice. The giant window.

CHRISTIAN WALKER

I think so.

DEENA PILGRIM

Christian Walker understand because once great hero to own world.

Makes perfect candidate for task offered.

Selfless. Brave, good.

Know precisely how to wield power bestowed.

2- Profile, two shot. The floating figures. The city goes forever in the distance. Walker looks to her. Getting excited. This is real. This is happening.

CHRISTIAN WALKER

What <u>kind</u> of power?

DEENA PILGRIM

Question: accepting offer?

CHRISTIAN WALKER

I don't know. What kind of-?

DEENA PILGRIM

All that Christian Walker needs. Question: accept?

3- Same but the camera is turning over her shoulder. The glorious world around them. Deena watches walker.take the step.

CHRISTIAN WALKER

Who killed the last Millennium?

DEENA PILGRIM

Do not know.

Conjecture: an accident unrelated to his task as Millennium guard. Very good guardian. One of finest.

CHRISTIAN WALKER

And it doesn't bother you to know what happened?

4- Same but the camera is turning over her shoulder. The glorious world around them. Walker is kind of stalling.

DEENA PILGRIM

Insignificant to goals of bigger picture.

Bigger picture is correct phrasing?

CHRISTIAN WALKER

Yes.

DEENA PILGRIM

Many metaphors in Christian Walker's people.

CHRISTIAN WALKER

Can I think about it?

5- Same but the camera is turning over her shoulder. The glorious world around them. Walker is stunned. Deena smiles warmly.

DEENA PILGRIM

Already have.

CHRISTIAN WALKER

You know my answer.

DEENA PILGRIM

Yes.

CHRISTIAN WALKER

Then why are you asking?

DEENA PILGRIM

Christian Walker's society custom of politeness.

Question: Answer...?

PAGE 19-

1- Walker, exhales it, as if its the answer to every problem he has ever had. Its god asking you to carry the Ten Commandments.

CHRISTIAN WALKER

Yes.

2- Deena smiles warmly as the world starts to glow white hot behind her. The pyramid circular window they were hovering is glowing white from the inside.

DEENA PILGRIM

Congratulations.

3- Walker is floating towards the white. She and the church and everything is fading out in light that is pouring from the circular and pyramid church window.

4- Walker's body lunges as it is being transformed and treated on a cellular level to handle the power that he will have with the suit.

His body is being carried through the its being carried into the pyramid circular window of the church. Into the piercing bright light.

PAGE 20-

1- Page tall. A wall of fire takes hold of walker's full nude, backlit figure. He is screaming in unholy pain. His back arches as the blue fire pummels him.

2- Tight on Walker. He screams. Eyes tight.

3- Tighter on Walker. He opens his eyes wide. Horror. Pain. Screaming. His pupils course blue fire.

4- Tighter on his eye. There's a form of blue fire in his eye. Its the form of...

PAGE 21-

Full page.

A tiny floating nude form of Walker floats before a giant form of a bird like alien bird made completely of blue and white fire. Egyptian bird.

The fire bird god is tilting its head down at Walker and yelling something.

PAGE 22-

1- Walker's p.o.v. Looking up at The fiery Egyptian bird head of fire.

2- Walker screams. Panic fear, his body is on fire. He is looking up at us. The bird. His horrified face is overwhelmed in the face of this alien god.

3- The bird eye looks down at us.

4- Walker's wide eye crackled blue

PAGE 23-

Full page shot.

Christian Walker is now the Millennium. In uniform. His arms down in front of him. His head down humble. Considering how he feels in this new role.

He is a hero reborn.

He is in costume. He is glowing. He is alive. He is back. Bands and cape.

Whips of white blue energy pour off of him. The fires fading.

PAGE 24-

1- Over millennium's glowing shoulder, Deena floats there. Pleased. A warm smile. The alien city-scape is behind her for miles and miles.

DEENA PILGRIM

Now a warning.

2- Walker squints. What the fuck?

CHRISTIAN WALKER

Now a warning?

3- She says this with a calm air of authority.

DEENA PILGRIM

Story will travel across universe of predecessor's demise and Christian Walker's appointment to Millennium.

There will be those who attack Christian Walker's world solely to test- to see if Christian Walker is weak.

Or to discover if Christian Walker's lack of experience leaves world weak for conquest.

4- Walker is bursting with emotions. He doesn't know where to begin or what to feel. He is alive for the first time in decades.

DEENA PILGRIM

Christian Walker will be tested.

CHRISTIAN WALKER

I- I have so many questions.

DEENA PILGRIM

Will visit. Will eat foods and talk words.

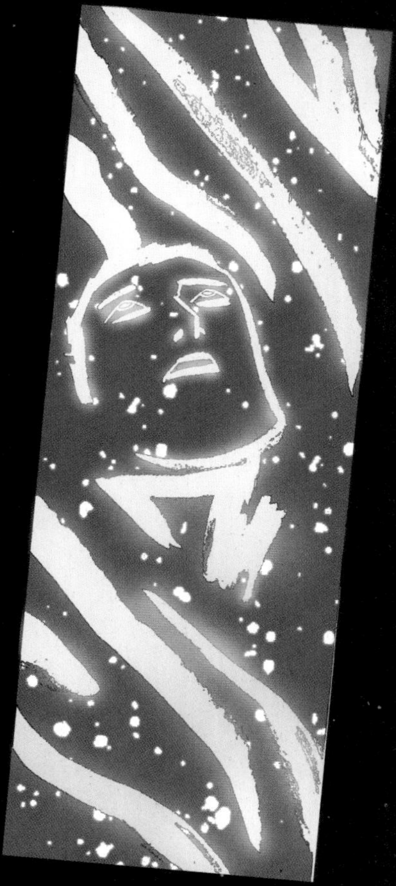

5- Walker looks down. Looking down. There is a pool of grey and silvery liquid on the floor right under his feet. Perfect circle. A pool of silver. a new kind of liquid effect.

DEENA PILGRIM

For now there is nothing that wouldn't be better taught by experience.

6- Over Deena's shoulder, Walker looks up- panic. The circular pool rises up to enclose his hovering feet and ankles.

CHRISTIAN WALKER

Wait, I want-

DEENA PILGRIM

Time to go home.

Christian Walker's world needs its protector.

5- Walker is shocked as the silvery black liquid is half covering his hovering body.

6- Walker's p.o.v. Through the silvery liquid. Blurry, liquid images of the two superhero woman, but clearly they aren't woman. They are aliens.

We can barely make out Deena's big grey heads. Is it the liquid distorting her?

7- Inside the liquid. Walker's eyes roll up in his head.

PAGE 25-

Black page.

Thin stripes of color towards the bottom.

PAGE 26-

1- Int. Walker's dark living room- Same

Walker is in his living room. On his knees. Not hunched, but looking at his slightly glowing hands in awe.

He is In his costume. Shocked. Stunned. Just dealing with what has happened to him.

His room is exactly like he left it. If not for the costume we would think it was a dream. In the background the small hallway to the bedroom and bathroom. Its dark.

2- Over Walker's head, looking down. His arm bands crackly with energy. He is empowered.

3- Same as one but tighter he is lost in thought when the sound of the toilet flushing.

Spx: fluuuush

4- Opposite angle. Walker snaps out of it. He looks at the off panel toilet in shock. Someone is here.

Retro girl, Calista, is coming out of his bathroom and whipping her hands as she does. In costume.

RETRO GIRL

Walker??!

Don't freak, I needed to take a squirt and you were the closest-

PAGE 27-

1- 2/3's of a page. Over Calista/ Retro girl's shoulder, past the hall and into his living room.

The glowing, kneeling figure of Walker staring at her in shock. Walker on the floor. That secret didn't last long.

2- Calista, in the hall doorway, leans into the door a little as he mouth drops. That is totally shocking. Walker is a superhero again???

PAGE 28-

1- Int. Club Cinderella- main stage - night

The rather attractive woman from the beginning of the issue.

Think actress Jeanne Tripplehorn in basic instinct, with a wild fire in her eyes and wearing all things a three piece men's suit.

> ### JOY
>
> If I ever got to meet someone from another planet.
>
> I don't know <u>what</u> I would ask them.
>
> I mean, there's millions of questions.
>
> The secrets of the universe might at our fingertips.
>
> A perspective on the universe that's <u>completely</u> different from ours.

2- Same. She thinks about it and smiles to herself.

3- Same. She tries not to laugh at her own joke.

> ### JOY
>
> I'd probably fuck him.
>
> Him or her or it.
>
> I'd have sex with them.

4- Same. She shrugs and smiles.

> ### JOY
>
> I mean, Just for the anecdote.
>
> Just to have something to say at parties!
>
> Or when people start telling their naughty stories.
>
> "I fucked two guys once..."
>
> "Really, I fucked a Jupitarian."
>
> "What's that?"

5- Same as 3.

> ### JOY
>
> "Guy from Jupiter. Let him fuck me in the ass.
>
> "Wasn't all that."

To be continued...

SKETCH GALLERY

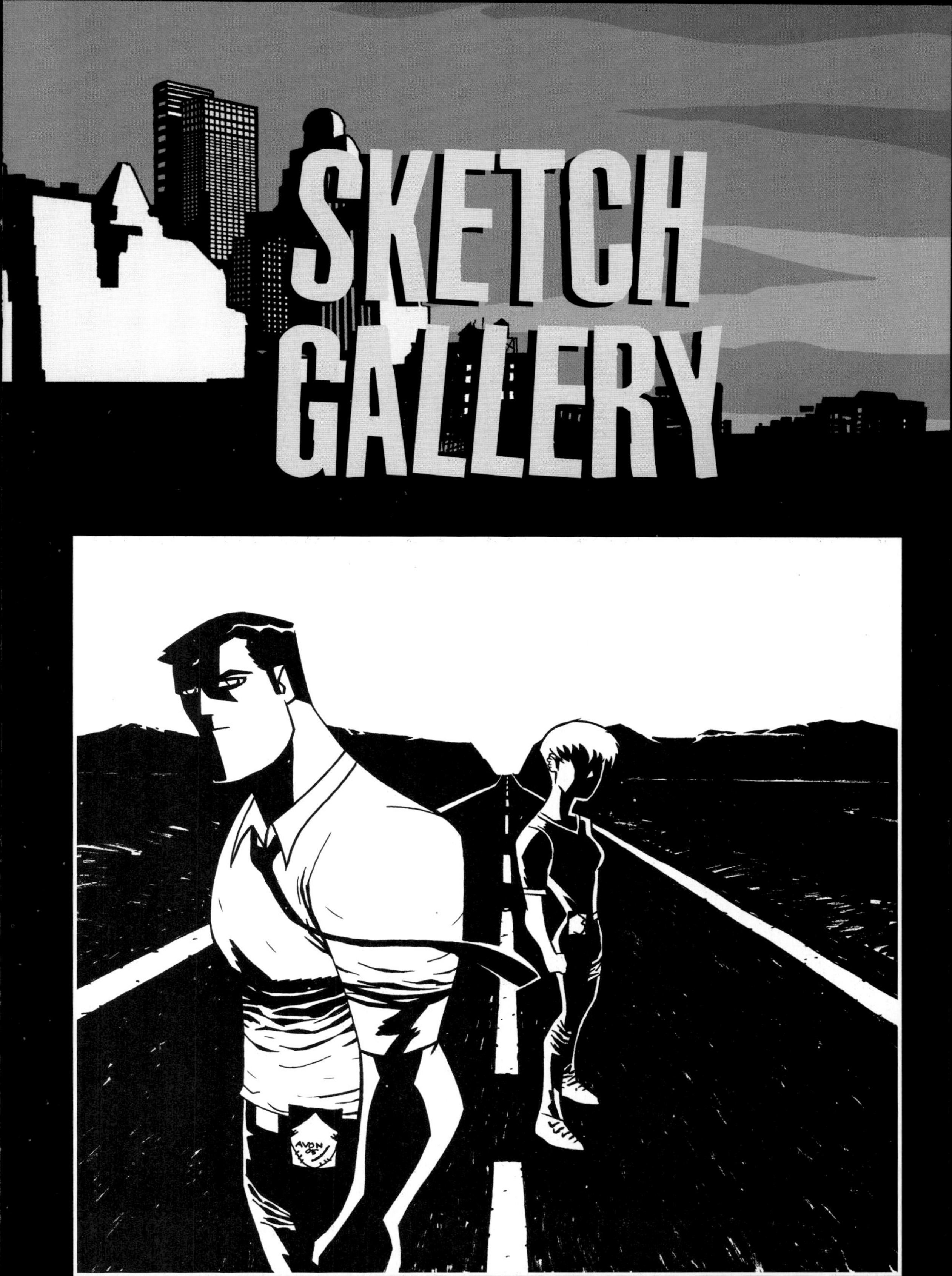

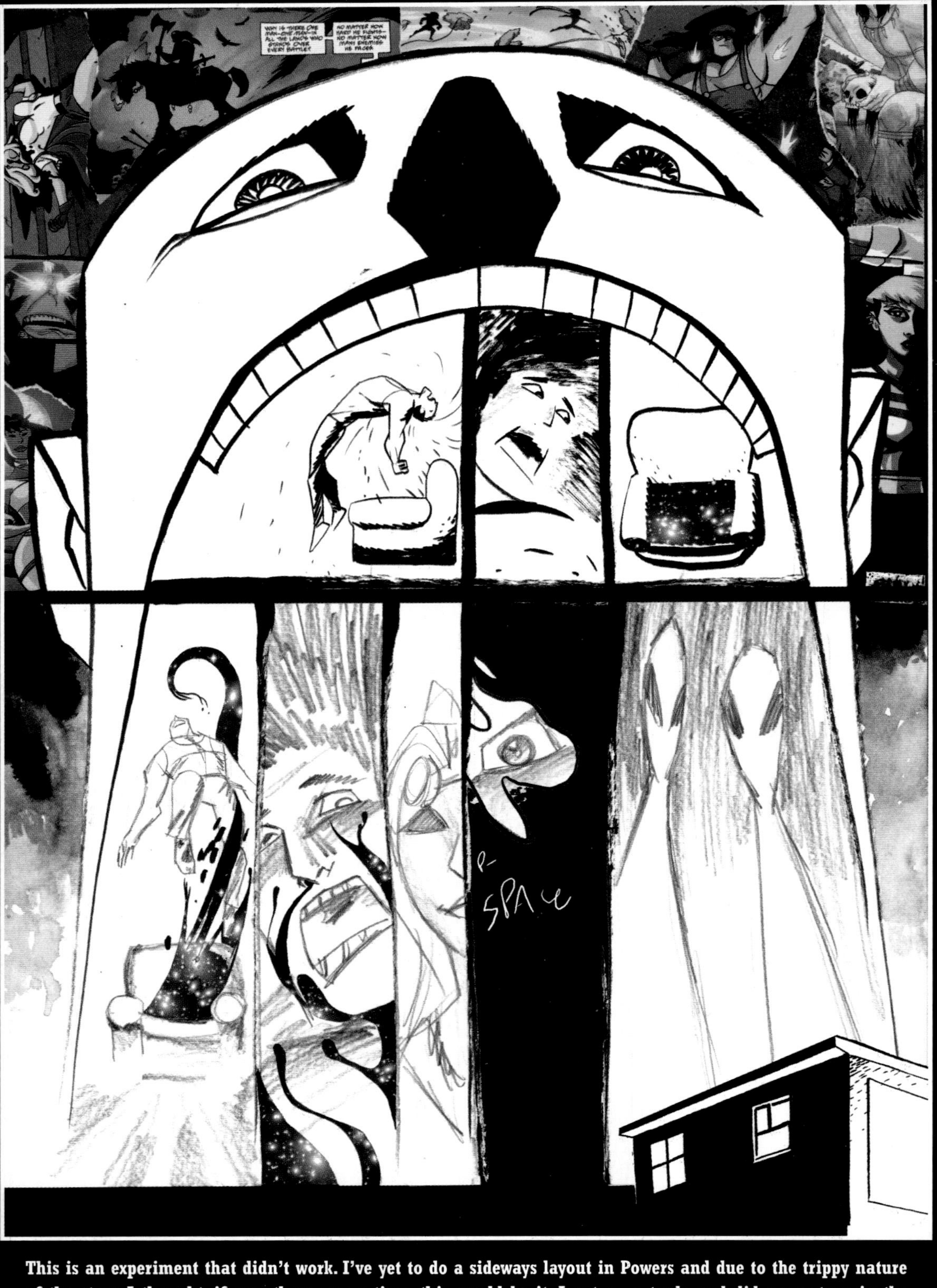
WHY IS THERE ONE MAN—ONE MAN—IN ALL THE LANDS WHO STANDS OVER EVERY BATTLE?
NO MATTER HOW HARD HE FIGHTS— NO MATTER HOW MANY ENEMIES HE FACES
SPACE

This is an experiment that didn't work. I've yet to do a sideways layout in Powers and due to the trippy nature of the story I thought, if ever there was a time, this would be it. I cut up a trade and did a montage in the background. The originals are pasted onto the page and I just allowed myself to be loose and sketchy on the rest. The final is better, but this sure was fun to do!

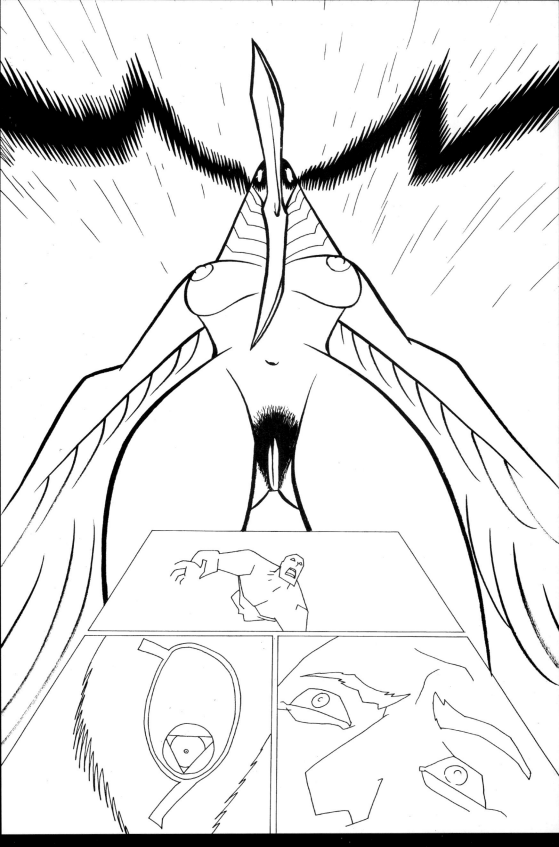

Ah, the original Bird Vagina page. Here is another good call by Brian to change things as Walker clearly looks afraid of the Vagina and we all know he's a fucking stud. I bet Calista's words from issue one came back to haunt him "Oh my god, so that's a clitoris."

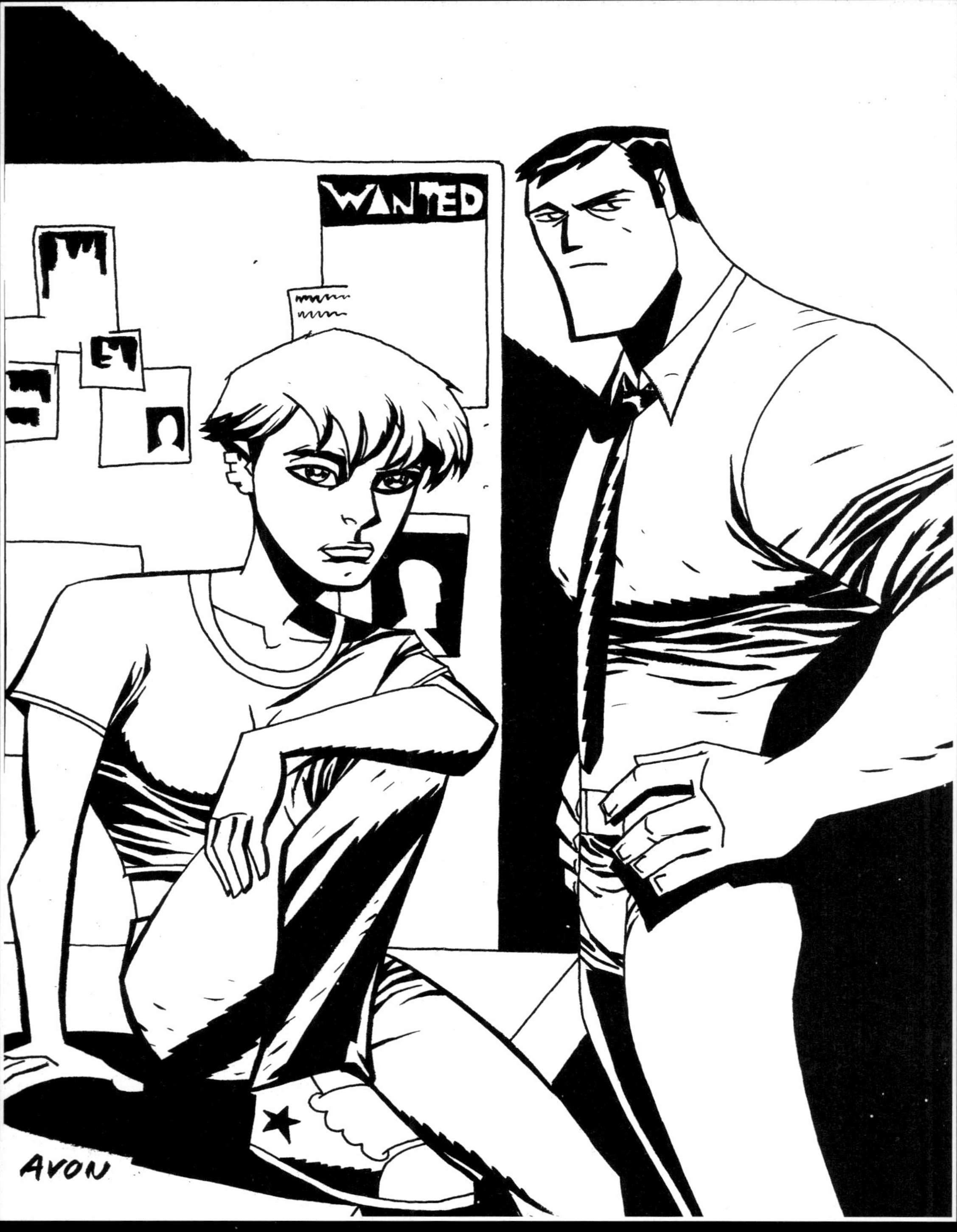
WANTED
AVON

A random commission. Deena's head is funny looking.

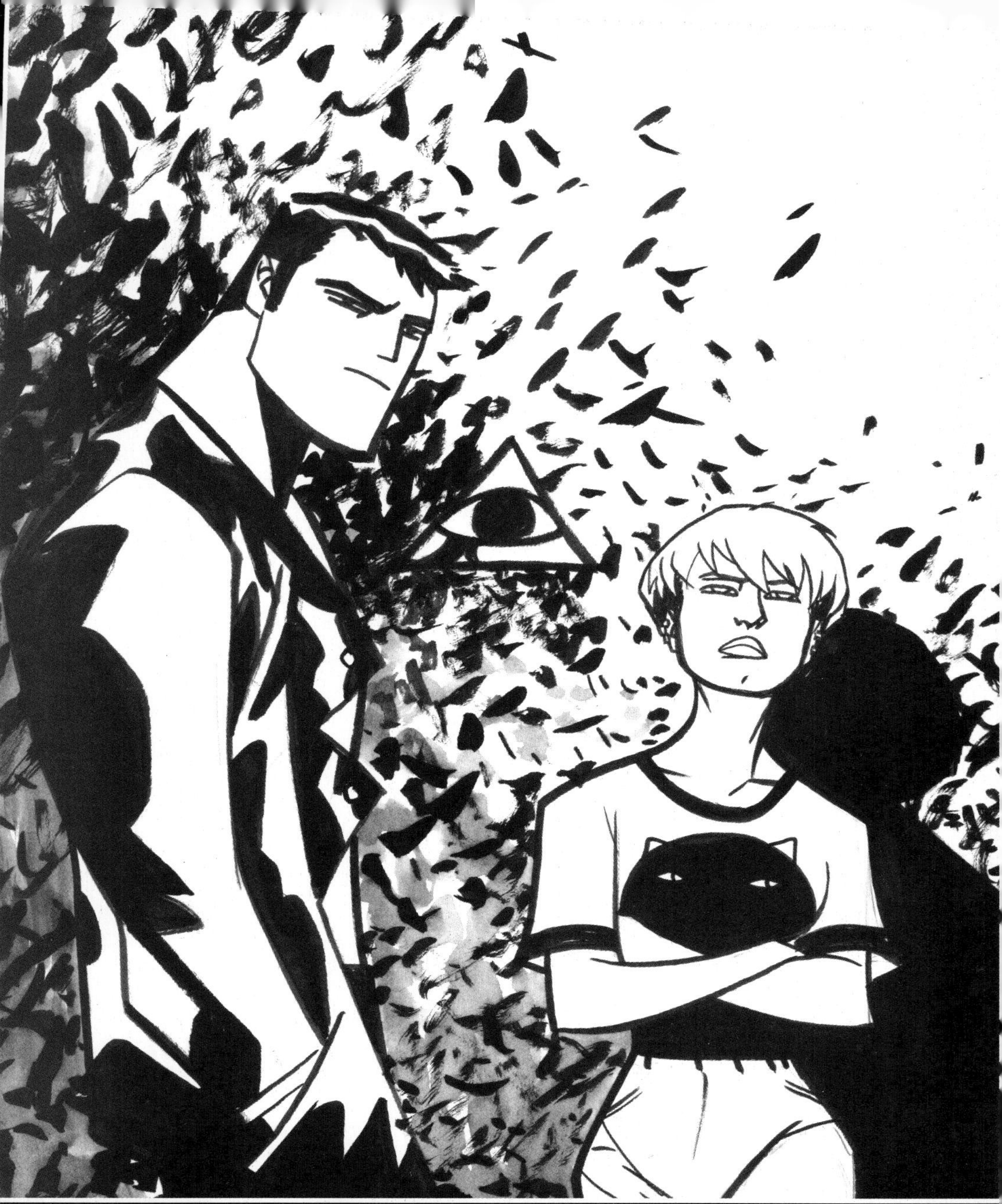

This was a birthday gift for Jen Grünwald, Marvel editor supreme and MOB MOLL! Below is a stamp made by Jim McLauchlin of the Heroes Initiative.

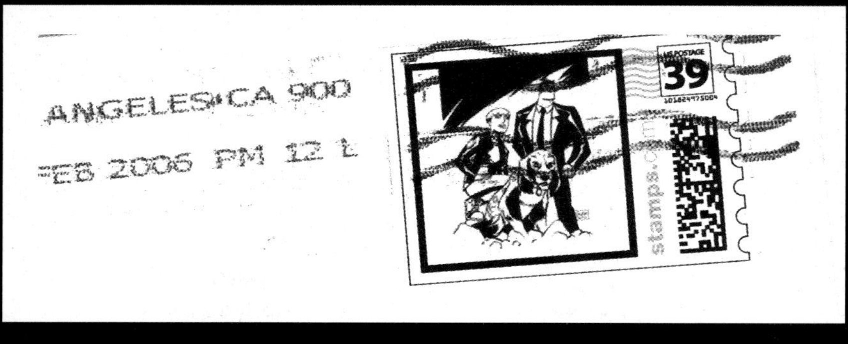
ANGELES CA 900
FEB 2006 PM 12 L
US POSTAGE
39
stamps.com

Please visit their site and give them your support: http://www.heroinitiative.org/

By the authors...

POWERS
- Who Killed Retro Girl?
- Roleplay
- Little Deaths
- Supergroup
- Anarchy
- The Sellouts
- Forever
- Legends
- Psychotic
- Powers Script Book

By Bendis...

- Jinx
- Goldfish
- Fortune and glory
- Torso
- Alias / The Pulse
- Secret War
- Ultimate Spider-Man
- Daredevil
- New Avengers
- House of M
- Total Sell Out

By Oeming...

- The Six samurai
- Bastard of the Gods
- Hammer of Gods
- Ship of Fools
- Parliament of Justice